CAPITALIST DEVELOPMENT AND CRISIS THEORY
Accumulation, Regulation and Spatial Restructuring

Capitalist Development and Crisis Theory: Accumulation, Regulation and Spatial Restructuring

Edited by
M. Gottdiener
Professor of Sociology and Chair, Urban Studies Program
University of California, Riverside

and

Nicos Komninos
Assistant Professor of Urban Planning,
Aristotelean University of Thessaloniki

St. Martin's Press   New York

First published in the United States of America in 1989

Printed in China

ISBN 0–312–02102–X

Library of Congress Cataloging-in-Publication Data
Capitalist development and crisis theory.
Includes index.
1. Capitalism.   2. Business cycles.   3. Saving
and investment.   I. Gottdiener, Mark.   II. Komninos,
Nicos
HB501.C24273   1989   338.9   88–15848
ISBN 0–312–02102–X

To the memory of Gregory Garwick and Thora
Paulson — M.G.
To Elena and Alexandros — N.K.

Contents

List of Figures

List of Tables

Acknowledgements

The editors would like to thank James O'Connor and Basil Blackwell Publishers for permission to publish a revised version of the introduction to *The Meaning of Crisis: A Theoretical Introduction* (1987); Ernest Mandel for his permission to publish a revised version and translation of chapters 25 and 26 of *La crise* (Paris: Flammarion, 1982), and for permission to publish a revised version of 'The Infernal Logic of the Debt Crisis' which first appeared in *International Viewpoint* (1986).

The editors would also like to thank Olga Varveri for her translation of the material from *La crise* and for helping in the translation of 'Three Crises' by Alain Lipietz. In addition, we wish to thank Simon Winder, our editor at Macmillan, for his kind attention to our project.

Finally, M. Gottdiener would like to thank the Academic Senate of the University of California, Riverside, for intramural grant support which aided the completion of this collection.

Notes on the Contributors

Mike Berry is head of the Department of Planning, Policy and Landscape, Royal Melbourne Institute of Technology. He co-edited *Austalian Society*, is co-author of *Urban Political Economy: The Australian Case* and author of *Marxist Approaches to the Housing Question* and *The Political Economy of Australian Urbanization*.

Klaus Busch is Professor of Political Science at the University of Osnabrück. He is the author of *The Multinational Firms: A Contribution to the Laws of Internationalization of Production* (Frankfurt/Main, 1974), *The Crisis of the European Community* (Koln u. Frankfurt, 1978), and co-author of *Structures of the Capitalist World Economy* (Saarbrucken, Ft Lauderdale, 1984).

John Bellamy Foster is Assistant Professor of Sociology at the University of Oregon. He is the author of *The Theory of Monopoly Capitalism* (Monthly Review Press, 1986) and co-editor of *The Faltering Economy: The Problem of Accumulation Under Monopoly Capitalism* (Monthly Review Press, 1984).

M. Gottdiener is Professor in the Department of Sociology at the University of California, Riverside and Chair of the Urban Studies Program. He is the author of *Planned Sprawl: Private and Public Interests in Suburbia* (Sage, 1977), *The Social Production of Urban Space* (University of Texas Press, 1985), *The Decline of Urban Politics: Political Theory and the Crisis of The Local State* (Sage, 1987). Editor of *Cities in Stress: A New Look at the Urban Crisis* (Sage, 1986), co-editor of *The City and the Sign: An Introduction to Urban Semiotics* (Columbia University Press, 1986).

Thomas Krämer-Badoni is Professor of Regional and Urban Sociology at the University of Bremen. He is the author of *Zur Legitimitat der Burgerlichen Gesellschaft* (Frankfurt/New York, 1978), and the co-author of *Zur Soziookonomischen Bedeutung des Automobils* (Frankfurt, 1971), and *Die Kneipe: Zur Soziologie einer Kulturform* (Frankfurt, 1987).

Juergen Haeusler is Assistant Professor of Political Science at the University of Frankfurt. He is the author of several articles on energy politics, industrial policies and political parties.

Hartmut Häusermann is Professor of Regional and Urban Sociology at the University of Bremen. He is the author of *Die Politik der Burokratie* (Frankfurt, 1978), co-editor of *Sud-Nord-Gefalle in der Bundesrepublik?* (Opladen, 1986), co-author of *Neue Urbanitat* (Frankfurt, 1987).

Joachim Hirsch is Professor of Political Science at the University of Frankfurt. He is the author of numerous books and articles on state theory. His latest publications include 'Der Sicherheitsstaat' (1980) and as co-author, 'Das Neue Gesicht des Kapitalismus' (1986).

Bob Jessop is Lecturer in Government at the University of Essex. He has worked for many years on issues in the theory of the capitalist state and on topics in the political economy of post-war Britain. He is the author of *The Capitalist State* (1982), *Nicos Poulantzas* (1985), *The Political Economy of Post-war Britain* (1988), as well as many articles on these and related themes.

Desmond King lectures in Politics at the University of Edinburgh. His main interests lie in state theory, political economy and urban politics. He is the author of *The New Right: Politics, Markets and Citizenship* (Macmillan and Dorsey Press, 1987), *The Cities* (Methuen, 1988), and co-author of *The State and the City* (University of Chicago Press, 1987), as well as numerous articles.

Nicos Komninos is Assistant Professor of Urban Planning in the Department of Urban and Regional Planning, Aristotelean University of Thessaloniki. He is the author of five books and numerous articles on spatial development and crisis, city planning theory and methodology, design ideology and practices, including *Theory of Urbanity* (1986) in Greek, three books dealing with contemporary crisis, spatial restructuring and new forms of local regulation.

Alain Lipietz is an economist at CEPREMAP in Paris, France. He is the author of numerous articles and books on contemporary political economy including *Crise et inflation: pourquoi?* (1979), *Le Monde enchanté* (1983), *L'audace ou l'enlisement* (1984), *Mirages et miracles* (1985).

Ernest Mandel is Professor at the Vrije Universiteit in Brussels. Among his numerous books are: *Marxist Economic Theory, Late Capitalism, Trotsky, a Study of the Dynamics of His Thought, Revolutionary Marxism Today, The Long Waves of Capitalist Development, The Second Slump* and *Delightful Murder — The Meaning of the Second World War*.

John Milios lectures in political economy at the National Technical University in Athens. He is editor in chief of the theoretical sociological and economic journal *Thessis* (in Greek) and he is the author of articles on capitalist development and political economy.

Hyman P. Minsky is Professor of Economics at Washington University, St. Louis, MO. He was educated at the University of Chicago and Harvard and is author of *John Maynard Keynes, Can It Happen Again?, Stabilizing an Unstable Economy*, as well as numerous articles in professional and public journals.

James O'Connor is Professor of Sociology and Economics at the University of California, Santa Cruz. Prior to this he was Professor of Economics at San José State University. His latest books are *The Meaning of Crisis: A Theoretical Introduction* (Basil Blackwell, 1987) and *Accumulation Crisis* (Basil Blackwell, 1985).

1 Introduction

M. Gottdiener and N. Komninos

In the 1960s the older industrialised countries (OICs) of Western Europe and the United States experienced socio-economic well-being unprecedented in their histories. Prosperity was not simply a consequence of powerful economies. Rather, the OICs grew because, ever since World War II, they had augmented economic management with political and cultural accommodations to development. Both the emergence of the modern welfare state and the rise of a mass consumer culture contributed in their own ways to complementing basic productivity gains in national economies. The concordance of economic, political and social forces around robust growth stimulated analysts to talk about an end to ideology and to remark about the emerging similarities between advanced industrial societies across the globe. European and American welfare statism converged around a core set of structural features including accommodations between workers and capital, the presence of state regulation, the feeding of consumer demand, and an integration of world capitalism through institutions such as the EEC and the IMF. Metropolitan spatial development played itself out against the backdrop of this larger structure which has come to be called the world system.

The two decade period of post-war prosperity for the OICs was driven by a certain 'regime of accumulation' based upon a correspondence between levels of capitalist industrial production and levels of consumption dependent on the purchasing power of labour. This so-called 'intensive' form of accumulation for capitalist society[1] held the crisis tendencies of capital in check principally by matching the supply of commodities produced by domestic industry with domestic demand. However, because the necessary correspondence is not inherent in the capitalist mode of production, state regulation and the provision of use values for both capital and labour also became necessary. Thus, the intensive regime of accumulation required also a certain 'mode of regulation' and it was precisely upon the latter need that the modern welfare state was based. Along with the development of a mass culture of consumption and spectacle, welfare state provision sustained the necessary reproduction of labour and helped to

1

coordinate worker claims on surplus value with the tendency of profit rates to fall.

Today, however, the older industrialised countries have experienced a decomposition of the correspondences between the sectors of production and consumption and have reached the limits of Taylorist and Fordist[2] forms of work organisation that sustained continuous productivity gains in the past, and, as well, a certain effective form of labour reproduction managed by the state. A central role in this collapse of the post-war regime of accumulation was played by the slowing productivity rates in the major industrial branches (chemicals, automobiles, steel and coal) coupled with periods of intractable inflation (the so-called 'stagflation'). Eventually, this trend helped to force changes in the mode of surplus value extraction for basic industry.

In addition to the crisis experienced within the OIC manufacturing sectors, several other factors also played decisive roles in the break-up of the post-war regime of accumulation in recent years. Labour unrest and accelerating worker demands, for example, during the late 1960s threatened the mutual accords which served as the backbone for the correspondence between capital's needs and worker claims on surplus value. Fiscal and monetary strains, in addition, along with the inflation crisis brought about debt problems for governments at every level. Such tendencies also accelerated in the 1970s as a result of the oil price shock which, for a time, spun inflation out of control, and increased the upward pressure on wages.

Finally, the 1970s ushered in an era of intense international competition which penetrated the calm of world system co-operation, eventually calling this concept itself into question. Global competition attacked unproductive and obsolete industries within the OICs thereby undermining directly the old regime of accumulation. This latter trend also accelerated during the 1980s due to the efforts of Japan and several 'newly industrialised countries' (NICs), such as Taiwan, Singapore, Korea and Brazil, which surfaced because of their own ambitious efforts in promoting export manufacturing and international competition.

By the late 1970s institutionalised accommodations between capital and labour under corporatism in the OICs could not withstand the triple pressures of industrial decline, inflation and declines in the rate of profit. The welfare state reeled under the mounting debt crisis and its inability to reproduce labour while simultaneously also reproducing the general conditions of production under the new constraints of fiscal austerity. Consequently, the mode of regulation also characteristic of post-war industrial society began to crumble along with its regime of accumulation and a global need for restructuring within the OICs manifested itself.

In the 1980s the combination of economic and political crises in the OICs, global competition involving the NICs and the OICs and a world debt crisis of monumental proportions forced an extended period of restructuring in many countries. Restructuring also affected fundamentally the socio-spatial organisation of OIC metropolitan areas through the complex articulation of economic change, political interventions, labour requirements and characteristics, and the effect of spatial design on valorisation and realisation relations of capital. Traditional cities were afflicted by industrial decline, the diffusion of the productive system across the national space, deconcentration of the urban population and the secondary, tertiary and even quaternary economic activities, a growing unevenness in incomes and the social polarisation of housing provision, and, finally, the degradation of social equipment and urban infrastructure along with the selective building up of certain places through gentrification and robust investment in real estate. The result of recent restructuring is a landscape found in traditional metropolitan regions within the OIC of progressive unevenness in socio-spatial change and of extremes between the affluent and the poor, and, the well-cared for places and blight which seem to exist side by side.

Almost paradoxically and along with decline, restructuring has also given birth to new landscapes of growth. The so-called 'silicon landscapes' appeared, such as high-tech industrial parks, technopoles of growth, corridors and routes of development outside the city, and so on, which correspond to expanding industrial branches linked to defence-related industries and new forms of co-operation among industry, research and the state. During the 1980s it became fashionable to speak of geographical splits and regional uneven development, such as the distinction between the traditional city and suburb, or the 'sunbelt-frostbelt' contrast. Regional inequities and their social consequences along with the spatial transfer of value to new domestic and foreign growth poles brought forth new state policies as well that involved a new relation between the state and localism.

In short, today the spatiality of the OICs can be characterised by a lower and sometimes negative rate of urbanisation along with the presence of deconcentration which corresponds to the new phenomenal form of late capitalism[3] that has replaced the traditional industrial city. Furthermore, today there exists a new centrifugal industrial mobility, a spatial diffusion of production and the transfer of growth activities to new places both domestically and across the globe, a domestic deterioration of the traditional physical and social metropolitan environment, the recommodification and retreat from collective consumption by the welfare state, and, finally, growing social inequities in employment, income, housing and social care.

It is precisely this multi-dimensional readjustment of capitalism's 'regime of accumulation' that has been characteristic of development over the last decade and which will be in effect for some time to come. Every industrialised society in the West has had to change the way it does business. Fundamental transformations have occurred at all levels bringing social, political and spatial, as well as economic, issues into consideration. The old accommodations between planning and economic growth, the welfare state accords and the conflict between capital and labour, the management of debt and global finance, and capital investment in local development have all become obsolete and candidates for change in the face of new realities caused by the needs of crisis adjustment.

As major consequences of this multi-dimensional restructuring, traditional political ideologies, such as socialism and conservatism, institutionalised planning schemes, and social welfare programmes have all been questioned and discovered to be inadequate for guiding social organisation in the future. Consequently, new forms of national politics and worker social movements have appeared in the OIC that resist easy characterisation by old labels.

Given all that has occurred of substance during the past decade, current attempts at understanding crisis and restructuring among industrialised nations have been wholly inadequate. Inquiries have followed the more traditional avenues of academics and have produced myopic studies that stick to individual disciplines and limited points of view. The multi-dimensionality of the present patterns of change is lost on single-minded treatments encapsulated in individual academic fields, such as human geography or international economics. More importantly, without an interdisciplinary understanding of contemporary industrial restructuring, theoretical perspectives remain hopelessly inadequate and out of date. This collection seeks to remedy this conceptual and theoretical failure. It is both interdisciplinary and geographically diverse. The editors have brought together a series of original papers from eminent political economists, sociologists, geographers, and planners from the United States, the United Kingdom, France, Germany, Belgium, Australia and Greece that focus on different aspects of the growing imbalance between economic restructuring and state policies that have resulted in crises of regulation and leadership.

The following discussions are about present day patterns of capitalist development and the ways that growth has been linked to crises and restructuring. Papers contained in it document empirically contemporary changes but they also seek out new ways of understanding the fit between social, political and economic forces in the development of the world capitalist system. The past decade of restructuring calls into question accepted ways of conceptualising the nature of capitalist industrialisation. There already exist a considerable variety of partial explanations for the current crisis. These include: problems with the costs of energy following the 1970s oil shocks; problems with inflation which also reduces purchasing power and demand; the reduction of investment due to lower rates of profit and rising labour costs; a re-orientation of investments towards greater rationalisation and involving the entire globe; the growing ineffectualness of the Fordist welfare state; and, the impact of technological innovations which create new markets and restructure labour, industry and space.

Along with the above observations there are also more substantively articulated theories of contemporary crisis developed by political economists working in the main traditions of Neo-classicism, Keynesianism and Marxism. A starting point of the Neo-classical approach to crisis is the principle of the impossibility of a true crisis in the sphere of real economic relations of production and exchange. Because of the rational behaviour of economic actors, according to this approach, competition establishes equilibrium through a system of prices compatible with the latter. Also, particular equilibriums occur in the market for products, in the market for factors of production and in the money market. Consequently, the existence of systemic stability and equilibrium, despite temporary perturbations and ill-fits among particular equilibria, are assumed as the overarching system's property by the Neo-classical approach.

Neo-classicists acknowledge that techno-economic laws of production and exchange do not extend to the fields of money and circulation, and, this separation may lead to crisis. Money and circulation introduce discontinuity and crisis in the economic system and, therefore, are the main objects of state intervention. Consequently, monetary policies of the state, which are based on its own political interests and not pure economic considerations, become a permanent agent of perturbation that upsets the natural tendency of markets to arrive at equilibrium. A stable conviction cutting across all Neo-classical approaches, consequently, is the disjuncture between self-regulating workings of the private market and the disequilibrating tendencies brought about by the need for regulation and carried out by a politicised and bureaucratic state.

A questioning of the efficiency of the market system and of endogenous trends that naturally generate equilibria are the starting points for the Keynesian approach to crisis. By criticising the Neo-classical law of outcomes, the quantitative theory of neutral money, and the Neo-classical analysis of the labour market Keynesians arrive at a quite different conception of macro-economic processes. According to their approach a crisis may occur as a result of several factors including: limited returns to capital; counter-developmental policies; a failure of regulation mechanisms; high social costs of development and high functioning costs of capital, through augmented collective consumption; and, even de-investment processes, and so on. However, in the framework of the Keynesian approaches, a crisis does not assume any specific social function. It represents an absolute loss that can be avoided by astute state intervention.

It is also worth mentioning that there is an interesting division among Keynesians in the explanation of the contemporary crisis of the OICs. One group attributes crisis to added value distribution between wages and profits, while another to differentiation of productive structure. The former point out that as wages reached extraordinary levels — especially after the 1960s — they hindered high rates of accumulation, investment and development. In the latter explanation, crisis is the direct product of de-investment characterising a long-term devaluation of capital caused by its use. This devaluation cost is integrated into prices, thus lowering returns to investment, public revenues and effective demand.

Finally, for Marxists crisis is not only possible but even necessary. Focusing on crisis conceptions in *Capital*, we may distinguish four complementary views: A crisis may be (a) a result of a growing imbalance between production and consumption, as production surpasses a level of consumption limited by exploitation; (b) a result of imbalance between sector I (producing the means of production) and sector II (producing goods of consumption), caused either by the anarchy of production or by the inherent trends of capitalism towards production of the means of production and fixed capital accumulation; (c) an outcome of a decline in the return to capital caused by the class struggle and reserve army reduction; and (d) an outcome of lower profitability due to the high organic composition of capital. In all cases the origins of crisis are the social contradictions of capitalism, and crisis is an endogenous mechanism of their regulation. Marx believed that crisis forced capital to restructure, if it could, until the eventual ultimate crisis of revolution. In the years since he worked it is apparent that the restructuring capabilities of capitalism as a consequence of crisis have yet to reach their limits.

The more contemporary Marxian approaches try to combine the above partial views derived from Marx's writings and have fashioned them into several coherent theoretical perspectives on the nature of crisis in capitalism. Two major attempts of this kind are represented by the theory of 'overaccumulation' and by the theory of regulation. Both deal with the manifestations, immediate causes, mechanisms and necessities of crisis. What is also important in these approaches is that they deal with modern capitalism and they introduce an historical differentiation of capitalist forms of development and crisis in their respective explanations. Therefore, they are capable of explaining the present crisis and its historical antecedents, rather than constituting some general theory of all capitalist crises in the past.

The discussions below are driven by a concern for the development of contemporary crisis theory, although the perspective most often adopted by the authors is some variant of the Neo-Marxian approach. The latter is the consequence of a general recognition that the current theories of crisis derived from the main traditions of political economy are presently inadequate. Overarching this collection and integrating its contributions is the requirement that individual authors address the current state of developmental theories. These papers seek to evaluate theoretically the relation between crisis and restructuring through a re-examination of some of the most central topics of modern social organisation, such as Keynesianism, welfare statism, and corporate capitalism. Theories of national growth, accumulation on a world scale, and industrial change are all examined and assessed. The inadequacies of old perspectives are exposed and some more recent approaches, such as the regulationist school, the theory of uneven development and 'modification' theory are introduced and deployed in several case studies.

In short, the following collection does something unique. It brings
the reader up-to-date regarding the current aspects of global capitalist
development and it revises our theoretical understanding of that
process. Interdisciplinary in both its scope and analysis, this book
assembles papers from a range of social scientists coming from *eight*
different countries who assess the relationship between crisis and
restructuring through empirical case studies and theoretical investiga-
tions. In the end, it moves towards the forging of a new perspective on
the nature of political, social and economic forces in the development
of modern, industrial society. The collection has a unifying theme,
namely, the desire to move away from one dimensional, deterministic
explanations of crisis, especially economic reductionism, in order to
forge approaches that consider political and cultural as well as
economic dimensions. A genuine attempt is made in the following
papers to move away from some one-dimensional approaches that
have appeared recently to explain fundamental restructuring in the
OICs, including technological reductionism, neo-Ricardian reductionism, World System Theory, the theory of the 'new international
division of labour', and so on. Instead it is the theme of contingency
and the interplay of various factors pushing capitalist development
that unifies the following papers.

The collection is divided into four parts. Three essays in Part I,
'Theories of Late Capitalism and Crisis', provide a theoretical
overview to the question of contemporary capitalist development and
restructuring. James O'Connor presents us with a summary of his
latest book, *The Meaning of Crisis* (1987).[4] He examines theories of
crisis subscribed to by mainstream economists, orthodox Marxists,
neo- and post-Marxists. These perspectives are termed market theory,
value theory, social theory and social psychological theory by
O'Connor and each provides some understanding of the problematic
nature of system integration. O'Connor argues against strict economic
determinism and shows that crisis possesses a subjective as well as a
structural dimension. The subjective realm of crisis allows individuals
to assert themselves in ways that can alter seemingly deterministic
crisis tendencies through politically motivated change.

Ernest Mandel's paper is a revised version and translation of
chapters from his recent book, *La Crise*.[5] He reviews theories of crisis
specifically with regard to an understanding of the period between
1974 and 1982. Mandel first provides a critique of conventional
Marxist overproduction theories of crisis which are considered limited
because they separate valorisation from realisation problems. Mandel

next provides an overview of crisis explanation. Crisis always upsets the functioning of the law of value under capitalism. Hence, restructuring efforts must be aimed at restoring the operation of the law of value. Essential to any true recovery, however, is a massive devaluation of capital and measures of rationalisation which can be installed to boost the rate of exploitation of the working class. Hence crisis always combines overproduction tendencies with under investment tendencies so that the deep level understanding for crisis and recovery, according to Mandel, is a more global approach to capital logic than often subscribed to by Marxists.

The translated paper by Alain Lipietz represents a third approach to crisis theory, namely, the regulationist perspective. Lipietz sees crisis and change as stemming from two different dynamics: the internal transformations of capitalism, which represent a kind of systemic force; and, the labour movement, which is a potentially anti-systemic, but at times also systemic, force. The two are related and Lipietz is quick to assure the reader that disequilibrating tendencies can arise from the actions of both capital and labour. His goal is merely to explain the relation between the two dynamics for the case of capitalist development as illustrated by three crises. Important in Lipietz's discussion is the isolation of types of labour struggle that can actually serve to 'develop' capitalist productive forces, thereby contributing to crisis resolution rather than the overcoming of capitalist hegemony.

Part II, 'Internationalisation of Accumulation: The Crisis of Integration, Trade and Debt', contains several studies of international development. John Bellamy Foster reviews current global crisis theories but from an important perspective, namely, the break up of US hegemony within the global hierarchy that served in the past to co-ordinate the post-war period of prosperity on a world scale for the OICs. Foster examines the mainstream 'Theory of Hegemonic Stability' or the idea that global order requires the dominance of a single nation, thereby justifying efforts at world leadership, if not imperialism. Foster reviews the rise, since World War II, and subsequent crisis of decline in US hegemony. Current foreign policy of the US is discussed in light of the present loss of dominance, thereby providing an interesting analysis of the Reagan administration's international activities and its adventurist relation to the Third World. The second part of Foster's paper provides a review of Marxian theories of global hegemony including: the internationalisation of capital thesis, dependency theory, unequal exchange theory, and the world system approach. Foster faults many of these perspectives for minimising the role of the Third World countries in the present crisis, treating them as weak and dependent on the OICs, and without autonomous powers of their own to influence the integration of the world order.

Klaus Busch is an exponent of 'modification theory' introduced for the first time in English in his paper. This approach is both a critique of world system theory and the perspective known as the 'new international division of labour'. The latter, also developed in Germany, has been imported earlier into the Anglo-American literature, especially as a label alone without substantive knowledge of its particular theoretical assumptions or limitations. The new international division of labour, like its parent world system perspective, requires as a basic premise that the law of value be assumed to operate at the global level itself. Modification theory challenges this assumption. According to Busch the existence of nation-states with their different currency areas prevents the global operation of the law of value except in a severely modified form. Investment decisions, in particular, are highly sensitive to exchange rates and to nation-state political policies. Busch uses modification theory to discuss attempts at integrating European economies by focusing on the history of the common market or the European Economic Community. By highlighting the problems arising from nation-state policies and differences in exchange rates in an empirical analysis, Busch analyses the contradictory successes and failures of the EEC, especially its long-term failure to achieve economic integration — an outcome Busch believes can never be altered under existing conditions.

John Milios explores modification theory by focusing on its contrasts with other approaches. He provides a thorough critique of the 'new international division of labour' perspective which has failed empirically to be borne out by studies on developing countries, especially the NIC in the Third World. As he remarks, 'The whole construction simply exaggerates the improvement, since 1970, of the competitive position, in the world market, of some third world countries'. As modification theory suggests, Milios finds that international investment takes place mainly among the OICs and Japan and it is this relationship that conditions growth everywhere.

Mike Berry provides an extended discussion of the Pacific Rim countries that amplifies the critique of world system theory and global political economy contained in previous papers. Berry documents in considerable detail the industrialisation of the NICs and South East Asian countries, such as Singapore, South Korea, Hong Kong, the

Philippines and Malaysia, as well as discussing the relationship between these countries and Japan, Australia, New Zealand and the US. Berry illustrates the uneven development occurring presently in this region produced by the uneven power relations between the countries. The nature of Pacific Rim development contradicts prevailing theories of growth and crisis held both by neo-classical and neo-Marxist political economists. Berry proposes an alternate explanation based on the internationalisation of capital thesis but modified to account for the nature of regional uneven development. As with the other authors in this volume, Berry tries to explain why the spectacular success of the NICs is a temporary phenomenon related to the absence of a global capitalist system and the decline of American hegemony.

The final paper in this section is a second contribution by Ernest Mandel. This time Mandel provides an account of the heretofore missing dimension of global crisis, namely, the overpowering level of debt. In previous work Mandel has already pointed out that post-war prosperity is by and large a product of debt financing.[6] Both the permanent war economy and what the regulationist theorists would call the neo-Fordist, consumerist regime of accumulation, have been made possible by immense levels of borrowing and the introduction of the modern system of credit. In his paper, Mandel extends his analysis of this phenomenon to examine the relationship between the OIC, the NIC and the rest of the Third World. Arguing against reductionist economic approaches, Mandel asserts that contemporary developmental theory must understand the complex relation between debt, credit, the phenomenon of capital flight by indigenous bourgeoisies, the combined political and economic activities of finance capital and the separate changes and movements occurring in corporate, industrial capital.

Part III addresses the mode of regulation and the crisis of the welfare state. One aim of this collection is to grasp the multi-dimensional nature of crisis and its relation to societal development. The previous section has been devoted more to an examination of economic theories of crisis. In this part we consider changes currently taking place in the mode of regulation, more specifically, the restructuring of the welfare state in the OICs. In this regard we have chosen to constrast the cases of Great Britain, West Germany and the United States.

Desmond King's lead off paper makes several contributions. First, it provides a general overview of the growth of the modern welfare state among the OICs. King carefully points out the role of political ideologies, party politics and the class struggle, along with economic factors associated with crisis restructuring in his survey. Second, King provides an informative account of the relation between the welfare state and the economy, especially through a focus on the process of 'decommodification' and the role of the state in the general provision of use values for both capital and labour. Finally, King discusses the present by comparing the rise of conservatism and the retrenchment of the welfare state, or 'recommodification' in the US and Great Britain.

For the case of contemporary political change and the interpretation of the relation between the modern state and the economy, more so than perhaps for the analysis of accumulation processes alone, the regulationist perspective provides the strongest available means for an understanding of current socio-political restructuring. For this reason the remaining two papers in this section have been chosen because of their original contributions to regulationist theory, that is, their analysis of the transition from Fordism to post-Fordism.

Bob Jessop, like Desmond King, also addresses the theme of the rise of conservatism; this time with a comparison between Thatcherism and the Kohl regime in West Germany. Despite the presence of a similar ideology of governance in the two countries, quite different paths have been taken in the restructuring of the welfare state, and Jessop explains this contrast. His paper commences with a general discussion of regulationist theory. This is more detailed and current than the remarks of Lipietz above. He provides an historical overview of the rise of Fordism in both Britain and West Germany illustrating many of the theoretical concepts deployed in his discussion of this perspective. Jessop explains crisis restructuring in terms of the transition from Fordism to post-Fordism and discusses the factors leading to the contrasting records of Thatcher and Kohl. He concludes with an analysis of the nature of post-Fordism that is applicable to other countries as well.

The theme of party politics and its role in the restructuring of the mode of regulation was touched on in King's paper. This subject is the central focus of the final paper in this section. Juergen Haeusler and Joachim Hirsch examine the transition to Post-Fordism in West Germany specifically through a study of political party changes. The authors provide their own overview of the regulationist approach which contrasts somewhat with that of Jessop. They quickly get to their main theme, however, namely the role of political parties as regulatory institutions. This is a significant contribution to the theory of the modern state. This analysis is more complex than approaches that merely focus on the role of the class struggle in conditioning the relation between the state and the economy. Finally, they discuss the present party crisis in West Germany and the potential trend of organisational fragmentation which is accompanying the transition to Post-Fordism.

Part IV concerns the impact of current societal changes on local areas and the relation between capitalist development and space. Hartmut Hausermann and Thomas Krämer-Badoni discuss the highly significant changes taking place in West Germany without which support for Kohl and the transition to post-Fordism cannot be attained. Simply put, West Germany is experiencing a shift in productive vitality similar to the 'sunbelt-frostbelt' change in the US. More specifically, the older industrialised and highly populated manufacturing cities of the north are experiencing a depression, while the modern, reindustrialised cities of the south are booming. Although high technology oriented business is one factor in the national pattern of uneven development, the authors point out other causes as well, thereby avoiding the current plague of high-tech determinism (see Gottdiener below), including global changes in competition, domestic political policy, and contrasting labour organisation. In particular, the authors document the explicit role of state regulation in the new spatial transfer of value leading to the reversal of fortunes between the north and the south. They conclude with a discussion of the social and political consequences of the north's decline and reflect on the patterns of change accompanying the transition to post-Fordism that will rule West Germany in the future.

Nicos Komninos examines the new patterns of capital accumulation and their relation to new spatialities that have appeared in Western Europe. Komninos provides a detailed discussion of the elements comprising restructuring forces including political aspects of regulation as well as new forms of accumulation that have arisen as a consequence of crisis adjustment. He then discusses restructuring's impact on spatiality, especially the new forms of uneven development and social inequality. Komninos characterises contemporary changes in terms of four associated processes: de-industrialisation, re-industrialisation, high-tech clustering and decentralisation. Finally, Komninos illustrates the way these processes have combined with new forms of regulation to alter local space.

M. Gottdiener examines the relation between crisis theory and socio-spatial restructuring with regard specifically to the US case. Gottdiener is critical of current approaches which assert that some new phase of capitalism is responsible for the restructuring of space in cities and suburbs. He suggests, instead, that such changes have a long history in the US. In contrast to approaches that are technologically deterministic, that stress production at the expense of other contingently related factors and that advocate the world system perspective, Gottdiener proposes a separate theory which contingently relates six social forces that have transformed space since World War II including: racism, the transformation of the corporate/bureaucratic form, the action of knowledge and technology as a force of production, the interventionist activities of the state mode of regulation, the operation of a relatively independent second circuit of capital involving real estate and labour sourcing.

In a final paper Hyman Minsky, an economist, discusses the significance of the stock market crash of October 1987 for crisis theory. He suggests that a major source of volatility in American capitalism is the chaotic financial market. Consequently, theories such as the neo-classical synthesis, monetarism, and supply-side economics, that assert the equilibrating powers of decentralised markets, have been proven false by current events. Minsky points out that money market volatility does not conform to standard business cycle or crisis theory views of capitalism. Between 1980 and 1987, for example, the Federal Reserve has had to intervene five times to bring stability back to financial markets. This changes the nature of economic regulation because policies are directed more towards controlling chaotic sources of instability rather than pursuing longer term strategies through the regulation of growth.

At present money markets and alternative channels of investment have become a new force in American capitalism. Pension funds, mutual funds, insurance companies and bank administered trusts all have a powerful and potentially destabilising role. Minsky calls this new stage of growth 'Money Managed Capitalism'. Due to microelectronics and so-called programme trading, managed money is active money. Managers now pursue active, short-term asset appreciation by fine tuning portfolios. The presence of managed money, which represents almost wholly a speculative enterprise, complicates the crisis base of capitalism and calls into question existing theories that stress the equilibrating nature of markets.

CRISIS THEORY AND THE RESTRUCTURING OF CAPITAL

Since the 1960s industrialised capitalist countries have been subjected to wave after wave of changes in the economy, politics and culture.

Some of these include: rapid innovations in new technologies, intense international competition, fiscal problems of welfare states leading to privatisation, the growth of a new middle class that has forced new social cleavages and styles of consumption, shifts in the structure of production in favour of export and/or defence goods, new forms of money, technopole growth and the decay of traditional urban centres, shifts away from the social engineering agenda of the welfare state, the weakened dollar and the breakup of US hegemony in the West, de-industrialisation, re-industrialisation, the progressive deconcentration of metropolitan areas, and new relations between capital and labour.

There is a logic to social change but it involves less the structural logic of capitalist dynamics and more the institutional logic that accounts for the need to coordinate economic and political processes in advanced industrialised societies. This 'regulationist' logic worked well for the stage of Fordism prior to the 1960s. With new conditions of production and consumption it is much less clear whether the necessary adjustments between the economy and the society will arrive at some clearly focused model of development that can inspire imitation in a number of countries. At present it seems as if different societies have embarked on their own modes of development which stand in subtle contrast despite similarities. Variety in the mode of development has resulted from differences among countries with regard to respective class capacities that guide change according to the conflicting interests of capital and labour. However, this is not the only factor; variation is also the product of differences in the institutional means by which technology is researched, developed and transferred or assimilated. Compare the great extremes of Japan and the USSR, for example. This second axis of differentiation has become a popular subject of study as industrialised societies gear up to compete in new rounds of international trade. Remaining neglected, however, by advocates of a new mode of society such as 'flexible accumulation' or periodised Fordism, is the slumbering potential of the working class as it absorbs each new shock apparently as yet without an organised and sustained collective response that has opposed the declining social wage and the assault on union power itself.

Differences among countries in the present transition are also the product of a third factor, namely, state policies which in turn relate both to the relative position of countries in the global system and to endogenous needs of societal reproduction and social control. Once again structural conditions, such as the operation of the law of value at the international level, are tempered by institutional and contingent factors, such as the operation of exchange rate differences on investment and product flows. Additionally, it would be hard to explain new forms of development in the US, including the process of capital deepening and the deconcentration of urban space without understanding the state's role in promoting a permanent defence-oriented economy and industrial and housing subsidies to both business and the middle class.

All this means that crisis theory, of the type once used by economists to explain the ebb and flow of country fortunes has lost much of its explanatory ability. More importantly, it can no longer be asserted that societal changes, such as the emergence of new forms of space, new technologies, or new institutional arrangements for the fiscal support of cities and the quality of life, can be attributed solely or even directly to changes in the realisation of profit rates and the operation of the law of value. The great pressure to rationalise investment flows has forced capital to renegotiate its terms with labour, cities, and even nation-states. As this adjustment process plays itself out in country after country, the effects of institutional, historical and contingent factors are deeply felt and the process of adjustment bears witness to the saliency of political, technological and cultural factors in addition to those deriving from the logic of accumulation. Furthermore, there seems no immediate end to these pressures for change. While capital can shift between countries using real time electronics, regulation still relies on the snails' pace of political and state-sanctioned policy initiatives. Policy lags behind and thereby provides a source of future crisis tendencies that are not products of the law of value.

Regulationist theory has attempted to grasp this more sophisticated arrangement of political economy. It does its best when explaining the multi-causal accommodations under Fordism. It is much less impressive in dealing with current changes and their variation among industrialised countries. In the future perhaps some more effective theory of contemporary social organisation, possibly itself an outgrowth of the regulationist effort, will no doubt appear. At present, however, we merely possess the threads of a new understanding. What are clear are the fundamental limitations of all one-sided arguments that have stressed single features of change, such as flexible accumulation or particular, and possibly temporary, changes in the capital-labour relation forced on labour due to the crisis conditions of job loss, that allegedly accounts for the new forms of state policies, business organisations and space. The papers in this collection argue for a more multicausal and contingently related process of change organised, in theory, around the necessity for some working accommodation between forms of regulation, modes of accumulation and paths of development within an increasingly structured global system of international competition. Precisely *how* economic, political and cultural factors lock step together in some yet to be devised post-Fordist mode of development must be left as a project for continuing and future work.

NOTES

1. M. Aglietta, *A Theory of Capitalist Regulation* (London: New Left Books, 1979).
2. Ibid.
3. M. Gottdiener, *The Social Production of Urban Space* (Austin: University of Texas Press, 1985).
4. J. O'Connor, *The Meaning of Crisis* (Oxford: Basil Blackwell, 1987).
5. E. Mandel, *La Crise* (Paris, Flammarion, 1982).
6. See E. Mandel, *Late Capitalism* (New York: Velos Press, 1975).

Part I
Theories of Late Capitalism and Crisis

2 An Introduction to a Theory of Crisis Theories

James O'Connor

INTRODUCTION

The purpose of this chapter is to outline a critical theory of crisis theories. There are four kinds of explanations of various aspects of the modern crisis put forth by bourgeois economists, non-orthodox Marxists, and neo- and post-Marxist theorists. These may be conveniently called market theory, value theory, social theory, and social psychological theory, respectively. The subject of bourgeois market theory is system integration of capitalist economy at the level of exchange or market relationships. The subject of neo-orthodox Marxist value theory is capitalist system integration at the level of the production and circulation of capital and capital accumulation. The subject of social theory is capitalist social integration and that of social psychological theory is personality integration. These approaches to crisis theory are based on four progressively less objectified and formal levels of abstraction from the palpable reality of capitalist daily life. It should be stressed that none of these approaches to the modern crisis of capitalism is more correct than any of the others. Rather, each is a successively more concrete, less deterministic, and more 'historically interior' interpretation than the one immediately preceding it. Each is an increasingly less partial and more substantive view of reality, which progressively subsumes (or sublates) the views antecedent to it.[1]

Another purpose of this article is to suggest a critique of economic determinism and note the explanatory power of neo- and post-Marxist social and social psychological theory in the realm of material life. The practical importance of this is to show that 'crisis' is not and cannot be merely an objective historical process (such as, for example, the turning point in an illness over which the victim has no control). 'Crisis' is also a subjective historical process — a time when it is not possible to take for granted 'normal' economic, social, and other relationships; a time for decision; and a time when what individuals actually do counts for something. This is congruent with the classical Greek meaning of

21

crisis defined in terms of uncertain or arguable evaluations of a disease or illness. In short, this article encourages the opening up of crisis theory to more interpretive and less deterministic approaches, meanwhile attempting to avoid simple subjectivism or voluntarism.

MARKET COMPETITION AND MARKET THEORY

The most objectified and formal level of capitalist society is the totality of exchange relationships which is conventionally called the 'market'. Exchange or market relationships are the process whereby property rights in labour power, raw materials, machinery, buildings, land, consumer goods, and credit are exchanged against one another through the medium of money, the 'universal equivalent'. In the capitalist market, real individuals are 'bearers of commodities' and 'commodity guardians' (to use Marx's expression) — mere personifi- cations of exchange relationships themselves. Hence real individuals objectify themselves and others in the sense that they abstract from their own and others' identities as workers, lovers, friends, women or men, members of ethnic groups etc., as well as their own irreducibly singular human natures, or what Walt Whitman called the 'me myself'.

The most abstract and also the most superficial crisis theory is bourgeois market theory or the theory of market equilibrium which is an account of disjunctures or breakdowns in the transfer of property rights between capitalist enterprises and individuals. These disjunc- tures or breakdowns appear to be the cause as well as the consequence of economic crisis because exchange relationships appear to be the central reality of capitalist life. This is so because they are the hidden way in which labour becomes social labour, or the basic social activity through which capital makes itself public or reveals itself. This may be illustrated by the fact that data about commodity prices, stock prices, interest rates, sales volumes, and other market information inundate the popular consciousness; that civil lawyers and judges do little else than try to ensure equitable and secure transfers of rights to property; that politicians promise little more than to support policies which will enhance the market value of their constituents' property; that the most common questions heard in developed capitalist society are: How much does it cost? and How much money is there in it?

Market theorists abstract from what is commonly called 'work' (excepting the issue of physical productivity per worker) or what Marxists call the imposition and exploitation of labour within specifically capitalist relations of production. This abstraction is natural because the capitalist labour process is a peculiar form of private property, a kind of social secret which the capitalist monopoly of private property in the means of production conceals from public view. The labour process is known therefore only to the degree that labour organisers, investigative journalists, sociologists of work, and others critically expose it to public scrutiny. Furthermore, market theory abstracts from social, cultural, and ideological relationships, not to speak of the real-life experiences of real human beings within and outside of the labour process.

Market theory is the foundation of the bourgeois world view which holds that modern crisis trends such as growing state deficits, inflation, unemployment, Third World debt, and so on are the result of market disequilibria and/or inadequate monetary incentives and penalties and/or (in macro-economic theory) disparities between physical production capacity and effective demand for commodities, excessively high interest rates, and so on. Neo-liberal bourgeois economists, in particular, regard market mechanisms as autonomous forces which tend toward stability and/or stable economic growth as a result of the free workings of competition and the price mechanism. However, stable equilibria or growing productivity and growth may be disrupted or distorted by excessive government, labour union, or other monopolistic interference with free competition, or by the wrong kind of government intervention. A well-known example is the neo-liberal view that the current problems of capitalism are in large part the result of excessive government regulation and public deficits and borrowing, which raise interest rates and hence discourage investment spending.[2]

PRODUCTION RELATIONS AND VALUE THEORY

The neo-orthodox Marxist theory of economic crisis is based on a more concrete level of capitalist society than market theory, namely, social labour and social class relationships. Emphasis is given to the theory of labour exploitation and its relationship to economic crisis and the theory of the contradiction between productive forces and production relationships.

The Marxist value theory of crisis is meant to be a two-edged sword. First, it is a critique of the self-objectification of human beings within exchange relationships and the labour process, that is, it is a critique of the capitalist ideology of commodity and capital fetishism. Second,

Marxist crisis theory is a reconstruction of the problem of capitalist accumulation and crisis. This is so because it is more totalistic than market theory and because it incorporates market theory in ways which transform the meaning or status it has in bourgeois economics. However, value theory retains the convention of abstracting from social-cultural life as well as real individuals, or 'real frogs in real gardens'. Value theory is the foundation of the traditional or neo-orthodox Marxist world view which holds that deficits, unemployment, inflation, and so on are the result of contradictions inherent in the process of capital valorisation, self-expanding capital, and especially contradictions between the production and realisation of capital arising from the exploitation of labour.

It is important to stress that traditional or neo-orthodox Marxists present their work as a critique of market theory including its reformist Keynesian variants. Neo-orthodox Marxists critique the former in that they theorise the relationship between value production and value realisation rather than market relations alone. They critique Keynesian crisis theory in that they theorise the relationship between value and surplus value production (and total revenues and their distribution between social classes) rather than the relationship between physical production capacity and effective demand. Neo-orthodox Marxists also critique neo-Keynesian crisis theory in that they theorise the relationship between changes in value and surplus value production (and changes in revenues and their distribution) rather than the relationship between changes in physical production capacity and changes in investment and consumption spending. Marxist economists are thus better able to understand the movements of capital as a whole in general and the process of accumulation through economic crisis in particular.

Marxist theorists believe that value relationships based on capitalist class domination and exploitation of labour are inherently unstable or crisis-ridden, and also that capitalism is inherently crisis-dependent. Economic crisis, however, may be postponed or displaced by imperialistic expansion, the growth of credit money, restructuring of physical production and social relationships between capital and labour, and capital mobility, among other ways, as well as by state fiscal, monetary, and other policies. A well-known example is the view that current problems of world capitalism are in large part the result of capital over-production and/or the tendency of the average rate of profit to fall, which threatens to bring about a general crisis, which, in turn, the dangerous expansion of credit money and fictitious profits postpones or displaces into the political sphere and state budget, or internationalises (for example, the creation of massive Third World debt).

The strength of neo-orthodox Marxism, however, is also its weakness. Marxist political economists have a powerful method to theorise global movements of capital, labour, commodities, credit, and money and, at the same time, a manifest inability to grasp their social and political meanings, hence real possibilities of social struggles and social movements. The basic reason is that neo-orthodox Marxists regard individuals and groups as personifications of capitalist production forces and relations, competition, and other categories of capital, and, in this sense, little separates them from bourgeois economists. The exception to this rule occurs during times of economic crisis when workers may discard their masks as owners of the commodity labour power and reappear on the historical stage as a political class or class-for-itself. Neo-orthodox Marxists thus define economic crisis in objectivist terms, or ruptures or breakdowns in the labour or capital markets, commodity markets, or production itself. Social crisis and political class struggle are seen as historical dependent variables dancing to the tune of the independent variable called economic crisis. Put another way, Marxists have a systems theory of economic crisis and a social and political theory of social crisis and political struggle, maintaining that the latter is dependent on the former. The Communist Party is then regarded as the embodiment of organised historical subjectivity and working-class emancipation, which may come about during economic crisis. The extreme sciencism and voluntarism, which has plagued Western radicalism for a century or more, originates in Victorian objectivist and individualistic (or great man) theories of history, respectively. It is based on the premise that social development is governed 'in the last instance' by economic laws, on the one hand, and strong-willed leaders or the fittest on the other. In this sense, there is little space separating Marx and Herbert Spencer, both 19th-century thinkers, in life as well as death. In fact, this premise conflates the theory of the conditions of capitalist accumulation with the theory of capitalist development historically understood, or a priori theory with interpretive dialectics.[3]

While bourgeois economists outline surface crisis phenomena, Marxists expose deeper crisis manifestations at the level of social labour and contradictions between capitalist production forces and relationships. However, both market relations and social labour are, in fact, abstractions at both the social and theoretical levels. Nowhere in the world are there pure exchange relations or processes of social labour (or value production and circulation) which are not inscribed and structured by cultural, ideological, and other social productive forces. Culture and ideology are embedded in market and production forces and relations in complex ways — the discovery of which brings us closer to real history. History and class struggle, therefore, are not structured by movements of social labour and capital alone, nor still less by changes in wages, prices, and profits, or market forces. They are ambiguously structured by culture and ideology, tradition and fantasy, personality development, and other social processes which cannot be reduced to material life strictly defined. Put another way, class struggle does not take place within the productive circuit of capital alone, nor still less the money and commodity circuits (e.g., wage struggle and struggle against inflation). Class struggle takes place within and against cultural, ideological, state, and other imaginary and real structures within which capital organises itself and which simultaneously organise the movements of capital.[4] Especially the variants of crisis theory which equate exploitation, crisis and class struggle need to be revolutionised to take into account this basic fact. Failure to do so makes a firm grasp of the 'concrete totality' of modern capitalism and imperialism as allusive as it was to the successive Communist Internationals of the 19th and 20th centuries.

SOCIAL RELATIONS AND SOCIAL THEORY

In modern neo-Marxist theories of social crisis, special notice must be taken of the fact that real individuals in historical time and space are implicitly or explicitly defined as personifications of social categories — ascriptive or demographic groups such as women, racial minorities, youth, and the elderly, on the one hand, and quasi-groups such as environmentalists and urban movements, on the other.[5] In this way, neo-Marxists retain the convention established within neo-orthodox Marxism of reifying the lived experience of real people in real history. However, critical theory and neo-Marxism are less abstract or more concrete than Marxist political economy, hence potentially more useful in the concrete analysis of concrete situations. Put another way, neo-Marxism at its rare best critically incorporates market and value theories in ways which transform their meaning in bourgeois and neo-orthodox Marxist thinking, respectively, and thus comes closer to representing the 'concrete totality' (in Karl Kosik's words) of the social, cultural, ideological, and political economic contradictions which constitute the modern crisis.[6] Social theory is the foundation of the world view which holds that unemployment, inflation, deficits, and other crisis manifestations are the result of contradictions within and between social and political structures and social action within and against developed capitalist social and ideological structures based not only on work and class but also gender, ethnic, national, and other identities. These identities, including the modern sense of self-hood, combine and recombine in complex ways which transcend reductionist science as well as individualistic and subjectivistic interpretations of the present as history.

Social theory at its best defines the modern crisis not only in terms of market relations and production forces and relationships, but also and more importantly in terms of popular interpretations of these categories, including dominant cultural symbols, lived ideologies, political illusions, family relations, and so on. The main tenet of social theory is that there is no such thing as an economy defined in either bourgeois or neo-orthodox Marxist terms, hence no economic crisis strictly defined, hence, in turn, no strict theory of economic crisis. Instead, there is a theory of social and political crisis and struggle which are and are not part and parcel of economic crisis and economic struggle. In sum, both neo-orthodox and those neo-Marxist conventions which separate economic and social crisis in the form of systems theory and action theory are inadequate. The critique of the well-established dualism between objectivist and subjectivist approaches to crisis theory is based on the idea that modern economic, social, political, and cultural crisis interpenetrate one another in ways which transform them into different dimensions of the same historical process — the disintegration and reintegration of the modern world. It is also based on the idea that both neo-orthodox Marxism and many varieties of neo-Marxism mistakenly view the working class and/or particular social groups as merely crisis victims, who may or may not fight back depending on whether or not neo-orthodox Marxist-Leninist parties and neo- and post-Marxist new social movements succeed in their different projects of enlightenment. The critique of this view is based on the claim that the working class, social and cultural movements, the state, and society as a whole are themselves implicated in the development of the forms and contents of the modern crisis.[7]

PERSONALITY RELATIONS AND SOCIAL PSYCHOLOGICAL THEORY

The premise of personality crisis theory is that the most concrete level of social life is the day-to-day lived experiences of real social individuals, that is, individuals who at one and the same time are containers of property and class relationships, ascriptively based relationships, and so on, and at the same time are irreducibly singular or unique persons. Everyday thoughts, feelings, and actions are more often than not accepted matter-of-factly, but within the context of personality crisis they also may be creatively innovated in self-conscious or unself-conscious ways, hence filled with uncertainty, surprise, real and false hopes and disappointments. Personality organisation includes forms of psychological repression, sublimation, and projection which guard against individual self-knowledge and also more transparent views and experiences of capitalist alienation, exploitation, and reification. Psychological repression also distorts communication between the inner parts of individual personalities as well as between individuals and groups. In this sense, personality organisation includes the social and cultural processes of the production and evolution of experience and meaning (not only fact and knowledge) as well as inner personality conflicts and struggle.

This account of personality crisis is a critique of the self-deceptions which individuals use to legitimate to themselves as self-defined moral beings and deceptions of others. It is also an exploratory account of the value of modern repression including forms of distorted communication, hence of possibilities of successful social integration into the structures of modern capitalism. Personality crisis theory is an analysis of the relationship between confused social integration based on repression of affect, unresolved inner conflicts, and distorted self-knowledge, on the one hand, and communication, social and system integration, and economic crisis, on the other. It is also an account of individual struggles against ideological individualistic identities and for a richer social identity, i.e., the way in which struggles against repressed affect are both causes and consequences of the development of a social individuality. In particular, personality crisis is essential for the imminent development of a social individuality; redefinitions of the self as a social being presuppose the successful resolution of personality crisis. Personality crisis theory also stresses the relationship between struggles for social individuality and the social construction of crisis as struggles within and against the capitalist state and political apparatus. Political struggle and its relationship to personality struggle both are defined not only in terms of means to particular material or social ends but also as ends in and of themselves. In this way, the old dreams of politics as the vehicle for the good and just life, and individual identity as the vehicle of moral and rational, as well as expressive and aesthetic, public life might be reintroduced into crisis theory in useful ways.

NOTES

1. 'As an ontological category, the "subject" is the power of an entity to "be itself in its otherness." ... Only such a mode of existence can incorporate the negative into the positive. Negative and positive cease to be opposed to each other when the driving power of the subject makes negativity a part of the subject's own unity. Hegel says that the subject "mediates" ... and "sublates" ... the negativity. In the process the object does not dissolve into its various qualitative or quantitative determinations, but is substantially held together throughout its relations with other objects.' (Herbert Marcuse, *Reason and Revolution: Hegel and the Rise of Social Theory*, New York, 1954, p. 69).

2. A good account of this crisis theory of the great rebels within economics —Hobson, Schumpeter, and Veblen (whose works are well-known and are not discussed in this article) — is: Paul Mattick, 'Bourgeois Economics', *Economic Crisis and Crisis Theory* (London, 1981).

3. All 19th century social theory — whether Marxist, Durkheimian, or Weberian — lacks any plausible method to combine positivistic and interpretive approaches to history. There is a strong methodological resemblance between Marx's theory of the *conditions* of capital accumulation, Durkheim's theory of the *conditions* of social solidarity, and Weber's theory of the *conditions* of legitimate authority. The historical conditions, hence intellectual conditions, for 'post-scientific' theory in the 'age of capital' were lacking. Only in the late 20th-century world revolutionary epoch, that is, the epoch of permanent crisis, has theoretical history and sound interpretive approaches to theory and practice become possible. In short, the historical subject today is not capital as such, but social-cultural labour and production and reproduction relationships (for example, James O'Connor, *Accumulation Crisis*, Oxford, 1984, chapters 2 and 3).

4. *Accumulation Crisis*, op. cit., passim.

5. The term 'quasi-group' was coined by Jürgen Habermas, to the best of my knowledge.

6. Social theory is thus a critique of the critique which value theory makes of market theory. It is a dialectic of non-identity, hence open-ended and inherently self-critical.

7. *Accumulation Crisis*, op. cit., passim.

3 Theories of Crisis: An Explanation of the 1974–82 Cycle

Ernest Mandel[1]

OVER-PRODUCTION CRISES IN GENERAL: THE MARXIST EXPLANATION

The Marxist theory of the industrial cycle, like the academic theory, has suffered from the penchant of influential authors to advance monocausal explanations for periodic over-production crises. Two great 'schools' have arisen. One claims that the crises are caused by the under-consumption of the masses (that is, over-production of consumer goods), the other that they are caused by over-accumulation (meaning the insufficiency of profit to continue expansion in the production of producer goods). This debate is but a variant of the old debate between those who explained the crises by 'insufficient aggregate demand', and those who explained them by 'disproportionality'.

Both schools have made undeniable contributions to a deeper understanding of crises. But they both commit the error of arbitrarily dividing what is organically linked in the very heart of capitalist production. This is the origin of their inability to elaborate a comprehensively satisfactory Marxist theory of crises, beginning from the hints Marx left us in his major works.[2] This division is particularly astonishing since Marx himself explicitly stressed in his last writings — the manuscript of the third volume of *Capital* — that the explanation of the phenomenon of periodic crises must *combine* the problems resulting from the fall of the rate of profit with those of the realisation of surplus-value: 'The conditions of direct exploitation and those of realising it are not identical ... The first are only limited by the productive power of society, the latter by the proportional relation of the various branches of production and the consumer power of society'.[3]

The capitalist mode of production is *both* generalised commodity

30

production and production for profit by firms operating independently of one another. It cannot be one without the other. It is both a system oriented towards the production of a growing mass of surplus-value (of surplus-labour) and a system in which the real appropriation of this surplus-value is dependent on the possibility of actually selling commodities, which contain this surplus-value, at their production prices (returning the average rate of profit) or at prices permitting the realisation of super-profits. Any other interpretation of the capitalist mode of production dispels one of its intrinsic structural characteristics without which it would no longer be capitalist.

Formulae such as the following are especially mystifying: 'Capital appropriates more and more surplus-value because it is in capital's very nature to expand in value'. Such a formulation conjures away the conditions that limit realisation of the expansive tendency of capital, that is, the contradictions of the system. (It may be added in passing that it is also sadly tautological, of the same order as the assertion that opium is a sedative because of its soporific properties.)

The very nature of the 'basic cell' of capitalist production — the commodity — implies its necessary cleavage into 'commodity' and 'money'. The commodity is *simultaneously* the product of private and social labour. But this social labour, realised in the form of private production, cannot be recognised immediately and a priori as such. The commodity thus cannot present itself immediately as social labour; it requires conditions under which this representation becomes external to it, in the form of exchange value, in the form of money. But this a posteriori recognition of the social labour contained in the commodity is always problematical; it always depends on the actual sale of the commodity and on the price at which it is sold.

It matters little to the capitalist that a growing mass of surplus-value has been *produced* in the course of production if he obtains only a fraction of the counter-value of this surplus-value in the course of circulation. Production of surplus-value does not automatically entail its realisation. Thus, in the very division of the commodity itself in commodity and money, which is necessary if the exchange value of the commodity is to be realised, and in the contradiction between the use-value and the exchange-value of this commodity, we find the initial possibility of over-production crises.

Unlike pre-capitalist crises (or post-capitalist crises, for that matter), which are nearly always crises of physical shortage, that is, crises of *under-production of use-values*, capitalist crises are crises of *over-production of exchange values*. It is not because there are too few products that economic life is upset. It is because it is impossible to sell commodities at prices guaranteeing the average rate of profit — that is, because there are 'too many commodities' — that economic life is disorganised, factories close, employers dismiss workers, and production, incomes, sales, investment, and employment decline.

What are the causes of capitalist economic crises? Is it the 'over accumulation of capital'? Undoubtedly; in a moment we shall explain exactly what this means. But not in the mechanistic sense that if only wages had been lower and profits higher accumulation, and therefore growth, could have continued unhindered. For the 'over-accumulation of capital' is accompanied by an 'over-production of commodities', and lower wage levels certainly would not have prevented that! Indeed, Marx himself derided those who admitted that there was 'over-production of capital' while denying 'over-production of commodities'.[4]

Is it the 'under-consumption of the masses' (of society as a whole)? Undoubtedly this plays a role. On several occasions Marx emphasised that 'the ultimate reason for all real crises always remains the poverty and restricted consumption of the masses, as opposed to the drive of capitalist production to develop the productive forces as though the absolute [physical — E.M.] consuming power of society constituted their limit'.[5] This should not be understood, however, in the vulgar sense that crises could be avoided if wages were raised. For, it must be repeated, the capitalists have no interest in simply selling commodities. They are interested in selling them at *sufficient profits*. Now, any increase in wages beyond a certain threshold must inevitably reduce first the rate and then even the mass of profits and thus impede the accumulation of capital and new profits.

Is it the 'anarchy of production' and 'disproportionality' among various branches of production, rooted in private property and the generalised market economy? Again, this undoubtedly plays a role. Provided one does not present a 'harmonicist' vision of this explanation by claiming that a 'general cartel to regularise production' in all sectors would suffice to eliminate over-production crises. For under the capitalist mode of production, the disproportion between production and consumption by the 'ultimate consumers' is itself an *autonomous constituent element* of the system, side by side with anarchy of capitalist production.

Is it the 'falling rate of profit'? Once again, undoubtedly this is a factor, but not in the mechanistic sense of the term, which would imply a linear causal chain of the type: fall in the rate of profit → reduction of investment → reduction of employment → reduction of incomes → over-production crisis. Generally, there is an increase and not a reduction in investment on the eve of a crash, just as generally there is an increase and not a reduction in wages during the period of feverish activity that precedes the outbreak of the crisis. (Obviously, there are some exceptions to this rule. In West Germany investment did indeed begin to decline before the outbreak of the 1974–75 recession.)

To understand the real sequence linking the fall in the rate of profit, the over-production crisis, and the outbreak of the crisis, we must distinguish the phenomena of *appearance* of the crisis, the *detonators* of the crisis, their deeper *cause*, and their *function* in the framework of the intrinsic logic of the capitalist mode of production.

The capitalist economic crisis is always a crisis of over-production of commodities. This is neither a mere appearance nor the product of 'deformed ideological view'. The over-production crisis is a tangible reality which Marxism seeks to explain and not to drown in a sea of pseudo-theoretical verbiage.

Over-production always means that capitalism has produced more commodities than can be bought by available purchasing power if they are sold at their production prices, at prices that render the owners of these commodities the anticipated rate of profit. Whatever the deeper meanderings of the analysis, the first phenomenon that must be grasped is this sharp break in the unstable equilibrium between the supply and demand of commodities that prevails in 'normal times'.

Suddenly, supply exceeds effective demand to the point that it provokes a massive decline in orders and a significant reduction in current production. It is this sales slump, depletion of inventories, and reduction in current production which bring on the *cumulative movement of the crisis*: reduction in employment, incomes, investment, production, etc. And this occurs in both fundamental departments of production, that of producer goods (Department I) and that of consumer goods (Department II).

It matters little whether the slump begins in one or the other of these two departments. Empirically, it may be noted that most often it begins in Department II. This was the case for the 1974–75 and 1980–82 recessions (automobiles and housing). But this empirical fact expresses no particular intrinsic logic. There have been and can be over-production crises that begin simultaneously in both departments and others — less frequently — which begin in Department I, that of producer goods.

The forms in which over-production crises emerge must be

distinguished from the event that precipitates them. The detonator may be a financial scandal, a sudden panic, the bankruptcy of a great firm, or more simply a reversal of the cycle (generalised slump) in some key sector of the world market. The detonator can even be a sudden shortage of an essential raw material (or energy); such was the case in 1866, when the crisis was triggered by a shortage of cotton resulting from the civil war in the United States. But the detonator does not *cause* the crisis. It merely precipitates it inasmuch as it triggers the cumulative movement described above. In order for it to be able to trigger this chain of events, however, a whole series of preconditions must coincide, and these in no way flow automatically from the detonator itself.

For instance, the resounding bankruptcy of a great commercial company or a big bank generally will not strangle expansion at the beginning of a boom. It will have this effect only at the end of this phase, because all the elements of the impending crisis have already come together and are merely awaiting a catalytic event to break out.

The objective function of the over-production crisis for the development of the capitalist mode of production is another concept, which also must be differentiated from that of the forms of appearance of the crisis, its detonator, and its deeper causes. The objective function of the crisis is to *constitute a mechanism through which the law of value asserts itself*, despite capitalist competition (or the action of the monopolies).

At the beginning of every industrial cycle there is rationalisation, increased intensity of labour, and accentuated technical progress. (This is especially true during the epoch of the great technological revolutions which subtend the phases of accelerated capitalist expansion, such as the phase from 1940, or 1948, to the end of the 1960s.) In a market economy, a pronounced rise in productivity always means a fall in the value of commodities. (It matters little if this is masked by a depreciation of paper money. A price calculation in gold or in hours of labour-time would rapidly reveal this fall in value.) But a period of 'over-heating' is precisely one in which the capitalist owners of commodities — especially those industrialists who have been applying the most advanced techniques — are able, with varying degrees of success, *to hold the old values in force*, which assures them copious super-profits. The slump, over-production, and sudden breakup of the balance between supply and demand is precisely the mechanism that triggers the fall in prices. In other words, it imposes the new values of commodities that result from the rise in productivity, thus provoking heavy profit losses and a heavy devalorisation of capital for the capitalists.[6]

It may likewise be noted that the upturn and the beginning of the boom are precisely the phases of the cycle in which the massive renovation of fixed capital occurs in a manner rather concentrated in time, not staggered more or less proportionally over the years of its 'moral' duration. The cyclical movement is clearly thus stimulated, and tends to be reproduced through echo effects.[7] But since the periodicity of this renovation is not strictly predetermined, since it is itself a function of the conditions of profitability, the forecasts of market expansion, and the rate of more long-term technical innovation, it is more the result of conjunctural fluctuations than their source, even though it incontestably amplifies them and contributes to reproducing them on a regular basis.

All the preceding does not constitute an *explanation* of the crisis. We have said again and again that the crisis is a manifestation of the fall in the average rate of profit and that it also reveals an over-production of commodities. We still have to establish a more exact causal chain, incorporating a whole series of indispensable mediating factors which are located *both* in the sphere of production and in the sphere of the circulation of commodities, both in the sphere of competition and in that of the class struggle.[8]

At a certain point in the recovery, or in the upswing of the cycle, there is an inevitable increase in the organic composition of capital as a result of technological progress (which under the capitalist system is never 'neutral' but always essentially 'labour-saving', substituting machines for manual labour) and the swelling of investment that fuels the boom. For a certain period, this rise in the organic composition of capital can leave the rate of profit intact (this is the 'honeymoon phase', of the boom), when it is accompanied by a strong increase in the rate of surplus-value, a relative decline in raw material prices, and/or higher capital investment in the branches or countries where the organic composition of capital is lower.

But the very logic of the expansion undermines the conditions of this 'honeymoon'. The more the expansion accelerates, the more the industrial reserve army shrinks and the more difficult it becomes to increase the rate of surplus-value, because the relationship of forces on the labour market shifts in favour of the sellers of labour power, provided they are well organised. The longer the period of expansion lasts, the more difficult it becomes to maintain the relative decline of raw materials prices, because of the less elastic conditions of production in this sector (which is more dependent on natural factors). The longer and deeper the expansion, the more rare become the sectors (and countries) in which productive capital can find conditions of organic composition of capital structurally lower than in the essential sectors of the most industrially advanced countries.

Once a certain threshold has been reached, the totality of this inherent logic of the expansion provokes a trend towards a decline in the rate of profit. But neither prices not production are automatically, uniformly, and immediately adapted to these worsened conditions for the valorisation of capital (an adaptation that could 'mitigate' the cycle and avert a resounding crash).

The fall in the rate of profit accentuates competition among capitalists. Now, the technologically strongest firms and those with the greatest amount of operating capital command obvious advantages in this competition over the poorer or more backward firms. Since the former dominate the market, especially under conditions of monopoly capitalism, they seek to hold off the 'moment of truth' as long as possible — in other words, to maintain the old profit rate, and even the superprofits they enjoyed at the peak of the boom, for as long as possible.

The fall in the rate of profit simply means that *relative to social capital as a whole*, the total surplus-value produced is no longer sufficient to maintain the old rate of profit. It does not necessarily mean that the major industrial firms or the major banks immediately experience a fall in profit rates. The decline first appears in the following form: a fraction of *newly accumulated* capital can no longer be invested productively at the 'normally anticipated' conditions of profitability. This capital is then increasingly directed to speculation, risky activity which is less profitable.[9] The absolute volume of investment does not necessarily decline on this account. It can even increase. Neither do employment and the wage bill decline. They even stand at a very high, even maximum level. But investments, employment, and productivity (production of relative surplus-value) *no longer increase sufficiently* (that is, in sufficient proportion) to fuel the expansion by themselves, apparently without regard to the situation of the 'ultimate consumers'. Industry is no longer 'the best customer of industry'.

Now, this point of reversal of the cycle, generally 'concealed' by the continuation of the boom, coincides with two phenomena that further undermine the foundations of expansion.

On the one hand, under conditions of continuing expansion and intensification of speculation, a fall in the average rate of profit must entail *constantly greater recourse to credit*, and therefore an aggravation of the indebtedness of companies. This intensifies their resistance to any rapid adjustment of prices and profits, since the increased financial charges, combined with a fall in gross profits, would even more seriously reduce company profits. The credit boom is practically inevitable, since the banks strive to avert chain reaction bankruptcies, which could cause them severe losses. There is thus an imperceptible shift from a boom to an 'overheated' economy. For the time being, this further veils the forces inexorably preparing the crash.

This is true for capitalism in general.[10] But in the epoch of late capitalism, it acquires additional significance, as a result of the greater weight of credit (permanent inflation of credit, of private 'bank money') in the economy, as well as of the greater weight of the state. International deviations (differences) in the rate of inflation thereby trigger off partially desynchronised recessions during the long 'expansive' wave 1940(48)–68, to which increasingly synchronised recessions are substituted, once US hegemony, and the weight of the dollar as 'world currency', become revitalised.[11]

On the other hand, as the expansion, not to mention the overheating, develops, instances of excess production capacity, that is, potential over-production, *must* inevitably appear. The two fundamental features of the expansion during its 'honeymoon' phase — the increase in the organic composition of capital and the rise of relative surplus-value (the rise of the rate of surplus-value) — must inevitably result in an increase in the *mass* of commodities produced.[12] Under the capitalist mode of production it is impossible to reduce the unit value of consumer goods (which lies at the root of the rise in relative surplus-value) without substantially augmenting the total mass of commodities. Likewise, it is impossible to increase the production of machines and raw materials (production in Department I), which lies at the root of the rise in the organic composition of capital, without in the long run substantially augmenting the production capacity of Department II, even if to a lesser degree than that of Department I. The internal contradictions of the capitalist mode of production thus have the following results during the expansion:

(a) The rise in the rate of surplus-value $\left(\dfrac{\text{surplus capital}}{\text{variable capital}}\right)$ cannot neutralise — is not proportional to — the rise in the organic composition of capital $\left(\dfrac{\text{constant capital}}{\text{variable capital}}\right)$, because of

the intensification of the class struggle (the better position of labour on the labour market).

(b) Despite the progress of the '*roundabout ways of production*', Δ (c/v) *cannot* become proportional to:

$$\Delta\ \frac{\text{capacity for production of the means of production}}{\text{capacity for production of consumer goods}}$$

because of the mechanisms of competition and technological progress.

Under these conditions, the production capacity of Department II *must* rise more rapidly than the wage bill, particularly to the extent that capital succeeds in retarding the moment at which the rise in the rate of surplus-value begins to slacken or halts.

The more capital lies fallow, the more the increase in the *mass* of surplus-value is too slow for the accumulation of total capital, the more the rate of profit declines, and the greater grows the gap between the anticipated rate of profit and the rate of profit actually realised by a growing number of firms, the gap between their financial charges and their real revenues. They are therefore increasingly at the mercy of the slightest incident, which could cause bankruptcy. 'Super-abundance' of capital and 'shortage' of profits coexist and determine each other.

In order for the effects of the fall in the rate of profit to be *imposed* on all capitals, there must be a generalised slump and a fall in prices (gold prices), which entails a contraction of production in all sectors. The over-production crisis in turn *amplifies* the fall in the rate of profit. This had already occurred despite the fact that *production of surplus-value* was at a close to maximum level. With the reduction in employment and the emergence of unemployment or short working weeks, the total mass of surplus-value produced contracts, even compared with the level attained at the end of the boom and during the period of 'overheating' —despite the rising rate of exploitation of those workers still employed. (The mass of surplus-value produced had ceased to rise at the end of the boom.)

Schematically, then, it may be said that 'over-investment' provokes 'over-accumulation' which in turn brings on 'under-investment' and a massive devalorisation of capital. Only if this devalorisation of capital is sufficiently ample and if unemployment and the many measures of rationalisation vigorously boost the rate of exploitation of the working class can the fall in the rate of profit be checked and a new cycle of increased accumulation of capital be touched off.

The economists of the French Communist Party, like Boccara, who have worked on the crisis are handicapped by attachment to the concept of 'state monopoly capitalism', even though they have striven to combine analysis of the over-accumulation of capital with analysis of the over-production of commodities. The notion of 'state monopoly capitalism' leads them to confused and contradictory formulas such as 'excessive accumulation' or 'wasted accumulation':

> ... a formidable waste of accumulation has been caused by the exigencies of capital accumulation on the part of monopolies which benefit from financing of the public type. This waste of accumulation of capital and the need for profits to make that capital profitable and increase it even more constitutes the essential cause of accelerated inflation ... And, because of its colossal excess, the accumulation of means of production no longer furnishes sufficient outlets for compensation.[13]

Boccara seems not to remember that capitalist production is *always* production for profit, today just as at the dawn of the capitalist mode of production, and that the notion of 'wasted accumulation' in reference to the use-value of the commodities produced by the capitalists has no meaning in the context of this mode of production. If there is 'over accumulation' it is not fundamentally because the state has given 'too much aid' to the monopolies or because these monopolies 'badly oriented' their investments. It is fundamentally because the *totality* of the surplus-value produced does not permit a sufficient valorisation of *total* capital (that is, no longer guarantees the anticipated rate of profit). The manner in which this capital is shared out among various sectors is only a secondary factor which in itself cannot cause a general over-production crisis so long as the total surplus-value produced is sufficient for the valorisation of total capital.

There is one very simple way of gauging to what extent the advocates of the theory that crises are caused exclusively by 'under-consumption' and the advocates of the theory that they are caused exclusively by 'over-accumulation' are both partially correct and partially mistaken. Imagine the following dialogue of the deaf between two fervent defenders of these counterposed theories (let us say a reformist trade unionist of neo-Keynesian inspiration and an employers' representative of neo-liberal inspiration).

The neo-Keynesian starts off:

> Since there is a sales slump, which means an over-abundance of commodities, we must immediately raise wages in order to reabsorb unsaleable inventories and prime the pump. Otherwise there is no way out of the crisis.

Poor misguided soul! The crisis is primarily the reduction in investment (and therefore employment) because of the fall in profits. If you increase wages at this point of the cycle, you will further cut investment and therefore employment. On the contrary, we must reduce wages immediately. Then company directors will see higher profits coming in and they will proceed to make new investments and hire new personnel, which will turn the cycle up again.

Never have I heard such insanity! There is already a huge sales slump. If you reduce wages you will reduce the current purchasing power of the masses, you will reduce aggregate demand. If aggregate demand is reduced the sales slump will get worse and the market will be glutted with unsaleable commodities. Has anyone ever heard of employers investing to produce even more unsaleable commodities? If you reduce wages you will worsen the crisis instead of overcoming it.

The fundamental mistake made by both schools, a mistake which is quite common to academic schools that operate solely with macro-economic categories (the 'aggregate demand' of the Keynesians and the 'money supply' of the monetarists), is to presuppose a number of *mechanical and generalised adjustments* which actually occur only under certain precise conditions. A rise in household incomes really 'primes' the cycle only if it is accompanied by a rise in the rate of profit and a prospect of generalised expansion of the market. Otherwise increased investments do not follow. On the other hand, a rise in profits and investments permits the crisis to be overcome only if it is accompanied by an expansion in aggregate demand. Otherwise inventories of unsaleable commodities continue to weigh on the market and hold the economy in depression. Thus, if there is to be a new cycle of expansion in the production and accumulation of capital, there must be a *conjoint* strong expansion of the market (of the purchasing power of the ultimate consumers) and a pronounced rise in the average rate of profit. But this coincidence depends on the conjunction of many different circumstances.[14] It is impossible to produce it at any given moment through this or that government measure (or private agreement). Hence the uncontrollable character of the cycle.

One may wonder why, after 160 years of experience, the capitalists generally all move in the same direction rather than 'compensating' their reciprocal errors in forecasting. Why do all firms augment their investments during the boom (excessively), since that is what precipitates excess capacity and over-production? Why do they all reduce their investments during the crisis, which accentuates the slump and the decline in profits? Is it some irrational 'herd instinct' that makes them behave in this manner?

The answer is simple: what is rational *from the standpoint of the system as a whole* is not rational from the standpoint of each great firm taken separately, and vice versa. When the market is in a phase of strong expansion, all firms must attempt to cut themselves a large slice of the larger pie; they thereby precipitate 'over-investment' and excess capacity. When there is a slump, it is absurd for each individual firm to increase production capacity. On the contrary, the losses and the fall in prices (gold prices) must be reduced, which means that production must be reduced. This in turn leads to cumulative 'under-investment' at the macro-economic level.

The naive conviction of liberals that 'the common interest' is perfectly served if each individual pursues his 'private interest' turns out to be manifestly illusory at all decisive turns in the cycle — apart from the fact that it seeks to mask the contradiction between the interests of the capitalists and the interests of the wage earners. *Private property is the insurmountable obstacle to a smooth and continuous increase in investment*. It is thus the insurmountable obstacle to the disappearance of the cycle.

There will be those who charge that our analysis of the present crisis, as well as the Marxist theory of crisis sketched out here, lends excessive importance to phenomena relating to circulation, and therefore to demand. We would answer that in the final analysis fluctuations in the cycle are always fluctuations in accumulation, and therefore in the expanded reproduction of capital. But the process of reproduction of capital is precisely the *unity of the processes of production and circulation*, as Marx explained in great detail in the second volume of *Capital*. To attempt to explain the phenomenon of crisis exclusively by what occurs in the sphere of production (the production of quantity of surplus-value insufficient to assure capital an acceptable rate of profit), leaving aside the phenomena of the realisation of surplus-value — that is, circulation, which means the market — is in reality to eliminate a fundamental feature of capitalist production, namely that it is *generalised commodity production*. In Marx's words:

> Over-production is specifically conditioned by the general law of the production of capital; to produce to the limit set by the productive forces, that is to say, to exploit the maximum amount of labour with the given amount of capital, without any consideration for the actual limits of the market or the needs backed by the ability to pay; and this is carried out through continuous expansion of reproduction and accumulation and therefore constant reconversion of revenue into capital, while on the other hand the mass of the producers remain tied to the average level of needs, and must remain tied to it according to the very nature of capitalist production.[15]

And even more succinctly:

> The whole dispute as to whether *over-production* is possible and necessary in capitalist production revolves around the point whether the process of the realisation [valorisation] of capital within production directly posits its realisation in circulation; whether its realisation posited in the production process is its *real* realisation.[16]

In other words: to locate the causes of capitalist crises exclusively in the sphere of production (of surplus-value), implies the belief that output automatically creates its own markets, that is, a regression from Marx to Jean-Baptiste Say and his *loi des débouchés*. It thereby puts into question whether crises of overproduction are *immanent and unavoidable* in the capitalist mode of production as such.[17] Twenty-one crises of over-production in succession in 160 years (1825, 1836, 1847, 1857, 1866, 1873, 1882, 1891, 1900, 1907, 1913, 1921, 1929, 1937, 1949, 1953, 1958, 1961, 1970, 1974, 1981), and the first harbingers of the 22nd one, provide clear evidence that they indeed are.

A MARXIST EXPLANATION OF THE CYCLES OF 1971–75, 1976–82, 1982–88?

If we want to apply this general theory of crises to the explanation of the 1971–75, 1976–82 and 1983–8? cycles and more precisely to the origins and aftermath of the generalised recessions of 1974–75 and 1981–82, we must incorporate a whole series of particular elements that flow from the situation and from the specific contradictions of the international capitalist economy at the beginning of the 1970s. This recession, as well as the hesitant recovery that followed it and lent the period 1974–87 a clearly depressive character, must be understood as a focal point of *five different crises*:

A classical over-production crisis, limited in depth and duration by *deficit spending* and a large-scale expansion of credit, but marked by a clearly declining efficacy of these anti-crisis techniques.

The total expansion of the public and private debt in 1975 and 1976 must have been of the order of $400–500 billion. It climbed to $700–800 billion during 1980–82, and to more than $1500 billion in 1986–87.

In 1975–76 and 1980–82 loans to the weakest imperialist governments, to the monopolies hit hardest by the crisis, to the Third World countries, and to the so-called socialist countries *partially* took over from loans to consumers and the most solid capitalist firms. In 1986–87, a reversal took place: loans to the Third World and so-called socialist countries relatively declined, while the public debt of the US and the debt of businesses and private households relatively increased.[18]

The credit cycle has, until now, conserved a certain degree of autonomy from the industrial cycle, which permitted a repetition of the 1929–32 crisis to be averted. (This relative autonomy of the credit cycle is one of the fundamental characteristics of 'late capitalism' as it has been functioning for more than 40 years.)

The combination of the classical over-production crisis with the reversal of the 'long wave', which has ceased to work in an expansive direction since the end of the 1960s. High 'technological profits' — the monopolistic super-profits long realised by leading branches such as automobiles, electronics, chemicals, fabrication of scientific apparatuses, and so forth — are gradually declining or disappearing altogether.[19]

In a remarkable study, Orio Giarini noted in regard to the synthetic fibre industry:

> The cycle is reaching a certain maturity that could have been discerned back in the sixties: the new inventions cover only increasingly marginal possibilities of utilisation, disappointing the hopes for a great upturn. With time, research is being concentrated primarily on the improvement of the existing apparatus. *We have obviously entered a phase of decreasing technological yields* ... We see ... similar signs in other industries: in the sector of large computers ... for IBM, what had been planned for 1976 under the FS (Future Systems) programme has been postponed seven or eight years ... Likewise, ... civil aviation ... [20]

The disappearance of technological super profits is thus an additional important factor in the confirmation that the rate of profit *in the long term* will remain below the average of the 1950s and 1960s.[21]

A new phase in the crisis of the imperialist system, of which the rise in oil prices and the negotiations over a 'new world economic order' are only indirect reflections. Over a quarter of a century, imperialism was led gradually to shed the colonial system, to make the transition from direct to indirect domination of the semi-colonial and dependent countries, but without modifying (except marginally) the division of world surplus-value between the imperialist bourgeoisie and the owning classes of the semi-colonial countries. This endeavour finally ended in failure. At the beginning of the 1970s, the deterioration in the worldwide relationship of forces at the expense of imperialism compelled it to grant the ruling classes of OPEC a considerably larger share of world surplus-value through a sharp and enormous increase in oil profits. The exact share of world surplus-value thus redistributed is difficult to calculate. To give an idea of the order of magnitude, however, I would estimate it at some 7–8 per cent. This was later reversed partially by a predictable decline in oil prices.

An aggravated social and political crisis in the imperialist countries. This results on the one hand from the conjunction of the economic depression and a *specific ascending cycle of worker's struggles* until the mid-1970s, a rise in the combativity and politicisation of the workers in a whole series of imperialist countries, and on the other hand from the reactions provoked by the attempt of the imperialist bourgeoisie to make the workers bear the burden of the crisis and the redistribution of world surplus-value (see Table 3.1).

TABLE 3.1   *Evolution of strike struggles (in yearly averages)*

A   *Number of strikers (in thousands)*

	United States	Japan	West Germany	Britain	France	Italy
1951–55	2468	—	205	658	1415	2343
1956–60	1710	—	68	771	1414	1685
1961–65	1362	—	186	1512	2102	2971
1966–70	2653	—	111	1393	3755	4044
1971	3280	1896	536	1171	3235	3981
1972	1714	1544	23	1722	2721	4405
1973	2251	2232	185	1513	2342	8081
1974	2700	8500	250	1601	—	8464

B   *Number of strike days (in thousands)*

	United States	Japan	West Germany	Britain	France	Italy
1951–55	32 220	—	1193	2382	3894	4974
1956–60	32 320	—	707	4446	1980	5581
1961–65	27 300	—	486	2562	2794	13 017
1966–70	45 166	—	157	5540	32 138	17 676
1971	47 592	5777	4484	13 552	4392	14 799
1972	23 918	3871	66	23 909	3912	19 497
1973	27 949	4210	563	7200	3915	20 402
1974	48 505	9684	1051	14 740	3380	16 747

SOURCES: Huffschmid/Schui: *Handbuch zur Wirtschaftskrise in der BRD 1973–1976* (Pahl, Rugenstein Verlag, Cologne, 1976) p. 39, based on various West German sources.

These figures should be treated with caution; they are based on a mixture of government and trade union statistics. Nevertheless, they do provide an indication of a clear trend.

The conjunction of these four crises and the structural crisis of bourgeois society that has been developing under the surface for more than a decade has accentuated the *crisis of all bourgeois social relations and more particularly the crisis of capitalist relations of production.* The credibility of the capitalist system's ability to guarantee a constant improvement in living standards, employment, and the consolidation of democratic rights has been strongly undermined as a very function of the effects of recession.

Long waves tending towards stagnation in no way imply a permanent depression of material production over a period of 20 or 25 years. They are characterised by a succession of over-production crises and periods of recovery and rise in production, exactly like the long waves tending towards expansion. The industrial cycle continues to function as such. The difference is that during the long waves tending towards expansion the phases of recession are shorter and less profound, the phases of recovery and boom longer and more prosperous. On the other hand, during the long waves tending towards stagnation recessions are longer and deeper and recoveries shorter and less expansive. It is more difficult for the recoveries to turn into phases of prosperity in the real sense of the word. We have just lived through a striking confirmation of this.

The long-term tendency of the average rate of profit to decline had made itself felt since the end of the 1960s, even during the second half of the 1960s. The appearance of the excess capacity in a growing number of important industrial branches and the increasingly speculative character of the successive phases of prosperity were the most revealing signs of this. The 1972–73 boom was almost entirely speculative. Although the spectacular increase in raw materials prices during this phase also had intrinsic causes (under-equipment and excessively low growth rates in the production of raw materials during the preceding period) and represented a product of accelerated inflation throughout the international capitalist economy as a whole, there can be no doubt about its fundamentally speculative source. The total value of all future contracts in raw materials rose from $60 billion in 1964 to $340 billion in 1974. Enormous quantities of speculative capital flowed into raw materials exchanges, both to cover losses in the buying power of the dollar and other paper monies and to realise speculative profits, since a more or less lasting shortage of raw materials was anticipated.[22]

This speculative boom was condemned to collapse into a particularly serious recession since excess capacity was more widespread than at any time since World War II[23] and the acceleration of inflation compelled political and monetary authorities to erect a ceiling on the policy of expansion of credit. Thus, over-production, beginning in the automobile and construction industries, assumed the cumulative movement and scope seen in 1974 and 1975. As we demonstrated above, the partial attempts to restructure the world market and increase the rate of profit were not of sufficient scope to assure a lasting, cumulative, and rapid recovery.

In other words, the new outlets in the OPEC countries, the most industrialised of the dependent countries, and the so-called socialist countries, as well as the outlets created by the heavy increase in the public debt (the budget deficits), which in the United States was combined with a strong new upswing of household debt in 1977, did not fully compensate for the losses in outlets caused by massive unemployment, the more moderate recourse to credit by the big firms, the spectacular decline in mortgage credit over a two-year period, and the contraction of household debts in most of the imperialist countries. (This debt increased strongly again in the United States in 1977.[24]) There was some 'compensation' and therefore a recovery, but it was only partial and insufficient. There was a rise in the rate of profit, but not enough to fuel a real boom.

To give an idea of the difficulties an economic recovery would have to overcome to approach the average growth rates of the 1950s and 1960s, let us cite three sets of figures:

(1) The difference between peak pre-recession levels of inventories in key commodities for American industrialists and merchants and the lowest levels reached since the recession (June 1975) is only $10 billion. (The decline was from $273 billion to $263 billion.) By September 1977 inventories were already up to $237 billion, which, taking account of inflation, is equivalent to about $284 billion in 1974–75 dollars. Thus, there was some 'pruning' and 'devalorisation' of capital, but it was derisory, rapidly neutralised when the recovery began. The expansion of the market remains marginal. It is not at all sufficient to induce industrialists to make significant investments.

(2) The average annual growth rate of the productive capacity of manufacturing industry in West Germany was 6.1 per cent during the period 1960–65. It declined to 3.9 per cent for the period 1966–70. But it fell to 1.8 per cent in 1975, 1.5 per cent in 1976, and 1 per cent in 1977. Such is the objective effect of the enormous excess capacity weighing on the market. The severely limited reduction in the number of firms and in potential productivity — so far generally confined to small and medium-sized companies — has scarcely altered that excess capacity substantially.

Figures 3.1 and 3.2 eloquently indicate the extent to which it has become more difficult, from recession to recession, to reabsorb excess capacity. *That is the fundamental reason why there was no real boom after the 1974–75 recession, nor after the 1980–82 one.*

(3) *Despite the end of the recession, the volume of 'idle' capital has continued to grow.* In mid-June 1977 the total of investments in

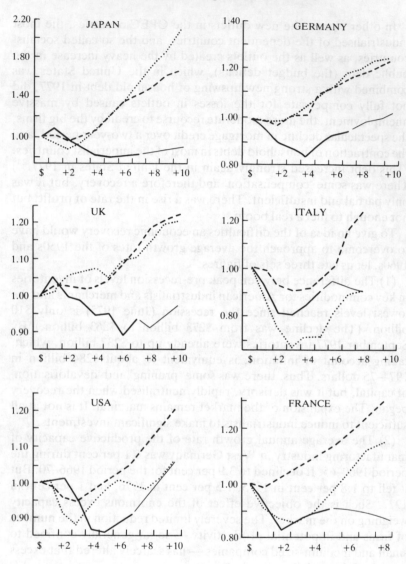

SOURCE: *Perspectives économiques de l'OCDE*, no. 21 (July 1977) p. 23.

FIGURE 3.1   *Cyclical evolution of productive investment in the private sector of seven major countries: 1955–78 (periodic peak in volume terms = 100)*

Real cycle: result ———   Previous cycles: average ------
Real cycle: prediction ——   Most acute previous recession ······

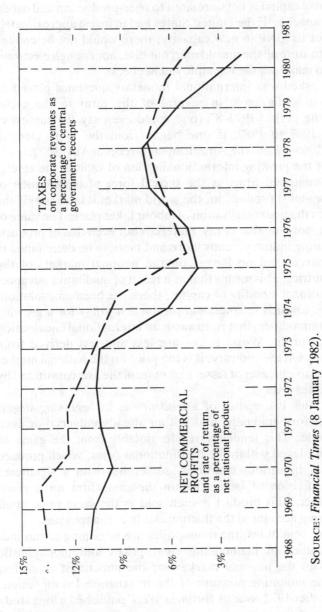

FIGURE 3.2 *Taxes on profits and corporate profits in Great Britain showing mutual decrease of taxes and profits (North Sea petroleum and gas figures are not included)*

SOURCE: *Financial Times* (8 January 1982).

Euro-dollars and Euro-currencies had attained $200 billion. At the end of 1977 it probably stood at $350 billion.[25] But this over-accumulation of money capital is not unrelated to over-production and excess production capacity. 'If the United States had to invest approximately 20 per cent of its GNP in new capacity, there would not be enough warehouses to store all the unsold merchandise, nor enough electronic calculators to make out the unemployment checks.'[26]

It may be asked why international monetary questions played an increasingly unsettling role in several of the turns in the cycles throughout the period 1972–87 (one could even say the successive cycles from 1967 to 1987, if one began from the West German recession of 1966–67 and the American mini-recession of 1967).

Because of the growing internationalisation of capital, the emergence of multinational firms as the typical form of organisation of large-scale capitalist production, the world market is increasingly the arena in which the real socialisation of labour takes place. The value of commodities, not only that of raw materials but even that of products of manufacturing industry, tends more and more to be determined in the world market and no longer on the national markets of the capitalist countries. This means that as a result of qualitative advances in the international mobility of capital, there has been an evolution, little by little, towards *international production prices* for a growing number of commodities, that is, towards an international equalisation of the rate of profit. World prices are less and less derived from national prices. On the contrary, it is the price on the national market which deviates to a greater or lesser extent from the axis constituted by the world market price.

Obviously, this is a matter of a *tendency in its beginning stages*, coming to the fore gradually, and not an already universal or even widespread rule. This tendency results notably from the game of compensation played within the multinational firms, which produce simultaneously in various countries, sometimes with a significant international division of labour within the same firm for a given finished product. This product is then sold at the same price in all countries, taking account of the fluctuations in exchange rates.

Under these conditions, the monopolies are beginning to run into serious difficulties in maintaining rigid prices and monopolistic super-profits on the national markets of the imperialist countries, because of the mounting pressure of the international competition. The 12 December 1977 issue of *Business Week* published a long study on the erosion of the old practices of monopoly pricing in the United

States and the growing application of 'more flexible' and 'more differentiated' prices. Here again, it is a matter merely of the beginning of a turn in the trend and not at all a generalised change. Protectionism, cartelisation, and centralisation of firms all represent attempts, widely utilised during the present cycle, to protect monopolistic super-profits. In the longer run, however, their efficacy is dubious, because of the growing internationalisation of capital and of production itself.

Under these same conditions, attempts by national bourgeois governments to 'regularise' the cycle at the national level are also meeting growing difficulties, mediated precisely by the fluctuations in the balances of payment and exchange rates of national paper monies. The transition to floating exchange rates was an attempt to take into account this weakening of the independence of action of governments in face of the imperatives of the law of value, which is increasingly asserting itself, particularly on the world market. But the results have been mediocre and ever more dubious, even for the most powerful imperialist government, that of the United States.

The more national governments manipulate the money supply, volume of credit, and artificial exchange rates, the more protectionist policies are applied and the internationalised productive forces rebel against these manipulations, the more the laws of the market — the law of value — trigger compensatory mechanisms that render these government measures ineffective or even counter-productive.

A number of governments, not only in the Third World but also in imperialist countries (Portugal, Italy, and Britain; and tomorrow it will probably be the turn of Spain and France), faced *diktats* from the International Monetary Fund (IMF) during the 1972–78 cycle when discussion arose as to whether their balance of payments deficits, which had suddenly risen beyond the 'normal' average, could be covered by substantial international loans. Some have claimed that the personnel of the IMF represent an ominous conspiracy of American imperialism (or of 'American-German imperialism') against the 'peoples of the world'. The reality is at once more sober and more ominous.

From a 'technical' standpoint, the representatives of the IMF, as good bankers, grant large loans only if minimum conditions of repayment are guaranteed. Now, for the countries suffering from rising balance of payments deficits, the ability to repay loans *in foreign currency* obviously depends on increased currency holdings, that is, the elimination of the balance of payments deficits and a growing

positive trade balance.[27] Depending on whether they are feeling the
pressure of this or that faction of the international bourgeoisie, these
technocrats can be more or less accommodating in regard to this or
that government. (They were much more accommodating in regard to
Pinochet than they were in regard to the Portuguese Armed Forces
Movement in 1975, for example.) Essentially, however, this is merely
a classic confirmation of the rule that the function creates the organ.
The organ *cannot* act otherwise than to carry out the mission for which
and by which it was established.

Behind this technical mechanism, however, stands a socio-economic reality which must be kept in view. The technique does not simply
drop from the sky. Nor does it correspond to 'eternal economic laws'.
It results from an institutional framework that corresponds to specific
social relations and class interests. What is commonly referred to by a
coy and mystifying euphemism as the 'open' economy is not equally
open to everyone. It is open to money; to the owners of large sums of
money. Once accumulated beyond a certain threshold this money is
spontaneously and continuously transformed into capital, that is, into
a potential capacity to appropriate a fraction of surplus-labour. It is
able to undergo this transformation into capital only because the
means of production are private property and there is a class of
hundreds of millions of people throughout the world who have access
neither to these means of production nor to the means of their own
subsistence; they *must* therefore sell their labour power to the owners
of the machines and of agribusiness.

Since production is increasingly organised on an international scale,
national borders must be 'held open' to inflows and outflows of capital
as well as commodities. Because of contemporary technique, industrial capitalism could not survive if its capital and commodities were
hermetically sealed within the boundaries of small national states, any
more than it could have arisen in the countries and dukedoms of the
Middle Ages.

In the context of the intrinsic logic of capital, however, so long as
there is no world government, no world money, and no world arbiter
to rule in sovereign fashion over the increasingly sharp inter-imperialist conflicts and the conflicts between the imperialist bourgeoisie and
the ruling classes of the dependent and semi-colonial countries,
borders can be 'held open' to inflows and outflows of money-capital
only if everyone submits to certain objective 'rules of the game', which
precisely permit the law of value – that is, the logic of capital –
to arbitrate these conflicts and 'resolve crises'. *The International*

Monetary Fund is merely the embodiment of this objective logic, regardless of the minor liberties it may take on secondary questions, depending on which imperialist interest groups command hegemony (it is not always the same groups).[28]

We maintain that this explanation of the role of the IMF is at once more sober and more ominous than the 'conspiracy' theory. For it implies that whatever the composition of the body, and whatever the inclinations of the governments represented in it, there is no way to escape its *diktats* in the long run, unless one breaks with the logic of capital, along with the capitalist mode of production and all the international institutions that sustain it.

Such is the fundamental explanation of the gravity of the 1974–75 and 1980–82 recessions and the morose character of the recoveries of 1976–78 and 1983–85. Hovering over the future recession is the triple threat of a major bank crash, the insolvency of some important dependent or semi-colonial countries, and a crisis or collapse of the dollar. As may be seen, the partisans and apologists of this system certainly have no grounds for optimism.

But the system is not at all at the end of its tether. It still commands significant reserves in most of the imperialist countries, enormous reserves in the richest ones (primarily but not exclusively the United States, West Germany, Switzerland, Japan, the Netherlands, Sweden, Belgium, Canada and Australia) and substantial reserves in those imperialist countries more deeply affected by depression (primarily Britain and France, but even Italy and Spain, which are worse off). It commands substantial reserves in the richest OPEC countries, Brazil, Hong Kong, Singapore and South Africa. And above all, it combines these still considerable economic reserves and resources with an arsenal of political, ideological, and military weapons to be used in the service of a cause it will pursue tenaciously for long years: a substantial new rise in the rate of profit through a sharp upturn in the rate of surplus-value.

Such an upturn is impossible without a very severe political and social defeat for the proletariat of the imperialist countries, the colonial revolution, and/or the bureaucratised workers' states during the coming decade. A defeat of this kind would not necessarily have to take the form of a victory of fascism or a victorious war of aggression against the Soviet Union, the 'people's democracies', or the People's Republic of China aimed at substantially enlarging the geographic arena of the valorisation of capital — although if the defeat assumed catastrophic scope it could threaten to take these forms. It is incontestable, however, that we are approaching battles comparable to those of the 1930s and the beginning of the 1940s, as a result of the iron logic of the accumulation of capital. The international working class now enjoys much more favourable conditions than in the past to emerge from these battles victorious, even if it is weaker than in 1976–77. This results from long-term structural unemployment, the feat of unemployment, and the absence of a credible overall alternative to crisis-ridden capitalism, a product both of the capitulation of the mass parties of the working class to capitalist crisis management policies, and of the specific system crisis of the USSR and the East European 'people's democracies'. But the stakes are enormous. Because of the gravity of the crisis of the system, the accumulation of weapons of massive destruction, and the new rise of irrational and pathological tendencies towards contempt and hatred for humanity among the possessing classes and a portion of the ideologues and politicians in their service, the present crisis confronts humanity with an apocalyptic version of the alternative 'socialism or barbarism': 'socialism or collective annihilation'.[29]

Basically because the Marxist theory of crises incorporates the historical end-results of the class struggle between capital and labour over a certain time span (the long-term fluctuations of the rate of surplus-value) into its mechanism,[30] it does not imply an automatic turn from a 'long depressive wave' into a 'long expansionary wave'.[31] In our opinion, such a turn is not on the agenda in a foreseeable future. We therefore consider as either theoretically or empirically unproven the hypothesis of an intrinsic 'regulation' (self-regulation) of the capitalist system, which has been widely circulated of late.[32] The main arguments advanced by the proponents of that hypothesis are the beneficial effects of the 'new technologies' on the system, the shift of manufacturing output to semi-industrialised Third World countries with a much higher rate of surplus-value, the reorganisation of the labour process in the imperialist metropolis which also strongly increases the rate of surplus-value, and the effects of large-scale devalorisation of capital.

All these tendencies are indeed operating. But they could trigger off a new 'long expansionary wave' only on one condition: if their cumulative effects would be of such an amplitude as to unleash a massive upsurge of profits and of accumulation of capital, as occurred around 1893 (imperialism!) or 1940 in the US (1948–50 in West Germany, Western Europe and Japan). In our opinion, this is impossible without social and political upheavals on a world scale similar to those of 1893 or of 1940–48. And such upheavals are nowhere on the horizon.

The error of judgement of the proponents of the theory of (self) regulation of capitalism appears most clearly when one poses the simple question of the *overall effects on the world economy* of each of the tendencies which they stress. What new techniques or new products have opened up new markets and cumulative industrial growth comparable to those of postwar auto and housing (domestic electrical equipment) booms? In how far has the shift of manufacturing output towards the Third World been accompanied by an expansion and not by a stagnation of world trade, actually tending to reduce 'world demand' rather than to increase it, precisely because wages are much lower in the semi-industrialised countries than in the imperialist ones?[33] To what extent have 'robots' and fully automatised production techniques substituted themselves for semi-automation in the West? What part of large-scale corporations and banks have gone bankrupt? The concrete answers to all these questions clearly prove that none of the basic causes of the present long-term depression have been eliminated.

NOTES

1. A revised version and translation of chapters 25 and 26 of *La Crise* (Paris: Flammarion, 1982).
2. Especially chapter 17 of *Theories of Surplus Value*, chapters 15 and 30 of volume III of *Capital*, chapters 16, 20 and 21 of volume II of *Capital*, and the passage on crises in Engels' *Anti-Dühring*, which was at least reviewed and corrected, if not actually drafted, by Marx himself.
3. *Capital*, vol. III, p. 244.
4. *Theories of Surplus Value*, vol. II, pp. 496–9.
5. *Capital*, vol. III, p. 615.
6. Inability to grasp this concatenation constitutes the fundamental weakness of the otherwise remarkable study by Makato Itoh, 'The Formation of Marx's Theory of Crisis', in *Bulletin of the Conference of Socialist Economics*, vol. IV, no. 1, February 1975. The author is trapped in an imaginary dichotomy: either a theory of over-accumulation or a theory of over-production.
7. The same remark applies to Jacques Attali, who attributes 'two rather different conceptualisations of the crisis' to Marx (*Ruptures d'un systéme économique*, p. 34). In the same symposium P. Dockes and M. Rosier underline, on the contrary, the complementarity of a crisis due to over-accumulation with a crisis due to underproduction, as is

done in the present study. The more rapid turnover of fixed capital, which I mentioned in *Late Capitalism*, was strikingly confirmed by a study of the Planning Bureau of the Netherlands, which reported that the age of the oldest machinery in use dropped from 45 years in 1959 to 17 years in 1973. It also reported, although too mechanically and one-sidedly, that the relative rise in wages was stimulating an increasingly 'young' investment of fixed capital, which tends to reduce employment (H. den Hartog and H. S. Tjan, 'Investeringen, lonen, prijzen en arbeidsplaatsen — Een jaargangmodel met vaste coefficienten voor Nederland', Central Planning Bureau, The Hague, *Occasional Papers*, no. 2, 1974).

8.   ' ... the real crisis can be represented only on the basis of the real movement of capitalist production, competition, and credit' (Marx, *Theories of Surplus Value*, MEW, vol. 26/2, p. 509).

9.   Marx, *Capital*, vol. III, p. 246.

10.   'If the credit system appears as the principal level of overproduction and excessive speculation in commerce, this is simply because the reproduction process, which is elastic by nature, is now forced to its most extreme limit; and this is because a great part of the social capital is applied by those who are not its owners, and who therefore proceed quite unlike owners who, when they function themselves, anxiously weigh the limits of their private capital' (Marx, *Capital*, vol. III, p. 572).

11.   Ernest Mandel, *Late Capitalism*, chapter 14, on the relative autonomy of the credit cycle.

12.   'Thus, to the very extent that it [machine production] increases in scope, the mass of products must increase ... ' 'The same with the *productive force*. On the one hand, the necessary tendency of capital to raise it to the utmost, in order to increase relative *surplus time*. On the other hand thereby decreases *necessary labour time*, hence the worker's exchange capacity. Further, as we have seen, relative *surplus value* rises much more slowly than the force of production, and moreover this proportion grows ever smaller as the magnitude reached by the productive forces is greater. *But the mass of products grows in a similar proportion ....* But to the same degree as the mass of products grows, so grows the difficulty of realising the labour time contained in them — because the demands made on consumption rise' (Marx, *Grundrisse*, p. 422).

13.   Paul Boccara, 'La Crise', *Economie et Politique*, no. 251–3 (June-July-August 1975) pp. 54–5.

14.   A typical example: Paul Mattick writes in *Marx and Keynes* (London, 1969) p. 79: 'The slump on the market must be caused by the fact that labour is not sufficiently productive to satisfy the needs of the accumulation of capital. It is because not enough has been produced that capital has been unable to expand at the rhythm necessary to fullyrealize [the value of] everything that has been produced.' In other words: if profits and investments had risen adequately, there would have been no slump in the sale of consumer goods. Marx held a categorically different view, as is quite clear from the quotations above.

15. *Theories of Surplus Value*, vol. II, pp. 534–5.
16. *Grundrisse*, pp. 410–11.
17. The proponents of the theory of 'state capitalism' supposedly existing in the USSR, which has now avoided crises of over-production for nearly 70 years, are forced to put into question that inevitability.
18. Huge debts were incurred for speculative purposes, for example, take-overs and mergers nearly completely financed by credit.
19. 'Even if only because revolutionary technical innovations are becoming rather rare, in the future the formation of fixed capital should no longer expect to attain the level of the years of expansion, even if activity picks up vigorously' (*Notices économiques* of the Union de Banques Suisses, November 1977).
20. Magazine *Futuriletes*, autumn 1977.
21. Note, for example, the spectacular collapse of prices of quartz components, semi-conductors, pocket calculators, and so forth.
22. Concerning 'speculative purchases of raw materials' during the period 1972–74, the 47th annual report of the Bank for International Settlements wrote: 'At that time, cover and speculation purchases engendered by great fluctuations in exchange rates played an important role, and this movement was accelerated in some cases by the growing supply difficulties in raw materials. This situation is perfectly illustrated by the accumulation and hoarding of considerable stocks of basic products by industrialists' (47e *Rapport Annuel*, op. cit., p. 38). A graph printed in the same publication indicated that the raw materials stocks held by the transformation industries in the imperialist countries, which had risen on the average only 0.5–0.8 per cent per quarter between 1968 and 1971, were rising at something like 2–3 per cent in 1972, 1973, and the beginning of 1974; in other words, the rate of growth quadrupled.
23. During the 1980–82 recession, manufacturing industry's capacity utilisation fell from 78.1 per cent in December 1980 to 66.4 per cent in April 1982.
24. During the first ten months of 1977 consumer credit rose 45 per cent (!) compared with the 1975 level (*Business Week*, 16 January 1978). Once again, the (mini-) boom in automobiles in the United States in 1977 was a boom in inflation of credit. The same is true for the 1983–85 recovery. At the end of 1985 household debt reached the record height of 19.2 per cent of disposable income (*Neue Zünder Zeitung*, 23–24 November 1985).
25. 'The Euromarket is thus increasingly becoming an extraterritorial centre of deposits for idle capital, whether short-term or long-term .... Today, in many great industrial countries of the western world, there are not only jobless people, but also "unemployed capital"' (*Frankfurter Allgemeine Zeitung*, 20 October 1977).
26. *Business Week*, 16 January 1977.
27. Hence a doubly perverse effect of debt (service) repayment on the world economy. On the one hand, there is a flow of resources from the 'poor' to the 'rich' countries, that is, the exact opposite of the requirement for a gradual reduction of the 'development gap'. On the

other hand, inasmuch as world trade is relatively stagnant, the semi-industrialised countries can only increase their share of world exports of manufactured goods at the expense of the imperialist countries' shares in export and output, that is, by exporting unemployment to the lender countries.

28.   'The IMF has, to a certain extent, always had a role of policing countries' balance of payments and of advising members to undertake adjustments when they are in chronic disequilibrium.... An alliance [!] between the IMF and the commercial banks would be facilitated by the fact that these institutions have similar [!] views of what adjustment policies deficit countries should adopt, although their reasons may differ slightly. In the case of the IMF, it is a question of historic institutional orientation: the Fund was created to oversee the world's monetary system, and exchange-rate stabilisation is its primary responsibility. Since chronic balance of payments deficits and a high rate of inflation are the main cause of deteriorating exchange rates, the IMF naturally [!] places great emphasis on policies that will eliminate such deficits and slow domestic inflation. For the private bankers, it is a matter of self-interest: they want to make sure that the countries to whom they have lent money will earn enough foreign exchange each year to meet their loan repayments' (Report of the Church Commission, *International Debt, The Banks and U.S. Foreign Policy*, Washington 1977, p. 63).

29.   Let us mention just two extreme forms of inhumanity which have been on the rise for years: the use of 'the food weapons' (see Emma Rothschild, 'The Economics of Starvation', *International Herald Tribune*, 12 and 14 January 1977), which even takes the form of projects deliberately to reduce the population of the Third World countries through starvation; and the spread of practices of torture in *dozens* of countries (see the torture report of Amnesty International). For other merely 'potential' tendencies towards barbarism, note the proposals to use lobotomies, (that is, cerebral mutilation) to discipline those who 'deviate from the norm' (see especially Michel Bosquet, *Ecologie et Politique*, Paris, 1975), and the proposal of the parliamentary leader of the CDU in the Bremen state legislature to burn the books of non-conformist authors, such as collections of the poetry of Erich Fried.

30.   See Ernest Mandel, 'Partially Independent Variables and Internal Logic in Classical Marxist Economic Analysis', *International Social Science Council*, vol. 24 (1985) no. 3.

31.   On the asymmetry of the turn of the 'long waves', see Ernest Mandel, *Long Waves of Capitalist Development* (Cambridge, 1980).

32.   On the theory of regulation see especially David M. Gordon, 'Stages of Accumulation and Long Economic Cycles', *The Political Economy of the World System* (Beverly Hills, 1980) and Michel Aglietta, *Régulation et Crises du Capitalisme* (Paris, 1976).

33.   In constant dollars, world exports were, in March 1986, 3 per cent *below* the recession level of 1981.

4 Three Crises: The Metamorphoses of Capitalism and the Labour Movement[1]

Alain Lipietz[2]

'A new revolution will not be possible without a new crisis, and the emergence of the former is as certain as that of the latter.' Two years after the *Communist Manifesto* and the failure of the European revolutions of 1848, Karl Marx published the elucidating and yet optimistic account of the *Class Struggles in France*. This exposition constitutes a prophecy, on which a century of subsequent millenarian rationalism within the labour movement is based. To demonstrate the inevitability of crisis was a rationalist attempt. To deduce from it the necessity of revolution was a form of millenarian faith.

Undoubtedly, this creative faith has been shattered in the labour movement — after the great depression in the late 19th century, and after the crisis of the 1930s, the present, third major crisis of capitalism (if one may consider that the events of 1848 mark the final point of a long transition, rather than a genuine capitalist crisis), there do not seem to be any revolutionary aspirations left today.

On the contrary, common opinion appears preoccupied with an optimistic and liberal version of Schumpeterian analysis: the thesis of regeneration of capitalism through its own crises, which corresponds to that of 'creative destruction'. Aborted revolutions and successful reforms did their part in convincing people (who had the option of either being delighted or regretful) that doubt may be quite a reasonable attitude. Similarly, in the beginning of the present century, the founder of Italian Marxism, A. Labriola (1899) referred to the first 'crisis of Marxism':

> If there is no form of domination which is not met with resistance,
> there is no resistance which, following the pressing needs of
> everyday life, does not degenerate in a submissive way... For these

59

reasons, historical events viewed superficially as if through an ordinary monotonous narration appear to invariably repeat themselves, like the images seen through a kaleidoscope ... There is no history in which these processes are genuine; this is translated in common language as 'history is an annoying song'.

In the complex dynamics of 'historical capitalism' (Wallerstein 1985), transformations *internal* to the system' seem to have prevailed over disputes *between* the 'system' and the 'anti-systemic forces'.

At this point, it is useful to look into the relations between the above two elementary 'dynamics', that is, between that which is internal to the system, and that which arises from the opposition of the system to the anti-systemic forces. Naturally, since the latter are by definition a part of the system, a connection between the two dynamics has always been acknowledged. So, the primary dynamic essentially concerns those forces which contribute to the maintenance of the fundamental relations of capitalism and its logic of accumulation: the dominant classes, the states, the firms and so on. With all the contradictions these entities face, they have learnt how to overcome their inevitable compromises so as to *continue* their domination. On the other hand, the contrast 'capitalism/oppressed workers' mobilises forces that, although internal to the system, do not take any advantage from its maintenance and would rather *move out* of it (according to the general Marxist wisdom).

This fictitious dichotomy is quite demobilising. It is fictitious because it induces the functionalist idea that, in the long run, system reforms result from self-regulation. This principle of self-regulation is supposedly immanent to the system, a sort of 'long-term invisible hand', which plays the role of the market forces in the short-range regulation of the micro-economic forces, thus resolving macro-economic and social contradictions. It is demobilising in the sense that it places the oppressed classes in a very difficult situation: either one cannot succeed (in periods of expansion), or one has to improvise (in periods of crisis), with the additional risk of falling from Scylla to Charybdis. So, the principle 'A bird in the hand is worth two in the bush' leads more surely to the conservative attitude, since 'acquired advantages' in periods of prosperity are tangible, and since experiences of 'moving out of the system' turned out to be quite unfortunate. This is the culture of the 1980s: the Wind of the West gets the better of the Wind of the East, contrary to Mao's hopes.

In any case, the 1970s have taught us several important points. First, socialism is not 'outside' of capitalism. The words of Lenin – 'The corpse of capitalism cannot be nailed in a coffin and thrown into the sea: it is here, it is decomposed among us, and it is contaminating us' are joined by those of Mao – 'The revolution will take a thousand years, ten thousand years' – and are corroborated by the actual outcomes of the Russian and Chinese Revolutions. We have been convinced that we cannot move out of capitalism through a revolution as an innocent person leaves prison through the front gate: one can simply 'reduce' the oppositions which characterise it, and which only seek to reappear. On the other hand, the processes of 'reduction' do not constitute a continual, peaceful phenomenon: they implicate crises, wars, revolutions, and changes in political regimes. Furthermore, a retrospective analysis of capitalist growth has led some historically informed economists to show that capitalism has been subject to mutations, which have occasionally benefited wage earners as well.

This was the case of the analysis in terms of the regime of accumulation and modes of regulation (Aglietta 1976; Boyer and Mistral 1983; Lipietz 1979, 1985; Mazier *et al.* 1984). Through the continuous encounter of various contradictions of accumulation, capitalism has simultaneously developed in the privileged epochs separated by the 'major crises' firstly, a scheme for growth (regimes of accumulation), and secondly, forms of control with respect to these schemes (modes of regulation). Such mechanisms tend to resolve capitalist contradictions for some time, although not definitely. Moreover, these mechanisms resolve contradictions in a *different* manner each time. With the terms 'mechanisms' and 'controls' I underline the indirect way such a conception is connected with that denounced above: the idea of a principle of 'overregulation' helping capitalism pass from a mode of regulation or a particular regime of accumulation to another, whenever positive effects of preceding patterns are diminishing. This is a retrospective illusion, allowable since it is a deliberate one (an 'a posteriori functionalism'), in the sense that it illustrates a research programme: the identification of the forces and processes which have historically created these new patterns.

Disregarding the necessity for such a concrete analysis could lead some addicted to this kind of theorisation to introduce the temporal succession of regimes of accumulation and modes of regulation as an inevitable result of an internal 'dynamic', as if inherent in the genetics of capitalism. In fact, this succession is nothing more than a 'diachrony', the product of a concrete history. Elsewhere, the rational eschatologism of the Marxist labour movement has tried to reduce the dynamic of history to an abstract conceptualisation of historical capitalism: the unavoidable development of a more and more exploited mass of people getting consciousness of themselves. To mistake for the self-regulated and finalising dynamic a process which is but the mark of hazardous times, involves the risk of inappropriate abstractions. The same holds even if it is legitimate to identify the *tendencies* characterising the structures we have defined as 'abstract' from the concrete. So, it would be of little use to be interested in crises, if they do not constitute the final crisis. They would just function towards the realisation of these tendencies, they would just be the necessary though anecdotal circumstances that follow a predetermined dynamic.

When I refer to 'two dynamics', that of the system and that of the confrontation between the system and the anti-systemic forces, I am simply taking literally the largely illegitimate dichotomy that considers two interlaced processes functioning in concrete time as autonomous.

In the present necessarily schematic and principally exploratory analysis, we will explore one hypothesis only: the articulation of the two 'dynamics' could permit a clarification of the first one. In other words, the struggle of the anti-systemic forces would play a crucial role in the transformations of the system itself. Under this general formulation, this is not an original idea. However, it may be interesting to elaborate on it in a way that involves the history of these forces, and the history of the modes of regulation and regimes of accumulation. In order to delimit the subject even further, we will essentially restrain ourselves to the consideration of one anti-systemic force, that is, to the labour movement. We will also deal only with a partial aspect of historical capitalism – the history of the norms of production and consumption, and the forms of wage regulation.

In the following, we will proceed to put the present crisis, as well as the preceding ones, into perspective. In the first two parts we will present the dichotomous versions of the two dynamics in caricature form: the labour movement facing capitalism on the one hand, and the transformations of capitalism on the other. In the third part, we will draft their interaction. In the fourth, we will examine the present crisis, and we will end our analysis by some concluding remarks on the history of capitalism and that of its more or less independent offspring (namely the labour movement).

It is not worth underlining the multitude of issues we are thus leaving aside such as the inter-capitalist and inter-country contradictions, and the contradictions between dominant and dominated countries.

NEW JERUSALEM VERSUS BABYLON

Let us start with an exposition of the two 'dynamics' – capitalism/ labour movement, and internal transformations of capitalism – using the general *tendency* to stylise them when separating the former from the latter. This is a rather arbitrary exercise, as no author can strictly keep within such a dichotomy. It is a caricature that purports to underline the usefulness of bringing them into perspective.

An additional difficulty was reported above, which is that as the labour movement is a part of historical capitalism, it is even more arbitrary to distinguish its performance as opposition to the system from its performance in the system itself. However, this relatively pertinent distinction is currently acceptable if it is thought of as a distinction between the labour movement 'for itself' and 'in itself'. Such a distinction, which brings Hegel to Sartre through Marx and Mao, in reality refers to the essence of the historical process. Within the latter, a certain pole in a dialectic (that is, one specified through its simple opposition to the other pole), can be transformed into an autonomous subject which is eventually contesting the relation which defines it. Being a questionable conceptual tool, this distinction manifestly points to an actual problem: if, according to Marx, people make history on the basis of conditions, and in accordance to a vision of the world inherited from the past and consolidated into the present, they may well adopt, under the pressure of these conditions, a group behaviour that aims at a consolidation or a reversal of the above conditions. As a result, there is sufficient room for two histories: one according to an objective dialectic, and another specified by the activities of actors operating 'for themselves' in their struggle to handle or destroy this dialectic.

Rationalist millenarianism

In 1842, young Marx pointed out in the *Contribution to a Critique of Hegel's Philosophy of Right* that the proletariat was the only force that had earned nothing from the French Revolution (a democratic, bourgeois one). He also suggested that the proletariat incarnates not only the ferment of reversing the existing order itself, but also, considering the universal character of its suffering, a class that cannot free itself unless the entire humanity is liberated. Marx expresses here rather clearly the mentality of the emerging labour movement, from the babouvisme to the circles of artisans who were to form the first communist groupings. If June 1848 marks the first invasion of this class in the political scene according to autonomous political objectives, it should not be surprising that the militant generation, from the supporters of 'utopian' and 'scientific' socialism to anarchists and Marxists, who thought and lived during this first period of the labour movement (until the Commune of Paris in 1871), resembled in many ways the Christian sects from the death of Christ to the end of the 1st century AD.

In fact, most of these intellectuals and highly skilled craftsmen (and Marx himself in his youth) were 'radical democrats'. They were dreaming of 'their revolution' as a completion, in their life-time, of the French Revolution, considered as a failure. Later, Marx will fight against the confusion between 'bourgeois' and 'proletarian' revolutions, but at this stage the distinction was all the more unclear, as in most parts of Europe bourgeois revolution was far from being achieved.

Moreover, these prophets are intellectuals, or individuals in the labour class. The great majority of workers, including the organised ones, are just fighting for their place within the post-Bourgeois Revolution system and they are pure reformists (not even radical). The ambiguity will be permanent in the first grass-root structures of the labour movement, the Job Centres which both seek jobs within wage relations, and fight against these new relations, trying to create other, co-operative ones.

Yet, the 'prophets' will have a major importance, since they will contribute to define the official ideology of the future fully-developed labour movement. So, it is important to grasp their general idea of the relation between labour movement and capitalist reality.

According to an image well-favoured in 'utopian socialism' (notably Owen), capitalism appears as a Babylon whose prisoners are waiting for the collapse to (re)discover New Jerusalem. The militant vehemence and the ideology of the members of the movement, like the work of theologists, aim at either confirming or proving that the system is going to perish soon, that the partial struggle is just reinforcing the army that has camped at the foot of the city, that tomorrow it may rise for an attack, and that it is time to prepare the plans for a new city. Some are even ready to go away and create 'colonies' in the New World, according to the new plans. The conflict between the proponents of the scientific and utopian socialism essentially places the point of equilibrium between elements that, in capitalism, *push* towards socialism, and elements which, due to the 'dream that Humanity has in head', *pull* out of capitalism. Marx quickly passed from the second to the first position, which he developed into rationalism, but without giving up eschatologism, even in the most analytical of his books, *Capital*. This 'rationalist millenarianism' considers itself as non-utopian and is presented as deductive, being based on an analysis of the *contradictory* character of the capitalist relations of production. Such a thesis appears in the famous *Preface of 1859 to a Contribution to the Critique of Political Economy*:

> The bourgeois mode of production is the last antagonistic form of the social process of production – antagonistic not in the sense of individual antagonism, but of an antagonism that emanates from the individuals' social conditions of existence – but the productive forces developing within bourgeois society create also the material conditions for a solution of this antagonism. The prehistory of human society accordingly closes with this social formation.

The same idea is met in *Capital* (Book 1, p. 32):

> The monopoly of capital becomes an obstacle to a mode of production that has grown and prospered through it and under its auspices. Socialisation of labour and centralisation of material resources have reached a point that they cannot fit under their capitalist cover any more. This cover is falling to pieces. The time of capitalist ownership has come to an end. The expropriators are expropriated from their course.

This conception of overcoming capitalism presupposes a certain unity of the elements in struggle: the two poles remain external to each other, and whatever establishes their unity also establishes the victory of the one over the other. In the case of the productive forces, the content of socialisation is independent from its form (a socialisation performed by the owners or exploiters). Of course, it is capitalists who have socialised the productive forces – however, the latter are socialist productive forces! The chrysalis has turned into a butterfly coming out of its cocoon, according to the prophecy in the *Communist Manifesto*:

> The development of industry, whose involuntary promoter is the bourgeoisie, replaces the isolation of workers (caused by competition) by their revolutionary union (which is due to their association) .... Above all, what the bourgeoisie produces are its

own gravediggers. Its fall and the victory of the proletariat are equally inevitable.

It is worth asking whether that external relation characterising the two adversaries in the structure of this dialectic does not have to presuppose or complement the neutrality of the productive forces. In this view, the latter are no more contaminated by their bourgeois form than the labour class itself. In some pages ('rediscovered' in the 1960s) Marx goes beyond the critique of the bourgeois character of the relation of properties, and goes as far as criticising the capitalist character of the productive forces themselves.[3] But these pages are mere exceptions before the universality of the conceptions shared by the intellectuals of the movement, from Cabet to Lenin. A radical contest of the 'progressive character of the productive forces' can certainly be found in the words of the authentic artisans and workers.[4] It can also be found in the work of Marx himself. However, it should be recognised that through its organisations and by its chanting the labour movement is not contesting the progressive character of the development of production as organised by the bourgeoisie; it is only contesting the distribution of outputs, and occasionally the management. Babylon provides the material basis for the construction of New Jerusalem.

It remains to clarify the arguments supporting the inevitable victory of the proletariat. These arguments encompass two tendencies: the reinforcement and automatic unification of the proletariat, as opposed to the weakening and increasing division of its exploiters. The second tendency reveals the importance of a theory of crises. Marx and some other theorists have played a key role in offering at least two types of explanation for past or future crises: one that is based on the fall in the rate of profit, and another based on the contradiction between production and realisation, that is, on underconsumption (or overproduction). However, that relates to the 'inner dynamics of the system' which we will discuss later. Let us now go on with the 'anti-systemic force'.

Strategies and tactics

Unfortunately, the growth of the movement, which at first seemed to unite the labour class (through the elimination of elements supporting 'pre-scientific' socialism), started to split up after the fall of the Paris Commune. Subsequent labour parties were constituted on a national basis (although theoretically federated by the Second International), and were faced with the question: to camp against or to establish within Babylon. This debate did not prevent their consolidation during the major crisis in the late 19th century, though it initiated a genuine international split before World War II. Curiously, the theory of crises serves well the theoretical argument in question.

'On the right' are the proponents of *insertion*. These theorists based their hopes on the numerical increase of the proletariat and on the democratic vote, which would presumably bring social democrats into power one day. It was a long-term strategy that despised agitation. They emphasised the theory of the fall in the rate of profit and the possibilites of regular accumulation, provided that the state is able to temper the anarchy of the market. Similarly, the great theorists of this approach, Hilferding and Kautsky, thought that the inevitable residual of intercapitalist competition and international rivalry would be reduced due to the 'super-imperialist' concentration of capitalist power in the hands of a very restricted financial bourgeoisie. In contrast, 'on the left' were the proponents of *rupture*. These theorists strove to prove that crises are able to shake the structure of Babylon in the short-term, as rivalries degenerate into wars. Consequently, the proletariat should keep itself prepared; it should not infiltrate the existing order, but surge from beneath the ruins. Rosa Luxemburg, a representative of this position, is also a great theorist of crisis due to overproduction. Lenin was initially faithful to the ideas of Kautsky, as far as the fight against the Populists was concerned. However, he turned against the 'traitor' when the 'social-chauvinist' logic of the social democrats was being pulled into the inter-imperialist war.

Naturally, Lenin is especially remarkable because he was the one who, under the cover of World War I, succeeded in what all of the socialists (theoretically) were calling for — the Proletarian Revolution. He was not the only one that undertook it, and if he succeeded, it was probably not only for objective reasons. Why Russia and not Hungary? Probably, because of the 'Kuneries'.[5] With Lenin, the sense of tactics breaks into the most radical version of the 'rupture' strategy. It begins with the introduction of a third term in the revolutionary dialectic, that of the 'centrist' forces. The latter are *for* the abolition of the past, but *against* the new order that the communists want to establish. The plurality of possible issues that emerged since the first *Letter from Afar* (March 1917) and the periodicity of crises that followed, structured the thought of Lenin, who was simultaneously a tactician and a theorist of the situation from February to October. His thought served as an example to all 'Leninist' analyses of political crises that comprise retrospective expositions, like those of Mathiez on the French Revolution. The three-fold range of issues (reactionary, reformist and revolutionary), and the periodicity of the process of a crisis, are not in fact new ideas as they have already been mentioned in Marx's *Class Struggle in France*. However, these are now working concepts implicating tactics, which Lenin (and later Mao) mastered in a remarkable way: rapid displacement of the principal contradiction and of the alliances, consequently of the objectives and the demands. Confrontation with Babylon descends from mythology to Clausewitz.

Yet, this major conceptual progress is immediately threatened. First, owing, to the particular character of the Russian Revolution, it over-accelerated due to the question of peace or war. This over-acceleration surprised Lenin with the phenomenon of 'reaching the extremes', 'characterised by an exacerbation of the revolution and the counter-revolution, and by a "weakening" of the intermediate elements for a more or less long time' [*Three Crises* July 1917]. Some, including Lenin himself, never forgot about the existence of the intermediate elements, and tried to bring them into work until the last moment, mainly after Kornilov's *coup d'état*. We may dare to say that this possibility of splitting between the non-revolutionary issues of the crisis constitutes *the* big Leninist innovation. It is the lesson Lenin learnt from 'his' revolution to be used by the international labour movement:

> The fundamental law of the revolution, confirmed by all revolutions and mainly by the three Russian Revolutions of the 20th century, is the following: if the revolution is to take place, it does not suffice that the exploited and oppressed masses be conscious of the impossibility of living as before, and that they claim changes. If the revolution is to take place, exploiters should not have the power to live and govern as before. This happens when 'those down below' *do not want*, and 'those high up' *can no more* live in *the old way*; it is only then that the revolution will triumph. Such a truth is expressed differently in these terms: the revolution is impossible without a *national crisis* (affecting the exploiters and the exploited) ['*The Child Disease of Communism*', *Leftism*, April 1920].

This concept of national crisis retrospectively clarifies the historical analyses of Marx (and later of Gramsci), as well as Mao's practice. However, it is immediately weakened by the 'reaching the extremes' phenomenon (that verified itself even in the Portuguese Revolution of 1974–75). This phenomenon tends to reproduce the simple opposition between Babylon and New Jerusalem. Such a reduction is encouraged by a weakness of the Leninist characterisations regarding the intermediate forces – 'the petit bourgeoisie'.

> Leaders of the petit bourgeoisie democracy lull the masses with promises of the possibility of an agreement with gross capitalists. Putting the matter better, they obtain token concessions from capitalists for a very short period of time, and for the benefit of the higher ranks of the labouring masses. However, in all cases of significant issues, the petit bourgeoisie democracy has always been in the barge of the bourgeoisie, for whom it was a weak appendage [*The Lessons of the Revolution*, September 1917].

Moreover, Lenin subdued the leaders of the reformist tendency of the labour movement in the 'petit bourgeoisie democracy', a characterisation that was destined to find itself a symbol during the German Revolution: Noske, a social democrat and butcher of the Labour Councils.

From that moment, the labour movement will be divided into two parts, and even into three. Firstly, the Soviet Union poses as the New Jerusalem under construction. On its side, communist parties of the capitalist world pose as supporters of New Jerusalem, although working at the foot of Babylon. Lastly, there are those who hope for extracting more than 'token concessions' from Babylon – revolution against reform, Marxism–Leninism against social-democracy. For the Marxists–Leninists, the emergence of the colonial question, which we have left out of this exposition, does no more than formally affect the analysis, as it underlines the importance of the intermediate forces (that is the national bourgeoisie and the peasants), only to immediately reaffirm (through the propagation of the rule of 'reaching the extremes') the necessity of a proletarian direction in the democratic revolution.

Today, few people look up to the USSR as the New Jerusalem. The analyses diverge on the reasons for such a defection, ranging from those who see a deviation by treason on this or that date (under Lenin, Stalin or Khrushchev), to those for whom the worm was in the fruit from the beginning, with the Bolsheviks representing a path to capitalist modernisation – this was the position of those on the

European far left in the 1920s such as Pannekoek and Gorter. In between are those who have tried to analyse the process of deviation as a process without subject, one that has resulted from a series of historical, determinable mistakes conditioned by the circumstances, although rectifiable in principle.[6] The revolutions that followed (in China, Cuba, Vietnam), have not yielded the expected outcomes. However, they modified for the first time during the 1960s, due to the questions raised by the masses (in a rather fleeting and ideological manner), what was presumed common knowledge in the 2nd, 3rd or 4th International: that Babylon provides at least the material bases for New Jerusalem. Such a radical contest of the neutrality, and even of the positivity of the productive forces remains the heritage, for the moment in limbo, of Mao and Che Guevara.

In the capitalist countries, communist parties and social democrats confronted the second major crisis of capitalism (that of the 1930s) under the worst circumstances. Communist parties concentrated on the tactics of 'class against class' (always in the name of 'reaching the extremes') and considered social democracy as 'the left side of fascism'. In doing this, these parties were not without reason, as we shall see when focusing exclusively on economic regulation. When the fascist threat forced the Soviet Union to recall the usefulness of the 'united fronts', the communists shifted to the opposite extreme: they made an alliance with Babylon against Assur. World War II ended with an attachment of East Europe to the Soviet system, the dispersion of Leninist seeds throughout the Third World, and the integration of powerful communist parties in their own national political life in France and in Italy. So, the 'communists in Babylon' found themselves reluctantly in the role of the social democrats.

Meanwhile, in the 1930s, some of these social democrats had started to realise, as in Scandinavia, that it was possible to establish within Babylon by extracting more than token concessions from capitalists, and for more than the 'higher ranks' of the proletariat. Gradually the social democrats in power, with or without the support of communists, were recognised as managers of capitalism, thus imposing norms of social democracy which their conservative adversaries would not contest for a while. When the French Socialist party took power in 1981, it was certainly the last to speak of a 'rupture with capitalism'. Unlike its northern counterparts it lost power after having only slightly transformed that society in a socialist sense.

Thus, the primitive ideology of the rupture seems to have been all burnt up, with the communist parties managing a Babylon they name Jerusalem, and the social democrats managing Babylon but guarding it against rebaptising. After some initial ripples, the present third major crisis of capitalism, far from having opened the way for a new radical thrust by the labour movement, and far from having favoured a 'reaching the extremes' process, seems to oppose only the proponents of different ways of managing capitalism, thus becoming the 'closed horizon of our time'.

METAMORPHOSES OF CAPITALISM: STAGES, CYCLES, AND REGIMES

Capitalism is susceptible to a stage-by-stage evolution: theorists of the labour movement have recognised this long ago and have proposed various types of periodisation according to their vision of evolution. In *Capital*, for example, Marx proposed a periodisation of labour organisation according to the dichotomy 'formal submission/actual submission', and according to the stages of cooperation and automation. His successors emphasised various forms of regulating inter-capitalist economic relations such as competitive regulation, monopoly or state monopoly. However, most often periodisation emerges only as the result of an immanent tendency (law of increasing deprivation of the direct producer, and law of capital concentration). Shedding some light on the tendencies of the long period of capitalism, and referring them to its invariant structure are interesting research undertakings by themselves,[7] on the condition that they do not reduce facts to these abstract laws, something that is not always avoided. More importantly, the mark of the 'rationalist millenarianism' can be seen in the recurrent assertion that the stage presently attained is the 'ultimate' one, immediately preceding the final crisis of capitalism, thus appearing as the ante-room of socialism.

Waves and long cycles

More academic in style, another Marxist strand that follows Parvus and Kondratieff introduces phases of a long duration regarding the movement of prices and revenues, thus setting off an important theoretical debate.[8] That is, should these 'cycles' (provided that they are worthy of the characterisation) be interpreted in the same way as the classic crises of the economic cycle,[9] or do they empirically manifest the trace of a more fundamental periodisation, each period marking a reorganisation of capitalism? Trotsky clearly refused to consider phases as cycles. That led one of his present students, Ernest Mandel (1980), to propose a methodologically seducing distinction, though many scholars (including myself) may object to the concrete content of his analysis. According to this author, reversal of the tendency at the peak of a long wave should be considered as endogenous, that is, it results from contradictions inherent to capitalism in the course of an ascending economic phase. On the contrary, reversal at the lowest point is exogenous and involves new inventions, a significant moment in the class struggle. This is a promising idea, as the wavy appearance of a continuing process is transformed into a discontinuous succession of forms new to capitalism. Each of these forms is progressing towards its highest and then to its decline; however, moving out of this decline is not automatically guaranteed. Unfortunately, such a promising idea (like the intuitions of Trotsky) tends to be overshadowed by the idea that the contemporary major crisis can be overcome only by socialism or barbarism.

It remains to give a characterisation to the long phases, according to the factor contingent to recovery. According to most theorists following Schumpeter, specification of these phases is based on their technological characteristics. One may have:

(1) a first cycle from 1789–1850, which ended in what I have called the 'final crisis of the transition', and was marked by the steam engine and the textile industry;
(2) a second cycle from 1850–95, which ended in the first major crisis of capitalism (1873–95) and was marked by the steel industry and the railways,
(3) a third cycle from 1895–1939, which ended in the second major crisis (1920–39) and was marked by electricity, internal combustion engines and the automobile,
(4) a fourth cycle extending from 1940 to the present crisis, in which it is not clear what it is marked by the most — the automobile (still?), electronics (already?).

Based on this summary description, it is easy to pin-point the major difficulties facing the explanation of long cycles by 'major innovations': the arbitrariness of their specification and of their periodisation (are the 1920s an ascending or descending period?) and even their characterisation as recurrent cycles (the descending years of the fourth cycle were marked by a stagnation rather than a recession, and by an acceleration of inflation).[10] However, like the theory of stages, the theory of long waves, and especially the above variant, once again puts emphasis on autonomy of the movement of 'those high up', of capital. Here, the history of leading sectors and technologies is just substituted for the history of capitalist concentration. This may appear as a move backwards, because economic history is reduced to the evolution of a technological parameter which remains unexplained.

Regimes and modes

The dismissal of technological determinism, coupled with the need to understand the truly new elements when passing from one period of growth to the next, has inspired a third current of thought: the analysis in terms of regimes of accumulation and of the mode of regulation. Also initiated from studies of long periods (that of M. Aglietta in the case of the US and of CEPREMAP (1977) in that of France), they are specified in econometric terms and primarily refer to gaps in *correlations*. More particularly, they deal with the reciprocal determinants of prices, wages, profits, production and productivity, rather than with variations in the magnitude of these indices.

Clarification of these gaps through an analysis of the forms of industrial organisation and of the institutional forms leads to periods of growth characterised as *regimes of accumulation*. The latter ensure, over a long period, a compatibility between firstly, transformations in the ways of production (defined by the dominant type of labour organisation), and secondly, the orientation of social consumption. Accumulation has the potential of being either extensive or intensive, and is centred on the production of the means of production or that of consumer goods, allowing for exports to a certain extent. However, a regime of accumulation cannot be supported solely by its own coherence — institutional forms and norms of actor aspirations (habitus) are needed to ensure the convergence of expectations and of behaviour towards the regime of accumulation. These *forms of regulation* concern the organisation of wage relations, of competition, the management of the money supply, and state intervention.[11] Based on the articulation of these partial forms of regulation, a *mode of regulation* results, which is characterised as more or less competitive (absence of an ex ante anticipation of macro-economic effects on micro-economic adjustments), or monopoly (normalisation and exploitation of an ex ante estimation of macro-economic effects on micro-economic behaviours). Since 1850, the end of the capitalist transition,[12] related analyses have generated the following periodisation:[13]

(1) An extensive growth,[14] based on the know-how of professional workers and centred on the means of production, with a competitive determination of prices, of wages, of the level of production, and with a 'circumscribed' state, strained by the depression of the late 19th century.

(2) This depression, 'the first major crisis of capitalism', took the form of recurrent crises. These were simultaneously due to firstly, significant tensions in the labour market at the end of the booms, and secondly a fierce war of prices for the distribution of outputs. So, it could be characterised as a crisis of the regime of accumulation (insufficient extraction of relative surplus value during the extensive phase of accumulation) with, secondarily, a deficiency in regulation of the supply/demand contradiction.

(3) It was succeeded by a phase of recovery thanks to the appearance of monopoly structures at the level of inter-capitalist competition (cartelisation and imperialism), and a tight stabilisation of the purchasing power of the labour class. To this 'improvement' of the mode of regulation was added a deep transformation of the regime of accumulation. If the latter remained primarily extensive and centred on the means of production, it contained the first effects of the Taylorist revolution at the level of the production process.

(4) World War I, a war of redistributing the world, permitted above all the propagation of the Taylorist and Fordist methods of production, thus initiating an intensive accumulation which stumbled over the second major crisis in the late 1920s.

(5) The time period from 1930–45 was characterised by a major crisis which was almost purely one of the global mode of regulation. The latter remained competitive in the sense that it was unable to incorporate a norm of growth of the consumption of wage earners into the regime of accumulation.

(6) The victory of the 'democratic side' in World War II at last facilitated concentrated mass-production towards durable mass-consumption, thanks to a strengthening of the monopoly regulation of the whole economy: contractualisation of wage relations, indirect wages, credit money, and state intervention. That regime of accumulation is called 'Fordism'.

(7) Finally, the present crisis is a combination, although in variable proportions according to researchers, of a crisis of the regime of accumulation and of a crisis of the mode of regulation. It is a 'mixed major crisis', possibly even more fascinating than that in the late 19th century. On the side of the regime of accumulation: the exhaustion of the gains of Taylorist productivity, and the increase in the composition of capital through Fordist processes lead to a fall in profitability (Lipietz 1986). On the side of regulation: its essentially national character is faced with the increasing internationalisation of production and circulation. Competition among states introduces a 'competitive stagnation'.

It is evident that the above conceptions are based on the same presumed methodology as Mandel's: moving into a major crisis is endogenous to the existing regime, it is the product of contradictions specific to *this* regime and to its mode of regulation. Interpretations about the reasons for the growth of contradictions within a regime may differ. Why these tendencies to a fall in productivity and to internationalisation? What is the importance of class struggles in these processes? The 'regulation school' is not unified about the answers. I gave mine in Lipietz (1984–85), emphasising the contradictions of labour organisation within core economies. But anyway, we think that the 'reasons for the crisis' belong to the history of the regime in crisis and must be understood within it. However, moving out of the crisis is a genuine 'finding', which is ignored by 'regulation theory' (despite ritual references to the effects of the social struggle on production and distribution). This is simultaneously the strength and the weakness of the above strand of research, which is content with depicting both new principles permitting stabilisation of a phase of growth, and new contradictions developing into a major crisis, and so on for every successive sequence, although without proposing a 'law' of the progression from each sequence to the next.

As a result, it is left to those interested to fill this gap. For instance, it can be assumed that there exists a permanent tendency (at the technological level, for example) and a permanent principle of accumulation, which periodically stumble over contradictions and have to search for a new regime and a new mode of regulation. In this conception, social struggles could only re-establish the unity of the system in a sort of 'inversed teleology' (in relation to the 'dialectic of rupture'). This would be an 'overregulation', a principle of long-term conservation through the metamorphoses of the capitalist system, following a kind of 'order by fluctuations'.[15] I am just as much sceptical about any 'regulating teleology of capitalism', as about the New Jerusalem eschatology. I do believe that social struggles could either lead to conservation or to deeper transformations of capitalism, may be out of capitalism. So, I now offer a consideration of the possible effects of that 'systemic anti-systemic force' (the labour movement) on the transformations of capitalism.

THE WORKING CLASS MOVEMENT, A SYSTEMIC ANTI-SYSTEMIC FORCE

To fill the blank that characterises the mystery of the end of major crises, we should evidently consider the intervention of social forces. The latter express themselves through specific propositions and struggles, thus setting off, consciously or unconsciously, issues which are never exactly as they were set at first. Fordism and Keynesian practices are not the clear or simple application of Ford's and Keynes' ideas having persuaded followers and adversaries alike. From the existing set of forces, at least three blocs (in the Gramscist sense of the term) can be distinguished: conservatives (who have benefited from World War I in the West), radicals (who won in Russia during the same time period), and reformists who can be either reactionary or progressive. Among the concurrent forces constituting these blocs, we will deal with the case of the labour movement.[16]

A shortcut: 'plan against plan'

A first simplistic approach, which nevertheless reflects well a part of reality, is to consider the class struggle directly in order to specify the great metamorphoses of capitalism. The way of Italian 'operaists', as manifested by the examples of Tony Negri or Sergio Bologna in the 1960s and 1970s, is typical. Their interpretation of recent Italian history is summarised below.[17]

Up to 1917, the labour class had been made up of professional workers possessing a certain know-how; big industry had not followed Taylorism yet. The Russian, Italian and German Revolutions were fought by the professional worker. Faced by the threat, capital reacted with Fordism, which destroyed the labour movement and substituted the professional worker with the 'mass-operative', thus undermining the possibility of an elitist (Leninist) type of proletarian organisation. This 'massification' of production engendered the crisis of overproduction in the 1930s; then, the Keynesian State intervened to expand labour consumption. There were two advantages to this: avoiding labour pressure ('based on labour reformism'), and initiating the planning of capital under the auspices of the state. However, such a response was contradictory because the high level of the organic composition of capital, constituting a 'technological way towards repression', set off a decrease in the rate of profit, which was not compensated by an increase in the rate of exploitation. So, the battle of the mass-operative against the 'State-Plan' was fought with respect to wage levels: either the 'State-Plan' would maintain the way of accumulation (that of the age of Fordism), or the proletariat would 'ruin the plans of capital'. Therefore, the situation shifted towards a 'simplification of the class struggle': the ratio of profit to wages directly expressed the 'commanding power' of the capitalist state over the working class in a political manner.

During the 1960s 'reformism overflew the flood plain'. The working class snatched the augmentations of wages which ruined the 'Italian miracle'; gains were spread over the 'entire proletariat' (such as the industrial-reserve army, the students, retirees and the unemployed). The 'class became proletarian over the entire social field'. The struggle shifted to the sector of public expenditures (capital of the 'factory-State'): budget reductions, abuse of absences due to illness, abuse of unemployment funds, and so on.

With the historical compromise, the Italian Communist Party proposed the reform of Keynesianism, which has by now become impracticable (for capital) and reactionary (for the proletariat). But the crisis triggered by capital is a genuine operation of destroying the productive forces, whose main target is the mass-operative engendered by automation. Such an operation of 'productive decentralisation' is seen as playing 'the society against the factory' through the increase in labour unemployment. By introducing even more automation and tertiarisation, it is faced with the generalisation of the 'social-operative'. When the 'movement' of students and 'under-employed' emerged in 1977, the 'Autonomous' following Negri have not hesitated to transfer the torch held by the Mirafiori worker in the 1960s to this incarnation of the social-operative.

Let's stop the film of this football match at this scene ... We have already recognised a simple *juxtaposition* of the two separated dynamics considered previously. Capital endowed with reason and working class endowed with goal are both caught in a titanic confrontation, where offensive follows counter-offensive, 'plan and counterplan' according to the title of an 'operaist' journal. The cyclic appearance of the confrontation undoubtedly results from the Clausewitzian principle that the defensive has a position superior to that of the offensive. The attempt to integrate the history of the labour movement in the history of capital is only imperfect or external.[18] The centrist blocs (those who negotiate the compromises stabilising the relations of power, and organise the collaboration of classes), appear as simple traitors, who change sides during the game. But the basis of the problem (which Lenin posed well, although he resolved it in a rather weak manner, denying any *real* mutual gains), is to understand why 'the masses' in the long run show confidence to 'leaders' who betray them. The solution is certainly not to follow the proposition of Lenin in *What is to be done?*: let 'qualified intellectuals import revolutionary consciousness into the spontaneously trade-unionist working class'.

To overcome this obstacle, we must understand that the essence of the labour movement is expressed by two aspects. As a 'class in itself' in historical capitalism, it should rather survive and struggle to keep its place and secondly, as a class that mobilises against capitalist relations, it should try to destroy them.

These two aspects are inseparably connected: if the labour class were not reproducing itself within the relations of capitalist production, there would be no tendency towards a struggle against the system. However, at the same time, these aspects are diametrically opposed: it is not the same to struggle for more wages and for more control within capitalist society, and to struggle for the abolition of wage labour and for workers' power. To these correspond two strategies, two tactics, and two contradictory forms of organisation. The same holds whenever the two strategies are temporarily confounded in a single tactic, or whenever the corresponding tendencies fight for hegemony over the organisational structure of a single union. This is because the struggle between two goals is placed on a unique basis of the material conditions offered to the labour movement within historical capitalism. That is why Marx could write in *Wages, Prices and Profits*:

Unions are useful, provided that they are the centres of resistance against the infringements of capital. They partly miss their purpose if they do not make appropriate use of their power. They entirely lose their purpose if they are constrained to fighting against the effects of the existing regime, instead of working at the same time towards its transformation, and towards serving their organised power like a lever for the definitive emancipation of the working class, that is, for the definitive abolition of wage labour.

In a similar manner Gramcsi,[19] who recognised a fundamentally positive element in the association of the proletariat when faced with the competition of the capitalist market, also recognised the material basis of reformism in the same association, without making any appeals to the 'treason of the sold leaders':

> The objective of association and of solidarity becomes the essence of the labour class, because it changes the psychology and the behaviour of workers and countries. This objective is expressed with the creation of new groups and organisations; they serve as the point of departure for historical development processes, which lead to the collectivisation of both the means of production and of exchange. (*La conquête du pouvoir*, 12 July 1919).

And yet:

> Workers feel that 'their' organisation has become such an enormous apparatus, that it has come to obey its own laws. These laws are implanted in its structure and in its functional complex; however; they are foreign to the masses who are conscious of their historical mission as a revolutionary class. They feel that their volition is not expressed in a clear and precise way through the present hierarchies of their institution [*Syndicats et conseils*, 10 October 1919].

From this point we should examine the role of labour organisations in the establishment of new regimes of accumulation and new modes of capitalist regulation. To this end, we will refer to two mutations successively by presenting the two major crises of capitalism whose outcomes we know already.

The union question and the crisis at the end of the 19th century

Summarising the period extending from the fall of the Commune to the beginning of World War I, W. Abendroth (1965) writes untroubled:

Existing labour parties at the national level had this in common, that, on the one hand, they wanted to transform the capitalist society of classes into a society without classes, and that, on the other hand, they were confronted with problems of a similar nature in their respective countries. They all wanted a democratisation of political power, improvement of work conditions and wages, security in the cases of illness, disability or unemployment. The forms of battle — union strikes and organisation of workers in parties and unions — were similar in the various European countries. In all cases, state interventions in social politics were considered as the means for action necessary for stabilisation, even within periods of economic crisis, of unions' successes in aligning worker standards of living with the rapid growth of productivity due to technical progress. State interventions were also considered necessary means for supporting those who had, even temporarily, quitted work because of illness or unemployment, or had definitely retired because of disability or old age.

Is this a retrospective illusion? An early identification of Fordism before World War I? Undoubtedly so. However, it is very interesting to understand why and how the labour movement unconsciously aspired to Fordism. Two theoretical and organisational debates took place before and after the first major crisis of capitalism, at the end of the 19th century, that can be clarifying in a useful way. Before the crisis, there was the struggle for union formation and the text *Wages, Prices and Profits* by Marx. After the crisis (and in fact after World War I), there was the triumphant recognition of unionism, and Gramsci's first critical writings in *Ordine Nuovo*. Between the two, there was a progressive stabilisation of labour purchasing power by indexing wages on prices, limitation of working hours, and the beginning of the struggle of capitalists for new sources of productivity.

In the processes of worker resistance and capitalist struggle for productivity, the history of capital and that of the labour movement are probably tied the most. As absolute surplus value cannot be augmented indefinitely (a day has no more than twenty-four hours), and as proletarians cannot live on air, capital cannot increase the rate of surplus if not by way of increasing productivity. However, individual capitalists tend to increase their *own* profit by underpaying or by over-utilising the work force, that is, by breaking with that which constitutes the essence of an 'agreeable' capitalist regime — established economic relations. Therefore, the declared struggle of the labour class is like the struggle of a party complaining in commercial court so as to make its adversaries stop the 'infringements' by playing according to the rules of the game. Moreover, society is endowed with conscious means against the abuse of its own organism, that is, political organisation, and in this particular case, the legislation of work.

This illustrates a specific type of labour struggle which 'develops' the capitalist productive forces. Its direct purpose is to impose prices and the *normal* usage of the commodities sold. Its lever is action at the legislative level, which spreads the partial gains and mitigates the perverse effects of the competitive game. Its result is the development of capitalist productive forces:

> Since the revolt of the working class forced the state to institute a normal day ... , that is, from the moment it ruled out increases in the production of surplus value by a progressive addition of working hours, capital has striven with all of its energy, and in full awareness, for the production of relative surplus value through an accelerated development of machinery [*Capital*, 1, Chapter 15].

These considerations permitted Karl Marx to describe in an excellent way the place and the limits of the union struggle before the General Council of the International:

> The periodic resistance of the wage worker against the reduction of wages, and the efforts he undertakes periodically to obtain an augmentation in wages, are inseparably tied to the wage system, and are provoked by the fact that work is assimilated into commodities, and is consequently subject to the laws regulating the general movement of prices. Concerning the limitations of the working day ... this is never regulated by anything different from legislative intervention .... This necessity of a general political action is the proof that in a purely economic struggle, capital is the strongest element. ... The general tendency of capitalist production is not to raise the average level of wages, but to lower, that is, to restore, the value of labour at its lowest limit. However, if these were the tendencies of the regime, shouldn't the labour class renounce its resistance to the infringements of capital, and abandon its efforts to eliminate the occasions presenting it with whatever could cause some amelioration of its situation? If it did that, it would degrade into a formless mass, crushed, starving for those it could not save any more. ... If the labour class retreated in its everyday conflict

with capital, it would certainly deprive itself of the possibility of
the most consequential moves. At the same time, ... wage workers
should not exaggerate the final result of this everyday struggle.
They should not forget that they are struggling against the effects
and not against the causes of these effects. ... They should understand that the actual regime, in all of its oppressive misery,
engenders at the same time the material conditions and the social
forces necessary for the economic transformation of society.
Instead of the conservative demand 'equitable wages for an
equitable working day', they should inscribe the revolutionary
demand 'Abolition of wage labour' on their flags [*Wages, Prices
and Profits*].

Before going on, let us remark that the above split is not between a
'purely economic struggle' and a 'political struggle', because the
struggle for a 'normal' day, a necessarily political struggle, has indeed
the same status as the struggle for wages. Marx talked about the
struggle against the 'infringements', while Engels used the same word
to define the relations between the capitalist state and individual
capitalists. 'Infringe' — what does this mean? It is to violate the
norms in order not to abolish them but to displace them with profit.
This is the behavioural tendency of private actors in a world of
competition. Natually, only the resistance of market competitors and
allies hinders the infringements. At the same time, the state can at
most stabilise further, and thus guarantee the fixed norms. However,
resistance to infringements is not a struggle against the system of
norms. On the contrary, it plays a certain role in the game of the
'coercive forces' (the law of value is another one), which constrain
capitalists to be true entrepreneurs and not *rentiers*. In brief, the
labour class develops the productive forces of capital, insofar as it
behaves as the capitalist merchant of its own labour force.

In this role, the labour class is just one of the elements in the
structure of the mode of production: it constitutes a 'class for itself'.
To this nature of class corresponds a specific *organisational form*
(otherwise the class would be just a collection of individuals), the
union, which is supplemented with a specific political representation,
the social democratic party. Such a historical form of worker
association is therefore a constrained form, which does not refer to a
class trying to establish in a new world, but to one defending itself in
a hostile world. And that is the form that stabilised after the major
crisis of the late 19th century. This is explained by Gramsci in *Ordine*

Nuovo, where he opposes unions to councils and soviets (flourishing in revolutionary Europe from 1917–22):

> During the present period, the proletarian movement does not exist but as a function of free capitalist competition. Proletarian institutions took certain forms not due to an internal law, but due to an external one under the formidable pressure of events and coercions deriving from capitalist competition [*La conquète de pouvoir*, 12 July 1919]. ...
>
> In a certain sense, we can maintain that these organisations constitute an integral part of capitalist society, and that they constitute an inherent function of the private ownership regime. In the present period, in which individuals do not have value unless they are commodity owners and make profit out of their possessions, workers are obliged to yield to the 'iron law' of everyday needs, and they have become sellers of their only property: their labour force and their professional intelligence. As they are especially exposed to the risks of competition, workers have accumulated their property in ever growing 'firms' employing increasing numbers of personnel. These firms have become an enormous apparatus of concentration of manpower, they have imposed prices and working hours, and have disciplined the market. They have engaged from outside or promoted from their own rank-and-files a devoted administrative personnel, which is experienced in speculation, has the ability to dominate the conditions of the market, is capable of stipulating contracts, of evaluating commercial areas, and of introducing economically profitable operations. *The essential nature of unions is competitive and not communist. A union can not be an instrument of radical renovation of society* [*Syndicats et Conseils*, 10 October 1919].

His radical conclusion is: '*Unionism is revealed as a simple form of capitalist society, and not as a potential way of overcoming capitalist society*' [*Syndicalisme et conseils*, 8 March 1920].

To sum up, during the first major crisis of capitalism (which corresponds to the period of the 2nd International), the labour movement forces capitalism to acknowledge its existence as a unique social class, and the right to defend its interests. That would lead to further improvement of the labour situation within wage relations — but precisely, *within* these relations.

With no treason, mourning is without reason ...

The question of the state and the crisis of the 1930s

It remains to consider that, at the beginning of the 20th century in advanced capitalist countries, the unions had gained at most the indexation of wages on rising prices. It is an exaggeration to state that they have obtained an indexation of purchasing power on productivity. Simply, econometric indicators seem to show that after the first major crisis purchasing power did not fall during the depressions more than it rose during the booms (Boyer, 1977). Indexation on productivity is a different matter. Unions should not simply struggle against the 'infringements' of rising prices, they should also *anticipate* them in order to appropriate a part of productivity gains.

At this point, a theoretical parenthesis is due. Struggling against the infringements presupposes a norm of distribution of value added, and therefore a norm of value of the labour force. The two ways this norm can be defined are firstly, the value of what is normally bought by wages, and secondly, a normal fraction of value added (Lipietz 1983). If capitalists change the norms of production by increasing productivity, conservation of the first norm implicates a fall in the second (hence the appearance of relative surplus value). However, is there a Marxist theory of the norm of labour consumption?

This is a delicate question. There exist formulations in *Capital* suggesting the independence of the history of the norm of labour consumption (which is described in chapter VI as 'historically given'), from the history of productive norms. However, in the pages where Marx seriously discusses the question, he advances two mechanisms implicating a restitution, be it transitory or definitive, which leaves a part of productivity gains to workers. First, in chapter XII of *Capital* referring to the relative surplus value, Marx states that under competitive regulation an innovative enterprise should *lower* its prices to gain parts of the market, and that other firms should follow. As a result, the consumer, (perhaps a worker) has at least temporarily a profit from productivity gains. Marx does not propose any mechanism that would eventually re-establish former purchasing power. Undoubtedly, this explains why, as early as in the late 19th century, the labour class tended to obtain, in an ex post manner, a lasting restitution of productivity gains.

However, Marx, again in *Wages, Prices and Profits*, appeals to the possibility of *anticipation*. An increase in wages extracted *ex ante* by the struggle leads to an enlargement of the market, to an increase in productivity, and finally to a fall in value of what is bought, consequently to an ex post restoration of the rate of distribution of value added. Marx was evidently carried away by the militant disposition of the text, however, he did not theoretically rule out that this mechanism of anticipation may become so widespread, that it can guarantee an increase in mass consumption according to potential productivity gains.[20]

Yet none of this can happen, if intercapitalist competition prevents it. For anticipation of spread, and for the new norm to be established as a fixed rate of surplus value, it should be imposed equally on all competing enterprises. To put it another way, firm unions are no more sufficient, sectoral collective bargaining is needed, and state regulation is needed. But the emergent labour movement was against any state, and later the young 3rd International that considers the quite anarchistic *The State and the Revolution* by Lenin as a bible, does not expect anything good from the bourgeois state.[21]

'State integration of economic affairs, against which capitalist liberalism used to stand, becomes an accomplished fact. The existence of capitalism not only in free competition, but also in a situation dominated by trusts…, is impossible in the future. The question is uniquely one of knowing who the agent of state integrated production will be: the imperialist state or the victorious proletarian state'. Who is talking? — an 'operaist' or an extremist proponent of State Monopoly Capitalism? No, this is the 1st Congress of the Communist International (1919)! The same was repeated in 1928: 'The tendency of the various factions of the dominant classes to act cohesively opposes the large masses of the proletariat not to an isolated master, but to the entire class of capitalists and their state.' If genius is needed to identify the tendencies of social relations in their emerging state, the essence of subjectivism is to affirm every ten years that the tendency is finally realised, ignoring other aspects of the situation… However, the subjectivism of the 3rd International still has a few things to teach us.

First, according to it, the interventionist state, being a state of capital, is necessarily a fascist state — the end of economic liberalism is going to join the end of political liberalism. Moreover, since the interventionist state often recruits its servants out of former 'left wing opposition' parties (social democrats in Northern Europe, the Democratic Party in the USA), the Communist International (CI) simply considers these parties as 'the left wing of fascism'.

Yet, at the same time that the CI notes the tendency of state capitalism, it insists on the obstacles to the realisation of this tendency. The more this model of state capitalism is realised in the USSR, and is presented as 'socialism', the more the persistent 'anarchy of the market' becomes the yardstick against which the deficiencies of western capitalism are measured. This is rather natural, since Marxism of the 3rd International definitely accepts Taylorism as the ultimate of social organisation within production units. Underlining the persistence of such an anarchy in the market became more urgent, as German Social Democrats adopted, under the influence of Hilferding in the Kiel Congress (1927), a conception of 'organised capitalism' as the necessary step towards a peaceful passage to socialism. According to this theory, the tendencies towards organising that are internal to manfacturing are propagated throughout the whole economy. They induce, thanks to the democratic game, a 'conscious regulation of the economy', which can 'overcome, on a capitalist basis, the anarchy of free competition inherent to capitalism'. Well, it is known that for Soviet economists the 'conscious regulation of economy' coincides with the definition of socialism!

The problem for the CI then becomes one of demonstrating that Social Democrats have not reached the point of imposing this 'conscious regulation'. For this reason, it emphatically underlines the failure of Roosevelt's New Deal, and mainly the failure of the National Industrial Recovery Act (NIRA), which was defeated by a coalition of private interests. At this point, it should be examined where such a critique comes from. Accusing capitalism for the failure of NIRA is like admitting that state integration of the economy is desirable, and that certainly capitalism cannot achieve it by itself. This theme can be found in an analysis of the New Deal by P. Baran and P. Sweezy (1969), and later in the German theorists of the 'derivation of the state'.

To put it in other words, at the height of the major crisis of regulation in the 1930s, the theoretical position of the CI, in view of the reduction of the anarchy of the market by the state, becomes unsupportable: 'The reduction has already happened, and it can only be fascist, and in fact it is impossible: only socialism can achieve it ... '
However, this reduction of anarchy evidently conforms to a strategic goal of the labour movement — the liberation of the blind forces of competition and the deliberate mastery of social production — *and* to the immediate interests of workers (because, we should not forget,

capitalists can profit from competition among workers through decreases in wages, while workers have to suffer from intercapitalist competition through layoffs). Finally, this reduction of anarchy conforms to the average-term interests of capital, and that makes it just as possible as the increase in real wages.

It is true that between liberals and communists, two opposed versions of monopoly regulation were in competition in the 1930s. The first, thought of as 'democratic', respected the autonomy of professional unions and labour unions — this is the social-democratic, or Roosevelt's, way. Such a version triumphed, together with the regime of accumulation that was based on mass consumption. However, it had to face diverse variants of *corporatist regulation* ranging from fascism (Italy, Germany, Portugal and Spain), to populism (Mexico, Brazil and Argentina). This alternative mode of regulation, which stabilised social demand in a centralised manner without necessarily raising purchasing power in relation to productivity gains, supported socially polarised and militarist regimes of accumulation (of Hitler), and regimes of import substitution (of Cardenas, Vargas and Peron), the fascist states of Southern Europe being intermediate cases. The passage from the one version to the other remains quite possible, as in the case of the 'neo-socialists' (certain French technocrats), who followed the regime of Vichy.

We do not follow here the intense debate which finally initiated the conversion of the entire labour movement into a struggle for maximum monopoly regulation.[22] In 1945, it was commonplace to proclaim that the institutions of the Welfare State, of minimum wages, of obligatory collective contracts, constituted 'social victory', (actually it was such), and even an 'introduction of socialist elements in capitalism' (which was quite contestable).

In reality, as in the case of recognising unionism, the struggle of the labour movement, in order to become enfranchised of some of the most disagreeable consequences of the functioning of the capitalist system, had established a new mode of regulation of the system in a more 'progressive' sense. Furthermore, the price paid for that was the abandonment of another strategical goal (after the abolition of the wage relation) — the destruction of the 'bourgeois state'. Finally, this price also included the renouncing of the struggle for 'taking over the tools, and taking over the machines', and the recognition of Taylorian methods.

THE PRESENT CRISIS AND THE QUESTION OF INVOLVEMENT

It is evidently impossible to analyse the present crisis in a retrospective discussion like the two precedent ones. We do not know what the outcome of this crisis will be, so we do not know its effects on the labour movement. However, the problems to be confronted can be pointed out. As the fall in the rates of profit of Fordism, and the international free-exchange competition will not permit a move out of the crisis by an increase in consumption,[23] at least the following problems will have to be solved:

(1) increasing productivity, without accelerating the increase in the composition of capital;
(2) affecting productivity gains (at the expense of investment, of public consumption, or of work time?);
(3) solving the crisis of the Welfare State (by accelerating the socialisation of revenues, by lowering taxes, or by making productive use of it through public utility works?);
(4) inventing forms of international regulation by reforming the monetary system, and by adjusting the rules of free circulation of commodities and the compatibility of social legislation among countries (by a certain protectionism, or by the introduction of transnational social legislation?).

The last three points pose enormous problems to the labour movement, although they are not completely new. The first point, in turn, implies a complete inversion of its tendencies, and we focus on this subject in the following.

First of all, the labour movement has not ignored the struggles over the question of labour organisation. The launching of the bourgeois Taylorist offensive has marked the great delaying battles from the professional workers such as the strike at Renault in 1913 or the 'strike of the needles' at Fiat in 1920. The anarcho-syndicalist or Leninist labour movement claimed emancipation of workers in the name of their ability to master the processes of production. The existence of a hierarchy of qualifications is not contested by Gramsci, but the entire productive force is considered as collectively possessing such expertise:

Each one is indispensable, each one is at his post and each one has a function and a post. However ignorant and backward the workers, however vain and 'dandy' the engineers, they are all finally convinced of a certain truth based on the experience of factory organisation: they all end up by acquiring enough communist conscience to predict what progress represents [to] the communist economy in relation to the capitalist economy... The worker can not conceive himself as a producer unless he understands that he is an integral part of the whole system of labour, which proceeds towards a final product, and unless he realises the unity of the industrial process demanding the collaboration of operatives, of qualified workers, of those employed in administration, of engineers, and of technical managers [*Ordine Nuovo*].

For such a 'social productive bloc' to exist, its kernel, the professional workers, should not be squeezed between the 'backward' and the 'dandy'. This type of worker, due to his self-management capacities, constitutes the main basis of labour organisations, and the heart of social movements till the French strikes of 1936 included, 'the soul of our country', according to Arletty.[24] However, after World War II, when Fordism triumphed, the labour movement seemed to have deserted the struggle against the capitalist reorganisation of work.

There are specific reasons for that in each country (and we are based here on the French experience), but it seems that the 'Fordist compromise' was sufficient to disarm the critique against Taylorism. This was true at least at the union level.[25] Since the 1960s, spontaneous struggles against the alienation of parcelised work, against its intensity and against the tyranny of 'the scientific organisation of work' have multiplied. Yet such a diffuse revolt has always been settled with augmentations of negotiated wages (or by formal re-classification), conforming to the Fordist compromise. The agreement of Grenelle, which in June 1968 put an end to the biggest labour strike of all times, supported this compromise in a spectacular way. It gave the green light to employers on the organisation of work against the predominance of monopoly (and union) regulation of wage relations in their other dimensions, wages, time and licencing rules.

Dealing with this paradox, D. and R. Linhart (1985) have offered several explanations:

(1) the acknowledgement of the index of purchasing power as the best measure of social progress;

(2) the acceptance of the neutrality of the productive forces and of the technical superiority of Taylorism, which was supported by Lenin himself (Linhart 1976);

(3) the thesis that the labour movement does not have to aid employers in managing production (this is the last instance of refusing Babylon, although the labour movement is already immersed in the collective management of society up to the neck!);

(4) the sociological and institutional factors pertaining in contemporary France (employer intransigence on questions of power thought of as decisive, and absence of unions in enterprises).

Let me introduce still another explanation: Fordism has never totally eliminated the qualified worker, and the stabilisation of this kernel, which constituted the immediate basis of unions (in particular of the CGT), became part of the compromise itself. Compromise which, in fact, was also a compromise on *power*: qualified workers were partly entitled (even more directly than the dandies) to the responsibility of framing the non-skilled workers. Let us add to this that the dichotomy 'qualified workers/non-skilled workers' was often parallel to a gender and racial dichotomy. It is then understandable that union organisations did not integrate the revolt of the non-skilled workers against Taylorism.[26]

In the case of non-skilled workers, the situation is more complex. There are 'savage' reactions against the organisation of labour. But during calmer periods, the conscious implication of workers, as much Taylorised as their job may be, is always required implicitly in order to make up for the unmanageable insufficiency of the directions of the Bureau of Methods. And there is a *consent* for it, because this participation permits workers to prove their dignity to themselves. It is also a way for them to prove the superiority of their know-how on Taylorist prescriptions (the so-called 'one best way'): a 'paradoxical consent', according to R. and D. Linhart. Such a clandestine know-how, and such an implicit participation cannot become systematised by the scientific organisation of labour. It cannot become mobilised for better management of the productive processes of the whole (because it is precisely individualised by Fordism), nor for a systematic improvement of machine operations. Now, the problems with the Fordist organisation of labour are precisely the 'constant flanery of capital' between two elementary operations (according to Zuscovitch), and the lack of flexibility in its chains of production.

Hence, the exhaustion of productivity gains, hence an increase in the composition of capital at the root of the present crisis.

The 'electronic revolution' does not resolve these problems by itself, it just confronts capital with a choice. It offers the possibility of incorporating a substitute for the 'paradoxical consent' into the 'hardware' and 'software' (which are both constant capital), thus permitting a reaction against the 'flanery of capital' by rendering it more intelligent. This solution, applied at Fiat in a situation where consent had been destroyed, ended up with extremely costly solutions (Santilli 1985). It completed the alienation of immediate producers by endowing each automatic shop with the reliability of an astronautic module. *Alternatively* — and this is the way preferred by the Japanese (Aoki 1985) and envied by most capitalists in the world — the management may mobilise the existing know-how and put it in the service of the firm by rendering it more transparent and systematised.

In this case, the labour movement finds itself at a cross-roads. Not only has it resigned itself to living within Babylon by negotiating the fruits of its labour and by demanding that the bourgeois state ratify its compromises, but it is also asked to participate permanently and wholeheartedly in the perfection of Babylon, throughout the entire system of productive processes, by implicating itself in the struggle for productivity and quality.

It seems that once more the labour movement, not only due to its extreme weakness, is preparing to cross that threshold in France as well as elsewhere. All depends evidently on what will be proposed to it as compensation. And once again the acceptance of such a compromise may conform with the immediate interests of producers, which is not, this time, incompatible with the most strategic objective that the Founding Fathers have assigned to the labour movement (that is, regaining control over workers' own creative activity). However, this compromise may result in a definitive acceptance of the logic of the whole capitalist system. This risk is inherent in the double situation of that 'systemic anti-systemic force' — the ambiguity of any historical action in order to transform/improve reality.

'Three times Randolph Carter dreamt of the wonderful city of Kadath' narrates Lovecraft in *The Dream-Quest of Unknown Kadath* (1939). After escaping from all the ambushes and after defeating Nyerlatho-tep, the Khaos Reptile, he would face the marvellous city whose roofs would shine in the dawn as fountains of gold or purple, and there he would recognise Boston, the town of his childhood.

Is the labour movement condemned to have searched so intensely for New Jerusalem, and to recognise finally that it has done nothing but improve Babylon? Perhaps, but just as Boston enriched by the dreams of childhood is not real Boston any more, the same happens with the world that the labour movement can contribute to build. This world is not the ferocious one which, from Manchester to Sao Paolo, gave life to it through the dirt and the blood. It is a world that the labour movement will have remodelled through the sacrifice, the martyrs and the activism of its humble militants. Born from capitalism 'on the basis of given conditions inherited from the past', the labour movement, together with the feminist, anti-inperialist and ecological movements, can write human history without having to step out of it. Nevertheless, it is by its refusal of the existing order that it will be able to make progress.

To those who seem dissatisfied with the meagre progress so far, I respond that the 'progressive' compromises which may be planned in order to move out of the present crisis are no more granted than the victory of the social democrats over Fascism was in 1938, and that the principal risk is not that the labour movement is integrated further into the system but that it disintegrates. To those who think that capitalism will always find new forms of regulation and a new regime of accumulation, I respond that these new forms are not of equal value, and that in the name of the ethical criteria of solidarity and of free creation, which characterise the labour movement since its beginning, certain compromises may open the way to a better future, though other reforms may crush under a foot of iron the cry of the oppressed.

We do not believe any more in 'progressivism', the ideology that the bourgeois leaders of the 19th century and the builders of a brilliant tomorrow in Stalinist Russia had in common. We do not believe any more that the development of productive forces will necessarily entail more equitable, rational and liberating social relations. But we do believe that there exist progress and retrogressions, and that struggling for progress is a just cause.

NOTES

1. Based on a contribution to the Conference 'The Present Crisis in Relation to the Preceding Ones', Binghamton, 7–9 November 1985.
2. I thank Yves Bucas-Français for his very useful comments on a first version of this paper, and Olga Varveri for her translation.

3. For a discussion of this debate see Lipietz (1979, conclusion of section III).
4. See the work of historians like those represented by the journal *Revoltes Logiques*. As Y. Bucas-Français (1987) has pointed out, the socialist intellectuals praised the development of productive forces in a modernist way (Saint-Simon), or even in a totalitarian, Orwellian way (Cabet). By contrast, the genuine workers in the 19th century labour movements expressed their hatred against work as it was organised by the industrial capitalist revolution. Now, most workers (including these) were *also* in favour of 'better' machines.
5. Leninist characterisation of the political feeling of Bela Kun, leader of the Hungarian Revolution.
6. Charles Bettelheim in *Luttes de classes en URSS* first supported the third position in volumes I and II, *Le Seuil/Maspero* (Paris, 1974 and 1977) and later the second one (volume IV, 1984).
7. See, for example, Lipietz (1979).
8. Such a discussion can be found in Dockes and Rosier (1983).
9. These are the cyclical crises of an intermediate period (seven to eight years), called 'Juglar'. They correspond to a modality of regulation within the framework of competitive regulation, and should be distinguished from the 'major crises', which are the subject of the present paper.
10. Ironically, in this case the exception (at the fourth trial!) would confirm the rule. It is like throwing three times tails and one time heads and deducing that the coins fell on the side of tails.
11. The question of the state has been especially studied by Delorme and André (1983).
12. Naturally capitalism was dominant in the most 'advanced' countries before this date; however, the coincidences underlying the crises (called 'crises of the Ancient Regime') reflect the preponderance of weather conditions on agricultural production.
13. Besides the studies cited here, see for example Dockes and Rosier (1983), Beaud (1981).
14. Indicators often show rapid mechanisation, and clearly suggest intensive accumulation (such as in France of the Second Empire). However, a transition from the production of former artisans towards mechanised production should be distinguished from the actual intensification of the capitalist mechanisation itself.
15. This is explicitly the initial position of G. Destanne de Bernis (1977). However, traces can be found even in the alternation of the singular and plural form in the title of the book *Régulation et crises du capitalisme* by M. Aglietta (1976).
16. I relate here certain developments by Lipietz (1979) on the relation between social struggles and productive forces.
17. See Negri (1978). For 1977 and 1978, see the articles of S. Bologna in the daily *Lotta Continua*.
18. Despite their intention, Dockes and Rosier (1983) do not really go further in presenting the major crises as 'crises of a disciplinary order'. In the conclusion to his contribution to this volume, James O'Connor is

right in outlining the shortcomings, not only of the 'capital-logic' (roughly speaking: the dynamics of the system referred to in the second part of the present chapter), but also of the 'operaist' version of the crisis as a class struggle. He proposes to consider the social movements not only as forces of 'social disruption', but also of 'social reconstruction'. What I intend to do in the end of this paper is a study of the 'reconstructive aspects' of the labour movement during crises. As we shall see, it is more 'reformist' than James O'Connor seems to imply.

19.   In what follows, we adopt the French translation (1976).

20.   In this remarkable text (which dates from 1865), Marx proposes the first idea of a joint revolution of the norm of wages and productivity.

21.   In the following, see Leclercq (1977).

22.   For France, see Kuisel (1981).

23.   See the French example in Lipietz (1984).

24.   In an interview to journal *Télérama* (July 1985). In fact, they are the soul of the 'poetical and social realism' that this actress incarnates (films by Carné-Prévent and so forth).

25.   Adoption of Taylorism by unions seems parallel to their conversion of the state. The 'reformist' unions, like the American unions (Nelson 1984) or the French ones (Moutet 1984), completely accepted it as a 'progress of rationality', and so as the source of future social progress, since the end of World War I. The revolutionary unions tied to the 3rd International kept their positions for a long time (due to the anarcho-syndicalist presence in their ranks), then, in the 1930s, they accepted Taylorism on the basis of the positions that progress cannot be arrested, and that this progress would destroy handicraft workers, who were considered as the basis of reformism (Ribeill 1984).

26.   In contrast, unions in Italy tried to channel the movement through Gramsci's conception of 'professionalism'.

REFERENCES

M. Aglietta, *Régulation et crises du capitalisme* (Paris: Calmann-Levy, 1976).

M. Aoki, 'Learning by Doing versus the Bounded Rational Control: An Approach to US-Japan Comparison of Industrial Organisation', *CEPR Publication*, 53 (Stanford University, 1985) mimeo.

P. Baran and P. Sweezy, *Le capitalisme monopoliste* (Paris: Maspéro, 1969).

M. Beaud, *Histoire du capitalisme 1500–1980* (Paris: Seuil, 1981).

J. P. Benassy *et al.*, *Approches de l'inflation: L'exemple Français* (Paris: CEPREMAP, Report to CORDES, 1977) mimeo.

R. Boyer, 'Les salaires en longue période', *Economie et Statistiques*, 103 (September 1977).

M. Boyer and J. Mistral, *Accumulation, inflation et crise*, revised edn (Paris: PUF, 1983).

Yves Bucas-Français, *Chemins de l'émancipation. Du travail et de sa perception au XIX siécle* (Univ. Paris VIII) mimeo.

R. Delorme and C. André, *L'Etat et l'économie* (Paris: Seuil, 1983).

G. Destanne de Bernis, 'Régulation ou équilibre dans l'analyse économique', in Lichnerowicz *et al.* (eds), *L'idée de régulation dans les sciences* (Paris: Maloine-Douin, 1977).

P. Dockes and B. Rosier, *Rythmes économiques. Crises et changement social: une perspective historique* (Paris: La Découverte, 1983).

A Gramsci, *Ecrits politiques*, vol. I (Paris: Gallimard, 1976).

R. Kuisel, *Capitalism and the State in Modern France* (Cambridge University Press, 1981).

A. Labriola, *Essais sur la conception matérialiste de l'histoire*, 2nd ed. (London-Paris: Gordon and Breach, 1970).

Y. Leclercq, 'La théorie de l'Etat et la IIIe Internationale', in ACSES (ed.), *Sur l'Etat* (Brussels: Contradictions, 1977).

R. Linhart, *Lénine, les paysans, Taylor* (Paris: Le Seuil, 1976).

D. and R. Linhart, 'Naissance d'un consensus', *Couverture orange, CEPRE-map*, 8515 (1985) mimeo.

A. Lipietz, *Crise et inflation: pourquoi?* (Paris: Maspéro, 1979).

A. Lipietz, *Le Monde enchanté* (Paris: La Découverte, 1983. English version: London: Verso, 1985).

A. Lipietz, *L'audace ou l'enlisement* (Paris: La Découverte, 1984).

A. Lipietz, *Mirages et miracles. Problèmes de l'industrialisation dans le Tiers Monde* (Paris: La Découverte, 1985. English version: London: Verso, 1987).

A. Lipietz, 'Behind the crisis: the exhaustion of a regime of accumulation', *Pev. of Radical Political Economy*, 18 (1986), 1–2.

Lovecraft, *The Dream-Quest of Unknown Kadath* (New York: Arkham House, 1939).

E. Mandel, *Long Waves in Capitalist Development: The Marxist Interpretation* (Cambridge University Press, 1980).

J. Mazier, M. Basleand and J. P. Vidal, *Quand les crises durent...* (Paris: Economica, 1984).

A. Moutet, 'La première guerre mondiale et le Taylorisme', in de Montmollin et Pastré (eds), *Le Taylorisme* (Paris: La Découverte, 1984).

A. Negri, *La classe ouvrière contre l'Etat* (Paris: Galilée, 1978).

D. Nelson, 'Le Taylorisme dans l'industrie américaine, 1900–1930', in de Montmollin et Pastré (eds), *Le Taylorisme* (Paris: La Découverte, 1984).

G. Ribeill, 'Les organisations du movement ouvrier en France face à la rationalisation (1926–1932)', in de Montmollin et Pastré (eds), *Le Taylorisme* (Paris: La Découverte, 1984).

G. Santilli, 'L'automatisation comme forme de contrôle social', *Travail*, 8 (June, 1985).

I. Wallerstein, *Le capitalisme historique* (Paris: La Découverte, 1985).

References to works by Marx and Lenin are given in the text without mentioning a particular edition.

Part II
Internationalisation of Accumulation: The Crisis of Integration, Trade and Debt

Part II

5 The Uncoupling of the World Order: A Survey of Global Crisis Theories

John Bellamy Foster

In every discussion of the current global crisis one single fact eclipses all others – the demise of undisputed US hegemony within the world hierarchy of nation states. Despite differing political persuasions, there seems to be widespread agreement among social scientists that it is only in this context that the chief threats of our time — namely, the spread of stagnation, the emerging currency and trade wars, the heightened conflict between centre and periphery, the international debt crisis, and the drift toward world war — can be properly understood and surmounted.

For liberal analysts of the global crisis what is known as the 'theory of hegemonic stability' has become the central focus of discussion and debate in this area. The problem is therefore narrowly defined as one of restoring stability to international relationships in the wake of declining American hegemony.

For radicals, in contrast, the dialogue on the causes and consequences of US hegemony is subordinated to the wider problem posed by a theory of imperial instability, or the uneven development of capitalism on a world scale.

The present paper will attempt to provide a critical rendition of prevailing mainstream views, demonstrating the importance of current insights into the rise and fall of hegemonic orders, as well as the contradictions that arise within this dominant discourse as a result of its self-limiting, non-critical outlook, and its lack of historical specificity. This will be followed by a reasoned scrutiny of radical perspectives, which, although seldom limited in critical range, often seem to lose sight of the concrete, conjunctural features of a crisis in which the fate of humanity still hangs on a thread, while dealing with such all-embracing global trends as 'the internationalisation of capital'. Throughout this inquiry it will be suggested that it is the downfall of US hegemony which constitutes the immediate terrain of struggle, that is the conjunctural crisis in which the deeper and wider structural or 'organic' crisis of imperialism is being 'worked out'. Such a perspective allows us to focus on current ruling class strategies for staving off disaster, and on the evolving counter-responses from below, while not losing sight of the root contradictions threatening to transform the entire regime of capital beyond its knowledge or control.

THE THEORY OF HEGEMONIC STABILITY

Most work on the deepening global crisis of capitalism emanating from within the mainstream liberal tradition has come to rest on what the international relations theorist, Robert Keohane has labelled 'the theory of hegemonic stability', or the notion that 'order [in the international sphere]... depends on the preponderance of a single state' (Keohane 1984, p. 12). The idea itself has a long history within the age-old tradition of political realism in international politics, and obtained renewed importance in the period between the two World Wars. As E. H. Carr observed in *The Twenty Years' Crisis* (1939), 'The mirage of the post-[World] War [I] years was, as we now know, the belated reflexion of a century past beyond recall – the golden age of continuously expanding territories and markets, of a world policed by the self-assured and not too onerous British hegemony ... ' (Carr 1939, p. 287). Indeed, the actual instability of the inter-war years, according to Carr, was due in large part to the failure of the US to assume the leadership role that waning British power had left vacant: 'In 1918 world leadership was offered, by almost unanimous consent, to the United States... [and] was declined ... ' (Carr 1939, p. 300; Kindleberger 1986, p. 296). Moreover, the best prospects for peace and stability after World War II had ended, Carr argued in 1939, still rested on the development of a 'Pax Americana'. Following in Carr's footsteps, later thinkers such as economist Charles Kindleberger and political scientists Robert Gilpin and Robert Keohane have (in the wake of declining US power) constructed a more systematic 'theory of hegemonic instability', designed to account for the rise and fall of international regimes.

Kindleberger's book, *The World in Depression, 1929–1939*, which first appeared in 1973, is often thought of, by mainstream international political economists, as the initial work that opened the way to the contemporary theory of hegemonic stability. In this study Kindleberger argued that the Great Depression of the 1930s, which afflicted the entire advanced capitalist world, had its roots in the fact that Britain was unable and the United States unwilling to assume the leadership role necessary for the stabilisation of international trade and monetary relations. More specifically, the US failed to assume responsibility for fulfilling five key functions: '(1) maintaining a relatively open market for distress goods; (2) providing a counter-cyclical, or at least stable, long-term lending; (3) policing a relatively stable system of exchange rates; (4) ensuring the co-ordination of macro-economic policies; (5) acting as a lender of last resort by discounting or otherwise providing liquidity in financial crisis.' (Kindleberger 1987, p. 289). It was the failure to fulfill these functions, he contends, that made the Great Depression so deep, long and wide.

Moreover, it is here that lessons can presumably be learned about the present and future, given current threats to global stability. Responsible leadership with respect to the above functions in the 1980s and 1990s, Kindleberger argues, might conceivably be provided by the US, by Europe or Japan, or even by international institutions to which some part of the economic sovereignty of nation states would be ceded. In contrast, the failure to stabilise the world economy through such responsible leadership would be reflected in one of the following possible outcomes: a struggle for hegemony by the US, Japan and the EEC; a situation, analogous to 1929 and 1933, in which one power is no longer able to lead and another power is unwilling to do so; or a stalemate in which each of a number of powers retains veto power over constructive actions by others. Each of the conceivable stable solutions is to be preferred over the possible unstable ones, since the failure to fulfill the functions of global leadership could lead to a catastrophic situation of the kind not seen since the Great Depression itself (Kindleberger 1986, pp. 304–05).

What made Kindleberger's analysis so significant was that it appeared at the time of waning US hegemony and increasing international economic fragility. The weakening of the gold–dollar standard that had been put in place by the Bretton Woods agreement at the close of World War II – a problem that had been building up since the late 1950s as a result of a growing US balance of payments deficit and a rise in foreign dollar holdings – reached absolute crisis proportions in 1971 with the appearance for the first time of an actual trade imbalance and a deficit in the private (in addition to government) sector of the balance of payments accounts. Between 1970 and 1971 the private sector (goods and services, investment and investment income, and tourism) experienced a drop from a surplus of $1.9 billion in the basic balance of payments accounts to a deficit of $3.5 billion, which, when coupled with the government sector deficit of $6.2 billion, resulted in a total balance of payments deficit in 1971 of $9.6 billion (International Economic Policy Association 1972, p. 8; Magdoff and Sweezy 1972, pp. 4–5). It was this situation, and the growing demand for gold in exchange for dollars, which led to Nixon's abandonment of the gold-dollar standard and its replacement in 1971 by what Robert Triffin was to call the 'paper-dollar standard', marking the end of undisputed US hegemony in the world economy (Strange 1986, p. 41).

Although it was the emergence of an actual trade imbalance along with a run on the US gold stock that drove home the point that US hegemony was rapidly fading, the chief source of balance of payments difficulties at this stage – and the real reason that it was necessary to delink the dollar from gold, resulting in the collapse of the international monetary system established at Bretton Woods – was to be found in the vast expenditures of the US government on the costs of overseas empire. As the International Economic Policy Association (or IEPA – a private advisory group financed and staffed by major corporations) declared in its 1972 study of the US balance of payments,

> Throughout the 1960s and into the 1970s government activities abroad produced deficits on the basic balance which swallowed up surpluses earned by the private sector. The government deficit averaged $3.5 billion for 1960 to 1964, and crept up to an average of $4.2 billion from 1965 to 1968, as the Vietnam escalation boosted military expenditures abroad. In 1969, the total government account deficit was $4.4 billion, in 1970, $5.3 billion, and in 1971, $6.2 billion. ... Military expenditures abroad have been the major contributor to the persistent government account deficits. ... The gross outflow on military accounts rose steadily from 1960 through 1970. It averaged $3 billion from 1960 to 1964, $3.9 billion from 1965 to 1968, and $4.9 billion in 1969 and 1970. ... The Vietnam War, of course, was the major cause [International Economic Policy Association 1972, p. 13].

Nevertheless, these hard facts behind the deficit were not sufficient to get the controlling interests in the US to back away from the 'absolutely essential' costs of empire. As the IEPA stated in its conclusion: 'The US government should continue to exercise the maximum feasible curtailment of all expenditures affecting the US balance of payments which are not absolutely essential for political, military or economic purposes' (International Economic Policy Association 1972, p. 88).

What such statements by corporate interests made clear was that the basic purposes and capabilities of US military activities abroad were not to be questioned; rather the object was to minimise waste while continuing to promote the global designs of the US state (Magdoff and Sweezy 1972, pp. 6–7). The reason was that there was a commonality of interest between the major multinational corporations and the government. Henry Fowler, then US Secretary of the Treasury, stated the following in 1965:

Indeed, while it is most difficult to quantify, it is also impossible to over-estimate the extent to which the efforts and opportunities for American firms abroad depend upon the vast presence and influence and prestige that America holds in the world. It is impossible to over-estimate the extent to which private American ventures overseas benefit from our commitments, tangible and intangible, to furnish economic assistance to those in need and to defend the frontiers of freedom ... in fact if we were to contemplate abandoning those frontiers and withdrawing our assistance ... I wonder not whether the opportunities for private American enterprise would wither — I wonder only how long it would take [quoted in Robinson 1973, p. 405].

Since the trade balance was deteriorating and a large surplus in this area was no longer to be expected even on the most optimistic assumptions (given the recovery of Western Europe and Japan from the devastation inflicted during World War II), and since, moreover, the costs of empire were virtually untouchable (given that the main beneficiaries were the US corporations themselves), the chief hope for a solution to balance of payment difficulties came to rest on the favourable effects of foreign direct investments. As the IEPA report noted:

In terms of the balance of payments, US direct investment has been consistently helpful, as income and royalties accruing to the United States from branches, affiliates, and subsidiaries have grown from $2.9 billion in 1960 to $9.3 billion in 1970, far outstripping capital flows. The net balance-of-payments contribution of direct foreign investment averaged $1.9 billion from 1960 to 1964, and rose to an average of $2.4 billion from 1965 to 1968. It reached $4.1 billion in 1969, dropped to $3.5 billion in 1970, and peaked again at $4.7 billion in 1971. Thus, in recent years, investment has made the major favourable contribution to the private sector of the balance of payments [International Economic Policy Association 1972, p. 35].

Even more importantly, the IEPA went on to explain that:

Estimates of the payback period, that is, the time in which a given investment pays for itself in balance-of-payments terms, vary widely. It would appear that ten years is a reasonable estimate for most well-managed operations; and on that basis, a strong case can be made for removing present direct investment controls so as to maximise future returns. America's income from foreign investments could be in the $15 billion range by the end of the decade. If that objective can be accomplished, these earnings will have played a major role in restoring stability to America's balance of payments; and, of course, once they have been 'paid for', the ongoing earnings are a major plus, with no off-setting liabilities [International Economic Policy Association 1972, pp. 39–40].

In essence, US strategy in the early 1970s involved relying on a combination of controlled devaluations of the currency and the promotion of foreign direct investment to solve the balance of payments difficulties. While the dollar devaluation was meant to close the trade deficit, the depreciation was never intended to be so great as to close the larger payments deficit resulting from government expenditures on military and other related commitments abroad; since a depreciation of this magnitude would have endangered the reserve currency status of the dollar and destabilised the entire international economic order. Instead, it was hoped that the return capital flow resulting from the outward expansion of the multi-national corporations – who after all were the main beneficiaries of the costs of empire – would close the payments deficit (or at least keep it within supportable bounds).

Ironically, even while such policy conclusions were being developed (partly at the instigation of corporate sponsored think tanks such as the IEPA), there was already plenty of evidence to suggest, as liberal theorist Robert Gilpin persuasively argued in *US Power and the Multi-national Corporation* (1975), that the giant, North American-based transnational firms were on balance by the 1970s mainly a force for the decline of US power in the world economy, not its preservation. 'Faced with a deteriorating balance-of-payments position', he noted, 'the United States government began to regard the multi-national corporations and their growing overseas earnings as the means to finance America's hegemonic world position' (Gilpin 1975, p. 156). But there was a catch to this dependence on multi-nationals to resolve the contradictions in the balance of payments: although these corporations tended to bring in capital in the short-run, the long-run effect was to weaken US competitiveness. 'In simplest terms, what the United States has been doing' (by promoting foreign direct investment) Gilpin wrote,

> is exporting or trading away its comparative advantages (technology, technical know-how, and management) and potential productivity gains in exchange for future foreign earnings. Insofar as the United States continues to move in this direction, it is converting itself into the type of *rentier* economy, that is, one which lives off investment income, that Great Britain became in the latter part of the 19th century [Gilpin 1975, p. 198].

In short, the US economy was following a path of hegemonic decline analogous to the one that Britain had proceeded down in the final decades of the 19th and the opening decades of the 20th centuries. 'As Murray Kemp has demonstrated, and as this study has argued with respect to Great Britain in the 19th century,' Gilpin wrote:

> there is a tendency for capital-rich countries to export too much capital and thereby weaken their own industrial base. ... Through the export of capital, technology, and managerial skills, the United States has strengthened its industrial competitors. Although this transfer of resources has been accomplished, except in Japan, by the extension of American control over important sectors of the foreign economy, this does not alter the fundamental fact that a shift in the locus of industrial power has been facilitated. For the sake of a long-term favourable balance of payments and the maintenance of a world market position, the United States economy has paid a price, in terms of real resources and productive capacity [Gilpin 1975, pp. 188–89].

Indeed, Gilpin followed Charles Kindleberger in arguing that the US economy was undergoing a fundamental 'climacteric' like the one that Britain had undergone after 1870, the main attribute of which was a 'crossover' in the role of overseas investment. As he put it, 'There is sufficient evidence to suggest that sometime in the 1950s or early 1960s American foreign direct investment became decreasingly a sign of industrial strength and increasingly one of relative industrial decline' (Gilpin 1975, p. 189). Under these circumstances, the only rational national strategy, he went on to suggest, would be to place greater emphasis on both internal investment and technological research and development, so that the US economy could retain its comparative advantages while maximising US value added.

In *War and Change in World Politics* (1981), Gilpin provided a more general, trans-historical analysis of hegemonic decline as part of an attempt to construct a universal theory of international political change from Thucydides to the present. Here he advanced the thesis that: 'Once an equilibrium between the costs and benefits of further change and expansion [for a hegemonic power] is reached [marking the end of its expansionary phase], the tendency is for the economic costs of maintaining the status quo to rise faster than the economic capacity to support the status quo' (Gilpin 1981, p. 156). According to this argument, each hegemonic power eventually runs up against the presumed universal 'law of diminishing returns', hindering its ability to generate the economic surplus necessary for political domination:

> In the absence of new spurts of innovation or a borrowing of technology from abroad, the growth of the wealth and power of a society begins to slow, describing an S-shaped curve. The society undergoes an economic climacteric as did Great Britain in the latter part of the 19th century, and many believe the United States is experiencing the same thing in the contemporary world [Gilpin 1981, p. 160].

Moreover, this problem of diminishing returns, on what economists call the 'supply-side', goes hand in hand with a growth in the share of total expenditures directed at non-productive consumption such as welfare and 'protection' (or warfare) on the 'demand side' of the economy. The dominant power in the world economy thus finds itself caught in a trap of providing 'international public goods' (imperial defence) that benefit the 'free riders' among its allies more than they do the hegemonic power itself, while simultaneously supporting growing consumption and moral decay at home. 'The divergence between costs and resources in turn produces a "fiscal crisis" for the dominant power or powers. The consequence of continuing disequilibrium and of the financial drain it entails if it is not resolved is the eventual economic and political demise of the dominant power' (Gilpin 1981, p. 157). Furthermore, the entire process – which, Gilpin believes, has the inevitability of a natural law – can be speeded up by technological diffusion. Hence, he suggests that, 'The greater longevity of the Pax Britannica relative to the Pax Americana is explained in part by the rapidity with which America's technological advantages were diffused to its economic and military competitors' as a result of foreign direct investment.

This theory of hegemonic stability, associated with the work of Gilpin in particular, can be reduced, as Robert Keohane has contended in *After Hegemony: Co-operation and Discord in the World Political Economy* (1984), to 'two central propositions': firstly 'that order in world politics is typically created by a single dominant power', and secondly 'that the maintenance of order requires continued hegemony' (Keohane 1984, p. 31). In the words of Charles Kindleberger, 'for the world economy to be stabilised, there has to be a stabiliser, one stabiliser' (Kindleberger 1986, p. 304). However, while it is clear that the rise of a hegemonic power often facilitates the creation of a set of relatively stable 'international regimes' — or global 'principles, norms, rules and decision-making procedures around which actor expectations converge in a given issue-area' (Stephen Krasner, quoted in Kindleberger 1986: p. 289n) — there is little reason to suppose 'that hegemony is either a necessary or sufficient condition for the emergence of cooperative relationships'. Nor is there any reason to believe, Keohane adds, that co-operative international regimes cannot persist after the conditions of hegemonic dominance have passed away (Keohane 1984, pp. 31–32).

In Keohane's view, the 'crude theory of hegemonic stability' represented by an analyst like Gilpin is a 'basic force theory', according to which outcomes are determined by the tangible resources of power (particularly economic and military) available to contending actors. Hence, this crude theory defines hegemony as a mere 'preponderance of material resources. Four sets of resources are especially important. Hegemonic powers must have control over raw materials, control over sources of capital, control over markets, and competitive advantages in the production of highly valued goods' (Keohane 1984, pp. 32, 34).

Although capturing a large portion of the truth, this type of 'basic force theory', Keohane contends, 'makes imperfect predictions. In the 20th century it correctly anticipates the relative co-operativeness of the 20 years after World War II. It is at least partially mistaken, however, about trends of co-operation when hegemony erodes. Between 1900 and 1913', he rather incautiously suggests, 'a decline in British power coincided with a decrease rather than an increase in conflict over commercial issues.' Be that as it may, it is essential to recognise that hegemony is not simply a question of power but also of leadership. As Carr (and many others) had pointed out, it was the failure of the US to assume the leadership role that its ascendancy as a world power 'rightly' gave it in the inter-war period, which accounted in large part for the breakdown in the international order that followed. Thus, for Keohane, hegemony is more properly defined as 'a situation in which "one state is powerful enough to maintain the essential rules governing interstate relations, and willing to do so"' (Keohane 1984, pp. 34–35; Keohane and Nye 1977, p. 44).

The world-historical significance of these objections to the crude theory of hegemonic stability only become apparent when one recognises that for Keohane – as the title to his book indicates – US hegemony has indeed faded, while the question of the rise of another hegemon to take its place is to some extent 'unthinkable', since it raises the issue of global holocaust. In his own words,

> Hegemonic leadership is unlikely to be revived in this century for the United States or any other country. Hegemonic powers have historically only emerged after World Wars; during peacetime, weaker countries have tended to gain on the hegemon rather than vice versa. It is difficult to believe that world civilization, much less a complex international economy, would survive such a war in the nuclear age. Certainly no prosperous hegemonic power is likely to emerge from such a cataclysm. As long as a world political economy persists, therefore, its central political dilemma will be how to organise co-operation without hegemony (Keohane 1984, pp. 10–11).

What are the actual chances of co-operation continuing 'after hegemony'? For Keohane the answer has to do with the durability of the international regimes constructed during the period of hegemonic domination. If these can be modified as the need arises and made to last, and if new regimes can be created even 'after hegemony', it is conceivable that peace can persist. After studying the weakening of the trade and monetary regimes represented, respectively, by the General Agreement on Tariffs and Trade (GATT) and the Bretton Woods monetary order, Keohane argues that the partial or wholesale breakdown of these institutional relationships has nonetheless not prevented considerable continuity in co-operation. With respect to GATT it is argued that the rules governing the regime are becoming tighter even as worldwide protectionist tendencies increase, holding out the hope that the growing crisis will lead to even greater co-operation and stability (Keohane 1984, p. 190). While the demise of the international monetary regime has partly disguised the fact that although 'international monetary co-operation in the early 1980s is certainly less institutionalised than it once was, and the rules are less clear ... the degree of discord is probably no greater than it was in the years between 1968 and 1971 ... ' (Keohane 1984, p. 187).

However, such wishful thinking, which perceives the dangers of the current international situation, and yet in the end only seems to close off the mind to any contemplation of the unthinkable, is unlikely to help preserve the world from the catastrophe that it fears. Indeed, the historical implications of Keohane's stance are best understood, as he himself makes clear, when placed in the context of the classical Marxist debate between Lenin and Kautsky about 'ultra-imperialism' (Keohane 1984, p. 43). While Kautsky, shortly before the outbreak of World War I (and again in 1915 and after the War had commenced), advanced the idea that ultra-imperialism, or the co-operative exploitation of the rest of the world by the leading capitalist states, was a distinct possibility in the near future, Lenin, writing in 1916, argued, against this view, that inter-imperialist war between the major capitalist powers was a characteristic feature of the monopoly stage of capitalism (Kautsky 1970; Lenin 1916). True to his own beliefs, Keohane – who in the lexicon of international relations theory sides with the 'institutionalist' perspective (those who believe that institutions can be designed to promote genuine co-operation between states of roughly equal power) rather than the 'realist' view (those who interpret diplomacy as war by other means) – goes on to suggest that it was Kautsky rather than Lenin who had the most accurate understanding of international relations. 'The successful operation of American hegemony for over a quarter-century after the end of World War II', Keohane writes, 'supports Kautsky's forecast that ultra-imperialism could be stable and contradicts Lenin's thesis that capitalism made inter-imperialist war inevitable' (Keohane 1984, p. 43).

These views no doubt carry an air of conviction. But the ahistorical nature of Keohane's assessment of the ultra-imperialism debate is revealed when the following considerations are taken into account. Firstly, the undeniable fact that Kautsky's analysis, which was developed prior to World War I, had failed to comprehend the true nature of the inter-imperialist rivalry leading up to two World Wars. Secondly, the unavoidable datum that while Kautsky's interpretation had envisioned the possibility of co-operation even after British hegemony had faded, it was only with the rise of a new, undisputed hegemonic power out of the ashes of global catastrophe that stability was finally restored. Lastly, the inexorable truth that it was the climb of the USSR to superpower status (a result that Lenin himself helped initiate through the Bolshevik revolution of 1917) – along with the continuing threat of anti-capitalist revolutions on the periphery of the capitalist world – that was to be perhaps the single most important *new* factor leading to the formation of a general Western alliance.

In any case, even if one wishes, like Keohane, to argue that Kautsky was somehow 'proven right' by the history of the world over the period 1914–71, and that there are no real barriers to international co-operation within the capitalist core, it can hardly be ignored that whatever degree of co-operation existed following the two World Wars and the Great Depression, this was dependent at least in part on the emergence of an American Imperium. What then are the prospects for continued co-operation 'after hegemony'? Keohane writes:

> The view taken here is similar to that of Kautsky and his followers, although the terminology is different. My contention is that the common interests of the leading capitalist states, bolstered by the effects of existing international regimes (mostly created during a period of American hegemony), are strong enough to make sustained co-operation possible, though not inevitable. One need not go so far as [Robin] Murray and [Stephen] Hymer in projecting the 'internationalisation of capital' to understand the strong interests that capitalists have in maintaining some co-operation in the midst of rivalry. Uneven development in the context of a state system maintains rivalry and ensures that co-operation will be incomplete and fragile, but it does not imply that the struggle must become violent or that compromises that benefit all sides are impossible [Keohane 1984, pp. 43–44].

Unlike Gilpin, who had been motivated from the start by a purely nationalistic concern with what in liberal analysis has come to be known as the 'hegemon's dilemma' – or the notion that by serving the interests of the world as a whole the hegemon steadily undermines its own position – and who was therefore concerned primarily with initiating a change in US policy with respect to consumption at home and technological diffusion abroad before it was too late (that is, before the US, through an uncritical exercise of its leadership role, fell prey to a decisive and irreversible climacteric of the kind that the British had already experienced a century before), Keohane, from a considerably less nationalistic perspective had focused on the question of international co-operation as a means of safeguarding world peace in the period 'after hegemony' (Strange 1986, p. 69). Nevertheless, it is the work of the former, rather than that of the latter, which represents the dominant view among leading mainstream commentators on international political economy (particularly in the US). Thus, Mancur Olson has argued in his very influential book, *The Rise and Fall of Nations* (1982), that the source of American decline is to be traced to the growth of 'rigidities' in the form of powerful interest groups (particularly trade unions) that gradually come to dominate the political landscape in those developed nations with a long history of stability, strongly suggesting that the US must find some way of getting its workers to fall into line as part of an overall strategy to re-establish a dominant position within the world capitalist order. Such views obviously fit well with the Reagan administration's more comprehensive strategy to 'make America strong again' by attacking institutions and policies that benefit workers and the poor at home, while promoting active interventionism abroad.

Indeed, the Reagan administration's singularly nationalistic goal of resurrecting American power knows few bounds, and can only be interpreted as an attempt to restore US global hegemony. Foremost among its objectives is control of the Third World. In a message to Congress on March 1986 the President provided a detailed outline of the policy that the media and international relations authorities had already dubbed 'the Reagan doctrine'. This message reaffirmed 'active American support' for the 'growing resistance movements [that] now challenge Communist regimes installed or maintained by the military power of the Soviet Union and its control agents – in Afghanistan, Angola, Cambodia, Ethiopia and Nicaragua' (Reagan quoted in Acharya 1987, p. 28). As Amitav Acharya has pointed out, two features distinguish this 'Doctrine' from a host of similar foreign policy 'Doctrines' that preceded it:

Firstly, its geographic sweep is much broader; in fact it is the first truly global doctrine of containment. In his message, Reagan targets the existing regimes in Nicaragua, Ethiopia, Angola, Afghanistan, and Kampuchea – thereby spread-eagling the entire Third World. In contrast the Truman, Eisenhower and Carter doctrines were essentially focused on the Middle East Region.

Secondly, while the earlier doctrines were meant to be deterrents to feared communist takeovers, the Reagan Doctrine aims at dislodging regimes that are already in power. ... In the new Cold War, Moscow is cast in the role of defending a status quo which Washington actively seeks to topple by assisting indigenous rebel movements or, to use Reagan's favourite phrase, the 'freedom fighters' [Acharya 1987, pp. 28–29].

Such a policy of the aggressive use of force to restore American domination, in the face of growing Third World revolution, is complemented by an increasingly beligerent use of economic pressure to re-establish US dominance in the areas of international trade and finance. Thus the US has developed a hawkish policy of 'opening international markets' by virtually whatever means possible. The 1987 *Economic Report of the President* flatly declares 'Governments that unnecessarily restrict the location and operation of foreign capital lower the welfare of their citizens by lowering their incomes. All investment policies that distort or impede trade alter the pattern of trade away from that dictated by comparative advantage and lower the economic well-being of both the countries that impose the laws and the rest of the world' (Council of Economic Advisers 1987, p. 142). Hence, it is in the role of the self-appointed defender of the best interest of all parties that the US has increasingly resorted in recent years to extraordinary pressures on other countries within the world capitalist economy, on the grounds that these countries have adopted various 'unfair trading practices'.

Pressure – partly through the IMF and a general creditors' cartel – has been greatest on Third World countries with large debt burdens, but the US has also acted (under Section 301 of the Trade Act of 1974) against the European Community and Japan. Faced with a deficit of approximately \$150 thousand million in 1986, on top of a stagnating domestic economy, the US has moved rapidly toward 'beggar thy neighbour policies' (Council of Economic Advisers 1987, pp. 125–45).

THE THEORY OF IMPERIAL INSTABILITY

Reagan administration strategies for controlling the Third World suggest that an understanding of global crisis cannot stop with a narrow conception of 'hegemonic stability', but must encompass the conflict between the developed and underdeveloped parts of the capitalist world, which is the principal contradiction of the system at the global level in the present historical period. And it is here that radical analysis, with its emphasis on imperial instability, has traditionally had the most to offer. Over the last two decades, Marxist theorists dealing with the contradictions of imperialism have generally divided into two traditions. The first of these traditions, with its roots primarily in Western Europe, views the present-day global conflict as primarily one of inter-imperialist rivalry. In this perspective, it is the growing rivalry between Europe and Japan, on the one hand, and the US, on the other, which is the central conflict in the capitalist world economy. The Third World enters this vision of inter-imperialist conflict mainly as a realm of often rapid economic development from which new rivals – the so-called 'newly industrialising countries', such as Brazil, Argentina, Mexico, South Korea, Taiwan, Hong Kong and Singapore – are emerging to further complicate the problem of rivalry.[1] Thus, thinkers within this broad stream of thought frequently refer to 'the internationalisation of capital' as a general trend resulting in an increasingly horizontal (rather than hierarchical) relation between states worldwide. Such views have come to be associated in various ways and to differing extents, with the work of such diverse theorists as Bill Warren, Ernest Mandel, Bob Rowthorn, Michael Kidron, Geoffrey Kay, Robert Brenner, Ricardo Parboni, Michel Aglietta and Alain Lipietz (Rowthorn 1980; Willoughby 1979).

The other broad tradition, with its roots mainly in North America, the Third World and Eastern Europe, focuses on 'the pillage of the Third World' as the central contradiction of the modern imperialist system. In this perspective, inter-imperialist rivalry is still secondary to what former US President Richard Nixon has called the 'Third World War' (that is the struggle for control of the periphery and its resources). The threat that the Third World poses to the system in this perspective has less to do with economic development – given the realities of dependent development – but emanates rather from the social revolutions taking place throughout the Third World, as imperialised nations and super-exploited classes try to break out of what seems to be a perpetual dependency by breaking with capitalism itself. A general analysis of dependent development along these lines is widely associated with the work of such distinctive theorists as Paul Baran, André Gunder Frank, Samir Amin, Harry Magdoff, Paul Sweezy, Immanuel Wallerstein, Arghiri Emmanuel, Clive Thomas, Richard Fagen, Fernando Cardoso, Peter Evans and Fidel Castro.

These broad traditions – which today are becoming less and less distinct as the generalisation of global crisis and the complexity of world development makes it increasingly difficult to focus on a single fault-line – have the advantage over mainstream discourse that, in focusing on such all-embracing alternative conceptions as the 'internationalisation of capital', and the world hierarchy of nation-states associated with the 'development of underdevelopment', they constitute truly global theories from the outset. Nevertheless, this sometimes leads to a scattering of vision, and a failure either to give adequate attention to the struggle for imperial hegemony within the core of the capitalist world economy or to perceive how this is related to revolutionary struggles within underdeveloped countries. It is true that some radical thinkers in the 'internationalisation of capital' tradition like Bob Rowthorn and Ernest Mandel were quick to appreciate the significance of the decline of US hegemony, but like many of their mainstream counterparts they placed this almost entirely within the context of 'Europe versus America' (or Europe and Japan versus America), putting relatively little emphasis on the consequences for US hegemony of the weakening of the American empire on the periphery of the capitalist world. As Rowthorn pointed out as early as 1971, 'European and Japanese capital is strong enough not only to fight back against American capital but also to counter-attack by expanding overseas' (Rowthorn 1980, p. 65). Although such views have insight, they tend to play down the key fact that the decline of the dollar, which constituted the proximate cause of the current crisis of US hegemony, was directly connected to the vast flood of dollars overseas associated with the seemingly endless US war against Vietnam. Indeed, those Marxists, like Amin, Frank, Magdoff and Sweezy, who kept the conflict between the advanced capitalist countries and the Third World at the centre of their analysis of the contradictions of global capitalism were labelled 'Third Worldists' by Mandel, Rowthorn and numerous others – even while the Vietnam War was still raging (Rowthorn 1980, p. 49).

In a similar vein, French theorist Michel Aglietta, commenting on 'World Capitalism in the Eighties' in 1982, presented the following 'four scenarios': (1) continuing world-wide stagnation as a result of high US interest rates; (2) 'the restored vigour of American capitalism' associated with a shift of world trade to the US–Japan axis; (3) a weakening of the US and a rise of the Common Market to an increasingly ascendant economic position; or (4) a global financial collapse originating in the centre of the capitalist system (Aglietta 1982, p. 35–41). Most notable in these alternative scenarios was the almost total disappearance of the underdeveloped countries from the picture. When the Third World did enter the analysis, in the work of Aglietta, or of other notable theorists like Bill Warren or Alain Lipietz (who was less inclined than Warren to deny the reality of dependence in the Third World) it was mainly in the form of additional rivals to the US, Europe and Japan – the so-called 'newly industrialising countries'. Such views are often accompanied by an interpretation of economic crisis in the advanced capitalist states that emphasises the supply-side constraints on accumulation, or the notion that costs are squeezing profits at the point of production. Low wages in the periphery are therefore seen as threatening advanced capitalism at its weakest point – the supply side (Lipietz 1987, p. 43).

In contrast to the relative de-emphasis on 'the pillage of the Third World' to be found in the work of those Marxian political economists with a strong European bias, theorists of 'dependent development', 'unequal exchange' or 'the world system' are distinguished by the fact that they locate this same problem much more centrally within their analysis, while at the same time providing a more comprehensive historical interpretation of the significance of declining US hegemony. Paul Sweezy told a Japanese audience in 1979:

> The period of undisputed US hegemony lasted somewhat more than a quarter of a century, after which it began to weaken as the defeated powers of World War II gradually recovered their strength. The global capitalist system always works most smoothly when there is one undisputed hegemonic power, and the eroding and ending of that undisputed hegemony always signals the onset of a time of troubles and crises. In both respects the post-World War II period has run true to form [Sweezy 1981, p. 80].

During the long wave upswing that followed World War II the contradictions of capitalism seemed almost to have disappeared. 'But underneath the surface and mostly out of sight, Sweezy argued, certain long-term tendencies were at work that pointed to stormy weather ahead. The most important, I think, were the following: (1)

over-investment, (2) vast expansion of the debt structure, (3) weakening of the international monetary system, and (4) growing inequality between centre and periphery.'

In the centre of the capitalist system there was a growing tendency toward 'over-investment' or over-building of productive capacity in such industries as steel, shipbuilding, automobiles and heavy chemicals, marked by rising amounts of unutilised productive capacity reflecting insufficient demand for final products. A great balooning of the debt structure of the capitalist economy occurred as the conditions of stagnation within production itself became more and more predominant – an expansion of debt which was to spread to Third World states as the Western banks sought out bigger and 'more reliable' borrowers. US global military commitments in general, and the Indochina War in particular, Sweezy suggests, led to increasing US balance of payments deficits and a swelling of dollars overseas (to as much as $1000 billion by 1980), thereby destabilising the gold-dollar standard. Finally, a widening inequality between centre and periphery produced growing social unrest (and greater demands on the US military to put down revolts) even while the extraction of surplus from the Third World worsened problems of surplus absorption within the metropolitan core itself. To sum up:

The consequence of all these co-existing, and largely interacting, trends and tendencies is twofold. In the centre we observe a faltering of the capital accumulation process, renewed stagflation, and an out-of-control explosion of the debt structure. In the periphery the scenario includes declining standards of living for the masses, accompanied by increasing political oppression: astronomical rates of unemployment, often reaching 30 to 40 per cent of the labour force; misery, malnutrition, even starvation, with no let-up in sight and no improvement in prospect. Both parties of the global system are thus in a state of at least latent crisis, and signs that breaking points are being reached are not wanting — the near US stock market and dollar panics of October 1978, the Iranian revolution, and more recently, a wild speculative increase in the price of gold, attesting to a distrust of *all* currencies. But apart from these specifics of the present situation, there is a much larger question at issue. The present crisis of the global capitalist system is shaped by forces that have been at work for more than a quarter of a century. They are still at work; in fact they are inherent in the system. Unless something unexpected, like a major war, intervenes, they will continue to work. It is unlikely that they can be stopped or controlled by national governments, and there is no such thing as an international government [Sweezy 1981, pp. 83–84].

According to this view, then, 'the underlying crisis of capitalism ... is an appalling and, by historical standards, extremely rapid deterioration in the conditions of existence of a clear and growing majority of humankind'. It is the inexorable working out of Marx's 'law' of uneven development, or 'the absolute general law of capitalist accumulation', according to which a growing disparate prosperity at the top is accompanied by an increasing relative misery at the bottom of society – a 'law' which finds its 'field of action' nowadays in 'the entire global capitalist system'. Moreover, it is this very same 'underlying crisis' – particularly in the context of the waning of US hegemony – 'that ineluctably generates tensions, both internationally and within countries, that threatens sooner or later to explode in a general conflagration' (Magdoff and Sweezy 1987, pp. 203–05).

Immanuel Wallerstein's historical reflections on the fragility of systems of hegemonic domination within the world capitalist system provide further reason for suspecting that the decline of US hegemony could lead to a war crisis of global proportions. According to Wallerstein's deliberately restrictive definition of hegemony:

Hegemony in the interstate system refers to that situation in which the on-going rivalry between the so-called 'great powers' is so unbalanced that one power is truly *primus inter pares*; that is, one power can largely impose its rules and its wishes (at the very least its effective veto power) in the economic, political, military, diplomatic, and even cultural arenas. The material base of such power lies in the ability of enterprises domiciled in that power to operate more efficiently in all three major economic arenas – agro-industrial production, commerce, and finance. The edge of efficiency of which we are speaking is one so great that these enterprises can not only out-bid enterprises domiciled in other great powers in the world market in general, but quite specifically in very many instances within the home markets of the rival powers themselves [Wallerstein 1984, pp. 38–39].

Using this restrictive definition, the only three instances of hegemony would be the United Provinces in the mid-17th century, the United Kingdom in the mid-19th, and the United States in the mid-20th. I would tentatively suggest as the maximal bounding points 1620–72, 1815–73, 1945–67 [Wallerstein 1984, pp. 39–40].

Based on these three instances, Wallerstein suggests a number of historical analogies relating to the rise and fall of hegemonies, which reflect re-occurring patterns in the interface between the political-structuring of the capitalist world system and the underlying economic forms:

The first analogy has to do with the sequencing of achievement and loss of relative efficiencies in each of the three economic domains. What I believe occurred was that in each instance enterprises domiciled in the given power in question achieved their edge first in agro-industrial production, then in commerce, and then in finance. I believe they lost their edge in this sequence as well (this process having begun but not yet having been completed in the third instance). Hegemony thus refers to that short period in which there is *simultaneous* advantage in all three economic domains.
The second analogy has to do with the ideology and policy of the hegemonic power. Hegemonic powers during the period of their hegemony tended to be advocates of global 'liberalism'. They came forward as defenders of the principle of the free flow of the factors of production (goods, capital, and labour) throughout the world economy. ...
The third analogy is in the pattern of global military power. ... In each case, the hegemony was secured by a thirty-year-long world war. ... World War Alpha was the Thirty Years War from 1618 to 1648, where Dutch interests triumphed over Hapsburg in the world economy. World War Beta was the Napoleonic Wars from 1792 to 1815, where British interests triumphed over French. World War Gamma was the long Euro-asian wars from 1914 to 1945, where US interests triumphed over German [Wallerstein 1984, pp. 40–42].

At present, Wallerstein goes on to argue, 'the US has lost its productive edge but not yet its commercial and financial superiorities; its military and political power is no longer so overwhelming'. Thus its Western European and Japanese allies are not as easily dictated to, while its ability to 'overwhelm the weak (compare the Dominican Republic in 1965 with El Salvador today) ... [is] vastly impaired' (Wallerstein 1984, p. 46).

Nevertheless, US dominance (if not exactly hegemony) within the capitalist world-economy persists, based on commercial, financial, military and political advantages. An individual might therefore reasonably conclude that, in the immediate future, there is little likelihood that an inter-imperialist war crisis will develop.

Ironically, the real immediate danger to world peace stems from the fact that, as Robert Cox and to a lesser extent Robert Keohane have emphasised, there is a 'consensual' aspect to hegemonic domination. In the words of the former, 'A hegemonial structure of world order is one in which power takes a primarily consensual form, as distinguished from a non-hegemonic order in which there are manifestly rival powers and no power has been able to establish the legitimacy of its dominance' (quoted in Keohane 1984, pp. 44–45; Cox 1982). Hegemony is thus not simply a question of power but of leadership and legitimacy as well.

Here it is necessary to recall that, in taking on the responsibility for protecting the 'free world' by containing revolutionary forces throughout the globe, in the immediate post-World War II period, the US promoted not only its own global ambitions, but also those of the other imperial powers, who shared in the systematic exploitation of the Third World. It was here that US leadership was most important, and it is here that (as a consequence of the Vietnam War) the growing limits of US power first became apparent. Not surprisingly, therefore, the Reagan administration has responded to the general crisis of the US imperial system by adopting a more agressive leadership role than ever before in the post-World War II period, hoping not only to stem the rising tide of revolution, but also – and of almost equal importance from a US standpoint – to bring its allies back in line, and therefore to obtain additional political leverage for American global designs. Moreover, this strategy is closely tied, in the minds of conservative policy-makers in the US, with overcoming the 'Vietnam Syndrome' – or the peace movement, as well as the more general anti-interventionist and anti-authoritarian sentiments among the underlying population, that remain as lasting legacies of the Vietnam War.

It is essential to recognise that, whether successful or not in its primary political objectives, an agressive *policy* of imperialism along these lines is bound to generate more frequent and wider wars, and could lead to a nuclear war crisis, if the US and the Soviet Union come into direct conflict in the Third World (as a consequence, for example, of a revolution in India).

Still, there is every indication that the Reagan doctrine is failing in every direction. American unilateralism, has at best helped to perpetuate limited European and Japanese co-operation in maintaining existing international institutional structures (which – now more than ever – have their greatest viability where the regulation of the Third World is concerned). Nevertheless, despite US pressures, its allies within the capitalist core have generally refused to follow its lead, to the extent that this would require subordinating their own interests within a larger 'historical bloc' associated with the Second Cold War. Nor have interventions in Lebanon, Grenada, Lybia and Central America served to break the resistance of the peace movement or to reverse much of the anti-interventionist sentiment in the US. Meanwhile Third World revolutions continue to take their toll on the world capitalist system.

Greater instability within the US-dominated imperial order can in fact be expected. To quote Harry Magdoff, 'What we have now is monopoly capital in an advanced stage of internationalisation, geared to expansion of finance and speculation, and stuck in stagnation' (Magdoff and Pollin 1987, p. 748). As the logic produced by the world glut economy and the global financial hypertrophy works its way through the entire system, the effects of the crisis will be transferred increasingly to the world's poor, with the result that a growing revolt from below is likely to be generated in both capitalist core and periphery.

What implications does the foregoing analysis carry for the future of world peace? Our analysis has shown that conservative attempts to reconstruct US hegemony in the context of a deteriorating US and world economy carry with them the dangers of ever wider war and potential global holocaust. The more progressive hope of co-operation among the advanced capitalist powers is, however, little more than wishful thinking 'after hegemony'; and derives whatever degree of viability it has from the common interest among the various ruling classes in the capitalist core in exploiting the periphery. On the other hand, radical analyses that focus too much on the conflict of 'Europe versus US' (or Europe and Japan versus US); on the presumed supply-side causes of crisis within the centre of the capitalist system; and on the pressures on the core exerted by the 'newly industrialising countries' of Asia, tend to underestimate the revolutionary imperative within the substratum of contemporary capitalist societies – as well as the importance for the imperial powers of suppressing such mutinies. Finally, a coherent analysis of the global crisis suggests that while there are incalculable short-term dangers associated with the current uncoupling of the capitalist world order, other long-term opportunities are to be found in the logic of socialism, which holds out the possibility that the poor and exploited of the world will be able to advance together. To avoid 'the common ruin of the contending classes' it is essential that the lower classes finally come into their own (Marx and Engels 1848: 2).

NOTES

1. The extent to which developments in the East Asian 'newly industrialising countries' are still most adequately viewed within a 'dependent development' perspective is shown in Evans, 1987.

REFERENCES

A. Acharya, 'The Reagan Doctrine and International Security' *Monthly Review* 38 (10) (March, 1987) pp. 28–36.

M. Aglietta, 'World Capitalism in the Eighties', *New Left Review* 136 (November–December 1982) pp. 5–41.

E. H. Carr, *The Twenty Years' Crisis* (London: Macmillan, 1939).

Council of Economic Advisers. *Economic Report of the President* (Washington DC: US Government Printing Office, 1987).

R. W. Cox, 'Gramsci, Hegemony and International Relations' *Millenium: Journal of International Studies* 12 (2) (Summer 1982) pp. 162–75.

P. Evans, 'Class, State and Dependence in East Asia', in Frederic C. Deyo, (ed.) *The Political Economy of the New Asian Industrialism* (Ithaca, New York: Cornell University Press, 1987).

R. Gilpin, *US Power and the Multinational Corporation* (New York: Basic Books, 1975).

R. Gilpin, *War and Change in World Politics* (New York: Cambridge University Press, 1981).

International Economic Policy Association, *The United States Balance of Payments: From Crisis to Controversy* (Washington DC: International Economic Policy Association, 1972).

K. Kautsky, 'Ultra-imperialism' *New Left Review* 59 (1970) pp. 41–6.

R. O. Keohane, *After Hegemony* (Princeton University Press, 1984).

R. Keohane and J. Nye, *Power and Interdependence* (Boston: Little, Brown, 1977).

C. P. Kindleberger, *The World in Depression, 1929–1939* (Berkeley: University of California Press, 1986).

V. I. Lenin, 1916, *Imperialism, the Highest Stage of Capitalism* (Moscow: Progress Publishers, 1975 printing).

A. Lipietz, *Mirages and miracles* (London: Verso, 1987).

H. Magdoff and R. Pollin, 'Toward a Socialist Strategy' *The Nation* (6 June 1987).

H. Magdoff and P. M. Sweezy, 'Balance of Payments and Empire' *Monthly Review* 24 (7) (December 1972).

H. Magdoff and P. M. Sweezy, *Stagnation and the Financial Explosion* (New York: Monthly Review Press, 1987).

K. Marx and F. Engels, 1848, *The Communist Manifesto* (New York: Monthly Review Press, 1964).

M. Olson, *The Rise and Decline of Nations* (New Haven, Conn.: Yale University Press, 1982).

H. L. Robinson, 'The Downfall of the Dollar', in R. Miliband and J. Saville, (eds) *Socialist Register* (London: Merlin Press, 1973), pp. 397–450.

B. Rowthorn, *Capitalism, Conflict and Inflation* (London: Lawrence and Wishart, 1980).

S. Strange, *Casino Capitalism* (New York: Basil Blackwell, 1986).

P. M. Sweezy, *Four Lectures on Marxism* (New York: Monthly Review Press, 1981).

I. Wallerstein, *The Politics of the World-Economy* (New York: Cambridge University Press, 1984).

J. A. Willoughby, 'The Lenin-Kautsky Unity-Rivalry Debate' *Review of Radical Political Economics* 11 (4) (1979) pp. 91–101.

6 Nation–State and European Integration: Structural Problems in the Process of Economic Integration within the European Community

Klaus Busch

Since the foundation of the European Economic Community in 1958, the process of economic integration in Western Europe has developed in a very contradictory way. While in the 1960s the customs union for commercial goods could be realised earlier than planned and even a common market for relevant agricultural products could be opened up, in the 1970s the plan which intended to realise an Economic and Monetary Union (EMU) (Werner Plan) and which was conceived to give a fresh impetus to integration, totally failed. Neither the monetary goals of the EMU project (fixing of exchange rates, establishment of a European Monetary Fund) and its monetary, fiscal, and economic policy goals (common European central bank, co-ordination of the budget policy of the member states, establishment of a supra-national economic policy decision centre), nor the legal harmonisation of plans worked out to establish a free circulation of goods, services labour and capital, could be realised.

After nearly ten years of failures in monetary and economic policy integration, in 1979 the EC, however, succeeded in establishing the European Monetary System (EMS), although with some reduction of the original EMU plans. This project is confined to monetary policy measures (fixed exchange rates, extension of the credit facilities, establishment of a European Monetary Fund), while renouncing the fiscal and economic policy aims of the Werner Plan. Although the European Monetary Fund has not been established yet, since 1979 the European fixed-rate system was less unstable than was the European exchange rate pool (the 'snake') between 1972–78.

In February 1986 the members of the EC tried again to intensify the process of integration by adopting the Single European Act (SEA). This supplementary agreement among other things schedules the gradual establishment of the EC domestic market until late in 1992. This should simplify the EC cross-frontier goods traffic by removing border controls and frontier formalities; technical obstacles (national production standards); and tax disharmony; and (by improving the access to government orders, especially in the fields of transportation, telecommunication, and energy supply) by creating a common market for traffic services and realising a European financial market by relaxation of national capital movements' control. With these efforts the EC is returning to the goal of the EMU plan, namely 'to realise a free circulation of goods, services, labour, and capital'. A comparison between the economically oriented parts of the SEA and the Werner Plan, however, reveals that the latest attempt at integration totally renounces the creation of supra-national bodies and initiatives in the fields of monetary, fiscal, and economic policy. It can also be observed that the European domestic market project has come into conflict with renationalisation tendencies in trade policy. Therefore, as long as certain national import quotas, quota regulations in the textile and clothing sector under the Multifibre Agreement (MFA), the different 'voluntary' export restraint arrangements of some EC member states with Japan in the automobile sector still exist, and, as long as production and delivery quotas are still fixed as a part of the EC steel policy, different EC markets within different economic sectors will remain separated from each other. These segmentational tendencies in some EC markets are inconsistent with the domestic market aim of the SEA.

Thus, the EC economic process of integration is contradictory in itself: phases of integration progress are followed by phases of integration retrogression, the latter are followed by reduced attempts at integration which, however, are not free from restrictive national state interventionist measures.

This chapter deals with the reasons for the ups and downs of the process of integration and the structural problems in the relationship between nation–state and the supra-national process of integration that hide themselves behind this delayed process of unification. It has been said in frequent criticism that setbacks in integration can be explained by a lack of political willingness and courage to overcome state nationalism. Here, I hold the thesis that political efforts of integration may be of only limited scope, governed by distinct borderlines, and cannot be overstepped except at the price of failure. I, thus, will demonstrate the possibilities and limits of overcoming the nation–state principle in the course of the economic processes of integration. First, the EC experiences with integration in the fields of monetary and trade policy shall be analysed, and subsequently the relationship between nation–state and the supra-national process of integration shall be assessed in a more theoretical fashion.

A PLAN FOR THE ESTABLISHMENT OF AN ECONOMIC AND MONETARY UNION (EMU) AND THE EUROPEAN MONETARY SYSTEM (EMU)

After the European Community gradually established a customs union in the 1960s, with the restrictions of tariffs and quantities of the intra-EC trade traffic being removed, it tried to push forward the process of integration by establishing an Economic and Monetary Union in the 1970s. Compared with the customs union, the Economic and Monetary Union involves a more qualitative deepening of the process of integration. While the customs union intensifies competition in the EC by gradually removing trade barriers, for example in the case of a country suffering deficits in its trade balance the exchange rate may be rectified, the EMU does not include this protective mechanism for weaker economies. It is, thus, a more decisive step towards realising a uniform economic area in the EC. Like the uniform British monetary system, where the Scottish economy cannot resist the superior competition of English industry by devaluating its own Scottish currency, or, as in the Italian case, the weakly developed south cannot compensate for superior north-Italian competition by establishing one's own monetary zone, in an EC monetary union those countries, whose competitive position has fallen behind, would have to compete with the other member states without the possibility of devaluating the exchange rate. Under these circumstances, the EC would promote a uniform economic system and the competition between the single capitals would be markedly stiffened.

A three-stage plan for the establishment of an Economic and Monetary Union

After the basic Den Haag decision in December 1969 to establish an EMU within the EC, in the spring of 1970 the Council of Ministers instructed a high-level group to draw up a plan which contained a gradual realisation of the EMU, under the chairmanship of the Luxemburg Prime Minister Werner. The work of this Werner Committee was primarily determined by an intensive debate between 'monetarists' and 'economists' about the initial steps for the establishment of the EMU. The 'monetarists', who primarily represented French interests, favoured the exchange rates being fixed as soon as possible, that is to install a monetary union. By this early monetary integration, the economic policy of the EC member states would be co-ordinated on a European level and, thus, entail the harmonious economic development of the community. In opposition, the 'economists' – with Germany as the main supporter – argued that the co-ordination of the member states's economic policy is the main basis for preventing strong foreign trade disequilibriums in the EC. Not until after the economic policy has been harmonised could the EC exchange rates finally be fixed.

This controversy reveals the different economic interests of the member states. France, struggling with crises in the balance of payments, was interested in pooling the foreign exchange reserves and extending credit facilities and financial assistance. In the case of an irregular economic development among the EC states, a system of fixed exchange rates would force financial transactions from member countries with balance of payments surpluses to members with balance of payments deficits. Germany, however, wanted to prevent just this interference with the foreign exchange reserves by harmonising the economic development among the EC members.

The Werner report suggests a compromise between 'monetarists' and 'economists': the three-stage plan for the establishment of an EMU intends a stringent parallel economic and monetary policy integration. On this basis, the Council of Ministers concluded an agreement about the gradual realisation of the EMU in the Community in the spring of 1971. According to the Council resolution the EMU plan should aim at the following: at the end of the process of integration the Community should:

(1) represent a zone which enables a free circulation of goods, services, labour, and capital without distortion of competition, however, without structural or regional disequilibriums, under circumstances which enable the economic subjects to develop their activities at the Community level; (2) create an autonomous monetary area within the scope of the international system with a

central bank system which is characterised by the complete and irreversible convertibility of the currencies free from fluctuations in rates and with immutable parity rates which is the prerequisite of a sole Community currency; (3) take responsibility and authority in the economic and monetary field so that its bodies can secure the leadership of the union. For this purpose, the necessary economic policy decisions are made at the Community level and the necessary powers are delegated to the Community bodies.[1]

This goal was to be realised within three stages up to 1980. In the first stage, from 1971–73, the short-term economic policy in the fields of monetary and credit policy as well as budget and fiscal policy would be co-ordinated on the basis of the medium-term economic programme of the EC. At the same time, the exchange rate fluctuations of the member state currencies *vis-à-vis* the dollar would be restricted to narrower margins than usual, due to the IMF Agreement by aimed actions on the part of the central banks.

A medium-term financial stand-by system amounting to 2 billion European units of account would support the member states in the case of potential balance of payments difficulties. In addition, the first stage would also comprise tax harmonisation, industrial and regional policy measures as well as the co-ordination of the capital market policy. The Committee of the Central Bank Presidents was instructed to make a report on the establishment of a European Monetary Fund, which was to support the EC exchange rate policy and to present the basic unit for the future European central bank system. The Federal Republic of Germany pressed for a precautionary clause to be built in, worded as follows: 'In order to support a smooth performance of the EMU plan and to especially guarantee the necessary parallelity between economic policy and monetary policy measures, the validity of the monetary policy regulations will be five years, from the beginning of the first stage on'.[2] Germany aimed at pursuing the policy of narrowing the margins of fluctuation just as long as the member states actually co-ordinated their economic policy. If these efforts to harmonisation should fail, then the medium-term financial stand-by system would also be given up.

The Council's draft as well as the Werner report did not go into details as to the future actions of the EMU. The Commission was instructed to submit a report on the progress of the co-ordination of the economic and monetary policy between the member states from 1 May 1973, and to make proposals about how to define the Community competencies in the fields of economic and monetary policy that were necessary for the establishment of an EMU. This should serve as basis for new measures, leading to the second stage of the EMU.

Shortly after the EMU stage plan was adopted in the spring of 1971, and the band experiment was scheduled on 15 June 1971, the international monetary crisis forced the EC states to temporarily put aside their plans. In the spring of 1972 they tried again to realise the first stage of the EMU. The Council of Ministers decided to fix the margins of exchange rate fluctuations between the individual EC currencies at ± 1.25 per cent, while the international margin of fluctuation fixed by the Smithsonian Agreement was of the order of ± 2.25 per cent. This system, known as 'snake-in-the-tunnel', functioned because the EC states fixed their exchange rates within the agreed margins by interventions of their central banks. Great Britain and Denmark also adopted this system practised since April 1972.

The 'snake-in-the-tunnel', however, was rapidly undermined by the uneven capital accumulation among the member states. In July 1972, shortly after the system had been installed, the pound sterling left this new monetary pool. The lira followed in February 1973. From that point in time, Great Britian and Italy let their currencies float. The necessary devaluation of the dollar early in 1973, and the revaluation pressure on the currencies comprising the snake system, led by the Deutschmark, made the EC states let their currencies jointly float *vis-à-vis* the dollar. Thus, the snake left its tunnel in March 1973. The margin of fluctuation among the EC currencies was fixed at 2.25 per cent. The pound sterling and the lira, however, did not participate in this joint float system. Norway and Sweden, in contrast, which are not members of the EC, took part in the European monetary pool.

In 1973, it became more and more obvious that a transition to the second stage of the EMU, planned for 1974, could not be realised. The EC countries had neither co-ordinated their economic policy as planned nor did the monetary concept of integration succeed, because Great Britain and Italy veered out. Since late in 1973, the problematic situation of the EMU has remained unchanged. Within the 'snake' the situation permanently changed, but the number of jointly floating currencies did not increase. One could not even notice a strengthening in economic policy co-ordination among the member countries. Between March 1973 and late in 1978, the following relevant shifts could be observed. Within the pool the Deutschmark was revaluated by 5.5 per cent in mid-1973, while the French franc stayed outside the currency pool between January 1974 and July 1975 and then retained membership until March 1976 when it abandoned the system once again until late in 1978. Great Britain, Italy and Ireland let their currencies float throughout this period. In August 1977 Sweden had to leave the EC currency pool and simultaneously the Danish currency was devalued by 5 per cent. Without the British, French, Italian and Irish currency and after the two associated Scandinavian currencies had left the system, the European exchange rate pool finally failed.

The European Monetary System (EMS)

Despite the failure of the EC Three-stage plan and the failure of any attempt to co-ordinate EC economic policy, in December 1978 the European Council decided to take a new run and to push forward EC economic and monetary policy integration by the establishment of a European Monetary System – to introduce a European Currency Unit (ECU), to fix the exchange rates among the EC currencies and to extend the credit mechanisms of the European Monetary Co-operation Fund (EMCF).

ECU is a currency unit consisting of ten currencies: 0.719 Deutschmarks, 1.31 French francs, 0.256 Dutch florins, 140 Italian liras, 3.71 Belgian francs, 0.14 Luxemburg francs, 0.219 Danish crowns, 0.00871 Irish pounds, 0.0878 pound sterling, and 1.15 Greek drachmas.[3] The European currency unit is taken as a numeraire to fix the central rates of European currencies, as a basis of the divergence indicator and as the denominator of operations in both the intervention and the credit mechanisms. Every five years or on application, the weight ratio of the individual currencies within the basket is checked and – if necessary – revised. Each currency has its own ECU-related central rate which is used to establish a grid of bilateral exchange rates. In the EMS, the margin of fluctuation of the exchange rates is fixed to ± 2.25 per cent (except Italy: ± 6 per cent). The central banks will only intervene in member currencies (and not in US dollars as before) to keep up the margins of fluctuation. Divergencies between member currencies are found out by means of the ECU-related rate. If the ECU price of a currency reaches 75 per cent of its maximum spread from the ECU parity (divergence indicator), the respective government is expected to intervene and/or to take monetary and economic policy measures and/or to change the central rates. If not, the authorities of the partner currencies are to be informed of the reasons. Changes in central rates can only be made by mutual agreement.

The participating states transferred 20 per cent of their foreign exchange reserves to the European Monetary Co-operation Fund (EMCF). These funds serve to finance the exchange rate interventions. Three forms of assistance can be distinguished: (1) the very short-term facilities, repayable within 45 days, destined to finance obligatory interventions and unlimited in amount; (2) the short-term facilities having a maturity of three months, (this period can twice be prolonged by three months), to cover a member state's financial needs resulting from temporary balance of payments deficits. For this purpose, the EMCF holds ready a credit volume of 14 billion ECU; (3) the medium-term credits with a maturity of two up to five years, contributing to tide over longer disequilibriums in the balance of payments. The EMCF disposes of a credit volume of 11 billion ECU. Contrary to short-term financial aid, this credit is connected with EC economic and monetary policy conditions.

The second phase of the EMS which was to start in March 1981, scheduled the supersession of the EMCF by the European Monetary Fund (EMF). The EMF was to be fitted with a proper legal status, become proprietor of the still national EMCF funds and was to control the EMS credit mechanisms. Up to now, this supersession has not been implemented.

A comparison between the EMS and the old EMU concept (Werner Plan) makes obvious that today the 'monetarist' concept of integration has achieved domination over the 'economist'. Contrary to the Werner Plan, which still intended a parallel integration both of economic and monetary policy, the EMS resolution of the European Council only says:

> Our main emphasis is put on strengthening the convergency of member states' economic policy, to improve stability within the scope of a wide-ranging strategy aiming at better perspectives for economic development and based on equal rights and obligations for all participants. We request the Council (ministers of finance and economy) to extend the procedure of co-ordination to achieve greater convergency.[4]

Thus, the EMS resolved to institutionalise economic policy competencies at Community level.

The introduction of the ECU and the divergence indicator are something quite new. Both elements originate from the currency basket model favoured by France, Italy and Great Britain. While in the grid-of-exchange-rates system two currencies always reach the points of intervention and thus two central banks have to interfere, by contrast, in the currency basket model it might happen that only one currency reaches the point of intervention and thus only one monetary authority would have to interfere. Germany rejected the latter model as it feared that it would have to intervene too often compared with other EC member states because of its stable currency. The German central bank would then be forced to make supporting purchases of other EC currencies and thereby, would have increased the domestic money supply and would have imported inflation.

Presently only the divergence indicator remains of the currency basket model. It involves the monetary authorities of the respective states which alone take corrective measures in the case of reaching the 75 per cent limit. Germany, however, largely succeeded in preventing too one-sided interventions by formulating the respective passages of the contract very imprecisely: 'The authorities concerned are expected to ... ' 'adequate measures' ... 'the other authorities are to be informed of the reasons ... '[5]

As the EMS was markedly 'monetaristically' orientated, the European Council's expectations that the new monetary system would 'support the convergence of economic development'[6] were unrealistic from the very beginning. Within the EC, economic development was, in fact, very unequal even after 1979.

Uneven economic development in the EC and the development of the competitive positions under the EMS

A regime of fixed exchange rates is only stable if the states involved develop similarly as far as international competitiveness is concerned. Table 1 gives data on productivity, inflation and real wages of the four major EC countries which are indicators of the development of competitiveness. A comparison between the date of the periods 1962–73 and between 1973–83 makes it obvious that the growth rates of the national product, of productivity and of real wages all decreased in the 1970s compared with the 1960s. This trend was produced by stagnation tendencies as a consequence of the over-accumulation crisis, while at the same time the rates of inflation markedly increased. The values among the individual states of these separate factors, however, deviate considerably from this parallel directed trend. Between 1973–83, for example, in Italy and France the real wages per employee, as an indicator of the strain on the costs of production, increased more rapidly than in Great Britain and Germany. The

TABLE 6.1 *Real gross national product,[1] productivity,[2] real wages[3] and consumer prices (the average annual percentage change)*

	Real gross domestic product		Productivity		Real wages		Consumer prices	
	1962–73	1973–83	1962–73	1973–83	1962–73	1973–83	1960–73	1973–83
Italy	5.0	1.8	5.5	1.2	6.0	1.9 (2.6)	4.2	17.4
Great Britain	3.3	1.1	3.1	1.6	3.2	1.3 (1.3)	4.7	13.4
France	5.5	2.3	4.5	2.1	4.4	2.9 (2.7)	4.3	10.9
Germany	4.4	1.6	4.3	2.2	4.6	1.9 (1.5)	3.0	4.7

1. Gross domestic product in constant prices.
2. Real GDP per person employed.
3. Real wage per employee deflationed with the GDP price index.
   Value in brackets deflationed with the consumer price index.

SOURCES: E. Wohlers and G. Weinert, *Unterschiede in der Beschäftigungsentwicklung zwischen den USA, Japan und der EG* (Hamburg: 1986) S. 60, S. 92; 'Jahresgutachten 1985/86 des Sachverständigenrates zur Begutachtung der gesamtwirtschaftlichen Entwicklung' (Bonn: 1985) S. 16.

difference between the increase in productivity and real wages makes obvious that in Italy and France the distribution of the national income shifted to the disadvantage of the share of profits, while in Great Britain and Germany the share of wages decreased. The difference between the rates of inflation is much more striking. Germany achieved the lowest rate (4.7 per cent between 1973–83) and Italy the highest value (17.4 per cent). Even the differences between countries with relatively high rates of inflation (Italy, Great Britain, and France: 17.4 per cent, 13.4 per cent, and 10.9 per cent) considerably burden a fixed-exchange-rate system.[7] In view of these distinct shifts in the competitiveness of individual EC countries, it is small wonder that the EC had not succeeded in establishing an interlinked system of exchange rates between 1972–78. At the same time, Great Britain, Italy and France, whose competitive position deteriorated, saw themselves obliged to leave the exchange rate pool. Otherwise, they would have suffered losses on the *domestic* as well as on the export markets.

It is all the more surprising, that since 1979 no participating country up to now has left the fixed-exchange-rate system, even temporarily. As shown in Figure 6.1, the rates of inflation within the EC countries strongly differed, even after 1979. Germany, Belgium and the Netherlands had the lowest, France and Denmark medium, and Italy and Great Britain the highest European rates of inflation. Between 1976–78, the Italian price index for consumer goods increased by 53 per cent and, between 1979–82, the cumulative rate of inflation already amounted to 75 per cent while the respective British data amounted to 46 per cent and 53 per cent for the same period. Compared with the period before 1979 then, between 1979–82 the differential of inflation rates within the European Community thus considerably increased.

In a regime of fixed exchange, such a fluctuating competitiveness among the individual EC states can only be tolerated by the countries disadvantaged, without weakening their goods-and-services account, if the system is able to react flexibly, that is the exchange rates have to be adapted very quickly to changed conditions of competition among the different countries. In the following, I will show that the EMS did not meet these requirements.

Table 6.2 gives a survey of all changes of the ECU central rate of the single ECU currencies between 1979–86. *Vis-à-vis* the ECU, the Deutschmark was revaluated by 18.9 per cent on the total, the Dutch florin by 14.4 per cent. All the other currencies have been devalued,

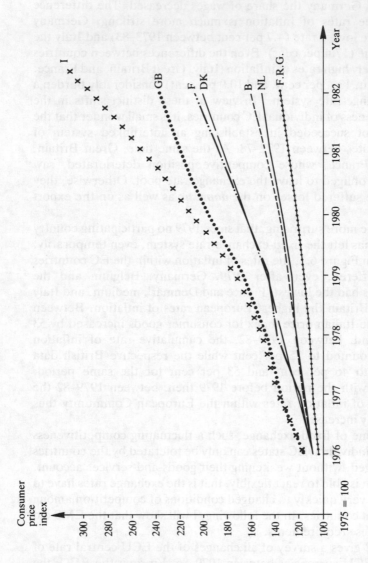

SOURCE IMF: International Financial Statistics, Yearbook 1982, calculated by R. Jaekel, *Die Integrationswirkung des Europäischen Währungssystems* (Hamburg: 1985) p. 83.

FIGURE 6.1 *Development of the Price Index for Consumer Goods in selected EC countries (1976–82)*

TABLE 6.2 *Change of the ECU parity of the EC currencies from March 1979 until August 1986 (per cent)*

Deutschmark	+ 18.94
French franc	− 15.64
Dutch florin	+ 14.4
Italian lira	− 22.26
Belgian and Luxembourg franc	− 8.48
Danish crown	− 9.35
Irish pound	− 13.38

SOURCE: 'Jahresgutachten 1986/87 des Sachverständigenrates zur Begutachtung der gesamtwirtschaftlichen Entwicklung' (Bonn: 1986) Tabelle 13, S. 85.

for example the Italian lira by 22.2 per cent, and the French franc by 15.6 per cent.

To compensate for the shifts of competitiveness resulting from the different EC rates of inflation, however, these adjustments of the exchange rates were insufficient. On the basis of a consumer price and wholesale price index, Jaekel calculated the real bilateral exchange rate of the Deutschmark for the period between 1979–81 *vis-à-vis* several other EMS currencies.

The results of his examinations are shown in Table 6.3.

TABLE 6.3 *Real changes of the bilateral DM exchange rate vis-à-vis different European currencies 1979–81*

Country	Index	CPI	WPI
Netherlands		+ 0.5	+ 1.9
Belgium		+ 0.8	+ 6.0
Denmark		− 3.3	+ 3.4
France		+ 15.6	− 8.0
Great Britain		− 57.0	− 52.3
Italy		− 23.1	− 25.2

CPI: Consumer price index.
WPI: Wholesale price index.
(+):   Revaluation of Deutschmark.
(−):   Devaluation of Deutschmark.

SOURCE: Jaekel, ibid., S. 107, 115, 125, 135, 142, 151.

Jaekel recapitulates:

In the basis period, the fluctuations of the bilateral real exchange rates *vis-à-vis* the Deutschmark were so weak that they had only little effects on the small EC countries' currencies (Belgium, the Netherlands, Denmark), and no significant distortions of foreign trade can be assumed. Compared with the period 1976–78 the Deutschmark tends to be revalued *vis-à-vis* the Dutch florin and with the Belgian franc between 1979 and 1981. As far as the French franc and the Italian lira are concerned, the 1979–80 period created increasing fluctuations of the real exchange rates connected with real revaluations of these currencies *vis-à-vis* the Deutschmark.[8]

The fixed-exchange-rate system of the EMS did not totally compensate the irregular development of nominal competitiveness by adjustments of the exchange rates and, thus, fundamentally and artificially distorted the competitive position between Germany, on the one hand, and France and Italy on the other hand. The development of German foreign trade with other countries participating in the EMS, makes obvious how strong the influence of the price component is (see Figures 6.2 and 6.3).

The strong increase of the German trade balance surplus towards France is most striking. From 1970–82, the positive balance increases from 6.8 billion DM to 17.2 billion DM and, thus, quadrupled. This development between 1979–82 clearly contrasted with that of the 1976–79 period, characterised by the Deutschmark revaluation (at that time the French franc did not participate in the currency pool). Within this period, German exports increased by 18.7 per cent and imports by 28.6 per cent. Between 1976–79, the German foreign trade surplus towards France, thus, decreased from 7.8 billion DM to 6.8 billion DM.

German foreign trade with Italy developed in a similar way. Between 1976–78, when the Deutschmark was revalued at 12.4 per cent (consumer price index) and 9.1 per cent (wholesale price index) respectively, (the lira did not participate in the system of joint float), the German trade surplus changed into a trade balance deficit. The Italian exports to Germany were raised by 36 per cent from 1976–79 while the German exports to Italy only increased by 29 per cent in the same period. The situation, however, fundamentally changed after the EMS was founded and the Deutschmark was heavily devaluated *vis-à-vis* the lira. The German deficit of 1.2 billion DM in 1979

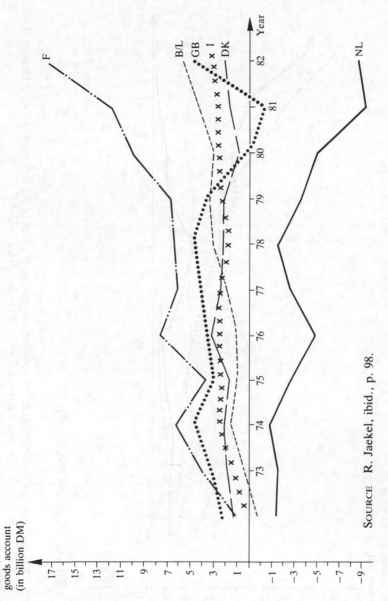

SOURCE R. Jaekel, ibid., p. 98.

FIGURE 6.2 *Bilateral Foreign Trade Balances between the FDR and other selected EC Countries (in billion DM) 1972–82*

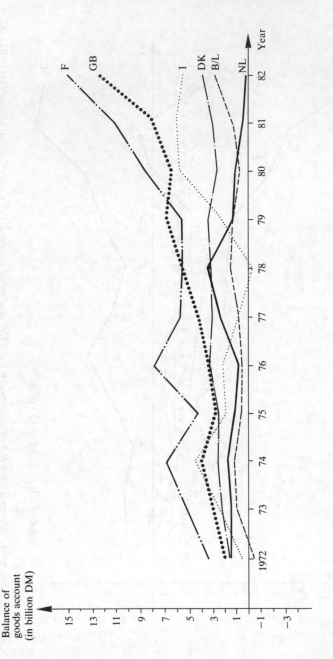

SOURCE   R. Jaekel, ibid., p. 101.

FIGURE 6.3   *Bilateral Foreign Trade Balances (15 specified sub-groups of goods of the industrial statistics) between the FDR and selected EC states (in billion DM) 1972–82*[9]

turned into a surplus of 2.8 billion DM quickly in 1980 which increased to 3.6 billion DM by 1982.

In spite of disadvantages in foreign trade, France and Italy did not leave the monetary union, as they did in 1979. This can be explained by the fact that both states were interested in a strong policy of austerity. Since the outbreak of the international economic crisis in the mid-1970s, in Italy as well as in France, socialist and conservative governments alike tried to improve the conditions of capital profitability by pursuing a policy of deflation. The only exception was the left-wing Keynesian economic policy of Mitterand and Mauroy between 1981–82, which totally failed. The attempts of French and Italian unions to resist the policy of austerity had to be overcome if there wasn't to be a weakening of the international competitive position of their respective countries. Wage cuts or wage retention were legitimated better by pointing to the deteriorated international competitiveness of the domestic economy than by referring to a low rentability of capital.

The German-British and German-Dutch development in foreign trade has been especially influenced by increases in oil prices in 1978–79 and by the regional changes of German oil import policy (from the Near/Middle East to the North Sea region). After 1979, the traditional German surplus in German-British trade thus changed into a deficit and the negative balance *vis-à-vis* the Netherlands increased. If one leaves aside these special factors and only considers the development of industrial goods trade making up at least 70–90 per cent of foreign trade between Germany and the EC states examined,[10] it becomes obvious that the real devaluation of the Deutschmark was accompanied by an increase in the goods account surplus in German-British trade in 1979–81. During that same period the surplus in German-Dutch foreign trade diminished, while the Deutschmark was revalued *vis-à-vis* the Dutch florin (see Figure 6.3).

The EMS, thus, did not contribute to greater convergence of the economic performance within the EC. On the contrary, some states (Germany) benefited from the EMS, while others (Italy and France) were disadvantaged. In Germany, artificial distortions of prices due to *false* real exchange rates within the EMS entailed additional investments and the creation of jobs. In France and Italy, however, the output and employment problems grew. As Jaekel observes,

> Summing up, it may be said – as far as the development of intra-EC trade is concerned – that the kind of exchange rate policy pursued

within the EMS had a more disintegrative character and could not contribute to diminish regional disparities which was an original aim of the EMS. The doubts which were raised towards the integration policy approach of the 'fixed-exchange-rate system' because of potential distortions of real exchange rates and impairment of foreign trade resulting therefrom, can be accepted.[11]

THE DOMESTIC MARKET AND NATIONAL EC PROTECTIONISM

After the three-stage plan to realise the Economic and Monetary Union failed, which also set back plans for a stronger integration of the domestic market within the EC, the Community required 15 years to pass before a new initiative.

On 17 February 1986 the 12 EC countries signed the Single European Act (SEA) in which they committed themselves to establish until 1992 a market with a free circulation of goods, services, labour and capital, that is a uniform domestic market without frontiers. Under this programme, the following measures were to be taken:

(1) Border controls and formalities, which complicate the EC goods traffic and which amount to 2–4 per cent of the gross domestic product are to be abolished.
(2) Technical barriers of goods traffic, i.e. national regulations about standards which restrict competition, are to be removed. Here, the hitherto existing policy of approximation of legislation shall be abandoned. Future harmonisation measures should be restricted to absolutely necessary criteria of health, security, and pollution control. Moreover, a mutual acknowledgement of national standards is to be aimed at, with reference to the decision of Cassis de Dijon of the European Court. Here, the principle of free circulation has to be applied, i.e. a commodity which has been legally produced and marketed within an EC state, may also freely circulate within the Community.
(3) As far as orders for the public services are concerned, intra-Community competition is to be intensified. Up to now, in the fields of energy supply, transportation, water supply, and telecommunications, normally only national companies obtain the contract in the case of public orders. This is to be abolished.

(4) The different, value-added taxing – different tax limits and taxation rates – are to be removed. The EC aims at adapting different excise duties and thus removing an important factor of distorting intra-Community competition.

(5) A common European financial market is to be created by removing national control of capital circulation and by concluding a common legislation for financial services. The European capital market is to be made more efficient as far as the allocation of savings and investments is concerned. Compared with the USA, the EC realises higher volumes of savings (430 billion ECU compared with 340 billion ECU) and, simultaneously, a smaller security issue than the US (142 billion ECU compared with 212 billion ECU).[12]

Within the EC, the realisation of the domestic market could lead to distinctly intensified competition between capitals and, thus, contribute to accelerate the process of accumulation and technical innovation, thereby also improving the international competitive position of the EC *vis-à-vis* the US and Japan. In 1984, the Group of Twelve realised a gross domestic product of $3525 billion: USA $3635 billion). Moreover, the EC population amounts to 320 million inhabitants, and, thus, exceeds the US population by 80 million.

It remains to be seen, how the EC will succeed in overcoming its national protectionist efforts. It is true that the SEA allows decisions on the basis of a qualified majority, contrary to the former EC rule of unanimity,[13] considering the multitude of decisions necessary to realise the domestic market (up to late in 1992 more than 300!); however, it is possible to enter various coalitions of a blocking minority, so that final negotiations within the Committee of Permanent Representatives will last until a common consent is found among all member states. The renationalisation tendencies of EC trade policy and the development of the EC Steel policy make it obvious that the protectionist potential of the Community should *not* be underrated.

National elements in EC trade policy

Although on 31 December 1969, after a transitional period, the initiative for trade policy was shifted from the member states to the Community, there was still place enough to pursue one's own national trade policy, which was intensively followed especially since the 1980s. This margin consists of:

(1) resorting to article 115 of the EECR; article 115 EECR enables the member states to exclude certain goods of non-member countries which freely circulate within the Community from Community procedures (indirect imports), if member states suffer economic difficulties by the imports. Between 1977–85, this kind of measure has been taken 1451 times: France 544, Ireland 317, Benelux states 210, Italy 203, Germany 27, Denmark 4. Those countries which chiefly suffered from these interventions were Hong Kong, Taiwan, South Korea and Japan.[14]

(2) keeping up certain national import quotas; even after the competencies of the trade policy have been transferred to the EC, the member states are still entitled to adhere to *existing* import quotas towards non-member countries fixed before 1970 and to autonomously change the latter. In 1982, as far as imports of industrial products are concerned France disposed of 257 quotas, Italy of 510, Greece of 199, while the number of quotas in the Benelux states and Ireland was less than 100, in Great Britain, Denmark, and Germany less than 50.[15]

(3) practising non-tariffic restrictions of imports; and especially the 'voluntary' export restraint arrangements concluded with export countries are often used as non-tariffic national import barriers, as the EC has no special regulations in this connection. A well-known example is the national agreements in the automobile sector concluded with Japan. France has restricted the Japanese share of automobile sales on the domestic market to 3 per cent of total sales, Great Britain to 10–11 per cent and Italy restricts the import of Japanese automobiles to 2200 units annually. The Benelux countries and Germany have no trade restriction agreements with Japan, except for 1981. The EC Commission is supporting these export restraint arrangements by allowing the member states the application of the article 115 EECR, which thus can suspend all indirect importation of Japanese cars through other member countries of the community.[16]

(4) using the regulations of the Multifibre Agreement. Under the Multifibre Agreement (MFA), the EC concluded several trade agreements with 23 Asiatic, Latin American, and East

European countries between 1983–86, which aimed at fixing import quotas for a series of 'sensitive' products. These import quotas will be divided between the EC states according to an 'apportionment formula of burden-sharing', in order to protect the respective national market and not the EC market. As far as EC imports are concerned, there exists a similar national principle of apportionment under the General System of Tariff Preferences for Developing Countries.[17]

These national elements of the EC trade policy are problematic for three reasons. Firstly, the EC goods traffic is subject to regulations because these national trade barriers have no effect without the application of article 115 EECR. Secondly, the different degrees of protectionism towards non-member countries in some economic sectors entail different pressures of adjustment among the EC states. This may result in distortions of competition between the single EC capitals. Just this latter problem normally should be avoided by a common trade policy in accordance with article 112 EECR. Lastly, the segmentation tendencies in some EC markets compromise heavily the contrasting goals of the common domestic market. Like article 115, which above all was intended to represent a transitory solution, EECR shows that protectionist 'remainders' can hardly be abolished, especially in times of general economic stagnation.

EC steel policy and national protectionism

To cope with the crisis of overproduction of the EC steel industry, in 1975, the EC Commission increasingly intervened in the market on the basis of the European Coal and Steel Community Treaty. By a system of basic prices for steel imports and by means of bilateral arrangements on import quotas with the main supplier countries, the Commission prevented competition with the EC market from non-member countries. By a fixed system of minimum prices, production and delivery quotas within the EC steel market, it guaranteed that the policy of restructuring of the EC steel combines (that is the technological modernisation combined with reduction of production capacities) could largely be implemented under maintenance of 'traditional' shares in production and trade.[18] In 1977, the EC Commission stopped the advance of the 'Bresciani' – little Italian Steel producers in the Brescia region – which were able in those days to offer concrete reinforcing bars much more cheaply than the EC competitors because they produced on the basis of a modern electro-steel procedure.

Likewise, until late in 1985 the EC Commission tolerated the massive and strongly diverging national subsidising policy which in Great Britain and France was mainly pursued to compensate for the technological backwardness *vis-à-vis* EC competition. In Italy, they worked, above all, to help preserve the social infrastructure (wages, personnel, working arrangements) fought for by the Italian trade unions.[19] The EC Commission also instituted a programme of reduction of production capacity for its member states which was not oriented towards the principle of competitiveness but towards the principle of 'equal sacrifices' among the member states.

Within the steel cartel built up by the EC Commission and operating under protection against world market influences competition between the single steel combines was largely avoided and the national states were thus enabled to keep up single steel sites by means of massive national subsidies, even if they were no longer competitive on the international level.

Although the EC Commission was fitted with large supranational initiatives (investment control, minimum prices, production quotas) on the basis of the European Coal and Steel Community Treaty, the Community was not in a position to pursue a steel crisis policy directed against the interests of the nation-states.

This historical review of crisis tendencies in the EC has drawn to a close. It is necessary now to examine these tendencies in a more theoretical manner. The remainder of this discussion will be devoted to this task.

POSSIBILITIES AND LIMITS OF OVERCOMING THE NATION-STATE

The description of the economic process of integration of the EC can be summarised as follows: (1) in the field of the EMU/EMS projects: a supranationalisation of economic policy initiatives, that is, creation of a European central bank, transfer of the fiscal policy to the Community, and so on, could not be realised; (2) in the field of trade policy: existing supranational initiatives of the EC were undermined by renationalisation tendencies; (3) in the field of industrial policy: the supranational initiatives of the EC Commission embodied in the European Coal and Steel Community Treaty were only exercised with a simultaneous maintenance of the interests of the nation-states.

This description raises the question of how the continuance of the nation-state interest can be explained. What type of rationality is possibly hidden behind these efforts to maintain nation-state structures within a process of integration? Most of the economic scientific experts consider it irrational that the nation-states maintain economic policy initiatives. They appeal to the nation-states to have the courage to give up this kind of give-and-take policy and to accelerate the process of integration by a supranationalisation of economic policy.[20] The growing interdependence of the national economies of the member states would lead to a decreased efficiency of the national instruments of regulation. The EMS system with fixed exchange rates would undermine national monetary policy and without a supranational monetary and fiscal policy European economic development could not be harmonised. Thus, the EMS could not work and the whole domestic market project would be threatened.

To my mind, this economic analysis neglects the necessity of nation-state structures for the maintenance of the international competitiveness of single EC member states' economies. It ignores the limits of such an economic process of integration due to the unequal conditions of capital accumulation among the member states.

Unequal capital accumulation and the crisis of integration

The unequal economic development within the EC, and the unequal development of productivity and inflation among the member states which are both responsible for the failure of the EMU project and which led to distortions of the competitive positions of single national economies under the EMS, cannot be removed by a supranationalisation of the EC economic policy because this development is primarily based on structural differences in the conditions of accumulation of the national capitals. Above all, four factors influence the unequal development of capital accumulation within the EC which cannot be eliminated by harmonising and supranationalising the EC economic policy.[21]

Unequal structures of capital

If unequally developed nations are facing each other, as in the EC, then the weaker developed nations normally can raise more quickly their productivity by higher growth rates of accumulation, because the organic composition of capital (the ratio of constant to variable capital) has a lower level and thus the average profit rate is higher. This unequal development cannot be avoided by supranationalising economic policy as economic policy cannot eliminate differentials in the organic composition of capital.[22] These unequal capital structures, which were already a problem for the Group of Six, have been made more problematic by Greece, Portugal and Spain entering the European Community.

Unequal wage struggles

Among the EC member countries the political and economic consciousness of the workers and the structures of the trade unions vary greatly. These differences have a great influence on the result of wage struggles and, therefore, on the relations of profits to national incomes, that is, the shares of profits. Next to the organic composition of capital, the share of profits is the second variable of the rate of profit, likewise a variable, which cannot be influenced by the economic policy of the state. An incomes policy at Community level wouldn't harmonise the different amounts of industrial strife (for example in Italy and Germany) and would not be able, therefore, to avoid unequal wage ratios among the member countries (see Table 6.1). Even with supranational initiatives in economic policy, there would be a great divergence in the willingness of trade unions or the working classes of the EC members to accept wage-control measures. The wage struggle, the struggle between workers and capital in its most direct form, is not susceptible to government action, especially not within the European Community, which knows such great national differences in the tradition of workers' movements.

Unequal rates of inflation[23]

Without regard to the monetary policy of the central banks, the divergence in inflation rates among nations is a result of structural differences among the single economies. The phenomenon that the less developed sectors of the economy, such as agriculture or services, register an above-average rate of inflation and that in less developed industrialised countries the rate of inflation of these sectors is much higher than those in more developed countries, should be explained as follows:

Firstly, the growth rate of productivity of the modern sector is higher than that of the traditional sector of the economy, owing to the different degree of international competition. Secondly, the nominal increases of wages in the economy as a whole are oriented to the wage policy of the modern sector. Because of its lower increase of productivity, the traditional sector does, therefore, bear a greater pressure of production costs, which entails higher rates of inflation. Thirdly, the differences of productivity between the modern and the traditional sector of the economy is accentuated in less highly developed countries. For this reason in less developed industrialised countries the aggregate rate of inflation has a higher level than in more developed countries, a phenomenon that is to be observed not only within the EC, but world-wide.

The monetary policy of the central banks does not possess the possibility of influencing this structural component of inflation, which is based on the sectoral inhomogeneity of the economy. A European central bank would *not* be able to harmonise the rates of inflation within the Community, because it could not neutralise the intra-EC differences in the degree of sectoral inhomogeneity.

UNEQUAL HISTORICAL CONDITIONS

The development of capital accumulation in individual countries is often influenced by special historical factors. In the EC there are two pregnant examples to be mentioned: the North-South problem in Italy and the decline of Great Britain as a World Power. The relative stagnation of the Mezzogiorno in Italy and the deteriorated international competitive position of Great Britain after World War II have diminished the economic development of the respective countries. A regional promotion policy and an export promotion policy may counteract these structural historical components in the development of accumulation to a certain degree, but they could not neutralise them totally. A supranational economic policy of the EC aimed at harmonisation of the economic development of its members would be bound by these historical factors of economic development too.

Since the economic development of the Community must be unequal – because of the above mentioned structural factors of capital accumulation – the member countries cannot renounce the initiative to rectify changes in the international competitiveness of their economies by means of national policy measures. In this context the most important instrument of the nation-states is monetary policy, which allows them to correct a sub-average development of the productivity and/or an above-average development of the rates of inflation through a realignment of currency values. The EC process of economic integration is, therefore, limited by distinct borderlines, which manifested itself several times during the concrete development of integration policy.

.The member countries with a lower development level cannot accept an Economic and Monetary Union characterised by a sole Community currency just because of their necessarily higher rates of inflation in comparison with the more developed members. Even if in the course of economic equalisation the less developed countries realise higher increases of productivity than the more advanced countries, they will be left to their own monetary policy owing to the higher rates of inflation often joined by above-average increases in wage costs, both of which result in a deterioration of their international competitiveness.

The EMU project didn't, therefore, fail because of the narrow-mindedness of the member countries, but because of real economic constraints which prevent a supranationalisation of economic policy initiatives. The EMS cannot, therefore, be completed by the establishment of a European central bank with a sole Community currency, because it will be confronted *permanently* with the necessity of adjusting the exchange rates to the changes in competitiveness within the Community. If the EC will continue the fixed-exchange-rates system, it will have to secure an adjustment policy with sufficient flexibility to avoid artificial distortions of the competitive position of the member countries. Alternatively the EC could introduce a free-exchange-rates system which, by agreements about target zones, would have to avoid an 'overshooting' of the exchange rates. No matter which system it chooses, however, both require the co-operation of the members to guarantee the consistency of the exchange rates with the underlying economic fundamentals. Only by voluntary attempts at supranationalisation might the EC 'free' itself of the dilemma of being dependent on the co-operation of nation-states, the cost of which, of course, would be growing economic disequilibriums within the Community.

These constraints in this way determine the limits of the process of integration in the field of monetary policy. However, their presence does not imply that there are also barriers of integration in the field of trade policy in a like manner; quite the contrary. If the autonomy of the nation-states in the key issues of monetary policy is guaranteed, then individual member countries will save their general competitiveness and the coercion to secure the interests of different economic sectors by protectionist measures will diminish. On the basis of the nation-state structure it is possible to use the advantages of free trade, that is, the growing international division of labour, to raise the macro-economic level of productivity, output and employment. The realisation of the EC customs union in the 1960s and in the 1970s has led to a general intensification of trade among the member countries, the beneficiaries of which were not only those countries with original strong export positions, like the Federal Republic, but especially those countries with originally weak trading positions. Italy and France could thus raise their intra-EC trade shares, namely, in the field of industrial goods.[24]

The objective of the SEA to deepen EC integration by abolishing several national trade barriers will certainly call to arms those economic sectors which now profit by protectionism, but this could nevertheless be realised, because *all* member countries would gain from the intensification of competition and the growing EC division of labour. Unlike the EMU, the domestic market project is not a no-win-situation, because the elimination of trade barriers is to be fulfilled on the basis of the well-balanced mechanisms of the nation-state. While the EMU is leading towards macro-economic disequilibriums among the participating countries, the deepening of the EC domestic market produces adjustment pressure on single economic sectors in each member country, which are, however, more than compensated by the macro-economic advantages. The trade and industrial policy experiences of the EC have demonstrated quite distinctly, that the protectionist pressure resulting from these sectoral disequilibriums will not be underestimated. These difficulties, however, do not imply fundamental barriers to the integration process. By co-operation they may be surmountable.

The contradiction of the EC process of economic integration is that, on the one hand, the structure of nation-states must be preserved to realise the above-mentioned limited possibilities of integration at all, yet the maintenance of nation-states, on the other hand, does contain the danger of destroying the integration process by reactivated protectionism. At the risk of decline the EC must learn to live with this insoluble contradiction.

NOTES

1. H. Lipfert, *Einführung in die Währungspolitik* (München: 1974) Anhang I, S. 324.
2. Lipfert, ibid., Anhang I, S. 330.
3. Great Britain and Greece do not participate in the EMS.
4. Entscheidung des Europäischen Rats vom 5. Dezember 1978, Teil B, 1., abgedruckt in: Informationsdienst, Deutscher Rat der Europäischen Bewegung, Januar 1979, Anlage zu *Europäische Zeitung*, 30. Jahrgang, Nr. 1, Januar 1979.
5. Ibid., part A, point 3.6.
6. Kommission der Europäischen Gemeinschaft, Verwaltungsrat für Wirtschaft und Finanzen: Das Europäische Währungssystem, in: *European Economy*, No. 3 (Brussels: 1979) p. 96.
7. For the development of the relative prices of the EC countries see Beate Reszat *Einflußfaktoren realer Wechselkurse* (Hamburg: 1985) Tabelle A-3, S. 226.
8. R. Jaekel, *Die Integrationswirkung des Europäischen Währungssystems* (Hamburg: 1985) S. 94.
9. It refers to the following specified subgroups of goods of the industrial statistics:
   27 iron and steel
   28 non ferro metals and semi-metal wares
   22 mineral oil products
   40 chemical products
   55 mechanical pulp, cellulose, paper and paste-board
   59 rubber goods
   32 engineering products
   33 commercial vehicles
   35 aircraft and spacecraft
   36 electro technical products
   38 ironwares, tinwares and metalwares
   50 office machines, data-processing machines and equipment
   58 plastic products
   63 textiles
   64 clothes
10. Jaekel, ibid., S. 100.
11. Jaekel, ibid., S. 156.
12. H-E. Scharrer, 'Die Einheitliche Europäische Akte: Der Binnenmarkt' *Integration*, Heft Nr. 3 (1986) S. 102 ff.
13. C-D. Ehlermann, 'Die Einheitliche Europäische Akte: Die Reform der Organe' *Integration*, Heft Nr. 3 (1986) S. 102 ff.
14. See G. Koopmann, 'Nationaler Protektionismus und gemeinsame Handelspolitik in der EG' Bodo B. Gemper (ed.) *Protektionismus in der Weltwirtschaft* (Hamburg: 1984) S. 30 as well as H-E. Scharrer 'EG-Protektionismus als Preis für die Verwirklichung des europäischen Binnenmarktes?' *Wirtschaftsdienst*, Nr. 12 (1986) S. 621.
15. See Koopmann, ibid., S. 31.

16. See S. J. Anjaria a.o., *Developments in International Trade Policy*, (Washington DC: November 1982) p. 88.
17. See H-H. Härtel a.o., *Neue Industriepolitik oder Stärkung der Marktkräfte? Strukturpolitische Konzeptionen im internationalen Vergleich* (Hamburg: 1986) S. 161 ff.
18. Concerning the development of the EC steel policy see K. Busch, 'Protektionistische Tendenzen im Welthandel und die Politik der Gewerkschaften' *WSI-Mitteilungen*, Nr. 4 (1984) S. 220 ff.
19. Between 1975 and 1985 the EC subsidies for the steel industry amounted to 110 billion DM in total. In 1985 for example, Italy and France subsidised their steel industry with 16 billion DM and 7 billion DM respectively. The German subsidies amounted to 1 billion DM only. See H. Kriwet, 'Die Stahlindustrie steht erneut vor Problemen' *Handelsblatt*, Nr. 250, (31 December 1986) S. 37.
20. See, for example, Cairncross/Giersch/Lamfallussy/Petrilli/Uri: *Wirtschaftspolitik für Europa – Wege nach vorn* (München und Zürich: 1974) S. 47 as well as G. Grimm, 'Europa in der Krise – Perspektiven für die Wirtschafts – und Währungsunion' K. Köhler/H-E. Scharrer (eds) *Die Europäische Gemeinschaft in der Krise* (Hamburg: 1974) S. 63 as well as H-E. Scharrer, 'Die Einheitliche ...' ibid., S. 113 ff.
21. The line of reasoning here advanced only in short is based on a detailed examination of the development and the reasons for the uneven development within the European Community, in: K. Busch, *Die Krise der Europäischen Gemeinschaft* (Köln und Frankfurt/M: 1978) S. 87 ff.
22. In the 1960s, Italy could thus realise higher average growth rates than Germany. In the 1970s, Italy lost this margin, which to my mind was due to the special character of the Italian crisis since late in the 1960s. The power of the Italian labour movement resulted in remarkable increases in wages, levelled out the regional wage differential and the wage differences between wage workers and salaried employees, men and women, and entailed a reduction of working hours from 43 to 40. Above all, the organisation of labour was changed to the advantage of the wage-dependents. As a result, the average profit rate of Italian capital heavily decreased and thus paralysed the accumulation of capital.
23. A more detailed description of this model can be found in: K. Busch, *Die Krise der Europäischen Gemeinschaft* ibid., S. 183 ff. In literature, this model is described as the Scandinavian model of inflation which has been developed by the authors Aukrust, Edgren, Faxen and Odhner. See also W. H. Branson/J. Myrman, 'Inflation in Open Economies. Supply-determined versus Demand-determined Models', *European Economic Review*, no. 1 (1976) p. 15 as well as E-M. Claassen, *Grundlagen der makroökonomischen Theorie* (München: 1980) S. 419 ff.
24. See also K. Busch, *Die Krise der Europäischen Gemeinschaft*, ibid., S. 34 ff.

REFERENCES

S. J. Anjaria, *Developments in International Trade Policy* (Washington DC: November 1982).

H. von Berg, *Die Analyse – Die Europäische Gemeinschaft – Das Zukunftsmodell für Ost und West?* (Köln: 1985).

R. von Borries, (ed.) *Europarecht von A–Z, Vom Gemeinsamen Markt zur Europäischen Union* (München: 1982).

W. H. Branson and J. Myhrman, 'Inflation in Open Economies. Supply-determined versus Demand-determined Models', *European Economic Review* no. 1 (1976).

K. Busch, *Die Krise der Europäischen Gemeinschaft* (Köln und Frankfurt/M: 1978).

K. Busch, 'Protektionistische Tendenzen im Welthandel und die Politik der Gewerkschaften' *WSI-Mitteilungen*, Nr. 4 (1984).

Cairncross/Giersch/Lamfallussy/Petrilli/Uri, *Wirtschaftspolitik für Europa – Wege nach vorn* (München und Zürich: 1974).

E-M. Claassen, *Grundlagen der makroökonomischen Theorie* (München: 1980).

C-D. Ehlermann, 'Die Einheitliche Europäische Akte: Die Reform der Organe' *Integration*, Heft Nr. 3 (1986).

G. Grimm, 'Europa in der Krise – Perspektiven für die Wirtschafts – und Währungsunion' K. Köhler/H-E. Scharrer (eds), *Die Eiropäische Gemeinschaft in der Krise* (Hamburg: 1974).

H-H. Härtel, a.o., *Neue Industriepolitik oder Stärkung der Marktkräfte? Strukturpolitische Konzeptionen im internationalen Vergleich* (Hamburg: 1986).

R. Hellmann, 'Das Europäische Währungssystem: Vorgeschichte und Motive' *Integration*, Heft Nr. 4 (1978).

D. Hiss, 'Das Europäische Währungssystem: Gründe und Modalitäten' *Integration*, Heft Nr. 4 (1978).

R. Jaekel, *Die Integrationswirkung des Europäischen Währungssystems* (Hamburg: 1985).

Jahresgutachten des Sachverständigenrates zur Begutachtung der gesamtwirtschaftlichen Entwicklung (Bonn: 1985).

Jahresgutachten des Sachverständigenrates zur Begutachtung der gesamtwirtschaftlichen Entwicklung (Bonn: 1986).

H-J. Jarchow and P. Rohmann, *Monetäre Außenwirtschaft – II. Internationale Währungspolitik* (Göttingen: 1984).

N. Kleinheyer and D. B. Simmert, 'Fünf Jahre Europäisches Währungssystem' *Wirtschaftsdienst*, Nr. 4 (1984).

G. Koopmann, 'Nationaler Protektionismus und gemeinsame Handelspolitik in der EG, Bodo B. Gemper (ed.) *Protektionismus in der Weltwirtshcaft* (Hamburg: 1984).

H. Kriwet, 'Die Stahlindustrie steht erneut vor Problemen' *Handelsblatt*, Nr. 250 (31 December 1986).

H. Lipfert, *Einführung in die Währungspolitik* (München: 1974).

B. Reszat, *Einflußfaktoren realer Wechselkurse* (Hamburg: 1985).

H-E. Scharrer, 'Währungsintegration und Wechselkurssteuerung in der

Gemeinschaft' *Integration*, Heft Nr. 4 (1978).

H-E. Scharrer, 'EG-Protektionismus als Preis für die Verwirklichung des europäischen Binnenmarktes?' *Wirtschaftsdienst*, Nr. 12 (1986).

H-E. Scharrer, 'Die Einheitliche Europäische Akte: Der Binnenmarkt' *Integration*, Heft Nr. 3 (1986).

H-E. Scharrer and W. Wessels, (eds) *Das Europäische Währungssystem, Bilanz und Perspektiven eines Experiments* (Bonn: 1983).

E. Wohlers and G. Weinert, *Unterschiede in der Beschäftigungsentwicklung zwischen den USA, Japan und der EG* (Hamburg: 1986).

7 The Problem of Capitalist Development: Theoretical Considerations in View of the Industrial Countries and the New Industrial Countries

John Milios

Capitalist development, that is, its economic and social characteristics, as well as the economic and social presuppositions for it, has always been a subject of special interest in Marxist theory. The issue of contemporary capitalist development, however, involves *new* conditions from those of the past that derive from today's socio-economic, political and theoretical conjuncture, namely, the world crisis of capitalism; the subsequent restructuring processes taking place in almost all capitalist countries; and, above all, the rapid processes of capitalist development in some countries which were until recently considered as 'peripheral' or 'semi-peripheral' (the 'new industrial countries' – NICs). These new conditions compel us to re-examine the theoretical premises of Marxism regarding capitalist development and underdevelopment.

THE EPISTEMOLOGICAL IMPEDIMENT: THE CONCEPTION OF 'WORLD CAPITALISM'

For at least five decades the Marxist theory of capitalist development has been dominated by the conception of 'world capitalism'. According to this conception the capitalist mode of production, that is the fundamental social structures and relations which constitute the 'specific difference' of a capitalist social order, is being reproduced in its adequate forms only on the world level. This also means that the

154

Marxist theoretical system, the capitalist 'laws of motion' which were discovered and formulated by Marx shall refer to the world level, to the level of 'world capitalism'.

According to this conception of 'world capitalism', development and underdevelopment constitute simply the two opposite poles of one and the same process: capitalist development of some countries –the imperialist countries – presupposes, or even causes, the underdevelopment of the majority of the world countries, the dependent countries, which are subjected to imperialist exploitation.

This simple and easily conceivable conception of 'world capitalism', which on the one pole creates 'development' and on the other pole 'underdevelopment' can, however, hardly be useful for a scientific investigation of social processes that are taking place today with regard to: the decline of Britain's economic and political power after World War II, the emergence of the New Industrial Countries (NICs), the modifications in the power relations between US, Europe and Japan, or accordingly modifications among the European countries themselves.

Furthermore, the concept of 'world capitalism' ignores basic aspects of Marxism's Critique of Political Economy. Marxism understands capitalism as a system of class power which manifests itself not only economically but also politically (through the capitalist state) and culturally – ideologically. It claims, therefore, that capitalist power has been constituted in its adequate forms only on the level of the separate capitalist society. A world economy is the result of the articulation of the different (capitalist) societies, which historically takes the form of the 'imperialist chain' (Lenin). The fundamental postulate of Marxism maintains that economic and social evolution and development mainly reflects the results of class-struggle between capital (capitalist power) and the working class. In contrast, dependency theories reduce class-struggle and class-power in the underdeveloped countries to mere results of the 'decisions' of the ruling classes abroad, in the developed countries. Therefore, the assumption that class-struggle is taking place on a world scale ignores the capitalist state, that is the 'political condensation' of social power in each country (and the perspective of its 'overthrow' – Lenin) and converts Marxism into the evolutionary dogma of 'economism'.

At present the theory of world capitalism is responsible for a number of misconceptions regarding current restructuring efforts of capital. Of these perhaps the most misleading is the notion of a 'new international division of labour'.

THE EMPIRICAL FAILURE OF THE 'NEW INTERNATIONAL DIVISION OF LABOUR'

The concept of 'world capitalism' has found its completest form in the 'neo-marxist' theory of Wallerstein (1979) about the 'world capitalist system'. According to this, the 'world economy' has been, since its formation (that is, since the 16th century) capitalist in nature, polarised in centre and periphery (with the simultaneous existence of a semiperipheral region), and dominated by monopolistic structures. Capitalism, this theory claims, can only exist as a world system, not as a national one (Wallerstein 1979).

Wallerstein's concept was thus applied in the early 1980s to explain the restructuring processes taking place in different countries, and first of all the emergence of the NICs of South East Asia. All these processes are considered as mere sub-cases of a change in the 'world capitalist system', which tends towards a 'new international division of labour'.

As Fröbel, Heinrichs and Kreye (1983, p. 28–31) maintain: 'For the first time in the history of world economy during the past 500 years, there has now developed, in a large and extending scale, in developing countries, a profitable base for the world market of manufacturing production ... We name this qualitatively new development of the world economy, the new international division of labour'.

The 'new international division of labour' is a result of the effort of the world capitalist system to find a solution for the international economic crisis by increasing again the rentability of capital. By transporting some 'work-intensive' industrial branches to the Third World, the production costs of world capitalist production are lowered, since wages continue to remain extremely low in these regions. The 'inexhaustible reserves' of a cheap labour force are, therefore, considered as the main reasons for the transposition of capitalist production to the developing countries. These tendencies are being strengthened by the new technologies, which tend to divide the production process into a number of distinct sub-processes, some of which can be performed by a labour force of low skill and specialisation. On the other hand, the development of transport and communication makes possible the scattering of these sub-processes in a large number of countries.

This concept of the 'new international division of labour' is, however, problematic, not only because of its theoretical premises but also because of its empirical inadequacy. The whole construction simply exaggerates the improvement, since 1970, of the competitive position in the world market of some Third World countries. In reality empirical studies suggest that we cannot talk about the transposition of any branch of capitalist production from the industrial countries to the Third World. As Busch suggests:

> From 1973 to 1980 the share (in international trade) of the non-oil-exporting developing countries was raised from 6.7 per cent to 8.7 per cent, at the expense, indeed, of the socialist countries, the share of which was diminished from 10 per cent to 8.5 per cent, but also at the expense of the capitalist industrial countries, the share of which was lowered from 82.2 per cent to 81.4 per cent. In sectors of iron and steel, as well as clothing and footwear and textiles, the losses of capitalist industrial countries were above average, their shares in the world exports were diminished from 83.6 per cent to 81.7 per cent and from 66.9 per cent to 61.8 per cent respectively. By contrast, developing countries were extended above average in the sectors of iron and steel, textiles and clothing, and also in machinery and transport equipment, as well as in 'other consumer goods'. It is worthwhile noting that their shares in the world exports of sector textiles and clothing increased from 21.9 per cent in 1973 to 26.7 per cent in 1980, while for 'other consumer goods' the corresponding data is 15.1 per cent and 16.3 per cent respectively [Busch 1984, p. 221–2].

The economism and 'technicism' that characterises the theories of the 'new international division of labour', allow them only to detect a tendency to transport the labour-intensive production processes to the low-wage countries. In reality, two distinct processes are taking place in the world market. First, and most important, in the whole post-war period, the most productive sectors of the most developed industrial countries (such as the US) have carried out direct productive investments, primarily in the less developed industrial countries (for example Western Europe) and to a smaller extent in the NICs. Second, the improvement of the competitive position of some industry sectors of the NICs is surely connected in the 1980s to the crisis of these sectors in industrial countries and with some tendencies to transpose production. However, the main tendency in the industrial countries is not to transpose but to protect their traditional sectors in crisis from international competition. The industrial countries of Europe and the US legislated during the last decade a tariff system (which was very severe for this period after the War) of protection from international competition, which also included competition from the NICs (Busch 1984, p. 216–26).

The improvement of the position in international competition of some developing countries and especially the South East Asian NICs is mainly the result of the consolidation of capital relations in these countries, the formation of a skilled collective work force and an increase in the rate of surplus value exploitation. Only under such transformations can the low wages of the NICs be a viable factor for location decisions. But what is most important is that these changes in the periphery are not at all a 'new' phenomenon, as the theory of the world system maintains. Much more substantial transformations on the level of the world market took place, for example, during the last decades of the 19th century, up to World War I and during the inter-war period. During this period, a number of 'agricultural' countries entered the realm of developed capitalist countries through radical changes in their social and productive structures (Ioakimoglou 1985a, 1985b). In the same historical periods, radical changes in the economic and political power relations between the leading imperialist countries also took place.

Thus, contrary to the expectations of the 'new international division of labour' theories, the share of the Third World in the total direct investment from the industrial countries continued to decrease during the last decades. Of the total American direct investment in foreign countries during 1960, only 36.8 per cent was directed to the Third World. This percentage was decreased to 28.9 per cent in 1970 and to 21.7 per cent in 1980. Similarly, the percentage of the total capital exports of West Germany which was directed at the Third World was 39 per cent in 1960, 29.4 per cent in 1970 and 25.9 per cent in 1980. Decreasing also during this time was the percentage of the British foreign investment that flowed to the Third World: 36.8 per cent in 1960, 28.9 per cent in 1970, 21.7 per cent in 1980 (Busch *et al.* 1984, p. 28).

The theory of the 'new international division of labour', therefore, is of very little help for the study of the contemporary transformations of capitalist production. On the contrary, international capital movements (which, as mentioned, mainly take place between the developed capitalist countries), as well as the phenomenon of increasing participation of the NICs in these movements, can be adequately explained on the basis of the Marxist concepts of the *Critique of Political Economy*, as it has been shown by *the theory of the modification of the law of value in the world market* (Busch/Schöl-

ler/Seelow 1971; Neusüss 1972; Busch 1974; Busch/Grunert/
Tobergte 1984).

As is also obvious from the mentioned empirical evidence on
internationalisation of capital, it is not the 'low wages' but the
profitability of investment (the rate of profit in a country), as it is
determined by the overall production and social relations, that is the
factor which 'decides' the direction of the international capital flows.

The rate of profit differs from one country to another. The
underdeveloped countries are positioned at the lower levels of the
international heirarchy in rates of profit, due to the weak domination
of capital over both pre-capitalist social relations and the working
classes, which leads to a consequent low productivity of labour in these
countries. The under-developed countries show, therefore, a rather
weak integration with international trade and capital relations and
movements. By contrast, the developed capitalist countries have
achieved much higher rates of profit, in international comparison,
mainly because of the high productivity of labour in the dominating
capitalist sectors of these countries. *Among these developed industrial
countries* the (national) rate of profit is in most cases higher in those
possessing a relatively lower organic composition of capital, that is, in
the relatively less developed *industrial countries*.

Let us now briefly describe the process of capital exports between
the developed industrial countries, as it is illustrated by modification
theory. The organisation of each national capital on the level of its own
national state, expressed for example in the existence of a specific
national currency for each country (absence of a unique international
currency for all countries), or the persistence of protectionist
economic policies which restrict international trade, does not allow the
formation of international *production prices* and thus the formation of
an international *general rate of profit* on the level of the world market.

International capitalist competition in the world market resembles
the competition of unequally developed individual capitals within one
and the same branch of a national economy (international market
prices, differentiated rates of profit of each national capital and so on).
The more developed *industrial countries*, which due to the higher
organic composition of capital generally possess a lower rate of profit
than the lesser developed *industrial countries*, realise extra-profits
through export trade and, therefore, increase their average national
rate of profit. The international differences between the rates of profit
decrease, because the weaker industrial countries (or national
industrial branches) lose in international trade. However, inter-

national competition is characterised by the following *modification*: the extra-surplus-value and the extra-profit of the more developed national capitalist countries in the world market, is gradually being annulled. This effect is caused (in the typically ideal case: absence of protectionist state measures), mainly by the undervaluation of the national currency price of the less developed industrial countries (which realise deficits in their balance of payments) and the overvaluation of the currency price of the more developed countries. The equalisation processes of the national profit-rates are cancelled at the same time as the more productive and the less productive countries both realise average profits in the world market. The capital of the more developed country, however, can regain the lost extra-profits in the world market only by direct investment in the less developed (but possessing a higher rate of profit) industrial country. In this way, capital flows overcome the protective mechanism of the currency equivalences by partly 'changing nationality' as capital invested abroad becomes incorporated into the accumulation process of the total social capital of the capital-importing country. These capital exports, which regionally take place mainly in one direction, create again a tendency towards equalisation of the national rates of profit for the different *industrial* countries.

It is therefore the case that world market competition between the commodity capitals of industrialised countries, rather than the 'overall interest' of 'world capitalism' shall be regarded as the basis for direct investment (that is the logic of capital flows) and the internationalisation of capital.

Direct capital investment in underdeveloped countries cannot, though, be investigated on the basis of modification theory, since this theory only refers to the relations between internationally competitive industrial capitalist countries. Capital imports in economically retarded countries are mainly either related to the profitable (social and technical) conditions of raw-materials extraction (or mining), or they aim to overcome the 'import substitutive' protectionist policies of the local governments (the so-called 'tariff-investment') (Schweers 1980, pp. 128–85).

MODES OF PRODUCTION AND (CAPITALIST) SOCIAL FORMATION

Let us now return to the theoretical premises for a Marxist theory of capitalist development.

The fundamental concept of Marxian theory, the concept of *Mode of Production* and, specifically, of a *Capitalist Mode of Production* (CMP), does not refer to an existing object nor does it concern the concept of an empirically conceivable reality. It is a theoretical category which refers to the specific difference of a specific (capitalist) social power and structure of economic exploitation. It refers to the 'kernel' of this type of social relation, the 'kernel' which differentiates this type of social relation from any other.

The CMP does not, therefore, refer only to the 'basic' social level – the capitalist economy. It also refers to the political and ideological levels (instances). Capitalist domination, that is the relations of power of capital over the working class, is therefore also consolidated as a *typically capitalist form* in political relations (that is, the *capitalist state*, with its 'relative autonomy' from the economy, as well as from the different bourgeois factions) and in ideological relations (the domination of *capitalist ideologies* which 'reflect', that is 'realise', social class relations as individual relations, as relations between individuals).

The historically formed typically capitalist coherence between the antagonistic social classes, in the ideological-cultural and the economic instances, takes the form of the 'Nation'. The state appears, in the framework of capitalist social relations, as the political consequence, or the political 'completion' of the nation and it takes the form of a national-state.

It now becomes obvious that, if Marxism relies on the concept of the CMP as its main theoretical category, that is only because on the basis of this category one can undertake a scientific investigation of existing ensembles of class relations, capitalist societies, capitalist social formations along with their international articulations.

The main theoretical inefficiency of the theories of 'world capitalism', especially in their 'neo-Marxist' versions, is that they fail to consider the 'political condensation' of class-power relations, materialised in the form of the national states. That is why these theories tend to define capitalism as a mere economic 'world structure'. These economistic theories ignore, therefore, not only the category of political power but also of social-capital, as the manifestation of the overall interest of class power in a capitalist society (social formation).

A similar direction follows another conception, which, failing to understand the processes of capital internationalisation, speaks about 'a territorial non-coincidence between capital and its domestic state' (Murray 1971), foreseeing thus the overcoming of national states. The national state is again conceived, from an instrumentalist point of view, as an ensemble of 'state functions', not as the specific form of the manifestation of capitalist political domination, that is, not as a 'political condensation' of capitalist class power.

But the economistic ignorance of the political instance of class power is as old as Marxism itself.[1] At this point we would like to remind the reader of two positions related to the Marxist categories of the capitalist mode of production and the capitalist social formation which will be of crucial interest for the theoretical understanding of capitalist development and underdevelopment:

The category of (capitalist) mode of production (C) MP does not refer to the concrete capitalist relations of power but to their 'kernel', to the basic aspects of their specific structure.   The consequence of the above position is that one should never consider (capitalist) social formations as the result of a mere 'articulation of modes of production'.

Let us consider here a known example. As is known from Marxist theory about the modes of production, the CMP (as well as every other MP) refers to only two classes, the bourgeoisie and the proletariat. Why then, in the existing capitalist social formations do there appear more than two social classes? According to the conception of the articulation of modes of production, this is only due to the existence in the social formations of more than one MP. But from which MP does there arise, then, the so called 'new-petty-bourgeoisie', to which belong, for example, in the capitalist enterprise, the technicians and the engineers? The articulation concept fails because of this contradiction at this point. Let us follow here the arguments of Poulantzas:

If we confine ourselves to modes of production alone, examining them in a pure and abstract fashion, we find that each of them involves two classes ... But a concrete society (a social formation) *involves more than two classes, in so far as it is composed of various modes and forms of production. ...* Thus in contemporary France, for example, the two fundamental classes are the bourgeoisie and the proletariat. But we also find there the traditional petty bourgeoisie ... the 'new' *petty bourgeoisie* composed of non-productive wage earners, *dependent on the monopoly form of capital* [Poulantzas 1972, p. 9].

The contradictions of the above passage concerning the 'new' petty bourgeoisie are obvious. Firstly, the so-called 'monopoly form of capital' can in no way be counted as belonging to the 'various [that is, other than the CMP] modes of production'. Secondly, the technicians and engineers, that is, production agents that belong neither to the capitalist-owners of the means of production – nor to the proletariat, do not first appear in the so-called 'monopolistic stadium' of capitalism. They appeared at the same time as big industry.

The only outlet from the above obvious contradictions is to consider the CMP not as capitalist social relations *per se*, but as their 'kernel'. Social classes are the result of both the expanded reproduction of the positions (and practices) that correspond to the capitalist division of labour, as well as the expanded reproduction of the agents who will occupy these positions. The CMP refers only to the 'kernel' of this process, to its main aspect: the expanded reproduction of the positions (and practices) in the capitalist division of labour. From this point of view there really exist only two types of social positions (and practices): those of capital and those of the working class. In the existing social formations the bourgeoisie has, though, assigned some functions and practices which refer to the organisation of capitalist class power to agents who don't belong to the class of the owners of the means of production. (Such practices are those ensuring the extortion of surplus value as, for example, supervised control of the production process, or those ensuring the coherence of capitalist society, as for example the members of the state repression apparatus). The result of this contradictory aspect of capitalist relations of power in the existing capitalist social formations (schematically: 'practices of capital' that are handed over to agents belonging to the exploited classes) is the emergence of the class of the 'new' petty bourgeoisie.

(Capitalist) social formations do not simply 'condense' social relations referring to different MPs (under the dominance of the CMP). They also 'condense' a history. This history is that of the modification of the mutual strengths in the class struggle of the antagonistic classes, within one and the same type of class power. In other words, condensation takes place through the history of the forms of capital power and of domination. For example, the fact that we deal with a capitalist social formation does not indicate that the working day will be 12, 10 or 7 hours, that the welfare state services will be more or less extended, that the workers' trade unions will be strong or weak, etc. We refer to the variety of the *'external' determinations* (external in regard to the structural-causal relations that constitute the CMP) which act through the structural connections of the social relations (Althusser 1978).

The question of development is neither about some changes in the 'articulation of the different modes of production', nor a modification of the capitalist laws of accumulation and the structural characteristics of class power. The question of development refers to the historical forms of appearance of class power, that is, to the concrete results of class struggle. Without the consideration of these concrete results, any theoretical approach to the problem of capitalist development can degenerate into pure formalism.

CAPITALIST DEVELOPMENT AND CLASS STRUGGLE

On the basis of these theoretical conclusions we will now consider the problem of capitalist development.

Our first conclusion is, of course, that the problem of capitalist development can in no way be stated with regard solely to a description of the CMP. The CMP is a category constituted by excluding all possible 'external determinations' in regard to the laws of capitalist accumulation and domination. Only at the level of this abstraction did Marx show that the 'absolute' domination of the CMP results in a continuous development of the productive forces, in a continuous capitalist development, which is only stopped temporarily, by the cyclic over-accumulation crises. As he states:

> productivity of labour in general = maximum of product with minimum of labour, which means: to cheapen commodities as much as possible. In the capitalist mode of production this becomes a law independent from the will of each separate capitalist ... However, this immanent tendency of the capital relation will be only realised in its adequate form – and will become a necessary condition, also technologically – as soon as the specifically capitalist mode of production will be developed, and with it the real subsumption of labour under capital [Marx 1969, p. 63].

The problem of capitalist development can be, therefore, stated *only on the level of the (capitalist) social formation. On this level, the existence of antagonistic (non-capitalist) modes of production, but also the ensemble of the 'external determinations' (in regard to the laws of capital accumulation which refer to the CMP) determine the possibilities or limits of the extent, the rates and the direction of capitalist development.* There are not, in other words, different types of the

CMP, or different 'models' of capitalism, some of which tend to 'development' and others to 'underdevelopment'. There are developed and underdeveloped (capitalist) social formations, as well as social formations which develop capitalistically with different rates, as a result of the overall class relation of forces which is consolidated mainly in their interior.

The confusion created by 'neo-marxist' theoreticians with regard to the Marxist categories of the CMP and the capitalist social formation (as well as some ambiguous formulations of Marx himself) has allowed analysts to maintain that Marx had incorrectly 'foreseen' that all countries will follow the same stages of capitalist development. In reality, Marx described on the one hand, the immanent tendency towards the development and revolutionising of the productive forces *in the case* of capitalist productive relations dominating the class struggle; on the other hand, he described the general conditions which make this domination of the CMP *possible*, but not 'historically inevitable' in a social formation. Marx wrote in 1881:

I have shown in *Capital* that the transformation of feudal production into capitalist production has as a starting point the expropriation of producers, which mainly means that the expropriation of the peasants is the basis of this whole process ... I restricted, therefore, this 'historical inevitability' to the 'countries of western Europe' ... Surely, if capitalist production is to establish its domination in Russia, then the great majority of the peasants, that is of the Russian people, must be transformed into wage-earners and consequently expropriated, through the previous abolition of their common property. But in any way the precedent of the West will prove here absolutely nothing ... What threatens the life of the Russian community, is neither a historical inevitability, nor a theory; it is the oppression by the side of the state and the exploitation by the intruding capitalists, who are becoming powerful with the support of this same state and to the disadvantage of the peasants [MEW, Vol. 19, p. 396 400].

The ensemble of determinations that are external to the CMP, that is, mainly, the power and force relations in the class struggle, decide both the possibility and also the rates of capitalist development. Having asserted this thesis which is fundamental to my argument, it is necessary now to develop it more precisely.

It is first of all obvious, that among the very important 'external' –to the CPM – relations that determine capitalist development, one has to count the international connections of a social formation in the framework of the 'world imperialist chain'. These connections are, of course, of both an economic (world market, internationalisation of production, international capital movements) and a political-military nature. The overall effect of the international relations may act to accelerate as well as to retard capitalist development depending on the type of articulation of the given social formation within the context of the world imperialist framework. This type of articulation is, though, determined by the economic and social structure of the given social formation. In other words, the decisive factor is again the internal economic and class relations. Imperialist suppression and exploitation does not constitute the 'General Cause' that creates power relations in the underdeveloped countries. Conversely, it is the structural characteristics of these power relations that impose the specific aspect or position of a social formation within the imperialist framework, that is, the specific forms of subordination for any country under imperialism. If, in the conjuncture produced by the class struggle, the capitalist social forces in one country succeed to establish an economic, political and social hegemony over both the working class and the classes belonging to the non-capitalist modes of production, so that a process of rapid capitalist development is intiated, then the international role of the given country can no longer remain that of an 'agrarian appendage' or of a 'raw materials supplier'. This is today exactly the case of the new industrial countries (Menzel 1985). This example, however, also pertains to the past experience of some of the old industrial countries where capitalist development was initiated later than that of Britain's industrial take-off (for example, the Scandinavian countries, Senghaas 1982).

The variable patterns of capitalist development can be considered, therefore, a result of the class struggle. Particular forms of the class struggle determine the historical ability of capital, of the bourgeoisie, in the interior of an existing social formation, to establish its power and hegemony on all social levels (economic, political, ideological).

The decisive socio-economic characteristic of the underdeveloped countries is, conversely, a social relation of forces, in other words, an ensemble of 'external' determinations, that hinders the expanded reproduction of capitalist power relations, which are, thus, 'confined', socially and spatially, in the so-called 'capitalist-enclosures' (Hurtienne 1981).[2] The 'neo-Marxist' assertion that all production forms oriented to the market are capitalist in nature cannot conceal this reality.

The ability of the bourgeoisie in the underdeveloped countries to expand its power over the antagonistic (pre-capitalist) modes of production and to cause the disintegration of the latter is, thus, the most important presumption of capitalist development. This process takes historically the form of *agrarian reform*, because agrarian property constitutes the basis of the pre-capitalist mode of production (Senghaas 1982). In most cases, agrarian reform does not tend to establish capitalist relations of production in the agrarian sector of the economy, but mainly serves to develop relations of simple commodity production based on the land ownership of the producers. This form of production[3] does not constitute an antagonistic economic system in relation to industrial capitalism, but, on the contrary, is an excellent example of the economic precondition for the accelerated development of the latter. The subjection of the peasants under state economic policy (fixation of the prices of agrarian products) and the credit system (purchase of production means through bank loans) guarantees low prices for agrarian products and a lowering, therefore, of the costs of reproduction of the labour force (Vergopoulos 1975).

In the social formations which are defined as 'developed capitalist countries', in contrast, there exists, therefore, only one mode of production, the CMP. Capitalist relations are articulated with only the form of simple commodity production in the agrarian, as well as in the non-agrarian sectors of the economy. The extent of the form of simple commodity production, its preservation in the different sectors of a capitalist society, or on the contrary, the rates of its dissolution, mainly depend on the increase of labour productivity in the dominant, capitalist, sector of the society (Milios/Theocaras, 1986).

Both empirical as well as theoretical considerations show that the higher developing rates, among the countries belonging to the group of the 'developed capitalist countries', are usually achieved by countries possessing a relatively lower level of capitalist development (Busch 1974, Busch 1978).

This 'uneven development' of the *developed capitalist countries* is to a large extent the result of the following factors: (1) the organic composition of capital is lower in the less developed countries; consequently the average national rate of profit is higher in these countries (a fact which is mentioned as verified by the main direction of the international direct capital movement: from the more developed to the less developed industrial countries); (2) in the less developed industrial countries, the social sphere of simple commodity production is more extended. At the same time there is, though, a higher rate of dissolution of this production form. The result is a larger 'reserve army', the existence of which tends to lower the price of the labour force; (3) in the more developed industrial countries there is a higher percentage of wage earners in the economically active population and therefore a higher wage quota, which results in a pressure on the general rate of profit.

It is obvious that the above mentioned three factors do not exhaust the variety of the 'external' (to the CMP) factors that determine the manner of capitalist development. Reality is always much more complicated and that is why general theoretical remarks can never substitute for, but only open the way to the 'concrete investigation of the concrete situation'.[4]

AN ILLUSTRATIVE EXAMPLE: CAPITALIST DEVELOPMENT IN GREECE; FROM EXPANSIONISM TO CAPITALIST DEVELOPMENT

The case of capitalist development in Greece since the formation of the first independent Greek state in 1830 constitutes an excellent example which illustrates the theoretical positions developed in this chapter.

Greek independence was achieved as a result of the War of Independence of 1821–30 against the Asiatic social order and the national oppression by the Turkish conquerors.

The social relations consolidated in the first Greek state are characterised by the absence of large land ownership and the direct or indirect domination of commercial and shipowner capital over a population, the majority of whom were independent peasants. In the period 1844–64 the liberal bourgeoisie state form and the respective representative parliamentary political system (including general voting rights for all the adult male population) were established. This is a development which takes place several decades earlier than in most European countries (with the exception of France).

These 'presumptions' of capitalist development did not, though, result in a corresponding industrial development of the country. The developing rates of the secondary sector of the Greek economy were very low for the whole period until the 1860s and below the European average for the subsequent 50 years.

An economic take-off occurred however, in the early 1920s. This process of rapid capitalist development was only influenced to a minor extent by the world capitalist crisis, and was thus continued until World War II and the German occupation of Greece. Thus, during the whole inter-war period Greek capitalism attained one of the world's highest rates of development.

Greek capitalist development was continued after the war and especially in the period 1962–79, with comparatively very high rates of growth. Indicatively, we mention here that the Greek per capita GDP was in 1961 30.3 per cent of the average per capita GDP of the nine EEC countries, and 44.7 per cent of the average per capita GDP of the EEC in 1978 in constant prices. Accordingly, the international economic relations of the country were restructured with significant domination of industrial products in exports, significant capital imports and the secondary phenomena of capital exports.

This whole picture of Greek capitalist development allows at first sight a 'world capitalism' explanation: Greece was positioned in the periphery of the 'world capitalist system' and that is why it developed slowly during the whole 19th century. This approach posits that a 'new international division of labour' after World War I enabled a type of 'dependent' capitalist development.

This explanation is, though, superficial and it is contradicted not only by the social and political features of the Greek state mentioned before, but also by two basic aspects of the Greek social formation which do not allow its classification as a so-called 'peripheral' society. Firstly, Greece possessed, on the world scale, a very dynamic capitalist faction, namely its shipowner capital. The Greek merchant fleet was, during the 19th century, the seventh greatest in the world. Secondly, Greece practised, since the formation of the first Greek state, an expansionist policy in the Balkan, Asia Minor and North African regions, aimed at the formation of a Greek empire from the river Danube to Alexandria and from the Ionian Islands to the eastern mountains of Asia Minor. This imperialist strategy was confronted since 1850 with the rising nationalist movements of the other Balkan populations, the English annexation of Egypt in 1881, as well as the national revolution in Turkey under Kemal Ataturk. Thus, Greece did not fulfil its 'Great National Idea' (as the imperialist strategy was named); it succeeded, though, until 1922 in tripling its national territory.

The annexation of the new territories caused the emergence of a 'land question' in Greece: the agrarian economy of these regions was characterised by the domination of large land ownership of a feudal kind.

The economic and social basis of 19th century Greek expansionistic imperialism was the dominant position of Greek capitalists and respectively Greek minority communities in all the regions involved. For example, Greek capitalists controlled 50 per cent of the industrial production of the Ottoman Empire, Greek merchants controlled 60–80 per cent of Egyptian exports and more than 30 per cent of Romanian and South Russian exports.

This scattering, and at the same time the dominant position of Greek capital abroad, determined the characteristics of Greek capitalist development, during the whole 19th century. Firstly, it made the imperialist strategy of the 'Great Idea' sound realistic. It then enables the rapid development of the Greek merchant fleet, which practically connected the Greek capitalists abroad with the Greek social formation. The Greek merchant fleet controlled more than half the sea transports to and from the Turkish ports, and the Greek flag was the first in the transports to and from the ports of southern Russia, and the second to the Danube. Lastly, it created an emigration stream from Greece to the prospering Greek communities abroad.

All these parameters impede the process of capital accumulation in the interior of the Greek social formation and on the contrary benefit the 'cosmopolitan' factions of Greek capital. This is, though, not a result of some kind of imperialist exploitation of Greece but a result of a specific imperialist expansion of Greek capital, as well as the Greek 'nation state'.

The 'Asia Minor Disaster', the defeat of the imperialist Greek invasion of Turkey in 1922, put an end to the era of Greek expansionism and to the respective scattering of Greek capital and the labour force outside Greece. In this way it opened the era of 'national homogenisation', social reform (for example, agrarian reform in the newly annexed territories) and, therefore, capitalist development.

More precisely, as more than one million refugees came in 1922 from Turkey to Greece, a new social and political conjucture and relation of forces was created in the country which enabled capitalist development. The whole process functioned by firstly accelerating the land reform. Then, in a short time, private property relations were established for the overwhelming majority of the farmers, a situation which resulted in a rapid increase in the productivity of agriculture and in a rapid decrease in the price of labour force reproduction. The inner market was enlarged and supplied industrial capitalism with a cheap and relatively qualified labour force. This change brought into Greece the money capital of the Greek Asia Minor capitalists, and lastly, it ensured a majority Greek population majority in the annexed regions of Macedonia and Thrace.

The high developing rates of Greek capitalism in the post-War period are furthermore connected with the defeat of the Greek left and labour movement immediately after the War, and the international political military conjucture of the 'Cold War', which enabled Greek capitalism to improve its strategic and economic position by actively participating in the western 'roll-back' strategic plans.

A CONCLUDING REMARK

Capitalist development is neither a result originating from the interest of the 'world capitalist division of labour' nor is it the 'destiny' of all countries. It is the inevitable outcome of capitalist social power and domination. The enforcement and expanded reproduction of the latter in a social formation is decided by the class struggle. It is, in other words, a contingent outcome that varies according to the specific historical circumstances of each social formation.

NOTES

1. Lenin, for example, criticised, in July 1916, the economism of the 'world-capitalism' conception: 'They don't want to think about either the frontiers of the state or the state in general. It is a form of imperialist economism, similar to the old economism of the period 1894–1902... Instead of talking about the state, they talk about a "socialist cultural circle", that is, they choose on purpose such an imprecise expression that all state problems vanish' [Collected Works, Greek edition, vol. 22, pp. 330–1].

2. This is the case in most countries in the world, in Africa, the Middle East, Asia and Latin America.

3. The simple commodity production does not consist of a special system of exploitation and surplus-labour extortion. We speak therefore not of a mode of production but of a (simple) form of production.

4. Such a 'concrete investigation' on capitalist development in four EEC countries, for the period 1952–75, was undertaken by Busch (1978). From these four countries, Great Britain had already in 1950 only 5.4 per cent of its total workforce working in the agrarian sector. It was, therefore, the capitalistically 'maturest' country. On the other hand,

Italy was the least developed country in the group of four (in 1950, 42.8 per cent of the total Italian population of labour worked in the agrarian sector). As predicted from the above remarks Busch found a tendency for the capital accumulation process in Italy to attain higher than average development rates, in comparison to the three other countries. However, the development rates for Italy leave behind those of *all* the other three countries only in the period 1961–70. The acute class conflicts between capital and the working class, as well as the development gap between northern and southern Italy were the main factors that impeded capitalist development in Italy. In contrast, Great Britain not only attained the lowest rates of capitalist development in comparison to the other countries, but in the 1960s it also lost its previous economic significance in Europe, to the benefit of both Germany and France. This relative decline of British capitalism is, however, not a mere result of its 'maturity', but is connected both with the social relation of forces in Britain, as well as to the international role which Britain unsuccessfully tried to play within the framework of the imperialist strategy of the West (that is, persistence in a classical colonialist policy; very high military expenses; persistence in the high price of sterling so that it can keep up its international role and so forth.)

REFERENCES

L. Althusser, 'Introduction' in G. Duménil, *Le concept de loi économique dans le Capital* (Paris: Maspero, 1978).

K. Busch, 'Ungleicher Tausch-Zur Diskussion über internationale Durchschnittsprofitrate, Ungleichen Tausch und Komparative Kostentheorie anhand der Thesen von A. Emmanuel' *PROKLA*, 8/9 (1973) pp. 47–88.

K. Busch, *Die Multinationalen Konzerne. Zur Analyse der Weltmarktbewegung des Kapitals* (Frankfurt: Suhrkamp, 1974).

K. Busch, 'Protektionistische Tendenzen im Welthandel und die Politik der Gewerkschaften' *WSI Mitteilungen* 4/84 (1984), pp. 216–26.

K. Busch, W. Schöller and P. Seelow, *Weltmarkt und Weltwährungskrise* (Bremen: 1971).

K. Busch, G. Grunert, W. Tobergte, *Strukturen der Kapitalistischen Weltökonomie* (Saarbrücken: Breitenbach Publishers, 1984).

A. Eikenberg, *Die paradigmatische Krise der Theorie ökonomisch unterentwichelter Gesellschaftsformationen* (Dissertation University Osnabrück, 1983).

F. Fröbel, J. Heinrichs, O. Kreye, *Die neue internationale Arbeitsteilung* (Reinbek: Rowohlt, 1983).

T. Hurtienne, 'Peripherer Kapitalismus und autozentrierte Entwicklung' *PROKLA*, 44 (1981), pp. 105–36.

I. Ioakimoglou (1985a), 'From absolute to relative surplus-value' (in Greek), *Thesis*, 11, pp. 21–47.

I. Ioakimoglou (1985b), 'For the anticapitalist outlet from the crisis' (in Greek), *Thesis*, 12, pp. 73–100.

K. Marx, *Resultate des unmittelbaren Produktionsprozesses* (Frankfurt: Neue Kritik, 1969).

MEW (Marx-Engels-Werke) vol. 19 (Berlin: Dietz Verlag, 1972).

U. Menzel, 'Die ostasiatischen Schwellenländer. Testfälle für die entwicklungstheoretische Diskussion' *PROKLA*, 59 (1985) pp. 9–33.

J. Milios, 'Internationalisation of Capital and Polarisation of Accumulation', *Proceedings of Lesvos Seminar on Spatial Structures* (1985).

J. Milios and Ch. Theocaras, 'Remarks for a Critique of the Capitalist Theories of Development' (in Greek), *Thesis*, 16 (1986) pp. 69–80.

J. Milios, *Kapitalistische Entwicklung, Nationalstaat und Imperialismus. Der Fall Griechenlands* (1987).

R. Murray, 'The Internationalisation of Capital and the Nation State', *New Left Review*, 67 (1971), pp. 84–109.

Ch. Neusüss, *Imperialismus und Weltmarktbewegung des Kapitals* (Erlangen: Erlangen, 1972).

N. Poulantzas, 'The Problem of the Capitalist State' reprint from *New Left Review*, 58 (1969, 1972).

R. Schweers, *Kapitalistische Entwicklung und Unterentwicklung* (Frankfurt: Menzel Verlag, 1980).

D. Senghaas, *Von Europa Lernen* (Frankfurt: Suhrkamp, 1982).

Statistical Guide, *The Greek Economy in Figures* (Athens: Electra Press, 1984).

K. Vergopoulos, *The Agrarian Problem in Greece* (in Greek), (Athens: Exandas, 1975).

I. Wallerstein, 'Aufstieg und Künftiger Niedergang des Kapitalistischen Weltsystems', in D. Senghaas (ed.), *Kapitalistische Weltökonomie* (Frankfurt: Suhrkamp, 1979).

8 Industrialisation, De-industrialisation and Uneven Development: The Case of the Pacific Rim

Mike Berry

> The Pacific Basin region contains a number of countries that have experienced some of the highest rates of economic growth in the world in recent decades: Japan, South Korea, Singapore, Hong Kong and Taiwan. It also contains five of the world's largest food producers: Australia, Canada, New Zealand, Thailand and the USA; and it accounts for large proportions of the capitalist world's production of key minerals: 49 percent of copper, 54 percent of lead, 60 percent of iron ore, 69 percent of tin and 80 percent of nickel. About half the exports and imports are traded within it, and as much as one third of all transnational [corporate] investment in the world is located there. [Crough and Wheelwright 1982, p. 34]

The national economies comprising the Asia-Pacific or *Pacific Rim* region present a bewildering diversity of cultures, individual histories and current levels of development. They also form an increasingly articulated and significant global economic region; 'significant' in the sense that developments within this region influence and reflect the structural forces and transformations under way in the developed industrialised countries (DICs), the so-called capitalist 'core' or 'centre'. With the emergence of the Pacific Rim, earlier theories based on simple core-periphery dichotomies appear increasingly inadequate as explanations of the pattern and dynamics of uneven development in the world economy.

Moreover, the Pacific Rim is emerging as an increasingly critical arena for the uncertain and dangerous games of super-power politics. From a post-war 'American Lake', the region has seen the piece-meal development of a Soviet economic and military presence, complicated by the continuing and unwelcome nuclear role of French neo-colonialism. Both the increasing strategic importance of the region and the increasing tensions within it are reflected in recent events like: (1) the refusal by the New Zealand government to allow US nuclear capable warships to enter New Zealand ports (and the US' over-reaction); (2) the increasing number of countries committed to attaining a nuclear-free Pacific, in the wake of hardening French policies (*Rainbow Warrior*), both with respect to nuclear testing and opposition to independence in New Caledonia; (3) the emergence of commercial ties between the Soviet Union and the small Melanesian nation of Vanuatu; (4) the Aquino coup in the Phillipines; and (5) the army coup against the democratically elected government in Fiji and confused responses of other nations within the region.

This paper attempts, firstly, to outline the broad contours of contemporary economic developments in the Pacific Rim, to trace the emergent patterns of uneven development, particularly with respect to the rapid economic growth of a select number of 'newly industrialised countries' in the shadow of the continuing internationalisation of Japanese and American capitalism.

Secondly, the paper compares and evaluates a range of theoretical approaches which have been offered as explanations of these developments. The approaches analysed include explanations drawn from orthodox or neo-classical economics, dependency theory, proponents of 'the New International Division of Labour' and other theories of the internationalisation of capital.

Thirdly, an attempt is made to relate developments in the Pacific Rim to the overall global patterns and rhythms of capital accumulation of a world economy in pronounced crisis and, in particular, to consider the manner in which selective industrialisation in South-East Asia is related to de-industrialisation and re-industrialisation in the established industrialised regions of the developed economies. Finally, the question of the crisis-induced circulation of capital through the urban built environment of the DICs is raised and related to the prior discussion of Pacific Rim industrialisation, using Australia as a focal case.

THE CONTOURS OF UNEVEN DEVELOPMENT IN THE PACIFIC RIM

The 1970s and early 1980s was a period of intensifying economic crisis in the capitalist world, marked by falling growth rates, rising unemployment and inflation, stagnant world trade and collapse and piece-meal reconstruction of the international monetary system. The oil price rise shocks further intensified but did not cause these developments, as the latter were structurally embedded in and are only explicable through an understanding of the historical expansion of capitalism as an economic, political and cultural 'world system' in the post-war period (O'Connor 1984).

However, as generalised as these crisis effects were, their impact was far from even, both through time and over space (for selected Pacific Rim countries, see Table 8.1). Real per capita growth rates slowed to around 3 per cent per annum in the developed industrialised countries (DICs) and much of the Third World. Nevertheless, growth in the upper-middle income lesser developed countries (LDCs) was noticeably higher, with countries like South Korea, Hong Kong and Singapore growing at around 7 per cent and some of the Association of South-East Asian Nations (ASEAN) at more than 4 per cent. The growth rate of the oil-exporting LDCs exceeded 5 per cent. Within the DIC bloc, the US grew at just over 2 per cent, while Japan surpassed 6 per cent. Among LDCs, the Philippines grew at less than 3 per cent, much less than its ASEAN neighbours, while Chile barely grew at all.

Using the year 1970 as a divider (and ignoring relative population growth): low-income LDCs grew constantly but at a lower rate than higher income LDCs; lower-middle income LDCs grew slightly more quickly in the 1960s than the 1970s, while the situation was reversed for upper-middle income LDCs; DIC growth halved in the 1970s with even Japan's rate of GDP increase falling behind the LDCs, in general; finally, the spectacular growth of the oil-exporting LDCs in the 1960s fell back to levels comparable to other LDCs in the 1970s. However, despite temporal variations, the superior growth perform- ance of South Korea, Hong Kong, Singapore and Mexico (the 'Newly Industrialised Countries' or NICs) and, to a lesser extent, ASEAN, is clear.

Further divergencies are apparent when dis-aggregating to the sectoral level. During the 1960s industrial growth in low-income LDCs matched that in the DICs, while the upper-middle income LDCs industrialised at a significantly faster rate with the NICs matching the

TABLE 8.1 Selected growth rates

| | Average annual growth rate (per cent) | | | | | | |
| | Real per capital GDP | Real GDP | | Industry* | | Manufacturing | |
	1960–82	1960–70	1970–82	1960–70	1970–82	1960–70	1970–82
THIRD WORLD COUNTRIES:							
Low income countries:	3.0	4.5	4.5	6.6	4.2	5.5	3.4
Lower-middle income countries:	3.2	4.9	5.3	6.2	5.8	6.5	5.5
Philippines	2.8	5.1	6.0	6.0	8.0	6.7	6.6
Indonesia	4.2	3.9	7.7	5.2	10.7	3.3	13.4
Thailand	4.5	8.4	7.1	11.9	9.3	11.4	9.9
Upper-middle income countries:	4.1	6.4	5.4	9.1	5.7	8.4	5.8
South Korea	6.6	8.6	8.6	17.2	13.6	17.6	14.5
Hong Kong	7.0	10.0	9.9	n.a.	n.a.	n.a.	n.a.
Singapore	7.4	8.8	8.5	12.5	8.9	13.0	9.3
Mexico	3.7	7.6	6.4	9.4	7.2	10.1	6.8
Chile	0.6	4.4	1.9	4.4	0.6	5.5	–0.4
Malaysia	4.3	6.5	7.7	n.a.	9.2	n.a.	10.6
High income oil exporters	5.6	16.7	5.0	n.a.	–2.8	n.a.	9.5
ADVANCED INDUSTRIALISED CAPITALIST COUNTRIES:	3.3	5.1	2.8	5.9	2.3	5.9	2.4
Japan	6.1	10.4	4.6	13.0	5.6	13.6	6.6
US	2.2	4.3	2.7	4.6	1.9	5.3	2.4
Canada	3.1	5.6	3.4	6.3	2.3	6.8	2.5
Australia	2.4	5.6	3.1	5.9	1.6	5.5	1.5

*The Industry category includes: manufacturing, construction, mining, electricity, water and gas.
SOURCE World Bank, *World Development Report* (Oxford University Press, 1984) Tables 1 and 2.

very high rate of growth of Japan. Industrialisation generally slowed during the 1970s and early 1980s, except in some of the ASEAN economies; and the most dramatic drop occurred in the DICs, including Japan. NIC industrialisation, on the other hand, continued at a high rate. Dis-aggregating further, to focus on the manufacturing sector, the story is much the same. The rate of manufacturing growth in the DICs more than halved during the 1970s, at a time when the NICs and some other Asian economies were booming. The sluggish industrial development of countries like the US, Canada and Australia (and many western European countries), during this period raised the spectre of 'de-industrialisation', the claim that capital is deserting traditional manufacturing industries in the heavily industrialised regions of the north-eastern United States, north-western Europe and south-eastern Australia, with significant employment loss and local-ised economic decline (Bluestone and Harrison 1982; Blackaly 1979; Harris 1984; Crough and Wheelwright 1982). The extent to which apparent DIC de-industrialisation is related to rapid NIC industrialisa-tion has been hotly debated and is taken up in detail, below.

The differential impact of industrialisation can also be glimpsed by comparing the changing sectoral shares of GDP (see Table 8.2). Whereas the share of industry fell slightly in the DICs between 1960–82, in favour of a growing tertiary sector, industry increased its share of GDP in the LDCs and NICs, generally at the expense of primary production. In most of the latter economies, the most rapid rate of industrial development was concentrated in infrastructural provision (such as water, roads and construction) rather than manufacturing. However, in the NICs and to a lesser extent ASEAN, manufacturing expanded to account for more than 20 per cent of GDP, thereby approaching the DIC average. Indeed, in South Korea, manufacturing now accounts for around 30 per cent of GDP, the level for Japan.

However, this broad sectoral analysis obscures the differences in the *structure* of manufacturing in developed, developing and under-de-veloped countries. Table 8.3 compares the distribution of value added across manufacturing sub-sectors in selected countries. Clearly, much of the recent manufacturing growth in the LDCs has been concen-trated in light consumer goods industries, especially textiles, clothing and consumer electronics. Capital equipment and heavy industry forms almost half of manufacturing value added in Japan and the US, significantly higher than other industrialised or industrialising econo-mies. Only in the NICs have these sub-sectors grown to account for

TABLE 8.2 *Sectoral share of industry, selected countries*

| | Share of GDP (per cent) | | | |
| | Industry | | Manufacturing | |
	1960	1982	1960	1982
THIRD WORLD COUNTRIES:				
Low income countries	26	32	13	14
Lower-middle income countries:	22	35	15	17
Philippines	28	36	20	24
Indonesia	14	39	8	13
Thailand	19	28	13	19
Upper-middle income countries:	33	41	25	22
South Korea	20	39	14	28
Hong Kong	39	n.a.	26	n.a.
Singapore	18	37	12	26
Mexico	29	38	19	21
Chile	35	34	21	20
Malaysia	18	30	9	18
High income oil exporters	n.a.	74	n.a.	4
ADVANCED INDUSTRIALISED CAPITALIST COUNTRIES:	40	36	30	24
Japan	45	42	34	30
US	38	33	29	22
Canada	34	29	23	16
Australia	40	35	28	20

SOURCE World Bank, op. cit., Table 3.

more than 25 per cent of manufacturing value added, thereby expressing a degree of 'capital deepening' similar to the smaller DICs, like Canada and Australia.

This pattern of Third World industrialisation was closely associated with – some would say driven by – rapidly expanding foreign trade. The export performance of the Asian NICs and ASEAN is compared with that of the advanced capitalist economies in Table 8.4. South Korea experienced massive export growth through the 1960s and 1970s, while exports from Hong Kong, Thailand and the Philippines were also growing much more quickly than for the advanced economies. However, this conceals a critical distinction between the

TABLE 8.3　*Distribution of manufacturing value added, 1981 (per cent)*

	Food textiles and clothing	Machinery and transport equipment	Chemicals	Other manufacturing
Philippines	51	10	7	32
Indonesia	36	7	12	45
Thailand	57	15	3	25
South Korea	39	18	11	32
Hong Kong	n.a.	n.a.	n.a.	n.a.
Singapore	8	55	4	33
Mexico	27	20	12	41
Chile	20	14	12	54
Malaysia	29	18	6	47
Japan	12	39	8	41
US	17	33	12	38
Canada	21	23	7	49
Australia	24	22	8	46

SOURCE World Bank, op. cit., Table 7.

TABLE 8.4　*Export growth, selected countries*

	Average annual growth in exports (per cent)		Percentage share of merchandise exports					
			Primary commodities and textiles and clothing		Machinery and transport equipment		Other manufactured goods	
	1960–70	1970–82	1960	1981	1960	1981	1960	1981
South Korea	34.7	20.2	94	40	—	22	6	38
Hong Kong	12.7	9.4	65	45	4	18	31	37
Singapore	4.2	n.a.	79	48	7	26	14	26
Malaysia	6.1	3.8	94	83	—	12	6	5
Thailand	5.2	9.1	98	83	—	5	2	12
Indonesia	3.5	4.4	100	97	—	1	—	2
Philippines	2.3	7.9	97	62	—	3	3	35
ADVANCED INDUSTRIALISED CAPITALIST COUNTRIES:	8.5	5.6	41	31	29	37	30	32

SOURCE World Bank, op. cit., Tables 9 and 10.

NICs and LDCs like Malaysia. Export growth in South Korea, Singapore and Hong Kong over the 1960 to 1981 period was associated with a substantial shift in the composition of exports away from primary and light consumer goods towards heavy capital equipment, a trend which was not reproduced in the Third World, as a whole. Thus, the significant degree of capital deepening which has characterised NIC industrialisation has extended beyond satisfaction of the expanding domestic market to the capture of markets world-wide. In this, the NICs are approximating the earlier developmental trajectories of the western European countries, the US and Japan.

Associated with significant changes in the volume and composition of world trade are complex changes in the origin and destination of exports (see Table 8.5). South Korea, for example, has cut its dependence on markets in the advanced economies and now exports more than a third of its total to developing economies. Similar changes have occurred in the Philippines and Australia. Conversely, Hong Kong, Indonesia and, to a lesser extent, Thailand, have moved in the opposite direction, becoming more dependent on DIC markets, while the destinations of exports from Singapore, Mexico, Canada and Japan have remained broadly stable, in proportional terms.

Clearly, the complex patterns of uneven development briefly sketched out here confound easy generalisations. Consequently a number of recent theoretical attempts to understand and explain the structural forces underlying these observable patterns are critically evaluated and compared in the following sections.

WHY IS IT SO?: COMPETING THEORETICAL ACCOUNTS

The brief outline of contemporary pattern of uneven development described above clearly raises problems for both conservative and radical theories which stress a sharp dichotomy between the developed industrial economies and the underdeveloped non-industrialised ones.

Prior to World War II, orthodox economic explanations derived this 'old' international divison of labour from the Ricardian theory of comparative advantage or costs. Advanced industrial economies came to specialise in the production and export of capital-intensive manufactured commodities, while underdeveloped countries specialised in the production and export of labour intensive agricultural goods and raw materials. This pattern of specialisation was seen to be both efficient in the sense of maximising economic welfare globally

TABLE 8.5   Origin and destination of merchandise exports (per cent)*

Origin \ Destination	Developing economies (oil importers) 1960	1982	High income oil exporters 1960	1982	Advanced industrialised capitalist countries 1960	1982	East European socialist countries 1960	1982
THIRD WORLD COUNTRIES:								
Low income countries	27	39	—	4	51	52	21	5
Lower-middle income countries:								
Philippines	19	27	1	2	73	69	7	2
Indonesia	6	24	—	1	94	73	—	2
Thailand	48	38	3	4	47	55	2	3
Upper-middle income countries:								
South Korea	28	29	—	4	67	63	6	4
Hong Kong	11	25	—	10	89	65	—	—
Singapore	45	20	—	—	54	77	1	3
Mexico	7	9	—	5	93	84	—	2
Chile	9	26	—	1	91	72	—	1
Malaysia	35	45	—	1	58	51	7	3
High income oil exporters	17	35	—	8	83	56	—	1
ADVANCED INDUSTRIALISED CAPITALIST COUNTRIES:								
Japan	30	27	2	4	66	66	2	3
US	37	42	—	8	61	47	2	3
Canada	9	12	—	1	90	84	1	3
Australia	21	44	1	3	75	49	3	4

*Some figures relate to 1961 and 1981 and result in slight discrepancies in percentage totals.

SOURCE World Bank, op. cit., Table 12.

and stable since it reflected permanent differences in levels of productive efficiency between the developed and underdeveloped worlds; all that was necessary was for free trade to reign and for the world's governments and central bankers to maintain an international monetary system which would facilitate expanding international trade.

However, after the War the ideology if not the reality of the old international division of labour began breaking down. Nationalistic Third World governments having thrown off the colonial yoke now aspired to rapid industrialisation in emulation of both the advanced capitalist countries and the Soviet Union. The international political and strategic interests of the Western powers now required support for at least a limited degree of economic diversification and industrialisation in the Third World, if only to forestall a general turn to the alternative socialist model. Underdeveloped countries were renamed 'lesser developed countries' (LDCs) with the optimistic implication that they could indeed follow in the path of Western development.

The neo-classical model

Neo-classical economics, as ever mirroring the dominant ideological concerns of capitalism, found new ways to explain and legitimate the industrial route to Third World development. Although ditching Ricardo's theory of value (that is, relative prices) and crude version of the Quantity theory of money, post-war development economists have faithfully retained the doctrine of comparative costs to both legitimate a free trade regime of international trade and associated international division of labour and, when added to an appropriate monetary theory, to explain it.

> In this way the modern derivations of comparative costs rely on what are essentially variants of Ricardo's mechanism: in all cases, the very nature of the desired solution requires monetary variables (price levels and/or exchange rates) to adjust in such a way as to transform any existing absolute advantage into a comparative one [Shaikh 1979/80, p. 292].

Thus, a particular LDC which is absolutely less efficient in producing all or most commodities, by comparison to its trading partners, will initially run up chronic balance of payments deficits, exporting little and importing much. In the neo-classical view, chronic deficits lead to forced adjustment through either exchange rate movements or the deflation of the general price level in deficit nations in comparison to the price level in countries enjoying balance of payments surpluses.

In the former case, currency devaluation makes the exports of deficit LDCs more competitive (that is, cheaper in terms of the currencies of other countries) and its imports from surplus countries more expensive in terms of local currency, a process which continues until at least some local industries become so competitive as to begin to sell on world markets while other local industries are able to undercut and replace some increasingly expensive imports. The trade deficit is therefore squeezed from both directions – rising exports and falling imports. The situation is precisely reversed in surplus economies with an appreciating currency leading to falling exports and rising imports, thereby reducing the surplus. The deficit LDCs will attain competitiveness and begin to export those commodities in which they initially suffered the *least cost disadvantage* – this is their comparative advantage. Conversely, capitalists in surplus countries will be forced to withdraw from those industries in which they initially enjoyed the smallest comparative cost advantage, to concentrate on those commodities where their much larger initial advantages have not yet been wiped out by an appreciating currency. The end result is a pattern of international specialisation in which national economies each produce and freely export those commodities for which it has a comparative advantage, always assuming that commodity and currency markets remain free, especially from the attempts by national governments to cushion their individual economies from the equilibrating forces at work.

Precisely the same pattern of specialisation – for example universal production and export according to the prevailing pattern of comparative advantage – will result in a situation of fixed exchange rates, assuming one of a number of variants of the quantity theory of money. This is the case whether or not trading economies are on the gold standard. Where countries are *not* on the gold standard, all that is required is for central banks in each to obey the dictates of 'sound finance', tightening monetary policy and reducing the domestic supply of money and hence domestic prices across the board when trade deficits build up at fixed exchange rates, and acting to increase the money supply and prices when surpluses accrue.

The major problem of the theory of comparative costs is that although when wedded to an appropriate monetary theory it offers an explanation of the process of international specialisation it fails to specify its content – that is to explain which industries are likely to be located in which national economies. In particular, the theory or law of comparative costs, in itself, fails to explain why manufacturing industry was and is heavily concentrated in the advanced economies instead of the LDCs and what prospects exist for this pattern to break down in the drive by some LDCs to industrialise.

Neo-classical economists get over this problem by effectively assuming away its source, uneven development due to the overwhelming productive efficiency of DICs over LDCs. Indeed the dominant vehicle for the neo-classical conveyance of the law of comparative costs, the Hecksher-Ohlin model of factor proportions, assumes identical conditions for production (and hence, potential efficiency) world-wide. In this abstract and unreal world comparative advantage will be determined by the prevailing or 'initial endowment' of factors of production. Those countries (like the DICs) which have the highest stock of accumulated capital relative to labour will have a comparative cost advantage in capital intensive industries like most of the manufacturing sector, while those countries (like the LDCs) with a high proportion of labour to capital will enjoy a comparative advantage in labour-intensive industries.

This model leads to the old international division of labour when it is allowed that manufacturing in general is significantly more capital-intensive than agriculture and resource related development. However, it can also be used to explain the partial and selective development of manufacturing industry in the third world. As particular LDCs accumulate capital, both through an increase in domestic savings due to the efforts of growth-minded nationalistic governments and via foreign aid, and as underemployed low cost labour is 'freed' from traditional agriculture undergoing modernisation, they begin to develop comparative advantage in labour intensive manufacturing industries. These dynamic new industries producing for both domestic and world markets will, it is argued, provide the major impetus to self-sustaining economic and social development, in the form of rising per capita GDP. Once started, the process is assumed to be self-sustaining since growth will both generate further savings for reinvestment and via the lure of greater material welfare (which neo-classical economists assume is a central and universal feature of human nature, the 'quaint' customs and values of many indigenous cultures notwithstanding) lead to the further rationalisation of inefficient industries and redeployment of unemployed and underemployed labour.

The policy prescriptions of neo-classical economics are clear. The governments of both DICs and LDCs should take steps to 'free up' market forces everywhere to allow an efficient allocation of resources within and between national economies, with capitalists in each specialising according to comparative advantage. Industrialisation in the LDCs will hence occur 'naturally' through expanding exports in an open and expanding world economy, not arbitrarily and 'inefficiently' by way of import substitution strategies which rely on import controls, tariffs and other direct government controls which 'distort' local factor and commodity markets away from production according to comparative advantage.

> The causative link is thus twofold: from trade liberalisation to export orientation, and from the free play of market forces to incentives for export, both of which, because they produce a Pareto efficient allocation of resources, will result in increased levels of industrialisation, exports and economic growth [Browett 1985, pp. 8–9].

This is the strategy of 'Export Oriented Industrialisation' (EOI), so beloved by orthodox economists and held to be responsible for the recent industrial surge of countries like South Korea and Taiwan (Balassa 1981; Little 1981, 1982; Lee 1981).

Indeed, it has been the striking economic success of the NICs over the past 15 years, as described in the proceeding section, that has partly resurrected the failing stocks of the neo-classical model in development studies:

> The performance of these NICs is impressive by any standard. The question is what factors account for this success. The dominant explanation (emerging from mainstream economics) is that these countries adopted the 'right' policies by liberalising imports, adopting 'realistic' exchange rates and providing incentives for exports; above all they managed to get factor prices right so that their economies could expand in line with their comparative advantage; reliance on market forces and integration into the world economy yield results superior to protection and dissociation from the world economy ... [Schmitz 1984, p. 9].

Westphal (1978, p. 375) might be speaking for all neo-classical economists when arguing that: 'Korea provides an almost classic example of an economy following its comparative advantage and reaping the gains predicted by conventional economic theory.'

However, the NICs do not merely provide an apparent justification of conventional economic analysis and policy prescriptions; they are also held to provide a blueprint for the potential development of all LDCs, if only the latter's governments will move from a protective strategy of import substitution industrialisation (ISI) to one of EOI. Universal development becomes in effect a purely 'technical' question of 'getting the factor prices right' and leaving the world market to distribute the mutual gains from trade and growth.

It is this harmonious picture of a world economy in motion, benefiting peoples everywhere, at least through continuously expanding material living standards, that has drawn heavy fire from a range of radical perspectives. To the neo-classical economists' claim that uneven development world-wide and economic backwardness in particular regions is due to the failure of governments everywhere to pursue the appropriate EOI policies, radicals assert that these inequalities are structurally embedded in the world economy as it actually develops through time.

Dependency Theory and Warren's critique

Historically, the radical critique arose during the 1960s, especially in Latin America. Following the earlier work of Paul Baran (1957), Frank (1967) argued that the growth in global capitalism had systematically subordinated Latin American economies to the continuing development of the industrialised economies of Europe, the US and Japan. These relations of economic, political and cultural *dependence*, Frank argued, resulted in general economic stagnation through the Third World caused by the manner in which these economies were integrated into the world market.

Fitzgerald (1983) has listed the main 'structures of dependence', so called. First, the economic surplus generated in the peripheral economies is transferred to or appropriated by capitalists in the advanced or metropolitan countries by way of chronically unequal terms of trade, transfer pricing by trans-national corporations, super exploitation of local labour and so on. Second, through direct investment trans-national corporations take over control of local raw materials and agricultural production. Third, the markets of traditional local industries are destroyed by efficient foreign competition and increasing indebtedness. Fourth, local producers in general are forced into production for export in markets dominated by large trans-national corporations enjoying monopsonistic powers. Finally, local class and state structures emerge which politically express and entrench the above described features of underdevelopment. In particular, the traditional landowning and mercantile classes tend to benefit economically (by appropriating a share of the expanding domestic and economic surplus) and defend their interests through the imposition of highly authoritarian, often military, regimes committed to the continuation of policies underpinning dependence.

Frank (1978) and others subsequently developed dependency theory by explicitly tying it to an historical account of the rise of global capital over the past 300 years. In this they paralleled the related approach of 'world-systems theory', associated, in particular, with Wallerstein (1974) and Amin (1974, 1976). Alternatively, Emmanuel (1972) offered a theoretical account of a specific mechanism for the routine transfer of surplus value from periphery to metropolis through international trade. In all cases, the major conclusion was that widespread Third World development had been and would continue to be blocked as long as these economies remained part of the world economy. Genuine development required economic autarchy and political revolution. The structure of exploitation and lines of political struggle were held not to exist within national economies but between them.

Dependency theory has been subjected to severe criticism over the past 15 years, both on theoretical grounds and in relation to its implications for political strategy (Limqueco and McFarlane 1983; Seers 1981). However, for our purposes, the main weakness of this approach is that it fails totally to account for the phenomenon of the NICs in the Pacific Rim. As Browett (1985, pp. 19–20) has argued, dependency theorists either ignore the evidence of significant development in countries like South Korea and Taiwan or claim that such development is somehow not real or sustainable.

A major catalyst in the developing radical critique of dependency theory was the work of the British Marxist, Bill Warren (1973, 1978, 1980). Central to Warren's analysis '... is the view that capitalism is a progressive force in the Third World. This argued both with reference to Marx's own writings and with empirical evidence of economic growth and industrialisation in the post-war period' (Jenkins 1984, p. 35). Warren was the first to systemically select and present empirical evidence of widespread Third World industrialisation. The continuing geographic expansion of capitalism would, he argued, continue to break down the archaic obstacles to economic and social development. Indeed to the extent that ' ... there are obstacles to development they originate not in current relationships between imperialism and the Third World, but in the internal contradictions of the Third World itself' (Warren 1980, p. 10).

Warren's thesis has drawn extensive criticism (for example Petras, McMichael and Rhodes 1974, 1978; Lipietz 1982; McEachern and O'Leary 1980) focused initially on the selective nature of his empirical evidence and the sweeping nature of the implications drawn from it. However, as the substantive nature of NIC development became generally recognised, the critique shifted from statistical interpretation to theoretical specification (Corbridge 1986, p. 57). Warren's descriptive account of Third World development rests on the same positivistic method and superficial theoretical construction as neo-classical economics. 'Thus, all the old indicators of economic growth (industrial output, GNP) are resurrected as evidence of the development of the forces of production. There is no attempt to penetrate these surface manifestations in terms of Marxist concepts such as value, surplus value, or the falling rate of profit' (Jenkins 1984, p. 37). More specifically, Warren is taken to account for not adequately relating internal developments in the Third World to those in the advanced economies nor to analysing substantial differences in development trajectories *within* the former. The force of this critique has been summarised as follows:

Ultimately, Warren's thesis is no more satisfying than those he criticises: he didn't provide a coherent explanation for the prolonged period of non-industrialisation in the Third World; he fails to explain the persistence of a vast number of scarcely industrialised countries; he fails to discuss the different patterns of industrial growth in advanced capitalist, Third World and socialist countries; he fails to provide a comprehensive framework to understand the inter-relationship between the changing nature of capital in the West and the process of industrialisation in the Third World; finally he fails to discuss the enormous inequalities in industrial development among Third World countries, both in terms of the changes in productive systems and in terms of their stages of industrial growth; moreover, he fails to consider the possibility of the de-industrialisation of specific Third World countries [Petras 1984, pp. 182–3].

Thus, recent theoretical efforts have been focused on attempting to move beyond both the extreme generalisations of stagnationist dependency theory and Warren's developmentalism but in a way which confronts the unrealistic assumptions, analytical weaknesses and ideological apologetics of neo-classical development economics. An effort is made both to relate the current process and contradictions of capital accumulation in the DICs to conditions in the Third World and to account for pervasive differences in the development outcomes within the latter economies.

The 'New International Division of Labour'

Most prominent in this context have been theorists of the so-called 'New International Division of Labour' (NIDL). Jenkins (1984, pp. 29–30) here distinguishes two variants: a neo-Smithian approach focused on changes in the world market for labour power and production sites and a neo-Ricardian one emphasising the capital export effects of a secular decline in the average rate of profit in the DICs.

The former approach, typified by Frobel, Heinrichs and Kreye (1980), holds that productive capital is switching away from the DICs towards underdeveloped countries offering plentiful low wage labour. This switch is driven, as always, by the structural capitalist imperative to maximise profits in a highly competitive world, but is made possible by the historical emergence on the world stage of three key pre-conditions. First, thanks to the disruption of traditional agriculture and rapid population growth in the Third World, large reservoirs of potential labour power are being produced and concentrated in accessible urban locations. Second, the development of the labour process in many DIC industries has led to the continuing de-skilling and fragmentation of jobs which can now be transferred more readily to low wage havens. Third, revolutionary improvements in transport and communications have allowed an increasingly diversified geographic pattern of production, both by reducing the impact of transportation costs of components and finished products and by allowing more efficient managerial control and co-ordination on a global scale. The approach is termed neo-Smithian after Adam Smith's emphasis on the impact of improved transport developments on the expansion of the world market and consequent extension of the detailed division of labour.

The neo-Ricardian approach, exemplified by Arrighi (1978) and Frobel (1982), focuses not on the conditions of Third World labour markets, as such, nor on internal changes in the labour process but emphasises the impact of distributional struggles in the DICs. The post-war growth of the labour movement in the developed economies has placed an institutional check on attempts to maintain profit rates through increases in the rate of exploitation. The strategic power of DIC workers is based, in this view, on the institutional growth of organised labour and the demise of the reserve army of unemployment during the long post-war boom. As profits are squeezed in the DICs, industrial capital is relocated to Third World sites where low wages and poorly organised workers offer the prospects of regained and enhanced profit rates. This move is further encouraged by the tax subsidies offered and anti-labour laws imposed by repressive local regimes.

The resulting international division of labour is 'new' in the sense that it entails a limited degree of industrialisation in the Third World. Industrialisation is limited both in its extent, since not all industries will find it possible or profitable to relocate, and in its impact, because it will cease if local conditions of accumulation, especially wage levels, approach DIC levels. Thus, NIDL theorists deny the possibility of genuine Third World development, stressing the enclave nature of most foreign investments by transnational corporations (TNCs) in the free trade or export processing zones of countries like Malaysia and the Philippines (Crough and Wheelwright 1982, pp. 34–57).

The opposite side of the coin of partial Third World industrialisation, in this view, is partial de-industrialisation in the DICs:

> The effect on the developed countries is to *de-industrialise* them partially. This process has begun in Australia, western Europe and North America, and of course one result of the higher unemployment is pressure to reduce wages. Non-trans-national companies are forced to relocate production facilities off-shore since they cannot compete against trans-nationals using the latest equipment and lowest wages. They either go off-shore, go bankrupt or get taken over by trans-nationals. The result is to accelerate the concentration of capital and tilt the balance of powers further against labour and national governments [Crough and Wheelwright 1982, p. 42].

The empirical correlation of partial Third World industrialisation and export growth, pin-pointed by neo-classical economics, is therefore seen by NIDL therosits as an integral element of the changing locational patterns of industrial investment. As capital and jobs are exported from centre to periphery, finished products are imported back into the mass markets of the DICs.

By pitching their analysis at the level of the world market, NIDL theorists align themselves with the exchange oriented world-systems approach and, unsurprisingly, reproduce the latter's general conclusion as to the impossibility of Third World development. NIDL analysis becomes, in effect, a modern variant of dependency theory stressing the prevalence of super-exploitation, political repression and debilitating industrial specialisation in the periphery. As such, it is open to serious criticisms, both empirical and theoretical.

The empirical objections, based on the data presented above, can be taken first and are as follows: (1) Many, if not most, Third World countries remain relatively undeveloped, showing little signs of real industrialisation – this in spite of very low wage rates and large pools of potential labour. Thus, these factors *might* be necessary but are hardly sufficient conditions for peripheral industrialisation. 'The notion of the growth of export industrialisation as a result of industrial redeployment from the advanced countries to the low wage areas, fails to account for the fact that there are a *range* of low wage areas, and those that are most involved in industrial exports to the Western countries are *not* the *lowest* wage areas' (Petras 1984, p. 197). (2) Some underdeveloped countries have experienced significant industrialisation but based primarily on domestic accumulation rather than foreign investment by relocating and expanding TNCs. (3) For many peripheral economies undergoing limited industrialisation, production for the home rather than export markets seems critical. This was certainly the case for the NICs until the mid-1960s. (4) The NICs, in particular, have and are experiencing a pattern and rate of industrialisation far in excess of the enclave model proposed by NIDL theorists. With the exception of Singapore, foreign investment has played a relatively minor role. NIC exports are increasingly directed towards the Asia-Pacific region rather than being dominated by DIC markets in general. Nevertheless, NIC industrialisation has not been prevalent in all fields but has been concentrated in particular industries in which low wages do not appear to be the only or even most important condition (Hamilton 1983), a point returned to below.

Moving on to the theoretical criticisms, we can note at once the difficulty in interpreting the significance of low wages in the periphery. Low wages may mask low productivity thereby reducing and perhaps swamping the potential labour cost advantage of peripheral location. In a related sense, some industries depend not just on low cost unskilled labour but on appropriate mixes of highly skilled labour absent in most peripheral economies. Industrialisation here will depend on the extent to which such labour can be acquired through immigration or indigenous production; in the latter case, the home state will normally play a crucial role (see below).

A second and much deeper theoretical weakness of the NIDL approach concerns its fixation on the appropriation of absolute surplus value through job fragmentation, de-skilling and recruitment of super-exploited Third World labour as the only or dominant mode of capital restructuring in the DICs experiencing pronounced economic crisis. As Jenkins (1984, p. 33) notes, this is akin to 'Babbage's Principle' which emphasised the tendency towards de-skilling and low wage labour which Marx used to analyse the early development of industrial capitalism, the stage of manufacture. However, NIDL theorists would do well to ponder the contemporary critique (in 1835) of Babbage by Andrew Ure and the use Marx made of Ure's insight in analysing the internal transformation from the stage of manufacture to that of machino-facture. For Ure, the way of increasing productivity was through labour-displacing technologies – in the extreme, complete automation. This, Marx argued, led to the extraction of relative (not absolute) surplus value, under the competitive drive of technological innovation, becoming the main level of accumulation in advanced capitalism.

> It is these mechanisms for restoring productivity through increasing relative surplus value and depreciating constant capital, rather than attacks on the working class in order to increase absolute surplus value, which are central to the resolution of the crisis. Consequently, periods of crisis are also characterised by intense competition as individual capitals battle for survival and to establish positions for themselves in readiness for renewed expansion [Jenkins 1984, p. 41].

In the current context, DIC capitalists therefore confront a range of strategic possibilities in reacting to the current crisis of falling profit rates; possibilities which do not require relocation to the periphery. Three related areas are apparent here: (1) the application of new productivity-enhancing, labour-displacing technology as already noted; (2) the increasing marginalisation of a proportion of the workforce in the DICs, who work under super-exploited conditions in recreated 'sweatshops' in the heart of the most advanced capitalist countries. In some cases, marginalised labour will be employed in sub-contracting relations to the technologically advanced enterprises noted in (1). For example, technological restructuring and managerial reorganisation in the Japanese automobile industry has resulted in the clustering of small supplier and component firms around technologically sophisticated but flexible production plants (Hill 1985). In other cases, outwork will reappear as DIC capitalists attempt to radically slash overhead costs and piece rates and avoid union organisation. The textile industry is a case in point (for an Australian study on outwork in Melbourne's clothing industry, see Cusack and Dodd 1978); (3) immigration of Third World labour to the DICs. Hence, instead of exporting capital to the periphery, DIC capitalists may import labour instead. An example is the so-called 'guest workers' system' in western Europe (Castles and Kosack 1973; Piore 1979; Castles 1984). Illegal migration is also important here – for example from Mexico to the US. Illegal migrants form a fertile source of super-exploitation in the DICs.

Thus, the current crisis-induced economic and spatial restructuring of advanced capitalism is not solely or even primarily centred on developments in the Third World. 'The internationalisation of capital and the decentralisation of accumulation takes place not only to the Third World but also within the advanced capitalist countries' (Jenkins 1984, p. 44). For example, the rapid growth of the south-Western 'Sunbelt' region of the US during the 1970s drew on each of the sources stated above – on the construction and operation of new, technologically advanced plants, the employment of 'sub-employed' or marginalised local labour and the super exploitation of legal and illegal Mexican migrants (Perry and Watkins 1978). Run-away shops need not run all the way to Asia.

The prospects for economic restructuring within rather than outside the spatial boundaries of the DICs have been enhanced over the past decade. In the first place, the current crisis has, as always, intensified the process of the centralisation of capital, which, as Marx argued, arises from the competitive drive to accumulate through displacing living labour by machinery in production. In other words, increasing centralisation by way of forced merger and takeover, both expresses the competitive need for and provides the financial and organisational base to achieve the extraction of relative surplus value. This, as argued earlier, reduces the competitive urge for DIC capitals to relocate in search of cheaper labour costs.

Secondly, we have seen the progressive reconstruction of the reserve army of unemployed in the advanced economies, due partly to the impact of generalised crisis and partly to technological displacement. To the extent that selective de-industrialisation has occurred in favour of the Third World, the resulting increase in DIC unemployment has also damped further peripheral capital relocation. In all cases, rising DIC unemployment reduces the competitive attractions of cheap peripheral labour.

Thirdly, the threat and limited reality of capital flight has exerted a disciplining effect on organised labour in the advanced economies, reinforcing the effects of the growing reserve army and reducing the collective opposition of DIC workers to economic restructuring brought about by technological change. At the political level, conservative or right wing labour governments have been elected and re-elected on platforms devoted to facilitating the restructuring process: privatisation, deregulation, enforced real wage cuts, a declining social wage and reduced protection have been imposed, to varying degrees, in order to boost profit rates and prospects for capital accumulation in the advanced economies. To the extent that these policies have been successful, the economic advantages of Third World relocation have been further eroded.

These considerations, taken together, suggest that the overall trend towards Third World industrial location, partly established in the 1970s, will be sharply checked and even reversed in the 1980s. De-industrialisation in parts of the Third World may result as particular industries are re-concentrated in 'systemic blocs' in the DICs and most dynamic NICs (Ernst 1982; Rada 1984).

Perhaps most striking is the case of the assembly of semi-conductors, one of the major sources of LDC manufactured exports. With the manual technology of the 1970s, Hong Kong production costs were 33% of those in America, with the semi-automatic technology of the 1980s, the advantage had fallen to 63%; but with automated assembly lines installed in 1983, production costs in Hong Kong were only marginally lower (8%) than those in the US [Kaplinsky 1984a, p. 81].

Kaplinsky argues that related technical advances in highly automated industries are also reducing the economies of scale in mass production industries, encouraging the relocation of production close to the final (DIC) market and undermining the NIDL logic of 'global factories' and world-wide sourcing. Elsewhere, he presents evidence to the effect that the new flexible, automated production systems, which he terms 'systemo-facture', are diffusing more quickly to DIC-based TNCs than indigenous Third World enterprises (Kaplinsky

1984b). This is understandable in the light of the preceding analysis. Relatively high wages and working class power under crisis conditions in the DIC have encouraged the move to more automated production in the competitive search for relative surplus value; conversely, low wages and docile labour in the LDCs have led to the extraction of absolute surplus value through super-exploitation, acting as a *brake* on technological development there, which systematically acts to under-cut any existing LDC cost advantages.

Production relocation against the NIDL trend may also be occurring in industries other than micro-electronics. The case of the automobile industry has already been noted and recent research has tended to '... downplay the world car and global sourcing trends and see a future geography for auto production that conforms more to a 'philosophy of manufacturing at integrated assembly sites', that is, a tendency toward the Toyota City system (Hill 1985, p. 29: see also Altshuler *et al.* 1984; Jones and Anderson 1983; Maxay 1981). There is even some indication that this reversal is affecting light consumer goods industries like clothing which, as noted in the preceding section, have formed the core of Third World industrialisation and export growth (Hoffman and Rush 1983). 'In our view what is clear is that the utilisation of the new technologies will significantly reduce the rate at which production is subcontracted to the Third World; less clear, but probably likely, is a significant degree of trade reversal with subcontracted production being pulled back from low-wage Third World states' (Kaplinsky 1984a, p. 84).

Clearly what we are currently seeing is a fracturing or differentiation of the crude international division of labour painted by neo-classical, dependency and NIDL theorists alike. Particular industries are being restructured under crisis conditions to express *different* spatial divisions of labour on a global scale. NIDL and related theorists offering a mono-causal and economistic account of these complex processes not only mis-specify the underlying technological logic of accumulation but ignore the critical role and impact of the state, imperial and peripheral, on the manner in which this logic is played out over space.

Thus, the third and final criticism of NIDL and related theory relates to its limited emphasis on the state and underlying class relations. The role of the DIC state in re-establishing profitable conditions for accumulation has already been noted. But it is in the limited and one-sided treatment of the Third World state that NIDL theory is most deficient. In this view, the state is primarily treated as a guarantor of a cheap, plentiful and docile supply of labour through extra-economic (that is repressive) policies. Lipietz (1982, 1984) has referred to this indigenous version of primitive accumulation as 'bloody Taylorisation'. A secondary state function pertains to the provision of taxation and other incentives for industrial production. However, the state in some Third World countries has clearly had an impact well beyond this sphere. Driven by the nationalistic struggles of de-colonisation such states have striven to provide the general pre-conditions – that is, physical and social infrastructure – necessary for industrialisation, often rigidly controlling investment and trade patterns through direct intervention, tariffs, import quotas, foreign exchange controls and the like.

> While nationalism in power has not led to the demystification of oppressive class relations, control over the *government* has led to a number of economic 'openings' or possibilities; the national intermediaries can bargain over terms of dependency, diversify the sources of dependency, increase revenues, create a framework for the development of internal markets through social expenditure and state investments, promote diversification of production, create the basis for the expansion of the national bourgeoisie – anchored in either the state or private sector or both – and the petty bourgeoisie (mainly public employees), and open up opportunities for statist development policies. These possibilities are in large part contingent upon the type of international and national class alliances which are formed as well as the bargaining strength of the classes within the alliance [Petras 1983, p. 206].

It will be argued below that it is precisely in those countries which have attained NIC status that active state intervention has historically been most decisive, resulting in a transition to a regime of accumulation and mode of regulation which Lipietz (1984) terms 'peripheral Fordism'.

Uneven development and the internationalisation of capital

It is now possible to outline a theoretical account of uneven development, drawing in particular on Shaikh (1979/80) and Palloix (1973, 1977), in order both to explain the recent developmental histories of LDC and NIC economies and offer tentative forecasts as to what their likely futures may be.

Shaikh has developed a Marxist theory of international value, pitched at a high level of abstraction – assuming free competition, free trade, minimal state intervention, relatively fixed exchange rates, and the universal presence of a commodity money (gold) – and explicitly opposed to the neo-classical approach described above. DIC capitalists will, he argues, have an absolute cost advantage over their LDC counterparts across most sectors and industries, due we should note, to their longer and much more extensive process of industrialisation, culminating in a vastly more productive technological base, more complex infrastructural supports, more developed economic linkages, more appropriate organisational forms and more skilled workforce. Consequently, the prices of commodities traded internationally will in general be regulated by domestic prices in the DICs (adjusted for transport costs). LDC capitalists unable to compete at home or abroad in most areas will be squeezed into those few areas in which they either have an absolute cost advantage, say due to natural fertility or climate, those commodities peculiar to it (such as raw materials), perishables (food before efficient refrigeration) or those commodities with fluctuating world demands which cannot always be fully met by efficient DIC producers (Shaikh 1979/80, p. 39).

Moreover, this radically unequal 'old' international division of labour will be self-perpetuating and will *not* be ameliorated by automatic adjustments leading to a more equal pattern of international specialisation due to comparative advantage. In this model, DIC economies will build up chronic (permanent) balance of payment surpluses while the LDCs will suffer chronic deficits. The latter will meet their deficits by transferring money (gold) to the DICs.

The overall decline in the supply of money in the typical LDC is expressed through declining bank deposits, damped in part by a decline in the circulation demand for money and demand for loan capital brought about by falling effective demand. A declining supply of loanable funds in the credit system leads to rising domestic interest rates which further reduces domestic production by squeezing private investment. In other words, the results of trade deficits can be summarised as: curtailed production, falling bank reserves and rising interest rates.

Precisely the opposite occurs in the surplus DICs. The overall money supply will increase, leading to rising effective demand and production, rising bank reserves and falling interest rates. The *critical point* here is that the general level of prices in both deficit and surplus nations will remain unchanged, since prices expressed in the money commodity, gold, will only change if the labour socially necessary to produce commodities relative to gold changes. By rejecting the Quantity theory of money and replacing it with Marx's, Shaikh severs the neo-classical link between changes in the money supply and movements in general prices. Thus, price adjustments will not bring about specialisation due to comparative advantage and balance of trade disequilibria will tend to be permanent.

But this is not the end of the story. How will deficit nations go on financing accumulating international debts? In the short term, money capital will flow from DIC to LDC in order to reap the higher interest rates, until interest rates are equalised in both countries (discounted for risk). Secondly, direct investment or the export of productive capital by TNCs will be concentrated firstly in taking over existing LDC export industries through the transfer of their crushingly superior technology and organisational forms, and secondly in starting up new export industries in order to reap surplus profits from the exploitation of low wage labour, as described by NIDL theorists. Capital inflow, both portfolio and direct, helps LDC debtor nations to balance their international payments in the short term but at the expense of locking them into an asymmetric pattern of international specialisation only marginally less extreme than the primary pattern described above. Foreign portfolio investment will stem the decline in domestic loanable funds held in the banking system but will only be lent to profitable local enterprises – those existing and new industries able to survive the competition of DIC capitals. The direct investment of incoming TNCs will create some new industries locally, as they co-ordinate their global productive activities to take advantage of wage and tax differentials and so on, but as argued at length above this process will be limited and in some cases strictly temporary, especially in a period of intensified global crisis.

Moreover, from the point of view of local capital the effects of foreign investment will generally be disastrous. With the influx of more efficient foreign capital, the domestic capitals in the affected industries will either be driven into marginal roles or forced into still unaffected (but internationally competitive) areas or into the new industries created in response to the needs of the foreign-dominated sector (Shaikh 1979/80, p. 45). Thus, the hardening pattern of specialisation will actually undercut the potential social basis of more generalised LDC development — an active and dynamic indigenous bourgeoisie which under other circumstances (such as in conjunction with an interventionist indigenous state) might realise that potential.

In the longer term the deficit LDCs will be forced to cut imports back to their low export revenue earning capacity as the continuing drain on gold or reserves (accelerated by loan repayments and disinvestment) further reduces local effective demand and the confidence of DIC exporters and investors that they will continue to be paid and repaid, respectively. Thereafter, LDCs will bump along at low levels of output, employment, investment, trade and development, marginalised regions in a highly asymmetric international division of labour.

The results of this model are not significantly affected by the introduction of a more sophisticated and realistic international monetary system. Whether national currencies are on the gold standard or not, the intermediation of national central banks will generally bring about the relations between deficit/surplus and capital movements identified in the basic model, through conventional management of currency reserves and domestic interest rates. Similarly, once the neo-classical fiction of perfectly free exchange rates is ignored, the model's conclusions also hold in the real world of partially flexible or 'dirty' currency floats that has characterised world capitalism since the collapse of the Bretton Woods agreement in the early 1970s (Strange 1985; Wegner 1985; de Lattre 1985). The governments of deficit nations will not allow their currencies to depreciate too far for fear of further worsening their balance of payments by dissuading foreign capital inflow and encouraging a speculative capital flight in expectation of further devaluation. They will therefore step in past a certain point through their central banks in order to prop up the currency and squeeze imports and attract money capital by a tight domestic monetary policy, as the theory suggests.

Shaikh's model is a generalisation of Marx's theory of value and money in the international sphere. It offers a theory of the internationalisation of capital as the unity of the circuits of commodity capital (international trade), money capital (international loan capital movements) and productive capital (production relocation by TNCs) to use Palloix's (1977) terms. NIDL theory, as Jenkins notes, is fixated on the circuit of productive capital; 'since the three circuits are different aspects of a single process of internationalisation, however, such an approach again gives a partial picture of this phenomenon' (Jenkins 1984, p. 43). It is only by grasping the complex unity of the three circuits that it is possible to understand both the underlying structural predisposition to extreme uneven development and to identify the key factors responsible for its partial relaxation during the past two decades.

This latter period has seen two historically specific developments which have partially and selectively relaxed the structural limitations on LDC development specified above. Firstly, the prolonged and rapid expansion of world trade during the 1950s and 1960s, at the rate of 8 per cent per annum overall and 11 per cent for manufactured goods (Kaplinsky 1984a, p. 77) in a world of GATT negotiated reductions in trade barriers saw traditional LDC exports grow significantly. Rising foreign exchange earnings financed the importation of capital goods necessary to facilitate indigenous technological development and rising productivity – and hence, the *potential* for export-oriented industrialisation. Booming DIC domestic economies, especially in mass consumer industries opened up market niches for new LDC industries, supported by the limited degree of TNC relocation noted above. (We exclude oil exporting LDCs here, since after OPEC oil prices rises they represent a special case of aggressive Third World government intervention, discussed below.)

Secondly, international trade levelled off in the 1970s, one manifestation of generalised crisis, and was increasingly financed by the circulation of private capital flows through the transnational banks. During this decade private medium and long-term loans rose from just over a third to a half of the net capital inflow to non-oil exporting LDCs (World Bank 1981). This pool of expanding international liquidity was increasingly concentrated in the Euro-dollar markets beyond the control of national governments and supra-national organisations like the IMF (Aglietta 1985). In short, until the 1970s, the international banks were switching large amounts of money capital from the most advanced DICs and OPEC to the less advanced DICs (like Australia and New Zealand) and certain LDCs (Griffith-Jones and Rodriquez 1984), which were thereby able to finance a greater flow of imports and faster potential rate of development than even their impressive export growth allowed.

These developments represented a huge transfer of capital from DICs to LDCs, both direct and indirect (via OPEC). The major form of direct capital transfer was, as Petras (1984 p. 185) argues, *not* by way of TNC relocation in search of higher profits. As the crisis bit in the DICs, idle capital built up in the banking system to be lent overseas at high interest rates. Thus, whereas foreign investment in the LDCs rose annually by 2.7 per cent during the 1970s, private loans rose by 20 per cent per annum over the same period (World Bank 1981). OPEC's contribution was to transfer capital by way of a massive monopoly resource rent on DIC oil dependence, re-lent to the LDCs.

It is important to stress that the forces outlined above tended to encourage the reproduction on an extended scale of the *pre-existing* patterns of economic specialisation, including the pre-existing inequalities between particular LDCs. These forces, by themselves, would not have been sufficient to modify the structural determinants of uneven development specified in Shaikh's model. However, once that model has been developed at a more concrete level to include the active role of LDC states, these historically specific forces can be seen to have facilitated a significant degree of industrialisation and diversification in the Third World, albeit very unevenly concentrated, in a few economies, the NICs. But, to repeat the conclusion drawn in the preceding section; 'while significant changes in industrial development are taking place among a select number of Third World countries, the aggregate growth in Third World share of world manufacturing output and trade is still small and it is growing at a snail's pace' (Petras 1984, p. 190). For most LDCs, the structural constraints embedded in the internationalisation of capital have continued to block development, a fact only reinforced by DIC trade barriers and corrupt local regimes.

The primary impact of the state in the NICs, as opposed to other LDCs, has been the historical creation of a physical and social infrastructure supportive of self-sustaining indigenous capital accumulation. This has had two aspects. First, the provision of what Marx (1973, p. 139) termed the general preconditions of production or fixed capital of an independent kind (Harvey 1982, pp. 224–29); that is transport and communications networks, power, water and the built environment for production and exchange. Without an appropriate infrastructure capitalist production for sale on the world market will, in general be unprofitable, dissuading foreign productive investment and pre-empting indigenous accumulation, no matter how low wages are relative to those in the advanced economies where infrastructural supports have been constructed by both private and public sectors over a century of industrial accumulation. Too much of the aid and other capital inflow to the LDCs since World War II has been squandered through nationalistic zeal on inappropriate programmes (the 'big dam' or 'national airline' phenomenon), or corruptly appropriated by a parasitic political elite (the 'Swiss bank account' phenomenon). Overall, the NICs have managed, under strong state direction, to avoid these tendencies and build up a strong infrastructural base for accumulation.

Secondly, in many LDCs state power has been retained and monopolised by a traditional land-based and merchant ruling class, whose dominance depends on the maintenance of existing class relations embedded in an articulation of pre-capitalist and merchant capital modes of production with the consequent subordination of any indigenous industrial bourgeoisie. This condition has been described by dependency theory but mistakenly seen as part of the *cause* of resulting underdevelopment; it is not the cause of underdevelopment, *per se*, but part of the reason why most LDCs have not broken out of this subordinate position in an international division of labour imposed by the forces described above. With or without an existing local parasitic or comprador ruling class, an LDC will continue to remain underdeveloped until an active local industrial bourgeoisie emerges to secure economic dominance, especially with respect to the circulation of financial and commercial capital, and grasp state power.

Historically, this happened in the Asian NICs. In the case of South Korea and Taiwan, as Hamilton (1983) argues, Japanese colonial rule had broken the dominance of the traditional landed ruling class before World War II, leaving a legacy of physical infrastructure, a dispossessed peasantry and a strong nationalistic thrust towards post-war industrialisation on the material basis formed by the partial integration of the colonies into Japan's industrial war economy during the 1930s and the war itself. For South Korea 'an impressive structure of manufacturing industries, supported by an adequate infrastructure of transport and communication was inherited from the Japanese' (Datta-Chaudhuri 1981, p. 52).

Post-war developments subsequently entrenched strong, US backed (aided and armed) anti-communist nationalist governments. Referring to the four Asian NICs Hamilton (1983 p. 151) comments: 'while accumulation in the fifties was slow by later standards, it was highly formative. The study of the four reveals that the primitive accumulation of capital is as much a political process as an economic one'. In Taiwan and South Korea, the state took over the large majority of manufacturing capital, selling off light industries to dispossessed landowners and wealthy merchants and operating heavy industry bequeathed by the Japanese through state-owned enterprises. However, by the mid-1960s many such industries had been privatised as accumulated capital was progressively locked into the industrial circuit. 'The importance of the process lay not in the amassing of fortunes by individuals or firms but in the creation of a condition in which capital could be accumulated *industrially*; in other words, it was the process of *transforming* capital from agricultural and merchant forms into industrial form' (Hamilton 1983, p. 153). Capital was attracted to industry by its expulsion from large-scale landownership. Land reform imposed by the state decisively broke the power of landed property. It also created a patchwork of fragmented, inefficient owner-occupied farms. Through coercive taxes (in kind) and forcible state purchase of grain at low prices the agricultural surplus product was appropriated by the state to feed the rising mass of urban workers. State-provided cheap food achieved two things; firstly, it helped keep urban wages low and hence profits from industrial accumulation high; secondly, it forced large numbers of rural workers and small-scale farmers to migrate to the cities in search of work and subsistence. The expanding urban proletariat was also swelled by foreign immigration, especially in Taiwan. Thus, the state intervened to engineer both dimensions of the process of primitive accumulation – the creation of a class of industrial capitalists and the creation of an industrial working class. It subsequently maintained a political regime most conductive to industrial accumulation, through the continuing suppression of trade unions and other opposition and by not introducing a developed welfare state which would have provided a safety net or alternative for unemployed workers.

The colonial histories of Singapore and Hong Kong were very different but the interventionist role of the state was almost as decisive as in South Korea and Taiwan (though less so in Hong Kong than Singapore). Hong Kong accumulation also benefited from the influx of refugees, capitalists and workers, in the wake of the Chinese revolution (Lee 1981). Capital was partly forced to switch from commercial into industrial circulation with the loss of the Chinese re-export market and the declining economic role of British capital and military power in the Far East. In Singapore the state embarked on a concerted policy of publicly financed industrialisation, focused less on indigenous primitive accumulation and more on the attraction of foreign direct investment (TNCs) and the immigration of Malaysian workers.

However, intervention in the provision of infrastructure and the process of primitive accumulation does not exhaust the potential developmental role of the LDC state. A number of authors have pointed to the systematic way in which NIC states directly regulated capital flows, exchange rates, import controls and labour markets in the post-war period, only partially and very selectively liberalising these policies in the 1970s to take advantage of expanding world markets (Amsden 1979; Enos 1984; Luedde-Neurath 1980; Evans and Alizadeh 1984). Thus, a lengthy regime of Import Substitution Industrialisation (ISI) in the NICs may have been a critical pre-condition for rapid industrialisation in the 1970s and 1980s by encouraging a growing local market for manufactured goods, local economic linkages and an indigenous class of industrialists with the state subsidised space to develop a technically adequate base for international competitiveness – to reduce the crushing absolute cost advantages of DIC capitalists, in some industries at least. The TNCs which were persuaded to relocate did so not simply for low wages but because of an adequate infrastructure and the lure of an expanding domestic market sheltered behind high tariffs.

In summary, the recent rapid rate of NIC industrialisation must be seen, in part at least, as determined by strongly interventionist state policies both prior and continuing. It was precisely these economies that were best placed to benefit from the expansion in DIC markets, the selective flows of foreign direct investment and the circulation of bank mediated financial capital during the 1970s. In the latter instance, the massive flows of Euro dollar finance, noted above, were heavily focused on the NICs:

> Private banks clearly preferred lending to developing countries with relatively high per capita income, as well as those whose recent growth record was more impressive. Poor countries (both in income levels and/or natural resources) were not considered to be sufficiently 'credit worthy' to attract significant flows. As a result, private bank lending was heavily concentrated among the upper- and middle-income developing countries. As a result the four largest borrowers (Mexico, Brazil, South Korea and the Philippines) accounted for well over 60 per cent of total accumulated debts on non-OPEC, non-OECD developing countries to international banks in December 1982 [Griffith-Jones and Rodiguez 1984, p. 53].

However, the impact of strong governments, expanding world markets and idle financial capital has only loosened, probably temporarily, the structural determinants of uneven global development. In the first place, as stressed above, most LDCs continue to stagnate, showing minimal signs of deepening or widening industrialisation, locking into traditional exports and suffering chronic balance of payments problems only temporarily shored up by the increasingly nervous international banks. Industrialisation, to the extent that it has occurred, has been largely confined to light manufacturing; ' ... only in seven (developing) countries is 30 per cent or more of the value added in manufacturing other than light consumer goods industries: India, Kenya, South Korea, Mexico, Brazil, Argentina and Singapore ... Clearly whatever industrialisation has taken place is overwhelmingly located in light consumer goods areas' (Petras 1984, p. 191; Taiwan was excluded from the count). Hamilton (1983, pp. 163–65) has argued that even in the NICs a few industries, especially textiles, clothing, footwear and electronic consumer goods have dominated growth, though, especially in South Korea and Singapore, some heavy manufacturing industries like shipbuilding, petrochemicals, electrical machinery and transport equipment have also developed (see Table 8.3 above).

Hamilton goes on to argue that part of the reason for this highly specialised pattern of rapid industrialisation follows from the structure of indigenous NIC industrial capital – that is, from the generally small-scale, unconcentrated nature of capital enterprise, prior to the structural drive to capital concentration and centralisation embedded in the full dynamic of capital accumulation historically experienced in the DICs:

> Therefore indigenous capitals crowded into those industries which required only small initial fixed capital outlays and involved technologies that were not subject to rapidly increasing economies of scale. These tended to be highly labour-intensive; big Western corporations had a firm hold on capital-deep production processes and even the advantage of very cheap labour could not ease the difficulty of loosening such a grip [Hamilton 1983, p. 170; but see the empirical study by Kin and Tschoegly (1986) which presents evidence suggesting that the four Asian NICs have moved some way towards a more diversified industrial structure, characteristic of the DICs].

Prospects for Third World industrialisation

What, then, are the likely prospects for Third World industrialisation, both inside and outside the NICs in the coming decades?

In general, as Cline (1982) points out, it would be impossible for all LDCs to achieve simultaneously the same rate of export-driven growth as the NICs; such an outcome would require the LDCs to collectively increase their manufactured exports by more than 700 per cent to account for two-thirds of DIC manufactured imports, a trend which would certainly spark strong protective responses by DIC states. However, as Browett (1985, p. 5) stresses, this 'fallacy of composition' argument does not answer the question as to whether the few existing NICs will go on industrialising nor whether a few LDCs will emulate them by attaining NIC status.

There are several contemporary developments which suggest that the prospects for significant LDC industrialisation are dim. Firstly, as was stressed earlier, the DICs are themselves undergoing major technological and organisational restructuring, leading to a spatial reconcentration of productive activity. Secondly, the relatively open and expanding DIC markets are closing in the wake of what has been called 'the new protectionism'. An increasing range of tariff and non-tariff trade barriers (NTBs) are being thrown up, especially against LDC exports (UNCTAD 1983). 'These included voluntary export restrictions, orderly marketing arrangements, quotas, preferential government purchasing policies, local content requirements, and subsidies ... Moreover, as in the case of tariff measures, NTBs appear to be disproportionately aimed at LDC exports and escalate as the degree of processing increased ...' (Kaplinsky 1984a, pp. 77–8). Rising effective protection levels in the DICs will further encourage TNCs to reverse their (limited) initial pattern of Third World production relocation. LDC states are relatively powerless to respond to these protectionist measures imposed by the DICs.

Thirdly, private international liquidity is drying up. The private banks, over-committed to debt-encumbered, stagnant LDCs, are sharply reducing and restructuring their lending policies. Moreover, as profit rates rise after major restructuring in the DICs, international financial capital will flow more strongly back into those economies, reinforced by the US government's need to finance its escalating public debt; by mid-1987 America's foreign debt stood at almost $250 billion. Finally, a slow down in the Euro-dollar markets associated with falling world oil prices has placed a brake on this source of finance for LDC borrowers. The capacity of LDCs to stave off balance of payments crises, still less finance and implement coherent long-term industrialisation, will depend more and more on access to IMF provided or sanctioned finance.

IMF loans carry with them a high degree of 'conditionally'; that is agreement by the LDC state to impose a package of neo-classical policies, including reduced protection levels and reduction in state provision and regulation to allow 'free markets' to allocate resources to bring about specialisation according to comparative advantage. In terms of the model presented here, this is a recipe for de-industrialisation, for a reversal of the trend toward limited and selective post-war industrialisation; in short, for a return to a state of chronic underdevelopment. Kaplinsky (1984a, pp. 88–89) has raised a fourth factor dysfunctional for continuing Third World industrialisation – the significant growth in military expenditure by LDCs, rising from 20 per cent of the world total in 1960 to 30 per cent in 1980. Militarisation draws resources away from productive alternatives; it places a drain on limited foreign exchange, since the drive for military dominance in a region leads to an escalating demand for very sophisticated and very expensive weapons systems supplied indiscriminately by arms manufacturers located in the DICs, especially the US; and it props up parasitic military regimes of which the classic past example is the Philippines under Marcos. Given the crucial geo-political significance of the South-East Asian and Central American regions to US foreign policy, regional militarisation is likely to intensify in the foreseeable future.

Finally, to what extent might the NICs transcend these constraining developments in moving towards a deeper and more diversified pattern of industrialisation? Already there are clear signs that the NICs are in line for sharper protective responses by DIC economies, especially the US (Randall 1986; Michaely 1985). Brazil, Mexico and South Korea have already accumulated foreign debts of more than $US 100 billion and will face difficulties in re-financing and extending credit through the international banks, for reasons discussed above. The South Korean government, at least, has reacted by partly opening its stock market to attract foreign portfolio (but not equity) capital (Kaletsky 1985).

The role of large pension funds is likely to be crucial here. Recent World Bank estimates suggest that US, Japanese and European funds now control more than $US 2000 million and are beginning to move into the growing stock markets of the Pacific Rim – especially South Korea, Taiwan, Malaysia and Mexico – as well as Brazil and India. In general, further NIC development will depend on whether, and the extent to which, indigenous industrial capital, adequately supported by facilitative state policies, can continue to restructure, technologically and organisationally, in order to compete effectively with DIC capitalists in a situation of sluggish world markets, financial stringency and rising protection levels. Of critical importance will be the foreign investment strategies of Japanese TNCs, closely supported by the Japanese government.

Recent Japanese direct investment patterns (see Table 8.6) have been dominated by three strategic aims; firstly, and quantitatively of most significance, investment in the US and Europe close to final markets; secondly, in LDCs (especially Indonesia) to develop crucial raw material supplies for export to Japan; and thirdly, investment in NIC industries, including joint ventures, in both intermediate component and final product areas (Modak 1985; Franko 1984; Sazanami 1986; Nemetz 1986).

TABLE 8.6   *Japanese direct investment, 1984–85*

	Investment $US million	% Share
Asia:	1 628	16.0
Brunei	5	0.1
Indonesia	374	3.7
Malaysia	142	1.4
Philippines	46	0.5
Thailand	119	1.2
Hong Kong	412	4.1
Singapore	225	2.2
South Korea	107	1.1
Taiwan	65	0.6
China	114	1.1
Other	21	0.2
North America	3 544	34.9
Europe	1 937	19.1
Latin America	2 290	22.6
Middle East	273	2.7
Africa	326	3.2
Australia	157	1.5
Total	10 155	100.0

SOURCE Awandohara 1986, p. 72.

Rising DIC protection levels will accentuate DIC location by Japanese TNCs to the distinct advantage of direct investment in the LDCs, but further NIC relocation may also occur in order to preempt or defuse the political backlash against Japan's chronic trade surplus, especially with the US. Such investment may take the form of joint-venture or sub-contracting arrangements whereby Japanese produced components are processed to final product stage for export to the US and Europe, thereby appearing in the trade figures as NIC rather than Japanese exports.

Kim (1986) has found that this pattern of 'global production sharing' (GPS) has increasingly characterised the Japanese-based electronics industry. Kim *et al.* (1986) have demonstrated that the GPS strategy now characterises a range of Japanese industries, especially the labour intensive areas and, less so, in technology-intensive ones.

Production for the *Japanese* market, however, is still strongly dominated by Japanese-located firms. What has occurred, however, is a degree of decentralisation to NICs in the production of component parts, especially in South Korea and Taiwan. There are, however, dangers here to the host NICs.

Although there are (many) examples of increased sales for NIC exporters in Japan, such exports are nearly all of parts, not finished products. This pattern of trade will not change the dominance of Japan in the production of value-added manufactured products for its home market, but by creating a string of parts-producing satellites, Japanese manufacturers will be able to control – to a worrying extent – the Asian regional structure of some manufacturing. The subjection and gearing of manufacturing capacity to Japanese needs according to the dictates of its own and foreign markets, could result in the formation of a multi-tiered sub-contracting system akin to the Japanese model, where costs are kept down by keeping in line competing sub-contractors [Roscoe 1986, p. 60].

The current demands for new protection measures against Japanese industry concentrated in the US Congress, is a *political* response to a chronic imbalance in international trade expressed by the *permanent* tendency of the Japanese economy to build up trade surpluses. Variable exchange rates and an appreciating yen have *not*, as neo-classical economics holds, automatically re-established balance. By continuing productive reinvestment, strategic market development and strategic foreign investment to both minimise raw material (including energy) costs and avoid high domestic wages, Japanese capital has been able to continuously expand exports. 'Japan has turned the economic theory of exchange rate trade adjustment on its head by a limited capacity to increase imports and an ability to sustain export volumes. It has also turned the theory of free trade based on comparative advantage on its head' (Walsh 1987, p. 13). Japan's political response to US protectionism may, as Walsh suggests, be to negotiate bilateral deals favouring American wheat, coal, beef and so on, in the Japanese home markets which would have a devastating impact on Australian (and Canadian) exports. It is this economic or trade threat to small Pacific economies like Australia that coercively ties the latter into America's regional nuclear and defence strategy. An independent foreign policy – for example involving the denial of port facilities to US nuclear warships – risks not just the loss of US markets, through the direct implementation of discriminatory trade barriers but indirectly the loss of Japanese markets as well.

In summary, in the short term the NICs are likely to benefit from the high value of the yen and protectionist responses aimed initially at Japanese industry. However, as noted above, in the longer term, NIC exports are unlikely to be left unaffected by the new protectionism, especially as DIC states come to recognise the degree of Japanese industrial re-exporting entailed. Nor will Japanese investment necessarily continue to flow as quickly into the Asian NICs in future. There are already signs that Japanese TNCs are looking towards Mexico and Brazil as more strategic bases for export launches to the American markets (Roscoe 1986, p. 62). High US interest rates continue to attract Japanese investors, reducing the potential drive of Japanese direct investment overall and making finance scarcer for NIC industrial capitalists. Japanese capital is also being partly switched into real estate development in selected DICs and oil-exporting LDCs in the search for higher profits, a point developed further in the next section. Nevertheless, if continuing Japanese financed NIC growth is problematic, the prospects for the non-industrialised LDCs is grim indeed.

During the past three to five years, while Japanese investment in the entire East Asian area has flagged (at least by comparison with booming investment in the U.S. and Europe) the fall-off has been distinctly more noticeable in the four major non-industrial members of ASEAN, than in the Northeast Asian NICs [Smith 1986, p. 57].

Finally, it has been stressed that the NICs relatively successful industrialisation drive has been critically dependent on the role of their domestic anti-democratic regimes. Parliamentary democracy has *not* been the 'ideal shell' for Third World capitalist development. Indeed, primitive industrial accumulation in the NICs has more closely approached the Soviet model than Western experience. To date, the NIC states have been able to maintain reasonably tight social control. However, as this is written, South Korea is experiencing its worst student and worker riots for a decade. If the Korean industrial 'miracle' falters, opposition forces may succeed in mobilising a significant political challenge to the current regime, thereby undermining the political basis of the current industrialisation strategy which has been so successful in the past.

Conclusion

During the past 20 years the Asia-Pacific region has become an increasingly important part of the capitalist world economy. The new and complex patterns of uneven development unfolding there suggest that conventional theoretical accounts of development, both conservative and radical, are inadequate to capture, still less explain, the full picture. It has been argued in this paper that in order to understand the emergence of the Pacific Rim as an integrated but diversified region, it is necessary to consider both the historically contingent factors encouraging limited and selective Third World industrialisation during this period, as well as the underlying structural forces which constrained development within such limited and selective lines. It has also been argued that *future* Third World industrialisation in both the NICs and LDCs is likely to be severely constrained by the reconcentration of industrial and financial capital in the DICs, the political responses of DIC governments to balance of payments deficits, the further weakening of class power of organised labour in the DICs and the continuing waste of resources in the LDCs on inappropriate development programmes and rising military expenditures.

REFERENCES

M. Aglietta, 'The Creation of International Liquidity' in L. Tsoukalis (ed.), *The Political Economy of International Money: In Search of a New Order* (London: Sage, 1985).

A. Altshuler *et al.*, *The Future of the Automobile* (Cambridge: MIT Press, 1984).

S. Amin, *Accumulation on a World Scale* (New York: Monthly Review Press, 1974).

S. Amin, *Unequal Development: An Essay on the Social Formation of Peripheral Capitalism* (New York: Monthly Review Press, 1976).

A. H. Amsden, 'Taiwan's Economic History: A Case of Etatisme and a Challenge to Dependency Theory', *Modern China*, vol. 5, no. 3 (1979) pp. 341–80.

G. Arrighi, 'Towards a Theory of Capitalist Crisis', *New Left Review* 111 (1978).

S. Awanohara, 'The "Big Player" as an Unloved but Vital Partner', *Far Eastern Economic Review* (12 June 1986).

B. Balassa, *The Newly Industrialising Countries in the World Economy* (Oxford: Pergamon Press, 1981).

P. Baran, *The Political Economy of Growth* (New York: Monthly Review Press, 1957).

M. Berry, 'The Political Economy of Australian Urbanisation', *Progress in Planning*, vol. 22, part 1 (1982).

M. Berry, 'Corporate Accumulation and the Corporate City' in J. B. McLoughlin and M. Huxley (eds), *Urban Planning in Australia: Critical Readings* (Melbourne: Longman-Cheshire, 1986).

F. Blackaby (ed.), *Deindustrialisation* (London: Heinemann, 1979).

B. Bluestone and B. Harrison, *The Deindustrialisation of America* (New York: Basic Books, 1982).

J. Browett, 'Industrialisation in the Global Periphery: The Significance of the Newly Industrialised Countries', paper presented to *Urban and Regional Impact of the New International Division of Labour Conference* (University of Hong Kong: 13–20 August 1985).

S. Castles et al., *Here for Good: Western Europe's New Ethnic Minorities* (London: Pluto Press, 1984).

S. Castles and G. Kosack, *Immigrant Workers and Class Structures in Western Europe* (London: Oxford University Press, 1973).

W. R. Cline, 'Can the East Asian Model of Development be Generalised?,' *World Development*, vol. 10, no. 2 (1982) pp. 81–90.

S. Corbridge, 'Capitalism, Industrialism and Development', *Progress in Human Geography*, vol. 10, no. 1 (1986) pp. 48–67.

G. Crough and T. Wheelwright, *Australia, a Client State* (Ringwood: Penguin, 1982).

M. Daly, 'The Revolution in International Capital Markets: Urban Growth and Australian Cities', *Environment and Planning A*, 16 (1984) pp. 1003–20.

M. Daly and M. Logan, 'Australia's Role in the Pacific Basin: Urban Impacts of International Capital Flows' in C. Adrian (ed.), *Urban Impacts of Foreign Investment in Australia* (Canberra: AIUS, 1984).

M. K. Datta-Chaudhuri, 'Industrialisation and Foreign Trade: The Development Experiences of South Korea and the Philippines' in E. Lee (ed.), *Export-led Industrialisation and Development* (Geneva: ILO, 1981).

A. de Lattre, 'Floating, Uncertainty and the Real Sector' in L. Tsoukalis (ed.), *The Political Economy of International Money* (London: Sage, 1985).

A. Emmanuel, *Unequal Exchange* (New York: Monthly Review Press, 1972).

J. Enos, 'Government Intervention in the Transfer of Technology: The Case of South Korea', *Institute of Development Studies Bulletin*, vol. 15, no. 2 (1984) pp. 26–31.

D. Ernst, *The Global Race in Microelectronics: Innovation and Corporate Strategies in a Period of Crisis* (Frankfurt: Campus, 1982).

D. Evans and P. Alizadeh, 'Trade, Industrialisation and the Visible Hand', *Journal of Development Studies*, vol. 21, no. 1 (1984) pp. 22–46.

F. T. Fitzgerald, 'Sociologies of Development' in P. Limqueco and B. MacFarlane (eds), *Neo-Marxist Theories of Development* (London: Croom Helm, 1983).

A. G. Frank, *Capitalism and Underdevelopment in Latin America* (New York: Monthly Review Press, 1967).

A. G. Frank, *World Accumulation* (New York: Monthly Review Press, 1978).

L. B. Franko, 'The Pattern of Japanese Multinational Investment', *Multinational Business* 1 (1984) pp. 1–11.

F. Frobel, 'The Current Development of the World Economy: Reproduction of Labour and Accumulation of Capital on a World Scale', *Review* 4 (Spring 1982) pp. 1–19.

F. Froebel, G. Heinrichs and O. Kreye, *The New International Division of Labour* (Cambridge University Press, 1980).

S. Griffith-Jones and E. Rodriguez, 'Private International Finance of the LDCs', *Journal of Development Studies*, vol. 21, no. 1 (1984) pp. 47–73.

C. Hamilton, 'Capitalist Industrialisation in the Four Little Tigers of East Asia' in Limqueco and MacFarlane, op. cit. (1983).

C. S. Harris, 'The Magnitude of Job Loss from Plant Closings and the Generation of Replacement Jobs: Some Recent Evidence', *Annals of the American Academy of Political and Social Science*, 475 (September 1984) pp. 15–27.

R. C. Hill, 'The Global Factory and the Company Town: The Changing Division of Labour, in the International Automobile Industry', paper presented to *The Urban and Regional Impact on the New International Division of Labour Conference* (University of Hong Kong: 13–20 August 1985).

K. Hoffman and R. Rush, *Microelectronics and Clothing: The Impact of Technological Change on a Global Industry* (Geneva: ILO, 1983).

R. Jenkins, 'Divisions over the International Division of Labour', *Capital and Class* 22 (1984) pp. 28–57.

D. Jones and M. Anderson, 'Competition in the World Auto Industry: Implications for Production Location', mimeo (University of Sussex, 1983).

A. Kaletsky, 'The Japanning of Asia', *Financial Planning*, vol. 14, no. 9 (1985) pp. 67–68.

R. Kaplinsky, 'The International Context for Industrialisation in the Coming Decade', *Journal of Development Studies*, vol. 21, no. 1 (1984a) pp. 75–96.

R. Kaplinsky, *Automation: The Technology and Society* (London: Longman, 1984).

K. J. Kim *et al.*, 'An Empirical Study of the Transnational Product Sharing of the Asian NICs with Japan', *Journal of International Business Studies*, vol. 17, no. 2 (1986) pp. 117–30.

W. C. Kim, 'Global Product Sharing: An Empirical Investigation of the Pacific Electronics Industry', *Management International Review*, vol. 26, no. 2 (1986) pp. 62–70.

W. C. Kim and A. E. Tschoegl, 'The Regional Balance of Industrialisation:

an Empirical Investigation of the Asian Pacific Area', *Journal of Developing Areas*, vol. 20, no. 2 (1986) pp. 173–83.

E. Lee, *Export-led Industrialisation and Development* (Geneva: ILO, 1981).

P. Limqueco and B. MacFarlane (eds), *Neo-Marxist Theories of Development* (London: Croom Helm, 1983).

A. Lipietz, 'Towards Global Fordism', *New Left Review* 132 (1982).

A. Lipietz, 'Imperialism, or the Beast of the Apocalypse', *Capital and Class* 22 (1984) pp. 81–106.

I. M. D. Little, 'The Experience and Causes of Rapid Labour-intensive Development in Korea, Taiwan Province, Hong Kong and Singapore and the Possibilities of Emulation' in E. Lee, op. cit. (1981).

I. M. D. Little, *Economic Development: Theory, Policy and International Relations* (New York: Basic Books, 1982).

R. Luedde-Neurath, 'Export Orientation in South Korea: How Helpful is Dependency Theory to its Analysis?', *Institute of Development Studies Bulletin*, vol. 12, no. 1 (1980) pp. 48–53.

D. McEacken and G. O'Leary, 'Capitalist Recession and Industrialisation in the Third World: Reflections on the Warren Thesis', *Journal of Australian Political Economy* 7 (1980) pp. 86–104.

G. Manay, *The Multinational Automobile Industry* (New York: St. Martins Press, 1981).

M. Michaely, 'The Demand for Protection Against Exports of Newly Industrialising Countries', *Journal of Policy Modelling*, vol. 7, no. 1 (1985) pp. 123–32.

N. D. Modak, 'The Asian Pacific Basin', *Canadian Banker*, vol. 92, no. 1 (1985) pp. 30–33.

P. N. Nemetz, 'The Pacific Rim: Investment, Development and Trade', *Journal of Business Administration*, vol. 16, nos. 1 and 2 (1986) pp. 1–5.

J. O'Connor, *Accumulation Crisis* (Oxford: Blackwell, 1984).

C. Palloix, 'The Internationalisation of Capital and the Circuit of Social Capital', in H. Radice (ed.), *International Firms and Modern Imperialism* (Harmondsworth: Penguin, 1975 [originally 1973]).

C. Palloix, 'The Self-Expansion of Capital on a World Scale', *Review of Radical Political Economics*, vol. 9, no. 2 (1977) pp. 1–28.

D. Perry and A. Watkins, 'Contemporary Dimensions of Uneven Urban Development: A Research Report', paper presented to the *Ninth World Congress of the International Sociological Association*, Urban and Regional Development Research Committee (University of Uppsala, Sweden: 1978).

J. Petras, 'New Perspectives on Imperialism and Social Classes in the Periphery', in Limqueco and MacFarlane, op. cit., (1983).

J. Petras, 'Toward a Theory of Industrial Development in the Third World', *Journal of Contemporary Asia*, vol. 14, no. 2 (1984) pp. 182–203.

J. Petras, P. McMichael and R. Rhodes, 'Imperialism and the Contradictions of Development', *New Left Review* 85 (1974) pp. 83–104.

J. Petras, 'Industrialisation in the Third World' in J. Petras (ed.), *Critical Perspectives on Imperialism and Social Classes in the Third World* (London: Monthly Review Press, 1978).

M. J. Piore, *Birds of Passage: Migrant Labour and Industrial Societies* (Cambridge University Press, 1979).

J. Rada, *International Division of Labour and Technology* (Geneva: ILO, 1984).

S. Randall, 'Seeing the Pacific Rim Beyond Japan: Problems in the American Business Press', *Business Forum*, vol. 11, no. 4 (1986) pp. 12–16.

B. Roscoe, 'The NICs: Bits and Pieces of a Promising Surge in Sales', *Far Eastern Economic Review* (12 June 1986) pp. 59–62.

Y. Sazanami, 'Japanese Trade in the Pacific Rim: The Relationship Between Trade and Investment', *Journal of Business Administration*, vol. 16, nos. 1 and 2 (1986) pp. 53–73.

H. Schmitz, 'Industrialisation Strategies in Less Developed Countries: Some Lessons of Historical Experience', *Journal of Development Studies*, vol. 21, no. 1 (1984) pp. 1–21.

D. Seers (ed.), *Dependency Theory: A Critical Reassessment* (London: Francis Pinter, 1981).

A. Shaikh, 'Foreign Trade and the Law of Value: Parts I and II', *Science and Society* (1979/80) pp. 281–302; pp. 27–57.

C. Smith, 'Tokyo's Neighbourly Urge', *Far Eastern Economic Review* (12 June 1986) pp. 56–9.

S. Strange, 'Interpretations of a Decade' in Tsoukalis, op. cit. (1985).

United Nations Conference on Trade and Development, *Non-tariff Barriers Affecting the Trade of Developing Countries and Transparency in World Trading Conditions: the Inventory of Non-tariff Barriers* (Geneva: United Nations, 1983).

I. Wallerstein, *The Modern World System* (New York: Academic Press, 1974).

M. Walsh, 'Whoever Governs, Trading Won't Be Easy', *Age* (26 June 1987).

B. Warren 'Imperialism and Capitalist Industrialisation', *New Left Review* 81 (1973) pp. 112–41.

B. Warren, 'The Post-war Economic Experience of the Third World', *Journal of Australian Political Economy*, 3 (1978) pp. 6–54.

B. Warren, *Imperialism: Pioneer of Capitalism* (London: Verso, 1980).

M. Wegner, 'External Adjustment in a World of Floating: Different National Experiences in Europe', in Tsoukalis op. cit. (1985).

L. E. Westphal, 'The Republic of Korea's Experience with Export-led Industrial Development', *World Development*, vol. 6, no. 3 (1978) pp. 347–82.

World Bank, *World Development Report, 1981* (London: Oxford University Press, 1981).

World Bank, *World Development Report, 1984* (London: Oxford Uuniversity Press, 1984).

9 The Infernal Logic of the Debt Crisis

Ernest Mandel[1]

The growing indebtedness of the so-called Third World countries and the chain reactions it is unleashing are only one aspect of a much broader phenomenon. The fundamental problem is the overheating of credit, the locomotive of the late capitalist economy. This must be stressed so that it will be clear that the present financial crisis is the organic result of the worldwide expansion that ensued during the post-war boom, which extended from 1940–48 to 1968–73.[2]

Far from being the result of the fecklessness of the underdeveloped countries, of their propertied ruling classes or their governments, this growing indebtedness is only a specific manifestation of the key role that the inflation of credit – and thus the swelling of all forms of debts – played in stimulating growth (or, more properly, in delaying the crisis) after World War II in all capitalist industrialised countries.

In reality, since 1940 we have been living in an age of permanent inflation. Inflation and indebtedness are to a large extent synonyms. Inflation is, in fact, essentially bank money inflation,[3] and inflation of credit and therefore a swelling of debts.

We have already pointed out on many occasions that after World War II, capitalism floated to prosperity on an ocean of debt. To grasp the importance of this phenomenon, you have first to look at its extent. Today just the debt denominated in dollars exceeeds the astronomical sum of $8 trillion. This broke down roughly at the end of 1985 as is shown in Table 9.1.

It is evident that the Third World debt that has provoked such ungenerous commentary from banking circles is only a modest part of the total world debt in dollars, scarcely more than 10 per cent. Since the Third World debt also includes that of China, it is spread over two-thirds of the population of the planet. A tenth of the debt for two-thirds of the people is hardly excessive.

The recriminations by banking circles reflect the bourgeois adage that 'only the rich get credit', put here in cruder terms, that 'you ought to have given credit only to the rich'.

217

TABLE 9.1   *Accumulated debt at end-1985*

Countries and regions	Debts in billions of dollars
US public debt	2000
US corporate debt	2800
US household debt	1900
Third World debt	0.950
Public debt (denominated in dollars) of other countries, both capitalist and workers' states	0.700

These debt figures have only an indicative value. They do not include the public and private debt denominated in 'national' currencies by all the capitalist countries other than the US. Nonetheless, they have a real operational usefulness inasmuch as they reveal the vulnerability of the US banking system and of the international monetary system based on a special role for the dollar.

Let me recall briefly by what mechanisms the inflation of credit and the swelling of debt in the short run cushion the main contradictions of contemporary capitalism.

Household debt makes it possible to reduce temporarily the gap between the growing production capacity of enterprises making consumer goods and the much more modest growth of the purchasing power of the masses. A part of consumer durables (above all houses and automobiles) are bought on credit.

Corporate debt makes it possible temporarily to reduce the gap between the rate of capital accumulation and the rate of increase in profits. It thereby makes it possible to attenuate for a time the effects of the tendency for the average rate of profit to drop. The tempo of accumulation is maintained, inasmuch as part of new investment (purchases of new machines, additional quantities of raw materials and so forth) is financed on credit and not by profits.

The swelling of the public debt makes it possible to mitigate momentarily the fiscal crisis of the state, that is, to reduce the gap between the rate of increase of public spending and the much slower increase in state incomes, especially in taxes.[4]

Of course, debt can only play this role of cushioning some of the contradictions inherent in the capitalist mode of production for a certain time and within certain limits. The sharpness of these contradictions means that more and more credit, and therefore more and more inflation, is needed to achieve this effect. This leads inevitably to an overheating of inflation. But once inflation overheats and goes beyond a certain threshold, it can no longer fuel expansion. It even begins to choke off growth. It then becomes one of the factors reversing the long wave of depression that is now underway.[5]

This process is what has led to the shift from the capitalist economic policy of Keynesianism (stimulating demand and therefore moderate inflation) to monetarism (re-establishing monetary stability at any cost, even that of stagnation and economic depression). It is not the shift in economic policy that led to the turn in the economic situation. It is the reshuffling of priorities in the bourgeoisie's objectives as a result of the changed objective situation that led to the alteration in economic policy, at a time when that change in the economic situation was already a fact.

After 1945, the number-one objective of the major capitalist countries (North America, Western Europe, Japan) was social and political stabilisation. That led to an orientation toward full employment and a preference for Keynesian techniques. After 1968 and especially after 1973, the absolute priority shifted back to boosting the rate of profit, if necessary at the cost of massive unemployment and sharpening social tensions.

BOURGEOIS INTERESTS DEFENDED BY INDIVIDUAL AGENTS

What characterises bourgeois society is, notably, the fact that the general interests of the bourgeoisie (expressed most often by the bourgeois state) are defended by individual agents (politicians, top civil servants, business people) who in 99 per cent of the cases cannot abstract from their own private interests.

The general expansion of credit after 1940 (1948) undoubtedly suited the general interests of the bourgeoisie. It was undoubtedly also stimulated by the banks, which do not in the first instance pursue the goal of serving the general interest of big capital. They seek above all to increase their own profits – banking profits. When the economic situation is good, when the barometer is high, the general interests of the bourgeoisie and the quest for private profit by the banks coincide to a very large extent. The banks then function as centres for the 'objective socialisation' of capital. They collect capital from firms and households that have a surplus and direct it toward those firms (and since World War II to a growing extent toward the households of the upper strata of the petty bourgeoisie) that need it to expand their investments and buying.

However, when the system is in crisis, this tendency for the general interests of the bourgeoisie to coincide with the profit-making interest of the banks is thrown out of kilter. The special interest of the banks — to defend above all else their incomes and their own profitability — can come into contradiction with the general interest of capital, which is to restore the profitability of the system as a whole, especially of the main trusts, monopolies and financial groups.

In seeking supplementary profits, the banks engage in practices that upset the stability of the system as a whole, at least in the longer run. State overseeing of the banks, which was extended after the traumatic experience of the 1931–33 banking crisis, is powerless against this problem, which is inherent in private ownership,[6] in competition and in the profit motive as the main driving force of the capitalist economy.

Banking profits come essentially from the difference between the interest rate for deposits and the interest brought by loans. The more bank deposits swell, the greater the incentives for the banks in extending loans at higher than average interest rates.

After the shock of rising oil prices in 1973, the incomes of a number of oil-exporting countries went to swell deposits in a series of American and British banks (and, to a lesser extent, German, Swiss and Japanese ones, as well as those in some other countries). These were the famous petro-dollars. The banks faced the problem of finding someone to whom to loan this new money capital. However, the long depression that had just begun in the imperialist countries at the same time reduced the demand for supplementary credit by firms and households, which were already excessively in debt. To find new debts, the banks therefore turned elsewhere, essentially to the Third World countries, and, to a lesser extent, to the bureaucratised workers' states. It was the banks that offered these loans to the Third World; it was not the Third World that came to the banks begging for them.[7]

The operation was stimulated by three special conditions that came together in the mid-1970s. First of all, there was a desynchronisation between the depression in the imperialist countries on the one hand and in Latin America and South-East and East Asia on the other.[8] Thus, the illusion was produced that the solvency of the dependent semi-industrialised countries, at least in these regions, was growing.

Secondly, these countries were subject to the imposition of higher interest rates, which they were obliged to pay because of the chronic capital shortage from which they suffer, when real interest rates — allowing for inflation — were very low and sometimes even negative in the imperialist countries.[9] Moreover, the private banks filled a gap left open by the abdication of the international capitalist bodies, or more precisely by the reluctance of the imperialist governments, and first of all Washington, to function in the general interest of the capitalist system in a time of crisis.

The sky-rocketing oil price had redistributed surplus value (and its capitalisation in the form of money capital on the international scale). The main losers from this redistribution were the so-called Third World countries that were not oil exporters. The chief gainers were the possessing classes of the oil-exporting countries. Balance-of-payments deficits threatened to choke off the capacity of the non-oil-exporting countries to import not only producers' goods but even vital raw materials for their growing industries and even food.

A problem, then, of recycling the petro-dollars was objectively posed. It was necessary to lend the excess from the OPEC countries to those countries with greater deficits. This in general, is what the private banks did. However, they did it in a precipitous and imprudent way and for the sake of big private profits. And here another phenomenon comes into play — the progressive decline in standards of the leading personnel of the international banking system.

During the whole period opened up by World War II, there was a considerable widening of credit operations and a no less spectacular extension of purely speculative operations in the framework of the world banking system. This expansion can be seen in particular from the time that the dollar became unconvertible, that is toward the end of the 1960s. Speculation turned toward raw materials, gold, currency exchange rates, land and works of art. It extended during the upturn in 1983–85 to gigantic fusions of firms manipulated by outside interme- diaries involving thousands of millions of dollars.[10]

In these conditions, more and more traditional directors (some would say flatly, on the shady side of the law) have turned up at the head of major branches of the big banks, or even at the head of these banks themselves.[11] They operate with a view to maximising their profits in the short term, without taking account of the risks. The result is a succession of unexpected gains and losses, seriously undermining the solidity of the banking system as a whole.

Speculation, personal corruption, crises of national solvency and crises of solvency of the banking system intertwine more and more. An impressive series of loans to Third World countries have been diverted, at the source, so to speak, to serve the private ends of bourgeois layers in those countries who are seeking to cover themselves against galloping inflation and the threat of revolutionary crises.

Capital flight has been fostered by foreign loans and it in turn increases balance-of-payments deficits, which lead to a new round of increasing debt. The debt spiral widens, for the benefit of the possessing classes and at the expense of the popular masses.

The scope of this capital flight on the part of the bourgeoisies of the main Third World debtor countries was recently assessed by the magazine *Intereconomics* on the basis of statistics from the Organisation for Economic Cooperation and Development (OECD), the International Monetary Fund (IMF) and the World Bank. This study gave the results shown in Table 9.2.[13]

TABLE 9.2   *Clandestine export of capital from selected countries*

Country	Clandestine capital exports 1976–82 (in millions of dollars)	In per cent of national debt to foreign banks*
Argentina	17 150	80.5*
Mexico	13 488[12]	54.0*
Venezuela	8454	65.4*
Indonesia	5164	34.2*
Egypt	3944	44.3*
Nigeria	2743	43.3*
India	2132	33.3*
Syria	1889	96.0*

*Short-term debt

This list is far from complete, since it does not include the flight of capital from countries such as Brazil, the Philippines, South Korea or Thailand. This capital flight is deemed not to exist, when everyone knows of glaring examples of such practices by the 'great families' of these bourgeoisies.[14] This statistical oversight arises from the fact that the figures cited are aggregates and do not cover, in the cases cited, either short-term debt or fluctuations in exchange reserves.

Once again, the ungracious commentary by imperialist financial circles about this capital flight in the so-called Third World countries is tainted by a large dose of hypocrisy. It is an unchallengeable fact that possessing classes of the Third World countries are rotten to the core. But it is also true that in order for there to be corruption, there have to be both the corrupted and the corrupters. The corrupters and their accomplices in this case are the imperialist banks.

Moreover, most of all there needs to be a general context favourable to an unbridled quest for private enrichment. This general context is called the market economy, the money economy and above all the generalised market economy, that is, bourgeois society, the capitalist mode of production.

Indebtedness went out of control in the Third World at the time I mentioned, at the beginning of the 1970s. At that time, the overall debt of the semi-colonial and dependent countries amounted to $150 000 million. Today, it exceeds $900 000 million. This sky-rocketing of the debt is not essentially a product of political developments, although these have played a not inconsiderable role, nor of plots and counterplots. It is the result precisely of the inner dialectic of the capitalist mode of production as a whole, both on the international scale and on the scale of the main countries concerned.

Once set off by the recycling of petro-dollars, the overheating of debt in the Third World has been kept going by a series of mechanisms that operate more or less spotaneously, or at least are not under anybody's control, neither the Third World governments or the possessing classes of these countries; nor the imperialist banks, the imperialist governments, or the bourgeoisies of the imperialist centres taken as a whole.

The inflow of fresh capital into the underdeveloped countries is only invested in part and therefore can only in part provide new resources. And, thus, it can only have a partial effectiveness in generating new income to pay the interest on the debt and to reimburse the capital borrowed. This is an initial source of imbalance and no doubt the main one.

THE LAW OF VALUE OPERATES IMPLACABLY

Part of this capital serves to cover the operating costs of the economy and the state, or to maintain it at a given level of activity — to finance the payment of higher oil prices or importing raw materials not covered by exports. Another part is diverted to parasitic speculation. Finally, a part is directly appropriated by the possessing classes and held outside the country.

The Third World countries' exports, which are supposed to increase in the long term to the point of being able to pay the service on the debt and reimburse the principal, are not growing everywhere or always to the desired extent. The law of value is operating implacably. It is redistributing on a world scale demand as well as supply, the allotment of the means of production and of labour power. However, this is precisely a spontaneous readjustment, that is, one that is chaotic, unpredictable, and above all, one that is desynchronised from country to country, to say nothing of continent to continent.

This gives rise to enormous imbalances, which it is no use trying to dismiss as 'temporary'. Everything is temporary by definition in the capitalist economy, except private property in general and the unbridled chase after it. But its precise distribution among the various capitalists, sectors and factions of the capitalist class, is always temporary. This is always being upset by new facts, that is, by the law of combined and uneven development.

Thus, the temporary rise in the oil prices gave a boost to possessing classes such as those in Saudi Arabia, Kuwait and Mexico, while the economies of Argentina, Brazil and India were violently shaken up. The tables were turned on the other hand with a spectacular improvement in the balance of payments of South Korea and Brazil, while Mexico and the OPEC countries were thrown into a tail-spin by the drop in the price of oil.

The overall expansion in the world market, then, has been less than what would be needed for all of the debt-ridden countries to expand their exports to the extent necessary for regular repayment of the debt.

This is all the more true because throughout the 1970s and the 1980s, the economies of the imperialist countries have been marked by long-term depression. This has held back any expansion of exports from the Third World countries to the imperialist centres. At times this trend has been strengthened by protectionist measures.

The example of the multifibre agreement concerning exports of textile products (including clothing) from Asia and Latin America is the clearest expression of such protectionism. There have been similar restrictions on certain food products (sugar, coffee and others).

Of course, the share of exports of Third World manufactured goods in world trade has increased spectacularly over the last decade. The US trade balance in such products has gone into the red (which is not true either for capitalist Europe or for Japan). Today, the US is importing more manufactured products from the dependent semi-industrialised countries than it is exporting to them.

However, it is a small number of countries that have profited from this rise and a small number of products – Brazilian footwear and steel, South Korean electronics, goods assembled in Hong Kong and other examples. This is too little to get the Third World out of trouble. It is not enough to defuse the debt time bomb. Given the fact that current production is not providing the resources necessary to cover the deficit in the balance of payments (their foreign currencies deficits), these countries have to borrow again in order to meet a part of the service on the debt and to meet part of the payments on the principal falling due.

According to the UN statistics published in 1985, interest payments on debt for 88 so-called Third World countries amounted respectively to 35 000 million dollars, $48 000 million, and $44 000 million in 1981, 1982 and 1983. They exceeded private credits received over these three years, and in 1983 they even exceeded by $5000 million all of the private and public credits received.

To this draining off of resources from the Third World, you have to add profits, dividends and so forth repatriated from the Third World to the imperialist centres. These hover around $12 000 million a year. For all three years considered, this figure exceeded the net inflow of investment capital.

According to the Economic Conference for Latin America and the Caribbean (ECLAC), there was a net transfer of resources from Latin America to the rest of the world of $30 000 million in 1985, if you add the current operations accounts and movement of capital. The president of this institution, Ortiz Mena, estimates that for the four years 1982–85, this drain amounted to a total of $100 000 million.

The inevitable result of this is overheating of the debt. More and more is being borrowed, not in order to increase production but to repay old loans and the interest on them. Overall, between 1973 and 1982, debt grew almost twice as fast as the national product of Third World countries that are not members of OPEC.

This circle is all the more vicious because the terms of trade — the relationship between the export prices and import prices — normally operate to the disadvantage of the Third World countries. Except for the brief spectacular flare-up of speculation between 1971–73 and for oil at the time of the two explosions in price, the prices of raw materials and semi-manufactures rise more slowly — when they are not falling — than the prices of manufactured products.

The deteriorating terms of trade, from which only a few semi-industrialised countries, such as South Korea, have escaped and then only for a certain time, are a heavy burden on the poorest countries. Even though it is less in absolute figures than those of the semi-industrialised countries, their debt is an unbearable burden.

The overall price of raw materials dropped from an index of 100 in 1979–81 to 72 in 1985, the prices of food products (cereals, sugar, bananas, soya bean cakes) to 56, and that of oil-bearing seeds to 65. The loss of resources (income from exports) suffered in this way by the Third World mounts up to a sum higher than the service on the debt!

Finally, for several reasons inherent in the economy of the imperialist countries, a good part of the period considered is marked by precipitously rising interest rates, especially in the US. But, while for the imperialist countries this rise was not catastrophic given the level of inflation, the same was not true for the Third World countries. Since their debts are denominated in dollars, every increase of one point in interest rates in the US increased the annual service on the debt by respectively $1000, $5000 or even $6000 million at the end of the 1970s and the beginning of the 1980s.

Once again, it is necessary to borrow more to cover these supplementary costs. And since the currencies of Third World countries have been hit by inflation rates higher than those of the imperialist countries, the rising interest rates accentuate the tendency toward a 'dollarisation' of the economy of these countries. Thus, a whole sector of economic activity and a growing part of savings are thereby removed from the control of the national capital accumulation.[15]

Thus, an ever widening spiral of debt has led to $900 000 million in Third World debts today and to a situation of *de facto* insolvency in most of the debtor countries. Of this sum, far less than half has been genuinely invested. Between a third and a quarter has been diverted abroad by the possessors. Another quarter has been held or received by the lenders themselves.

THE PERVERSE EFFECTS OF IMF PRESSURE

The overheating of the Third World debt has unleashed a four-fold destructive process affecting the world capitalist economy as a whole. Firstly, the *de facto* insolvency of the Third World countries threatens to bring down some of the main banks in the imperialist countries and, as a result, the credit system as a whole and the capitalist world's monetary system. Today, more than half of the Third World debt, about $480 000 million, is held by private banks.

Secondly, the Third World countries cannot meet the service charges on the debt – to say nothing of the principal[16] — without producing huge surpluses from their balances of payments. This means net outflow of currency, money capital, and thus of capital in general on a grand scale. But these countries are the poorest in capital and need more capital in order to be able to industrialise and modernise. A net outflow of capital can only result in a progressive slowing of the rates of growth and development. As Raul Prebisch has said, the IMF's remedy comes down to bleeding a patient suffering from anaemia!

Lastly, the massive outflow from the so-called Third World through interest payments on the debt would require a drastic restriction of imports. Leaving aside the inability of a great many semi-industrialised dependent countries to achieve such an expansion — for example, Mexico, which is at the mercy of fluctuations in the oil price — this would mean a no less drastic narrowing of the world market open to the imperialist countries, especially the less competitive, in particular the US. These imperialist countries would thus lose on two fronts. They would export less to the Third World and they would have to import more manufactured goods.

However, it would not be the same sections of the bourgeoisie that would gain and lose from such an infernal evolution of the world capitalist economy. The repayment mechanisms established by the IMF in general favour the banking sectors and recipients of dividends in the imperialist countries and go against the interests of the industrial and exporting sectors. Thus, the parasitic, usurious character of the imperialist system taken as a whole, above all in the US and Great Britain, stands to become more pronounced.[17]

The imperialist bourgeoisies more oriented toward exporting commodities and therefore more dependent on an expansion of the world market — such as West Germany and Japan — are therefore in favour of a more flexible policy toward interest on the Third World debt. This is the meaning of the doctrine proposed by the West German Social Democratic leader Willy Brandt.

Paradoxically, Brandt and Franz-Josef Strauss, the right-wing Christian Democratic leader, are working in tandem today as the real spokesmen of the European imperialists against American imperialism.

The threats that the overheating of the Third World debt pose for the world capitalist economy are thus real. But this does not mean that a fully-fledged generalised bank crash is inevitable.[18]

Already at the time of the big banking crisis of 1931–33, a saying was going around international financial circles that 'if the debt is $100 000, the debtor can't sleep, but if the debt is $10 million, it's the creditor who can't sleep'. If you multiply these figures by 10 or 100 to adjust for the inflation and the expansion that has occurred over the half century that has gone by since then, this saying is more pertinent than ever.

The American imperialists cannot allow Chase Manhattan, Citicorp, or Morgan Guarantee Trust to go under, any more than British imperialism could accept the collapse of Lloyds, Barclays and the National Westminster. The most likely eventuality, therefore, is a massive bail-out of the big debtors (in reality of the private creditors of these big debtors) by the international banking system and by the imperialist governments.

This amounts to a double nationalisation of the losses, partly at the expense of the toiling masses of the imperialist countries, partly at the expense of the popular masses in the so-called Third World countries themselves. The horse-trading going on now is essentially over the division of the sacrifices. The Third World bourgeoisies are interested above all in the technical aspects of the question — the timing and costs of debt rescheduling. Avoiding sacrifices for their own peoples is not exactly their main concern.

However, the success of such bailing-out operations, of which the Baker plan is only one partial example,[19] is not at all assured, precisely because no one controls the capitalist economy in its totality. It is marked by abrupt, spontaneous, largely unforeseen changes under the pressure of competition, and regulated only in the long term, and therefore blindly, by the law of value.

Thus, the plan for straightening out Mexico's finances, which was so labouriously set in motion by international bankers in 1982 and whose success they prematurely proclaimed, has just had the props knocked from under it by the plunge of the oil price.

Moreover, if every economist who understood the way the capitalist market economy functions could easily predict that the oil price would fall, no one could predict how sharp this fall would be, and exactly when it would come about, that is in February 1986.

All of this was provoked in part by British Prime Minister Margaret Thatcher's determination to defend the exchange rate of the pound sterling by all-out pumping of oil from the North Sea and by the heightening of overproduction that this policy brought out, with the resulting drop in the oil price. Another factor was the refusal of Saudi

Arabia to sit by and watch its share of the oil market shrink. This led to the coming apart of OPEC, and hence to the breakdown of prices, and hence to more overproduction, and so on.

Now, the Mexican debt has to be renegotiated a second time, as it was in 1982, and under worse conditions from the standpoint of the world market for oil and the social situation inside Mexico itself.

The evident fact of the interdependence of the economy of the imperialist countries and that of the Third World countries in the framework of the international capitalist economy gives some Third World bourgeoisies a not inconsiderable power for blackmailing the imperialist banks. These bourgeoisies tell the banks in such cases in effect: 'If you squeeze the lemon too much, we'd rather go under and drag you down with us'.

For this reason, Fidel Castro's scheme for a collective disavowal of the debt by all the Third World countries is not a purely propagandistic proposal. It can be a positive contribution to the anti-imperialist struggle on a world scale. It deserves the support of all anti-imperialist activitists, of all revolutionists and of the entire international workers' movement.

This plan should be a signal for mobilising the popular masses of the Third World and the support of the world proletariat for them, behind the demands that their respective governments disavow the debt.

Far from favouring any subordination of the workers to the national bourgeoisie, such a mobilisation would increase the class independence of the proletariat in the Third World countries, inasmuch as it would show that it is the working class and the workers' movement that defend national sovereignty against imperialism with a consistency that the bourgeoisie has shown itself incapable of. It would thus promote an alliance of the workers, peasants, urban poor and the urban petty bourgeoisie independent of the bourgeoisie.

Moreover, such a mobilisation would promote the direct class struggle of the proletariat and its allies both against the Third World bourgeoisies and against imperialism. Not only do these bourgeoisies continue to pay a usurious tribute to international capital but they strive above all to shift the bulk of the burden onto the backs of the popular masses, whose living standards are dropping disastrously.

FOR WORKERS' CONTROL OF THE BANKS

The IMF is bringing constant pressure to bear for balancing budgets and reducing public spending, which means above all reducing social spending, cutting subsidies for necessities, as well as paring down the volume of wages and employment in the public sector. The reactionary character of this pressure — we might even say its inhuman character, since it produces abysmal poverty and hunger in the literal sense of the term — is obvious.

However, it is not enough to denounce this pressure by the IMF. It is necessary to excoriate all those who yield to it, who give in to its *diktats*, not only out of cowardliness and political fear but also out of class interest. This is why the workers' movement should combine the demand for disavowal of the debt in particular with one for workers' control over banking operations, preferably by the bank workers themselves. This would offer a means for exposing and then for taking concrete steps against diversion, hoarding, private appropriation and clandestine export of currencies by the bourgeoisies, operations that contribute considerably to increasing the debt burden.

Will the Latin American bourgeoisies, to say nothing of all the Third World bourgeoisies, in fact form the united front for disavowing the debt that Fidel Castro has called for? That is not very likely. As the example of OPEC shows, crisis conditions heighten competition equally among capitalists, among the capitalist powers and the dependent countries, as well as within the Third World itself. Like the Indian bourgeoisie, the Latin American bourgeoisies will try to use the mounting pressure of the masses, as well as Fidel Castro's proposal, to blackmail imperialism. 'Reschedule the debt, give us new credits, or else we will follow the Cuban proposals?' This is all part of a gigantic tug of war that is going on now and whose exact result no one can predict.

A growing number of commitments will not be kept. An increasing number of debts will be purely and simply carried forward when they fall due. Continual extensions are not very different from default. This is why, it should be noted again, the real battle is being fought over interest, over service on the debt, rather than over the principal.

The interdependence between the bourgeoisies of the semi-colonial and dependent countries and the imperialist bourgeoisies is not purely an economic and financial one. It is also political and military. With revolution rising in many countries in the so-called Third World, imperialism remains the great protector and the last line of defence of the native possessing classes. This is true not only in Central America, in the Arab countries, in South Africa, in the Indian peninsula, in the Philippines and in South Korea. It is true in all such countries.

On the other hand, imperialism no longer has sufficient resources to rule the Third World directly. It relies on a relative consolidation of regional and local bourgeois relays. If the international banking system collapses, this would not only be a fatal blow to the imperialist centres but one just as fatal to the possessing classes of the Third World. If the revolution spreads in Central America and reaches into Mexico, it would knock directly at the door of the US.

This explains the desperate attempts of both imperialists and the Third World bourgeoisies to grope their way along, from compromise to compromise, from renegotiation and rescheduling, from the bailing out of one threatened bank to another. The fate of the international bourgeoisie as a whole is at stake.

However, the bourgeoisie does indeed have to grope its way, because it does not control all the parts in the mechanism. The interdependence I described remains an interdependence subject to the iron law of the bourgeois world. That is, a crisis weakens the feeble more than the strong, it increases the differences of wealth (and poverty) and power, it tends to magnify relations of dominance and dependence rather than to eliminate them. And, above all, the bourgeoisie is less and less able to control the actions and reactions of the popular masses.

NOTES

1. A revised version of an article in *International Viewpoint*, 5 May 1986.
2. The beginning of the 'boom' came after 1948 in Europe and after 1940 in the Anglo-Saxon countries and in Latin America, in so far as the latter were dragged along. In fact only some of them were, the outstanding example being Argentina. The end of the long boom for some came in 1968 and for others in 1973–74.
3. Deposits are the sum of bank deposits that can serve as means of payment. When the banks grant loans to their clients, these loans are generally registered in the form of bank deposits, and they therefore swell the volume of deposits. If the rate of increase of these deposits is greater than the rate of increase in material production, we can talk about an inflation of deposits, although the rate of circulation of this money has to be examined as a partially independent variable.
4. The fiscal crisis of the state has class roots (structural roots) in bourgeois society. The bourgeoisie prefers to lend money to the state rather than to pay taxes to it. Taxes give back nothing. Public loans pay back interest. Moreover, by keeping the state budget constantly in the red, the bourgeoisie keeps it perpetually dependent on short-term bank

loans, as well as state bonds bought by capitalists. The bourgeoisie thereby guarantees that this state remains 'its' property, bound to it by the gold chains of public debt.

5. On my theory of 'long waves' of capitalist economic cycles, see my books *Late Capitalism* and *The Long Waves of Capitalist Development* (Cambridge University Press, 1979).

6. The only banking system that has functioned with less hitches during the present crisis is the French one, precisely because the French banks are almost 100 per cent nationalised.

7. It might be objected that the Third World countries were 'willing victims' because they had a pressing and constant need for an inflow of foreign capital. But precisely because this need is constant, it cannot explain by itself the abrupt flare-up of their foreign debt during the 1970s.

8. See on this subject the excellent article by Jeffrey Bortz, 'La Dueda Latino-americano y los Ciclos de la Economia Mundial', in *La Batalla* (journal of the Mexican section of the Fourth International), no. 13 (November–December 1985).

9. The real interest rate is the difference between the nominal interest rate and the rate of inflation. In the US for example, an inflation rate of 8 per cent and a nominal interest rate of 7 per cent meant in 1977 a real interest rate of −1 per cent. In Third World countries this negative interest was still more pronounced, encouraging capital flight. For example, in Mexico on average for the period 1976–1982, the real interest rate for the peso was −0.8 per cent, in Argentina it was −6.6 per cent, in Brazil it was −14.7 per cent. After the sharp rise in the interest rates this situation was obviously reversed.

10. See many examples in the last chapter of my book *La Crise* (Flammarion, third edition, 1985), in which the data go up to April 1985.

11. See Anthony Sampson, *The Money Lenders* (Coronet Books, 1981).

12. Mexican sources even give the figure of $37 000 million.

13. Susanne Erbe, 'L'Evasion des capitaux dans les pays en developement', *Intereconomics* (November–December 1985).

14. The Marcos family and its allies alone are supposed to have deposited $5000 million abroad.

15. See the excellent article by Pierre Salama 'Dettes et dollarisation', in *Problemes d'Amerique latine*, no. 77, (1985).

16. To repay nearly £1000 000 million in capital borrowed, the Third World would have to come up with a balance-of-payments surplus of the same value. Even scheduled over 15 or 20 years, this would represent an additional annual outflow on the order of $50–60 000 million, besides interest and dividend payments, which is totally unachievable. The entire world tacitly accepts the assumption that the bulk of this debt is never going to be paid off.

17. At present in the US, a nominal interest rate of 10 per cent and an inflation rate of 5 per cent mean that the real interest rate is 5 per cent. In France, an inflation rate of 4 per cent to 5 per cent and a nominal interest rate of 10 per cent to 12 per cent mean that the real interest

rate is 6 per cent to 7 per cent, an actually usurious rate. In the US at certain times in the 1980s we saw nominal interest rates of 20 per cent, when inflation was under 10 per cent.

18. Nonetheless, partial banking crashes are multiplying, not just in Kuwait, Singapore, Malaysia, Argentina, Indonesia and the Philippines, but also in the US, in West Germany, in Italy, in Great Britain and in Japan.

19. The Baker plan put forward by US Secretary of the Treasury James A. Baker, aims at getting the private banks to increase their credits to Third World countries by $20 000 million, with something close to public guarantees and a sharp increase in capital and commitments from the World Bank.

Part III
Crisis in the Mode of Regulation: The Restructuring of the Welfare State

Part III

10 Economic Crisis and Welfare State Recommodification: A Comparative Analysis of the United States and Britain

Desmond King

This chapter examines the condition of the present-day welfare state in advanced industrial democracies. It sets out briefly the historical formation of welfare states with specific reference to the processes of decommodification and of consumption. This characterisation provides the basis for examining the impact of recent right-wing government attempts to withdraw the state from the provision of welfare facilities; and emphasises the importance of the accommodations reached between capital and labour in the formation and persistence of the welfare state, commonly referred to as corporatism. Through an analysis of the growth of the welfare state and the changes affected on Western political economies by its development we can address contemporary efforts to retrench the welfare state and to restructure these systems. It is argued below, for example, that there are inherent limits on the extent to which the state can disentangle itself from welfare policies arising from their character. Also, welfare state activities have altered the public-private boundaries of these policies which in turn have influenced the character and content of political cleavages and conflicts: significant cleavages have formed around public activities. If an account of these processes can be provided here — particularly of consumption and of decommodification, that is, the extension of activities in the political economy which are not guided by commodity-based market relations — this will provide greater purchase upon the nature of advanced industrial democracies. This is an ambitious task but an urgent one intellectually, given current political practices. What Offe (1984) terms 'recommodification' — that is, the retrenching of welfare state institutions and policies through a return to private sector authorities, in effect, a reversal of the process of decommodification — has profound implications for advanced industrial democracies and therefore must be studied carefully.

These theoretical concerns are given empirical reference by the emergence of right-wing governments in several Western industrial democracies determined to reduce the state's role, particularly in the area of welfare; and even where right-wing governments have not succeeded electorally many governments conventionally considered to be social democratic have sought to modify existing welfare commitments by the state. A rapid survey of OECD countries illustrates the universality of this process: Australia, Britain, New Zealand, Ireland, Denmark, Norway, Netherlands, the US, Canada and France – all these countries have had to initiate some control of welfare spending however modest or unsuccessful. However, it is in the US and Britain, under the Reagan and Thatcher administrations respectively, that this thrust to roll back the state and retrench welfare commitments has been most sustained and systematic, reflecting the influence of so-called 'New Right' ideology (see King 1987a for a critical examination of this doctrine). 'New Right' is a term with diverse meanings and applications both in theoretical formulation and in policy practices but certain core features can be identified: an advocacy of market mechanisms in place of state intervention; economic and moral criticisms of the welfare state; criticisms of interventionist economic policies; and advocacy of market mechanisms within all areas of public policy. In relation to the welfare state, New Right theorists claim that public provision of welfare erodes market processes and incentive structures while the size of the public sector crowds out private investment and reduces individual savings (a key source of investment in the economy). Some New Right critics also attack the moral consequences of the welfare state: it is alleged to lead to disintegration of the family and so forth. While the intellectual and policy influence of these liberal arguments is debatable, the elections of Ronald Reagan and Margaret Thatcher did appear to reflect some popular endorsement of such liberal economic priorities. In retrospect both administrations have been of considerable significance in restructuring the agenda within these two polities and in pursuing some retrenchment policies — though less than sought; this latter outcome reflects, it will be argued here, the form of the contemporary welfare state and its transformation of the political economy of advanced industrial democracies. For the purposes of this paper, we will concentrate on the American and British cases where the resurgence of right-wing policy objectives has been most developed.

THE GROWTH OF THE WELFARE STATE

There are a variety of explanations for the formation of the welfare state in Western industrial democracies. Neo-Marxists emphasise the pressure of working class organisations on the state; other social scientists highlight the increased societal pressure resultant upon massive economic, social and political change including urbanisation and economic growth; historians stress the calculations of political elites anxious to retain office with the support of the populace; and most recently, neo-Weberians have focused upon the activities of state officials in the formulation and adoption of welfare state policies (for an overview of explanations see Orloff and Skocpol 1984 and Flora and Heidenheimer 1981). A complete account of the growth of welfare institutions must incorporate elements from each perspective as well as acknowledging country-specific variables, a considerable task. However, there are some general points which we can extract. Firstly, welfare state policies and institutions follow economic transformation in Western societies — this is a necessary condition for their emergence. Secondly, the factors determining their original adoption differ from those facilitating their subsequent expansion. Thirdly, to a significant extent, the welfare state represents accommodations between capital and labour mediated through and by the state; such accommodations have frequently taken a corporatist form though some polities have resisted this arrangement. Fourthly, welfare policies and institutions have themselves influenced the processes of conflict and capital-labour accommodation underlying them — the two cannot be effectively separated. Before addressing these latter issues a brief overview of the growth of the welfare state is appropriate.

The growth of the Western welfare state falls into two periods: the period of formation and consolidation between the 1870s and the 1930s; and the post-1930s expansionary phase (see King 1988). This distinction between the origins of the welfare state and its subsequent consolidation is quite important analytically in that rather different variables structured state welfare policy during these two stages. The central issue of interest in this account is the role of organised working class pressure articulated through socialist or social democratic formulations of the transformative potential of welfare state institutions (see King 1988, Stephens 1979).

The first period is characterised by pressing and immediate political imperatives influencing national elites rather more than the realisation of coherently stated and pursued socialist or social democratic objectives. For example, in the 1880s Bismarck introduced social security and pension rights into the German polity to steal a march upon socialists and trade unionists who were campaigning on these issues (though see Tampke (1981) who maintains that this legislation reflected specific Prussian state welfare traditions). The experience from other countries reveals a similar configuration of contextual political factors influencing the introduction of welfare policies; as Flora (1981, p. 344) notes, 'virtually all political forces in Europe played a part in building up the welfare state: Bismarck, the authoritarian conservative, laid one of the most important foundation stones; Lloyd George and Beveridge, the Liberals, revolutionised the British welfare state; the Scandinavian welfare states were largely the creation of Social Democrats, while on the Continent the Christian Democrats made considerable contributions.' Flora's assessment should be qualified, however, in that the first sorts of influences were rather more pragmatic and reactive to immediate circumstances than the later ones which forged the conditions of the Keynesian welfare state consensus.

Thus the beginnings of the welfare state lie in the closing decades of the nineteenth century as the processes of industrialisation generated new material wealth and created a host of social and political pressures for ameliorative state policy. These social and political pressures could not be ignored by the ruling political elites if political stability was to be maintained; and such working class grievances provided a basis for inter-elite competition (mainly through the institution of political parties — intensified with the gradual extension of the franchise. Working class pressure for improved work conditions and social security and health policies — frequently articulated in unison with trade union organisations — constituted the primary challenge to which welfare state legislation was responding: 'up to 1914, and to a large extent through the inter-war period, the social forces most relevant to welfare state development were those of the working class' (Flora and Heidenheimer 1981, p. 28). However, the political parties formulating policy and institutional initiatives — the genesis of the welfare state — were not usually socialist parties, as Esping-Andersen writes:

> These early pioneers (for example, Bismarck) were quite prepared to build extensive schemes for social protection as a means to arrest class conflicts and subordinate workers to the state. Organised working-class participation in this era of welfare-state formulation was, at best, marginal; often it was oppositional. But liberals, too, played a pioneering role, although their primary efforts were dedicated to the establishment of social programmes that strengthened the market mechanism, such as voluntary contributory insurance and occupational contractual plans [1985b, p. 225].

The accommodation between capital and the state to the demands of the working classes for greater state responsibility in the areas of welfare were consequently accommodations undertaken pragmatically and under the immediacy of pressing political imperatives rather than coherent socialist or social democratic shaped objectives.

The first phase of welfare state establishment concludes by the 1930s for most Western democracies: Norway, Netherlands, Great Britain, Sweden, Finland, Denmark, Italy, France, Austria, Germany, Belgium and Switzerland. In these countries accident insurance, sickness insurance, old-age insurance and unemployment insurance had been implemented with the average year of initiation 1914, 1923, 1922 and 1930 respectively (see Flora and Alber in Flora and Heidenheimer 1981).

As already noted, absent from the first phase of welfare state growth is a coherent formulation of the appropriate content of such policies and institutions, in particular from a socialist — or least, social democratic — perspective. Such a formulation is a post-1930s phenomenon and reflects the influence of social democratic and labour parties committed to parliamentarianism. The support for these social democratic and labour parties lie principally with the working class in alliance with other class groupings such as small farmers in Scandinavia or segments of the white collar middle classes. Stephens stresses the importance of the organised working class to the achievement of welfare state policies and institutions; he argues that the 'strength of labour organisation (is) the key to the struggle for socialism' (1979, p. 55). This is particularly applicable to Northern Europe where the prolonged incumbency of left-wing parties, based electorally upon the working class and allied groups, provided the basis for implementing a range of policies collectively constitutive of the welfare state (and thus significantly constraining the power of capital) and allowing an expansionary role for the state. The political economy of Western industrial democracies has been transformed, to some extent, by these developments with the relationship between the state and economy a complex, interrelated one. The degree of this change varies, of course, with the nature and scope of the welfare state, an issue treated in detail below.

One important aspect of left-wing incumbency is its conducive consequences for the formation of corporatist relationships. One scholar links the structural economic property of openness to the creation of powerful (and centralised) trade union organisations: these latter are the basis for left-wing incumbency (because there is a well-organised labour movement around the working class) and can be incorporated into tripartite institutional arrangements between the state, employers and workers. Cameron contends that the high industrial concentration which is a feature of open economies facilitates high levels of unionisation, itself an 'important prerequisite for enduring leftist governments, since unionised workers provide the electoral basis of most Social Democratic and Labour parties' (1978, p. 1257). Industrial concentration encourages a wide scope of collective bargaining which necessitates a strong labour confederation. The conjunction of confederations able to negotiate with the state in corporatist institutions with trade union organisations capable of mobilising electoral support for left-wing parties establishes the conditions for prolonged incumbency and for state expansion of social welfare, social insurance and other social policies, including employment programmes. Thus, welfare policies and institutions can be viewed in part as the product of accommodation between the state and capital for working class support. The price of this support is the assumption by the state of responsibility for welfare, social security and education provision or what is frequently termed the 'social wage' (Friedland and Sanders 1986). In a related way, Hibbs (1978) contends that strikes are expressions of working class power aimed at attaining redistributive policies by the state. He argues that the success of such strike activity will depend upon the presence of left-wing governments. Even in the US, where labour has been muted historically, evidence of the impact of organised working class strength can be adduced from the outcomes of popular protests in the 1930s and 1960s, as Piven and Cloward (1977) maintain: they argue that popular protest movements forced the expansion of entitlement welfare programmes in the 1960s and 1970s. However, at a more general level, there is a key contrast between American and European experience regarding working class mobilisation and the implementation of welfare state policies: in the latter countries working class mobilisation through trade union movements has been far more significant than that found in the United States where trade unions have confined themselves to workplace negotiations (and only in the corporate economic sphere) (see Furniss and Tilton 1977) and where political parties advocating social democratic or socialist policies have been absent (see Katznelson 1981, 1985). This contributes to an explanation of the weaker, and more selective-based, welfare state in the US if the centrality of labour power to its realisation is accepted.

The contrast between the US and northern European countries illustrates also the differing role of corporatist arrangements in the formulation of welfare policies and institutions. Corporatist institutions require peak associations representing labour and employer groups — confederations of all worker and employer groups respectively — who have the power to extract consent from their member organisations; these peak organisations engage in tripartite negotiations with the state to determine economic and welfare policy.

The scope of these policy deliberations can be extensive (as for example in Sweden where union organisations influence national policy by insisting upon substantial social wage and solidaristic wage policies) or restrictive (as for example in Britain in the 1960s and 1970s where such negotiations focused exclusively upon pay rates). In the United States, the absence of relevant peak associations, and the propensity for trade unions to bargain successfully with employers for workers' conditions and concessions, has resulted in the absence of national corporatist practices; thus the possibility of national discussions about the development of welfare policies has been precluded:

> American Keynesianism has been conservative, choosing to deal exclusively with questions of demand and distribution. Peak association corporatism linking business, labour, and government is virtually unknown. There is no national capacity to plan. Employment policy is a pastiche of ameliorative programmes incapable of making a dent in structural and cyclical unemployment [Katznelson 1986, p. 308; see also Salisbury 1979].

The different corporatist traditions of the US, Britain and Northern Europe were significant to their respective responses to the post-1973 economic crisis: the contrasting unemployment rates of Sweden, Norway, Austria, Britain and the US are instructive of the value of national institutions, accommodating labour and capital interests, and committed to planning (see King 1987a, Therborn 1986).

But the general point here concerns working class pressure and welfare state formation: there is strong evidence appertaining to the central role of organised working class pressure in the consolidation of the welfare state in Western societies. The post-1930s expansion of state responsibility into the welfare sphere reflects the articulation of demands by organised labour movements for modifications in the political economy to advantage their interests. One method of formalising these demands is through the creation of corporatist institutions: the establishment of national, annual negotiations between employers, workers and the state aimed at achieving economic prosperity through industrial peace. Such institutional arrangements allow working class pressure for an expansion in the social wage to be articulated and integrated into public policy. Here we should note an important implication of the role of labour organisations in the consolidation of the welfare state: it implies that a decline in a unified working class through trade unions and/or solidarity of the working class may have the consequence of weakening the societal support bases of welfare state institutions; however, labour organisations have always relied upon cross-class alliances and it is necessary to forge new ones, as Esping-Andersen (1985a, p. 70) notes in relation to Scandinavia: 'social democracy's long-term prospects will depend on the political choices and party allegiances of the rapidly growing white-collar employee organisations'; it is important also that such cross-class alliances strive to reduce wage differentials between these classes and increase solidarity across them. To the extent that trade unions and labour organisations have supported political parties favouring the welfare state, then any weakening of the trade union movement can be expected to affect welfare institutions negatively. And, indeed, right-wing governments might pursue their reduced welfare state ambitions through a strategy of weakening trade unions, which is indeed the pattern under the Thatcher and Reagan administrations. Alternatively, if unionisation has extended into the public sector – the most dynamic employment growth area in the post-1945 era – and if such organisations share the objectives of earlier union movements about the importance of welfare policies, then this might constitute a new and powerful support base for the welfare state. Thus the relationship between a decline in working class size and welfare state institutions is a complex one not easily predicted.

The implications of welfare policies for the capitalist political economy should be appreciated: while it has been traditional (at least within a neo-Marxist perspective) to view welfare policies and institutions as activities assumed by the state necessary for capital accumulation and the reproduction of labour-power, it is also the case that welfare policies represent organised working-class pressure for important modifications in state policy. That is, the welfare state cannot be viewed simply as a legitimation activity undertaken by the state; it constitutes also the outcome of important struggles by labour organisations to alter the character of contemporary political economies. This is a point wich O'Connor (1984, p. 194) recognises:

It is unarguably the case that concepts such as 'social consumption' and 'social wage' are inconceivable in the absence of some kind of working-class perspective on economic and social policy. The same thing may be said about the growth of welfarism in general, both the origins and functions of which are explicable to a lesser or greater degree in anti-functionalist terms, e.g., in terms of popular struggle ... State action may be 'functional' or 'dysfunctional' for capitalist accumulation and social domination.

Contemporary political economies are evolving, transformative configurations shaped by capitalist needs undoubtedly but not exclusively: other groups in society and their struggles also shape state policy.

CONTEMPORARY WELFARE STATE FORMS

In sum, the welfare state cannot be viewed simply as a state-controlled legitimation mechanism: it certainly plays an important legitimising role but its expansionary nature (that is, its representation of diverse interests articulated through the electoral process) gives it a meaning beyond simple capitalist functionalist necessity; the social citizenship rights (King 1987a, King and Waldron 1987) manifested in welfare state policies and institutions are by their nature egalitarian in application. However, the extent to which these social rights will apply to all citizens is a function of the nature of the welfare state – in particular whether it is a marginial (selective, means-tested benefits) or an institutional (universal, no means-tested benefits) one to draw upon Korpi's (1983) useful analytical distinction. These two forms are ideal-types representing extreme opposites of possible welfare state forms, the first a minimal welfare commitment by the state, the second a comprehensive public provision of health, education and social security universally applied. Korpi distinguishes between them by the proportion of national income spent on welfare policy, the proportion of the population receiving some welfare state benefits, the universality or selectivity of welfare policies, the progressivity of the taxation system, the importance of full employment programmes and so forth:

> We would expect universalistic measures, directed towards large sections of the population, to be important in the institutional model of social policy. Selective policies directed towards subgroups of the population with specific needs will be relatively more important in the marginal model [Korpi 1983, p. 192].

The adoption of the different welfare state forms has consequences for the representation of interests in society, and thus for the social support bases of the welfare state: the coalitions of support underlying welfare state institutions will be more extensive for institutional than marginal forms:

> Generally we would expect that a marginal type of social policy would have much fewer possbilities than an institutional type of social policy in generating coalitions in its defence. A marginal type of social policy, predominant for example in the US, explicitly or implicitly draws a poverty line in the population and thus separates the poor and relatively small minority from the better-off majority of the population [1983, p. 193].

More recently, Katznelson (1986, p. 308) develops a forceful statement of the limited form of the American welfare state:

> Public housing is meagre and starved for funds. The welfare state lacks many programmes familiar elsewhere, especially in health and family allowances. It distinguishes between social insurance and means-tested welfare programmes. It developed late. And it remains small in size, capturing a comparatively limited share of tax revenues and national wealth.

This outcome relates back to the differences in working class organisation and mobilisation between the US and Britain alluded to earlier.

DECOMMODIFICATION

The development of welfare state practices and institutions has implications for the nature of work and for people's relationship to state structures. Work in the public sector embodies non-market criteria (that is, criteria about the social usefulness of certain goods, the need for minimum standards of health and education) in its decisions about production, allocation and consumption of goods; this contributes to the erosion of the pervasiveness of market criteria in these advanced industrial societies. Public sector work differs from market employment by its removal from a generalised commodity production form. In the public sector, labour is no longer treated as a commodity produced for exchange. According to Marxism, labour power becomes a commodity within capitalist economies; public employees are no longer wage earners in commodity production in this traditional sense. As Keane (in Offe 1984, p. 18) writes; 'State policies considerably decommodify the daily lives of the population by replacing "contract" with political status and "property rights" with "citizen rights".' Offe (1984, p. 264), a key exponent of this decommodification argument, expands thus:

> I speak of certain organisations as decommodified because their provision of use-values is no longer guided by the form of rationality appropriate to market behaviour. If we consider the 'products' of hospital workers, for instance, it is evident that it is not sold on the market and that, moreover, its quantity, quality, timing and geographic distribution are not directly determined by market criteria. This non-market rationality is also crystallised in many other categories of service labour. In my view, the continuous growth of decommodified organisations such as hospitals consequently tends to weaken and paralyse market rationality.

Offe believes further that decommodified spheres can become relatively autonomous and bases for political action: 'Areas of social life that have been decommodified by welfare state interventions can be developed, through political struggle, into relatively autonomous subsystems of life oriented to the production and distribution of use-values' (1984, p. 265). This has implications for those who produce and consume welfare state policies who, through their experience of decommodified spheres, may wish to resist pressures (for example, the policies of Thatcher and Reagan) aimed at re-introducing market criteria. Offe's argument is complemented by Prandy *et al.* (1983) who cotend that welfare state producers are affected by the nature of their employment relations which are significantly distinct from those in the private sector: 'Employment relations take on a different class character because they are no longer tied so closely to market principles' (1983, p. 151). This reflects processes of labour organisation and mobilisation outside the state. 'The link that we argue ... is between trade unions in the private sector, reflecting the particular interests of their members and pursuing alternative principles to those of the market, and those in the public sector which reflect the operation of such alternatives and hence a transformation of class relations' (1983, pp. 151–2).

This decommodification thesis has not gone without criticism, however. One important point concerns the commodity status of those goods and services associated with the welfare state and the extent to which they have ever been the equivalent of market-based commodities – this is especially applicable to the cases of health and education. Such a criticism has implications for right-wing pressures toward recommodification in that policies of the latter sort may be confined to marginal areas of the welfare state only, or to other areas of stable activity unrelated to welfare institutions. For example, the Thatcher government's most successful area of privatisation, outside nationalised industries, has been public housing. The possibility of pursuing such a strategy in the area of health, for instance, is denied by Harloe (1984, p. 230). 'Limitations on the levels of private incomes among more than a very tiny proportion of the population are a serious constraint on the expansion of private health care to provide more than a very partial replacement for the range of care provided by the NHS.' It is also the case, of course, that privatisation — so-called state disengagement — entails considerable state activity (King 1987a, Harloe 1984).

CONSUMPTION PROCESSES

Related to the growth of decommodification and the welfare state is the development of cleavages around consumption processes, cleavages distinct from conventional class-based ones; such consumption-based demarcations reflect strongly the growth of state involvement in the provision of public services. Consumption concerns privately produced goods and services as well as public ones — access to consumption will be different depending whether it is publicly or privately provided and whether people have the appropriate resources to determine which they consume (Dunleavy 1979, Taylor-Gooby 1986). This is elaborated upon by Dunleavy, who stresses the difference between market-based commodity production and state-based consumption services:

> The growth of the state does not *create* sectoral cleavages in consumption situations. Rather it adds a highly significant new dimension to a process of sectoral differentiation already evident in a muted form in the market processes of advanced capitalist society. ... State intervention to provide collectively-consumed services ... radically changes the level of politicisation and the nature of consumption cleavages. In some areas, such as education and health care, near-universal public provision effectively depoliticises sectoral issues, although in a distorted form such conflicts continue to exert a wholly disproportionate influence on the development of these urban public services. In other areas, notably housing and transport, the growth of urban public services, combined with a rapid increase in the importance of commodity forms of consumption has massively eroded the extent of private service provision [1979, p. 419].

Consumption cleavages arise, therefore, between those goods and services which are provided both privately or individually and publicly or collectively. The greater the fragmentation between these two forms of consumption, the more significant will be the resulting sectoral cleavage. With regard to state provision of consumption there are two groups of concern: those responsible for producing welfare services and those who consume, with some overlap between these groups. The key point is that such groupings derive from state services rather than from conventional economic or class positions, a point Cawson (1982, p. 76) notes: 'Sectoral interests which emerge from the activities of the state, especially those grounded in the various branches of the state itself, are not so deeply entrenched in class relations and may, in certain circumstances, be seen as being more significant class divisions.' The public sector is structured in terms of non-market criteria and is responsible for the production and allocation of goods and services by reference to non-market criteria. Collectively, this changes the nature of contemporary industrial democracies, consequentially. What are commonly termed market economies have large proportions of the workforce working according to non-market, decommodified principles, which alters the nature of these political economies.

Decommodification and consumption processes have proved fruitful, if controversial, perspectives upon the welfare state (in addition to Dunleavy 1979 and Offe 1984, see Franklin and Page 1984, Harloe 1984, Harrison 1986, Holmwood 1987, King 1988, Marshall *et al.* 1987 and Taylor-Gooby 1986). At the very least they emphasise its distinctive processes, reflecting aspects of its origin with organised labour, and their important political consequences. For example, Dunleavy (1979) argues that a citizen's relationship to public or collective and private or individualised consumption filters through into electoral behaviour: consumption cleavages will not provide a complete account of voting behaviour, but knowledge of consumption processes and people's relationship to them will contribute to such an analysis. The relationship between consumption cleavage and voting is not a causally direct one; rather consumption processes focus analytically upon the 'social bases of ideas about self-interest in the use of state or non-state services' (Taylor-Gooby 1986, p. 601).

What are the implications of these processes for the restructuring of the welfare state? First of all, a great deal hinges on the distinction between marginal and institutional welfare state forms. Clearly the extent of decommodification in a society (in terms of collective consumption processes and employment experience) will be positively correlated with the size of the welfare state and therefore those approximating institutional forms will have more entrenched decommodified processes. This will constitute an important source of resistance to cuts in welfare policies and institutions, drawing strength from working class constituents and from those working in the public sector. In part, this factor reflects whether welfare programmes are universal or marginal in form: if the former then their support base in society should be considerably wider (see King 1988 for a fuller presentation of this argument). Further, polities with more established corporatist structures, representing working-class interests, will be less amenable to right-wing pressures to retrench welfare provision; but in the absence of corporatist institutions:

It is employers and their managements who are of central importance [to restructuring policies]. It is they who take the lead in tapping new sources of labour supply and in developing new methods of organising production and new forms of employment ... It is the unions who are placed in the position of being able only to react to initiatives taken by others. Their attitudes to most manifestations of dualism have been hostile, but such hostility has not in fact been widely translated into effective counter-measures [Goldthorpe 1984, p. 336].

Under corporatist arrangements, unions will have an equal voice in policy formulation and thus can influence systematically the content and scope of any restructuring of welfare institutions. The robustness of these factors in the face of right-wing retrenchment policies are examined in the next section after a consideration of welfare state crisis arguments.

It has become common parlance amongst some social scientists — particularly neo-Marxists — to view the welfare state as a contradictory set of institutions doomed to inevitable crisis. For Offe (1984, p. 263, 264), this contradiction is linked to the process of decommodification:

In my view, this relationship between 'welfare' and capitalism is contradictory: under modern capitalist conditions, a supportive framework of non-commodified institutions is necessary for an economic system that utilises labour power as if it were a commodity ... [But] state institutions which assign legal entitlements to citizens become relatively 'rigid' or even irreversible.

Such a process may result in decommodified state institutions developing an 'independent life of their own'. In his influential book on state fiscal crisis, O'Connor (1973) argues a structural contradiction between accumulation and legitimation functions of the state under advanced capitalism — a contradiction likely to materialise in a fiscal crisis as state expenditures upon welfare (to meet its legitimation function) outstrip the resources allocated to investment (to meet its accumulation function). More conventional social scientists have argued also a welfare state crisis in the wake of the 1973 economic crisis in advanced industrial societies. Thus, for overload theorists, welfare policies represented an over-extension of state services spurred on by the Keynesian welfare state consensus: the commitment of public resources necessary to sustain such welfare policies inevitably strained the economy, according to these theorists (King 1975, OECD 1981, Rose and Peters 1978).

THE CONTRACTION OF THE WELFARE STATE? RECOMMODIFICATION AND RETRENCHMENT UNDER THE CUTBACK STATE

We noted at the beginning of this essay that most advanced industrial democracies have confronted substantial economic problems since the early 1970s which resulted in a weakening of the Keynesian consensus and in welfare state crisis. In the US and Britain these developments have been linked intellectually to the doctrines of the so-called 'New Right'; these theories have influenced the policy objectives of the Reagan and Thatcher governments in these two countries and it is these cases upon which we focus.

Both the Reagan and Thatcher administrations embody certain attitudes toward the welfare state and the public sector in general. The welfare state is considered a fiscal burden upon the private economy. It is also argued to affect detrimentally the economic incentives of citizens. In policy terms, the Reagan and Thatcher administrations have sought to reduce the aggregate size of the public sector and particularly to retrench or recommodify the state's provision of public welfare, health, and education services and of social security. And, in those areas which remain within the state's scope private market practices are to be introduced into routinised administrative conventions. Thus, areas of welfare state policy excluded from market processes were to be recommodified — that is, they were to be provided through market processes as commodities. In the US, of course, certain areas such as health had enjoyed little decommodification in the first instance: there has never been a national health service available to all citizens. In Britain, some areas such as education, had been only partially decommodified — the persistence of private, fee-paying schools alongside state schools qualified the scope of state decommodification in education. Nevertheless, it was clearly the intention of the Reagan and Thatcher governments to reduce even further the extant practices of decommodification and to enhance market processes in all areas of economic and social activity.

In any event neither administration has reduced the aggregate size of the public sector but each has succeeded in shifting the priorities of public spending in their respective polities, to the detriment of state welfare activities. In both countries social welfare spending has been cut in some area though rather less than desired by these two governments. In Britain the most dramatic area of retrenchment is in public housing, a direct consequence of the state's extensive privatisation in this area. However, with the exception of expenditure upon housing, public social spending on education, health and social services and social security all increased at a greater rate than the government intended. A similar pattern holds for the US: aggregate federal outlays have grown under the Reagan administration but, within this aggregate priorities have shifted away from social welfare spending toward defence. Expenditures on unemployment benefits and on medicaid/medicare increased but reductions were achieved in allocations to education and to means-tested assistance programmes. Most of the cuts presented to Congress in Reagan's first budget were realised but in subsequent years Congressional resistance to cuts — particularly in social security — was considerable. Overall, the thrust of agreed cuts in social spending reflected the piorities pursued by thc Reagan White House though they were less than sought.

Thus, in both Britain and the US the Thatcher and Reagan administrations have shifted public spending priorities away from social welfare but to a rather more modest degree than desired. How is this explained and what are the implications for efforts at recommodification? One powerful factor is economic: the impact of recessions in each country upon demands for social security and related benefits was considerable. An additional relevant factor in the case of the US is increased defence outlays. But there are additional variables deriving from the nature of the welfare state and its associated processes discussed earlier in this essay. Two factors are particularly significant: the extent to which the welfare state form approximates the institutional or marginal form (and the associated degree of decommodification); and the influence of cleavages deriving from consumption processes and patterns.

Consumption cleavages emphasise the different relationships to the state apparent amongst different social groups. Working class recipients, middle class professionals and welfare state sector employees all differ in their structural relationships to the state which influences the maintenance or retrenchment of welfare programmes. Those welfare programmes which are universalistic in form and therefore consumed by all three groups are more powerfully based in society than those programmes consumed by one group only, usually on the basis of means-tested selectivity. In addition, given the structure of state power under contemporary capitalism and the centrality of welfare state professionals to those state structures, we might well anticipate their effectiveness in resisting recommodifying initiatives and defending service provision. There is some evidence to support such propositions with regard to the Reagan and Thatcher administrations, in particular from the welfare programmes which have been least reduced under these governments. This, in the US, it is the universal social insurance programmes which have been subjected to the fewest cuts whereas means-tested entitlement programmes (for example food stamps and Aid to Families with Dependent Children) consumed selectively by the poorest section of society, have been cut significantly. A similar pattern applies to other welfare programmes consumed predominantly by the working class such as those focused on training and employment. The general point is that those programmes consumed universally in the US (and thus the closest representation of the institutional welfare state form) have weathered the cuts more effectively:

> Social Security has come to be anchored politically in a broad voting constituency – perhaps the broadest that exists for any American public programme – and it is defended by Congressional representatives, 'conservative' and 'liberal' alike, anxious to service the needs of well-organised constitutents [Skocpol and Ikenberry 1983, p. 141].

Analogous patterns obtain in Britain. The Thatcher privatisation initiative has been pursued most vigorously in areas of marginal concern only to middle class professionals and state employees — most strikingly, in the area of working class public housing. Within the National Health Service, privatisation or recommodification measures have been restricted to peripheral activities (like laundry services or catering) with no impact on the medical sphere. In education, the oft-vaunted proposal for voucher schemes has remained untested. Part of the explanation of these outcomes must lie in the different forms of consumption (universal or selective) and in the power of the constituencies of these different welfare programmes in both Britain and the US. Harloe reaches a similar conclusion in his critique of consumption-based cleavages and recommodification when he queries the likeliness of privatisation outside housing in Britain:

> The growth of political support for owner occupation can be readily agreed ... Whether a similar development will occur in fields such as health care and education is less certain and is dependent on the extent to which, as in the case of housing, privatised consumption becomes the norm for a really significant proportion of the population [1984, p. 232].

One factor militating against such developments is conceptions of citizenship rights represented in the political community. The welfare state embodies a set of social citizenship rights which are integral to the British political culture. Comparable rights can be identified in the US but their narrower scope and emphasised selectivity has necessarily rendered them less pivotal, though not insignificant, to American political culture. The difference between the two polities in this regard concerns the varying form of the welfare state. Given the greater stress on universality, Britain has a fuller welfare state in this sense and hence a stronger notion of social citizenship rights. That these citizenship rights are so central to British political and social norms helps explain the failure of the current government's recommodification initiatives within the sphere of welfare programmes. And, indeed, in the US the Reagan administration's proposed draconian cuts in federal welfare benefits were thwarted by a Congress aware of public support for such measures. Despite the increasing costs of such universal insurance policies to the American taxpayers, they remain entrenched, as Heclo records: 'After six years of conservative government in Washington and a subordination of almost all other policy concerns to a mounting deficit problem, the cost functions of the American welfare state appear to remain intact' (Heclo 1986, p. 191). Although marginal welfare state forms are weaker in their social support base than institutional forms, they do not lack entirely supporting coalitions and organised groups. Public support for social citizenship rights is less firmly rooted in the US than in Britian and less immediately associated with welfare state institutions; but it is much stronger for social insurance than public assistance policies. In this regard, these two countries follow a general pattern: the welfare state has become integral to the social structures and routines of advanced industrial democracies, and the dynamics determining their persistence include principles (especially, non-market decommodified practices) which imply a significant transformation of these societies, one unlikely to be destroyed by a conservative administration.

CONCLUSION: TOWARD THE REGENERATION OF WELFARE INSTITUTIONS

The discussion of the welfare state and contemporary capitalism in this essay has focused upon Britain and the US because these two polities have thrown up the most serious right-wing political movements of the post-1973 economic crisis period; and, compared to other north European polities, the British and especially American welfare state forms are relatively undeveloped:

> The paradox we find is that social democracy has been *least* challenged and weakened in those nations where its accomplishments have gone furthest (Norway and Sweden) while it has been most effectively attacked in nations where the process of social democratisation was only partial or marginal.... The effectiveness of the new right in both Britain and Denmark cannot be explained by the circumstances that the labour movements there have been exceptionally successful in altering the political economy, but rather by the incompleteness of their accomplishments [Esping-Andersen 1985b, p. 245].

The concentration on these two countries is not intended to convey complacency about the condition of the welfare state or to belittle the seriousness of the attacks mounted against its policies and institutions in advanced industrial democracies since the mid-1970s. However, the argument advanced in this essay is that the processes of decommodification and consumption derivative of welfare state structures create their own support dynamics and become integrated into the political economy in a way which precludes their easy destruction, though this is not impossible. However, the extent and hence effectiveness of these processes is clearly a function of the scope of the welfare state, itself an institutional representation of working class power.

The class structure of Western democracies has changed as the welfare state has matured: the traditional blue-collar working-class grouping holds a proportionately smaller position within the class structure than in the pre-1940s era, while the size of the white-collar middle class – including those employed by the state – has expanded.

Such changes have important implications for the persistence of the welfare state: given the centrality of organised labour to the foundation and consolidation of welfare state policies and institutions, a decline in working class numbers might be thought to weaken the social support base of these policies. This is one possible outcome. But such an outcome will be mediated, this paper has contended, by the form of the welfare state. Where this is more extensive then its structural position within the political economy will be greater and its support bases will extend from a narrowly defined working class into other sectors, including the middle class and state employees (see King 1987b for an extended discussion of this argument). Thus, a decline in working class numbers and in organised labour need not erode social support for welfare state institutions. Alternatively, where welfare state policies and institutions are rather more modest – as in the US – then the decline of organised labour is likely to be of much greater significance. Where welfare state policies are selective in distribution and where the state sector is less developed, then social support for these institutions may be weaker. The degree of decommodification in any given polity will reflect also the form and extent of the welfare state. The more extensive the latter, so the more important will be decommodified activities, and thus resistance to recommodifying policies will also be greater.

A central implication of this discussion is that for governments intent upon welfare state retrenchment, a weakening of trade unions is a logical strategy – especially if the welfare state has not attained the institutional form outlined earlier. And where there is an absence of corporatist structures then this strategy faces relatively weakly articulated resistance from organised labour. In this regard, Goldthorpe has drawn the useful distinction between dualist and corporatist structures, and Britain and the US lie closer to the former practice where trade union representatives have rather less leverage over public policy. Indeed, trade unions have suffered considerably under the Reagan and Thatcher administrations both directly (for example, legislation aimed at restricting their power and bitter disputes as in the American air traffic controllers' strike) and indirectly (for example, economic policies which increase unemployment reduce the base for union formation). A key aspect of the dualist structure is recommodification: that is, a systematic effort to reverse, or at least halt, the process of decommodification represented in the post-war welfare state evolution and the diffusion of commodification into areas previously protected. Goldthorpe (1984, p. 337–8) argues, correctly, that dualist tendencies are linked fundamentally to New Right type policies aimed at reducing the role of government in economic policy and at enhancing market processes. Such an argument has some validity, but the thesis of this paper is that such New Right *laissez faire* initiatives confront sources of resistance embedded within the processes and structures of the welfare state through their entrenchment of decommodified non-market practices.

Goldthorpe's categories of dualism and corporatism can be linked with recommodification and decommodification policies respectively. Where working-class organisations and trade unions are integrated into national policy — as for example in Scandinavia — the thrust of public policy is welfare state expansion (social wage growth) and increased decommodification. But where such national policy making structures have been abandoned (or are non-existent) in favour of dualism, then national public policy promotes economic interests over working-class representations for expanded welfare policies; recommodification and the enhancement of market forces become the core concern of public policy. The Reagan and Thatcher administrations constitute examples of this latter development. We can conclude by noting that through their erosion of trade union rights and weakening of welfare state institutions and policy priorities these regimes have had a significant impact upon the social structures of welfare; and through their usurpation of corporatism with dualism the avenues for effective working-class pressure have been limited further. But it is important still to record that aspects of welfare state structures (most notably their decommodification practices and embodiment of social citizenship rights) constitute consequential limits on 'New Right' recommodification objectives, not easily abrogated.

REFERENCES

D. Cameron, 'The Expansion of the Public Economy: A Comparative Analysis', *American Political Science Review* 72 (1978) pp. 1243–61.
A. Cawson, *Corporatism and Welfare* (London: Heinemann, 1982).
P. Dunleavy, 'The Urban Basis of Political Alignment: Social Class, Domestic Property Ownership and State Intervention in Consumption Processes', *British Journal of Political Science* 9 (1979) pp. 409–43.
G. Esping-Andersen, *Politics Against Markets* (Princeton University Press, 1985a).
G. Esping-Andersen, 'Power and Distributional Regimes', *Politics and Society* 14 (1985b) pp. 223–56.
P. Flora, 'Solution or Source of Crises? The Welfare State in Historical

Perspective' in Mommsen 1981.

P. Flora and J. Alber, 'Modernisation, Democratisation and the Development of Welfare States in Western Europe' in Flora and Heidenheimer (1981) see below.

P. Flora and A. J. Heidenheimer (eds), *The Development of Welfare States in Europe and America* (New Brunswick and London: Transaction Books, 1981).

M. Franklin and E. Page, 'A critique of the consumption cleavage approach in British voting studies', *Political Studies* 32 (1984).

R. Friedland and J. Sanders, 'Private and social wage expansion in the advanced market economies', *Theory and Society* 15 (1986) pp. 193–222.

N. Furniss and T. Tilton, *The Case for the Welfare State* (London: Indiana University Press, 1977).

J. Goldthorpe, 'The End of Convergence: Corporatist and Dualist Tendencies in Modern Western Societies' in J. Goldthorpe (ed.), *Order and Conflict in Contemporary Capitalism* (Oxford University Press, 1984).

T. R. Gurr and D. S. King, *The State and the City* (London: Macmillan and University of Chicago Press, 1987).

M. Harloe, 'Sector and class: a critical comment', *International Journal of Urban and Regional Research* 8 (1984) pp. 228–37.

M. L. Harrison, 'Consumption and urban theory', *International Journal of Urban and Regional Research* 10 (1986) pp. 232–42.

H. Heclo, 'General Welfare and Two American Political Traditions', *Political Science Quarterly* 101 (1986).

D. Hibbs, 'On the Political Economy of Long-Run Trends in Strike Activity', *British Journal of Political Science* 8 (1978) pp. 153–75.

J. M. Holmwood, 'The Political Economy of Social Citizenship'. Unpublished manuscript. Department of Sociology, University of Edinburgh, 1987.

I. Katznelson, *City Trenches* (University of Chicago Press, 1981).

I. Katznelson, 'Working Class Formation and the State: Nineteenth Century England in American Perspective' in P. Evans, D. Rueschemeyer and T. Skocpol (eds), *Bringing the State Back In* (Cambridge and New York: Cambridge University Press, 1985).

I. Katznelson, 'Rethinking the Silences of Social and Economic Policy', *Political Science Quarterly* 101 (1986) pp. 307–25.

I. Katznelson and A. R. Zolberg (eds), *Working Class Formation* (Princeton University Press, 1986).

J. Keane, 'Introduction' in Offe (1984) see below.

A. King, 'Political Overload', *Political Studies* 23 (1975).

D. S. King, *The New Right: Politics, Markets and Citizenship* (London: Macmillan and Homewood Illinois: Dorsey Press, 1987a).

D. S. King, 'The State and the Social Structures of Welfare in Advanced Industrial Societies', *Theory and Society* (1988).

D. S. King, 'Meso-corporatism and the Welfare State: A State-Centred Analysis'. Paper presented to the ECPR annual meetings, Amsterdam, 1987c.

D. S. King and J. J. Waldron, 'Citizenship, Social Citizenship and the Defence of Welfare Rights'. Unpublished manuscript. Department of Politics, University of Edinburgh, 1987.

W. Korpi, *The Democratic Class Struggle* (London: Routledge & Kegan Paul, 1983).

G. Marshall, C. Vogler, D. Rose and H. Newby, 'Distributional Struggle and Moral order in a Market Society', *Sociology* 21 (1987) pp. 55–74.

W. J. Mommsen, (ed.), *The Emergence of the Welfare State in Britain and Germany* (London: Croom Helm, 1981).

J. O'Connor, *The Fiscal Crisis of the State* (New York: St. Martin's Press, 1973).

J. O'Connor, *Accumulation Crisis* (Oxford: Basil Blackwell, 1984).

OECD, *The Welfare State in Crisis* (Paris: OECD, 1981).

C. Offe, *Contradictions of the Welfare State* (London: Hutchinson, 1984).

A. S. Orloff and T. Skocpol, 'Why Not Equal Protection? Explaining the Politics of Public Social Spending in Britain, 1900–1911, and the United States, 1880s–1920', *American Sociological Review* 49 (1984) pp. 726–50.

F. F. Piven and R. Cloward, *Poor People's Movements* (New York: Pantheon Books, 1977).

F. F. Piven and R. Cloward, *The New Class War* (New York: Pantheon, 1982).

K. Prandy, A. Stewart and R. M. Blackburn, *White-Collar Unionism* (London: Macmillan, 1983).

R. Rose and G. Peters, *Can Government Go Bankrupt?* (New York: Basic Books, 1978).

R. H. Salisbury, 'Why No Corporatism in America?', in P. C. Schmitter and G. Lehmbruch (eds), *Trends Toward Corporatist Intermediation* (Beverly Hill and London: Sage, 1979).

T. Skocpol and J. Ikenberry, 'The Political Formation of the American Welfare State', *Comparative Social Research* 6 (1983) pp. 87–148.

J. Stephens, *The Transition from Capitalism to Socialism* (London: Macmillan, 1979).

J. Tampke, 'Bismarck's Social Legislation: a Genuine Breakthrough?' in W. J. Mommsen (ed.), *The Emergence of the Welfare State in Britain and Germany* (London: Croom Helm, 1981).

P. Taylor-Gooby, 'The Politics of Welfare: Public Attitudes and Behaviour' in R. Klein and M. O'Higgins (eds), *The Future of Welfare* (Oxford: Basil Blackwell, 1986).

P. Taylor-Gooby, 'Consumption Cleavages and Welfare Politics', *Political Studies* 34 (1986) pp. 592–606.

G. Therborn, *Why Are Some Peoples More Unemployed than Others?* (London: Verso Books, 1986).

11 Conservative Regimes and the Transition to Post-Fordism: The Cases of Great Britain and West Germany

Bob Jessop

This chapter deals with the current transition from Fordism to post-Fordism in Britain and West Germany under the contrasting conservative regimes led by Mrs Thatcher and Herr Kohl.[1] It addresses the question why Thatcherism has been so important for this transition in Great Britain and why no comparable regime (let alone one dignified with the label of Kohlism) has developed in West Germany. An explanation is sought in two related sets of factors: firstly, the modes of regulation and growth associated with the growth of Fordism in these societies and secondly, the nature of their state and political systems. For it is these features which have shaped the crisis of Fordism in each country and conditioned the form of transition to a post-Fordist accumulation regime.

This explanation is certainly not exhaustive (nor is it intended to be) and other aspects are also relevant. But a 'regulationist' approach is fruitful in defining the nature of these regimes. The chapter is divided into three parts: first, a very brief account of Fordism, its crisis, and the nature of post-Fordism; second, an account of the forms assumed by Fordism in Britain and Germany; and, third, an account of their different responses to the crisis of Fordism with special reference to the role of the Thatcher and Kohl governments. It concludes with some more general remarks on the regulation approach.

REGIMES OF ACCUMULATION

Capitalist development has been associated with different regimes of

261

accumulation, modes of growth and modes of regulation. Accumulation regimes and modes of growth are concepts located at different levels of abstraction but their empirical referents are closely related. An accumulation regime comprises a specific pattern of production and consumption considered in abstraction from the existence of specific national economies. A national mode of growth comprises the pattern of production and consumption and a national economy considered in terms of its role in the international division of labour. Relatively stable regimes of accumulation and modes of growth involve a contingent, historically constituted, and societally reproduced correspondence between patterns of production and consumption. Their basic features include: the various conditions governing the use of labour power, the features of the wage relation, the dynamic of investment and forms of competition and the monetary and credit system (Mazier *et al.* 1985, p. 9). A mode of regulation comprises 'the totality of institutional forms, networks and norms (explicit or implicit), which together secure the compatibility of typical modes of conduct in the context of an accumulation regime, corresponding as much to the changing balance of social relations as to their more general conflictual properties' (Lipietz 1985, p. 121; cf. Bowles and Edwardes on 'social structures of accumulation', 1985). The nature of the state and government policy are among the most important aspects of a mode of regulation. They are also increasingly significant as elements in international competition as governments seek to promote the flexibility and adaptability of whole societies (Dauderstaedt, 1983, p. 15).

Fordism

Fordism can be analysed as an accumulation regime, a mode of growth and a mode of regulation. In all three cases it involves a typical relation between mass production and mass consumption but Fordism needs to be specified more fully as one moves from a regime of accumulation through modes of growth to modes of social regulation. Recent studies of Fordism differ along two main dimensions. The first concerns the relative weight given to the nature of the labour process as opposed to the overall social structure of accumulation or pattern of societalisation (*Vergesellschaftung*). Both aspects are important and each conditions the other. Societalisation patterns cannot be derived from the labour process alone; and the latter is always overdetermined by various social and political factors. The second dimension concerns the relative weight accorded to national economies and modes of regulation as opposed to the international aspects of Fordist expansion (such as US hegemony, complementarities among different national modes of growth and the nature of peripheral Fordism). A thorough account would consider Fordism in all these respects (see Jessop 1988). Since this chapter is concerned with the radical break instituted by Thatcherism and the policy correction engineered through the West German *Wende* (turn), however, we will focus on the social and political aspects of two national modes of growth and regulation. This means concentrating on the national circuit of production-wages-consumption in its relation to the international economy and national modes of regulation.

Twelve general features of Fordism in advanced capitalist societies can be identified:[2]

(1) the development of mass production — especially in the consumer goods sector but also in some branches of capital goods — based on a dedicated, serial production process (often coupled with the mechanisation of transfer activities through such techniques as the moving assembly-line or the continuous flow production process);

(2) the predominant use of machine-paced, semi-skilled labour rather than skilled craft labour and non-Taylorised unskilled labour;

(3) managerial concern with the scientific organisation of the *collective* labour process in an enterprise rather than with the fragmented labour performed by the de-skilled individual worker (that is, the dominance of Fordism over Taylorism);

(4) the role of the wage (as opposed to domestic labour, subsistence agriculture or labour migration) as the principal mechanism and/or reference point in securing the reproduction of labour-power; this applies not only to industrial wage-labour but also to primary activities (capitalist argiculture) and tertiary sector activities (commerce, trade, finance, management, etc.);

(5) the consolidation of collective bargaining over wage rates (tied to inflation and/or to productivity increases) and working time, with the result that firms were better able to forecast wage costs and consumer demand;

(6) the predominance of the *mass* consumption of standardised, mass-produced commodities and/or of the *collective* consumption of goods and services provided by the state as opposed

to the consumption of non-standardised, typically hand-made or craft-produced commodities and/or home-produced goods and services;

(7) the role of marginal product differentiation (for example annual model changes), in-built obsolescence and advertising to encourage mass demand and the growing role of consumer credit facilities in financing mass consumption;

(8) the central role of mass consumption in integrating the circuit of capital so that the expansion of the capital and wage goods sectors are mutually reinforcing;

(9) monopolisitc regulation based on rigid 'mark-up' pricing rather than liberal, flexi-price product markets — coupled with movement out of obsolescent product lines into new production techniques and products;

(10) the central role of private and public credit in validating full employment levels of demand: private credit issued by the banking system underwrites private consumption as well as fixed and circulating capital whilst state credit is mobilised for demand management purposes as well as public investment;

(11) the increased importance of the state in securing the conditions for capital accumulation and the reproduction of wage-labour by adapting markets to the rigidities of Fordist mass production (only partially compensated through such forms of micro-flexibility as (de-)stocking, labour hoarding, subcontracting) through management of the wage relation, labour market policies, and demand management to smooth out fluctuations and to secure stable, calculable growth and thereby to encourage investment;

(12) the development of the welfare state as a mechanism to establish a minimum social wage, to generalise mass consumption norms and to coordinate the capital and consumer goods sectors.

Several studies from different positions in the regulation school suggest that Fordist accumulation depends on specific but contingent balances among different moments in the circuit of capital. For example, Lipietz (1985) presents a value-theoretical analysis; Boyer and Coriat (1987) focus on the Fordist wage relation; and Hirsch and Roth (1986) examine social and political blockages in the mobilisation of counter-tendencies to the tendency of the rate of profit to fall. In general we can say that continuing Fordist growth depends, firstly, on securing a balanced distribution of revenue between profits and wages so that the balance between mass production and mass consumption can be maintained; and, secondly, on preventing any tendency for the capital intensity of Fordist production techniques to increase from being reflected in a fall in the overall rate of profit — typically because productivity has failed to keep pace with that increase. This means, as Boyer and Coriat have shown, that wage indexing must be neither too high nor too low relative to increasing returns to scale, the propensity to consume, and the relation between investment and demand. If it is too high, profits and investment will fall; if it is too low, the mass demand to spur investment will be too weak (Boyer and Coriat 1987; Bowles and Edwardes 1985; Przeworski 1985). Thus Fordism thrives best where firms engage in oligopolistic pricing (which finances investment) and wages are tied to productivity below the growing returns to scale from new investment (so that mass consumption can also expand) (Boyer and Coriat 1987; Hurtienne 1986).

The crisis of Fordism

The crisis of Fordism is evident in all twelve areas noted above and has various economic, political and social causes. The more one moves from the labour processes to broader aspects of the mode of regulation, the more do political and social factors become central in explaining the forms assumed by the crisis of Fordism. We will deal with these factors in relation to the specific modes of regulation and growth in Britain and West Germany (see below) and will focus here on two sets of limits grounded in the labour process proper.

Firstly, there were technical limits to the introduction of rigid fixed capital and the realisation of its attendant economies of scale. Not all branches of production are amenable to Taylorism and Fordism and the scope for further productivity increases became relatively exhausted once these techniques had been generalised as far as possible. In addition, once the post-war boom slackened, the limited forms of micro-flexibility even when coupled with demand management proved inadequate. Political commitment to full employment also meant that 'reserve army' effects were limited to secondary markets and this delayed or halted the recovery of profits during downturns (Boyer and Coriat 1987).

Secondly, there has been growing working class resistance to the Taylorist and Fordist production process. This has also spread to other economic sectors. There was a growing absenteeism and labour turnover, a worsening rate of manufacturing defects, more frequent but often localised strikes with fundamental repercussions for the overall continuity of production and the growth of disputes and strikes over issues other than the abstract, universal categories of money and time (Albers *et al.* 1976; Crouch and Pizzorno 1978; Mazier *et al.* 1985, pp. 32–3; Hirsch 1985).

These problems have prompted a search for new forms of production which could overcome the rigidities of Taylorism and Fordism and also counteract working-class resistance. These responses were initially located within the Fordist pattern (for example job enrichment or bureaucratic controls). But post-Fordist responses have latterly become more important with the move to automation and robotisation and accompanying attempts to recompose the labour force (Hirsch 1985a; Kundig 1984; Mazier *et al.* 1985, p. 294; Morville 1985; Roobeek 1986).

FORDISM IN BRITAIN AND GERMANY

These general models of Fordism and post-Fordism have obvious limitations in comparing different social formations. For each national mode of growth has its own specific features deriving from its own mix for Fordist and non-Fordist elements and its particular industrial and political profiles. This is why the conceptual instrumentarium of the regulation school moves from abstract notions such as regulation to more concrete concepts such as national modes of growth (Boyer 1986b). Each national economy also has its own specific mode of insertion into the international economic system and the forms of crisis and this is reflected in its tendency to ascend or fall in the hierarchy of nations (Mistral 1986). Britain and West Germany clearly differ in both respects. The nature of Fordism in each society is different and so are their insertions into the international economy.[3] This has affected the forms of crisis and the forms of transition to post-Fordism.

Flawed Fordism in Britain

Fordism first struck firm roots in Britain in the 1930s. But the economic expansion and prosperity which this brought to *some* regions only became general in the years of the post-war boom. The extension of the Fordist wage relation was not so much rooted in the expansion of an auto-centric mass production system as in two other factors: the post-war settlement (1942–48)[4] with its precocious commitment to full employment and a universal welfare system and the favourable economic conditions created by an advantageous shift in the terms of trade with less developed economies and the sellers' market created by economic growth in the other advanced economies. The Keynesian welfare state (hereafter 'KWS') system provided the political shell and the organising myth in and through which a Fordist regime of sorts extended its hold over most parts of British society.

The extension of Fordism in Britain was flawed at all three nodal points in the virtuous circle of mass production-high wages-mass consumption. Productivity did not increase to the same extent as in other countries; the Fordist wage relation was defective; and mass consumption was financed through demand management and the social wage as well as productivity increases.

The relative retardation of Fordist mass production was reflected not only in lower levels of productive investment but also in two other aspects of investment. It was more often 'add-on' in nature, that is, concerned to compensate for deficiencies in existing techniques and processes of production rather than to introduce entirely new processes and products. And British firms failed to reach the same levels of *productivity* from similar production processes, machinery and so on, which were obtained in other advanced capitalist economies. This failure becomes even clearer if one discounts the impact of the higher levels of productivity and investment which were obtained by incoming *foreign* concerns and/or from British firms setting up on *greenfield* sites.[5] Its long-term impact was evident in recurrent balance of payments problems tied to poor productivity, inflation and progressive de-industrialisation.

The voluntaristic collective bargaining system also contributed to the problems of Fordism in Britain. Trade unions were organised on overlapping craft, industrial and general lines and this resulted at plant level in multi-unionism; employers' associations at branch or industry level were weak, peak organisations lacked power and there is still no peak organisation for business as a whole. In the private sector bargaining was dencentralised, fragmented, informal, *ad hoc* and disorderly; its scope and outcome depended far more on the prevailing balance of forces between 'the two sides of industry' than on any insitutionalised procedures and rules of engagement. There was only a long-term and imperfect link between productivity increases and real wages; and labour market conditions had little impact on collective bargaining. In the short term, stagflationary tendencies became more marked. This was not reversed by increasing state intervention through wages policies (as often concerned to support the exchange rate as to further industrial policy) nor growing centralisation in the 1960s. Instead the combination of relative decline and global crisis provoked greater conflict among all three social partners from 1969 onwards and this led to repeated attempts to reform industrial relations.

Thirdly, despite the failure to consolidate mass production, the British state was committed, through the post-war settlement and the continuing bipartisan consensus about jobs for all, to validating full employment levels of demand. Industry's failure to complete a thorough-going Fordist transformation in relevant sectors was there-fore reflected in a structural propensity to compensate for deficien-cies in domestic production through the import of mass consumer durables. This was not compensated by the export of capital goods – indeed increasing import penetration and export failure were also evident here. An expanding welfare state further aggravated these problems through an increase in public sector employment and the growth of the social wage – both of which served to generalise Fordist mass consumption norms. Overall the economy was affected by rising unit wage costs, rising imports of mass consumer goods, expanding social expenditure, and an emergent fiscal crisis.

This flawed Fordism was reinforced by the manner in which Britain was inserted into the international economy. British firms tended to look towards imperial markets in Africa and Asia and/or to the more slowly developing and fragmented markets overseas (Latin America) at a time when fast growth and integrated mass markets were found in North America, Japan and Western Europe. This reinforced the traditional industrial profile of British firms and did little to encourage modernisation. These problems were aggravated by the dominance of financial capital within the market hierarchy in Britain and by government's concern to maintain the reserve and transaction roles of sterling even when this meant deflation. Modernisation and growth policies were blocked by this external dependence. Conversely the weakness of Fordism led to payments problems which affected the City's role and at one time seemed destined to restrict it to the overseas sterling area. The result was a gradual descent down the international hierarchy.

The crises which have unfolded over the last twenty years in the British political economy involve more than the economic and political forms of the Keynesian welfare state. They are rooted in the failure even to complete the transition to Fordism in key respects and the emerging crisis of Fordism on a world scale. In particular this flawed Fordism has had significant effects both during the post-war boom and during its collapse.

Firstly, because the boom years were mistakenly identified with the Keynesian welfare state system, efforts were made to shore this 'KWS' system up through corporatist bargaining over prices, incomes, and productivity and through eleventh hour, state-sponsored Fordist modernisation aimed at securing economies of scale through mergers, more stable growth through indicative planning and re-industrialisation through investment subsidies. But the corporatist strategies lacked a continuous tradition of social partnership instituted before the economic crisis,[6] a corporatist social base in well-organised industrial unions and strong business associations and corporatist structural supports. Likewise state intervention was attempted without first constructing an interventionist state with the strategic capacities to define, co-ordinate and implement a coherent industrial policy (Jessop 1980). Industrial policy for the purposes of Fordist modernisation was too often confused with job preservation and/or regional policy and too often subordinated to exchange rate, fiscal and electoral priorities.

And secondly, the flawed character of British Fordism aggravated the impact of the second oil shock and the deflationary policies pursued by the Thatcher government, leading to a rapid process of de-industrialisation. But mentioning Thatcherism takes the present story ahead of itself and we must first deal with Fordism in West Germany.

Export-oriented Fordism in Germany

Fordism in West Germany has also assumed a specific form. This can only be understood by considering how its economic, social and political systems were reconstructed after 1945 and how it was inserted into the international economy during the 1950s. Whereas Britain survived the war undefeated and its organisational and institutional structures remained much the same, the occupying powers led by the US presided over the reconstruction of West Germany's systems of industrial relations, unions, parties, governance and education.[7] In addition the heavy industrial base which the future Federal Republic inherited after the division of Germany could only operate at full capacity if it found markets abroad.

Thus the German post-war settlement was quite different from that in Britain and it was considered somewhat later (1949–52). The labour movement secured co-determination and worker participation but was also obliged to work within the limits of a strong market rationality embodied in the social market economy (*soziale Marktwirtschaft*). This involved the dominance of private sector capital, a key co-ordinating role for banking capital, only limited direct and open state intervention and a welfare state organised along corporatist rather than liberal lines. The distribution of powers between federal and regional (*Land*) government and the legally entrenched autonomy of the central bank (*Bundesbank*) made it difficult for the federal state to engage in *dirigisme* and/or demand management[8]; but high levels of nominal taxation and access to Marshall Aid (together with counterpart funds) did enable the federal state to discriminate among different economic activities through selective tax concessions and subsidies. The Erhard government encouraged investment, exports and capital formation in specific industries and, despite rhetoric to the contrary, penalised consumption and imports (Abelshauser 1982, pp. 49–51; Markovits and Allen 1984, pp. 91–102; Deubner 1984, pp. 519–23). This pattern of massive tax concessions and subsidies has continued to the present (Webber 1986, pp. 25–8).

The German post-war settlement also gave a central role to the unions and employers' organisations in managing the wage relation. The industrial relations system was marked by a strong juridification — or the penetration of law into industrial relations, well-organised social partners (with a system of unitary industrial unions and highly organised employers' bodies[9] at both regional and national level), and commitment to wage bargaining. Protected from state interference through the legal principle of *Tarifautonomie*, unions and employers met each other on two levels. Whereas unions bargained over wages and hours at industry and regional levels, works councils (*Betriebsraete*) negotiated over conditions at plant level. In bargaining the social partners take account of conjunctural factors (especially export markets) as well as past productivity gains (Hager 1980, p. 6; Markovits 1986, pp. 416–17; Streeck 1985, p. 16).

The post-war expansion of German industry was marked less by mass production of consumer durables than by an export-oriented capital goods sector.[10] The expansion and productivity of this key sector depended less on Fordist economies of scale and the semi-skilled labour of the Fordist 'mass worker' than on technological rents and the highly skilled labour of *Facharbeiter*. Mass consumer durables (for example cars) penetrated West Germany more slowly than in other big West European countries and were important only from the mid-1960s onwards (Deubner 1984, p. 510). Likewise the consumer goods sector has lost out from internationalisation of the West German economy and has suffered from rapid import penetration (Deubner 1984, p. 512).

Initially sustained by the clear undervaluation of the DM, this export orientation has since become structurally necessary. For West Germany's industrial profile and production are oriented towards foreign markets, and conversion to serve the home market would be difficult – especially as the capital goods sector is so dominant (Deubner 1984, p. 506). This sector lies at the centre of a relatively coherent industrial core.

The development of this core is co-ordinated and, where necessary 'crisis-managed', in at least three inter-related ways: through the system of universal banks, which control four-fifths of shares[11]; through formal cartels, cross-investment, interlocking directorates, and subcontracting ties; and, especially from 1966–67, through regional and federal government (Dyson 1986; Esser 1986; Webber 1986). The state system has been active in promoting modernisation since the 1960s in order to maintain West Germany's position at the top of the international hierarchy in civilian capital goods: it has invested in nuclear energy, infrastructure, production technologies, industrial research and development, education and so forth (Hager 1980, p. 5). From 1966 there has also been a shift towards state sectoral intervention and Keynesianism. More recently *Ostpolitik* has had important commercial as well as political implications. Finally, although they play no significant co-ordinating role (except in structural crisis cartels), the trade unions recognise West Germany's export dependence and generally support the modernisation strategies necessary to maintain a high wage export oriented economy (compare Deubner 1979).

The dominance of the capital goods sector (and export-oriented industries more generally) has underpinned a virtuous circle in wage relations. Exports long maintained full employment, monopolistic pricing at home maintained profits, real wages tracked productivity, and the social partners took account of the export market in collective bargaining (Henkel 1980, p. 29; Boyer 1986a; Markovits 1986).

The crisis in the West German mode of growth took, as might be expected, a form different from that in Britain. The crisis is one of a mature, export-oriented mode of growth rather than a flawed, uncompetitive Fordism. The first export-led slump came in 1975 but the problems were already apparent earlier in slackening productivity and declining profits. They provoked the social-liberal coalition to develop the *Modell Deutschland* solution in the early 1970s. On the macro-level this sought to secure the international competitiveness of German capital through corporatist arrangements aimed at modernisation and austerity. It also sought to block the movement from economic to political crisis by integrating the unions into the crisis-management process (Huebner 1986, p. 375). The continuing problem has been to maintain export-driven growth despite high wages and a slackening in productivity increases in Fordist sectors (such as cars).

A crucial role in this adaptation process has been played by the state at regional and federal level: it has provided finance to modernise old branches and to develop high value-added products for export, promoted international co-operation to stabilise existing export markets and create new ones; financed retraining of the labour force; underwritten the social costs of change; and mobilised union support at plant, branch, regional and national levels in an effort to minimise the political costs of modernisation (Esser 1986).

Even this strategy was meeting real difficulties by 1981–82. These included union disquiet with the austerity programme and mass unemployment, growing hostility from employers to labour and the state, a deflationary policy on the part of the *Bundesbank*, blocking moves by the union parties in the upper chamber (*Bundesrat*), and internal conflict in the coalition and its two member parties (Scharpf 1987). Thus, for the social democratic government, the game was up. The crisis was followed by the Wende (1982–83) and a christian-liberal coalition government committed (at least rhetorically) to 'more market, less state' and to renewing the social market economy (Webber 1986 p. 2). In practice this involved a self-correction of the model, however, without giving up the economic attack on the world market (Huabner 1986, p. 376).

This modification of the prevailing crisis-management strategy contrasts strongly with the British case. In the latter it has been essential to dismantle the obstacles to Fordism and, in an unfavourable economic position, to secure the conditions for post-Fordism. In West Germany the prevailing strategy has been one of adapting the export-oriented model to new conditions and of promoting its self-reorganisation through concerted action.

THE TRANSITION TO POST-FORDISM

The first responses to the economic crises of the 1970s occurred within the existing modes of growth and regulation. Thus Britain saw corporatist strategies which tried to maintain full employment and social welfare demand management as well as state-sponsored Fordist modernisation based on mergers and industrial reorganisation. The attempt failed. The collapse of the Social Contract between the Labour government and the unions in 1976 brought this phase to an end. This was followed by a period of austerity, retrenchment and social democratic monetarism and, in the wake of the notorious strike-ridden 'Winter of Discontent', the election of the first Thatcher government.

The initial West German response also involved attempts to shore up the existing mode of growth and regulation. This was expressed in the *Modell Deutschland* programme and a more selective form of social partnership; and its was intended to strengthen the economy's export-orientation. When this strategy began to falter, the SDP–FDP coalition still pursued a step-wise, corrective programme rather than forcing a radical break. An austerity programme was adopted to promote investments, reduce social costs and promote technological change (Schmidt 1982). However, as mass unemployment continued to rise, the SDP became more isolated and divided. The *Wende* expressed the exhaustion of the SDP's approach rather than the collapse of the strategy itself and the christian-liberal coalition has given the model a new inflection rather than trying to overturn it completely. The nature and limits of this continuity will occupy us below.

Thatcherism and Post-Fordism

In the late 1970s a consensus gradually emerged about the need to break with economic demand-management and political crisis-avoidance and to embark on radical supply-side economic policies and more confrontationist politics. Thatcherism gave the growing popular disquiet with the Keynesian welfare state system some direction by placing it at the forefront of the electoral strategy of a major political party. It also provided a focus for an economic and political offensive which emanated from key sectors of the establishment and was directed against the post-war settlement in general and the gains of organised labour in particular. This was initially presented in terms of reorganising British society in accordance with the doctrines of the social market economy and the strong state. In the wake of the 'Winter of Discontent' (with its post-war strike record) this alliance brought Thatcherism to power.

But the rhetoric of authoritarian populism and the empty formulas of monetarism were unequal to the tasks of effective economic and political management. Thus the first Thatcher government already faced the problem of developing a more coherent strategy to manage the economy and to consolidate its own power. Its approach evolved in a trial-and-error fashion, at different rates in different areas and with varying degrees of success. Since the mid-1980s it has crystallised around the neo-liberal accumulation strategy based on flexible accumulation and a hegemonic project based on popular capitalism. These are counterposed to the corporatist, Fordist modernisation strategy of the 1960s and to the social democratic, One Nation welfare state project first established through the post-war settlement. The recent election (June 1987) has provided striking confirmation of the two nations, popular capitalist project (Jessop *et al.* 1987) and the third Thatcher government is already embarked on a re-invigorated neo-liberal programme aimed at creating the conditions for post-Fordism.

This involves more than acting as the economic midwife to post-Fordism. The social, political and cultural factors which obstruct this transition in Britain must also be tackled. The current strategy operates on a broad front. In particular Thatcher faces the problem that British industry can no longer compete in the old post-war technologies nor, perhaps, become competitive in the new. Many of the structural and institutional obstacles to Fordist modernisation are even more acute now and would present *any* government (and not merely Thatcher's) with real problems.

The most distinctive feature of Britain's neo-liberal transition to post-Fordism are its new-found position as the principal *site* for international (mainly foreign) financial institutions. The groundwork for this specialised role was laid in the 1960s with the rise of the Eurodollar markets but it has been consolidated under Thatcherism through the abolition of exchange controls, deregulation of financial institutions and services and favourable tax treatment. Thus Thatcherism has abandoned national capital to global competition and is actively promoting international capital instead of managing the tensions between these fractions as past governments have unsuccessfully attempted (Kastendiek 1987, p. 26). The City has also gained from a second defining feature of Thatcherite economic strategy: its commitment to privatisation as a means of raising revenue and reducing the economic weight of the public sector. Related measures have been adopted to encourage inward investment from multi-national enterprises. In addition many schemes have been introduced to promote small business through deregulation, investment schemes, tax breaks and direct state sponsorship. In all these measures the primary emphasis is on the market-driven character of reorganisation. Although state intervention still continues, it is not guided by any overall industrial programme or concern to secure the coherence of Britain's industrial base.

In other West European countries the unions have been weakened by conjunctural factors and changes in general economic policy. In Britain there has been a sustained political attack on the trade unions as well as direct intervention in their internal affairs as part of a labour exclusion strategy (Crouch 1986; Hyman 1987). Thus, whereas previous governments had tried to strengthen the position of responsible national leaderships within the unions and in collective bargaining, Thatcherism aims to weaken union leaders and return the unions to their members, confining them to plant level bargaining within the limits of post-Fordist market rationality.

The Thatcher governments have also made efforts to make labour markets more flexible. So far these efforts have been less concerned with re-skilling the labour force than with increasing the flexibility of wages, hours and working conditions. In addition to industrial relations, employment and social security legislation, the second Thatcher government gave a central role in this respect to the Manpower Services Commission. In its third term Thatcherism will reinforce these policies through measures to encourage more flexible pay schemes related to regional labour markets, profit-sharing and wider share ownership.

Thatcherism has also been busy recomposing the welfare state. Despite claims that the welfare state is safe in Conservative hands, it is steadily being reorganised. Whereas the social democratic state was based on citizens' rights, universal benefits and a rising standard of financial or material provision, the neo-liberal social security state is discretionary, means-tested and minimalist. As far as individual welfare is concerned, the government is promoting popular capitalism as a substitute for the nanny state: house-owning, pension-owning, share-owning and private medical insurance are subsidised through tax relief and are regarded as substitutes for council housing, adequate state pensions, income support and free health service. Where individuals and families cannot (or will not) make adequate private provision, a basic, no-frills state system will be provided, subject to rationing by queuing and/or involving minimalist, revolving 'social funds' administered on a local, discretionary basis. As regards collective provision or collective consumption, increasing emphasis is being placed on adapting public services to the needs of industry. This involves two different policies – private tendering for services under public management and/or growing centralisation of services at the expense primarily of local government.

Lastly, the Thatcher governments have been busy reorganising the state system. Already in the first two periods of office efforts had been made to 'Thatcherise' it in various ways. These included: civil service reorganisation and politically-motivated promotion to key official posts; enhancing Treasury control over all areas of government and using its financial powers to force restructuring; downgrading or ignoring established channels for tripartite or corporatist negotiation involving the trade union movement; reinforcing the police apparatus and redefining 'subversion'; reducing the financial and political autonomy of elected local authorities (notably by abolishing metropolitan councils and the Greater London Council which had proved important sites of resistance to Thatcherism but also through a series of annual legal and administrative changes to reduce, redirect and control local spending); establishing powerful but locally non-accountable bodies such as urban development corporations to modernise the inner cities for and on behalf of capital; radically restructuring the education system through education spending cuts and systematic interference in all areas; expanding the Manpower Services Commission (MSC) into a major force in training (especially for young people and other groups of the unemployed); and embarking on a programme of privatisation and deregulation. It should be stressed that many of these changes are motivated more strongly by issues of political strategy than they are by questions of economic rationality. They are undermining political forces committed to the Keynesian welfare state system and constructing new interests in the transition to flexible accumulation and popular capitalism. Their cumulative effect is to provide long-term structural underpinnings to the neo-liberal strategy currently being pursued.

The third Thatcher goverment is now embarked on a final assault on the social democratic settlement and its political supports. Particularly significant here are four areas where political power is being reorganised. The expansion of urban development corporations to remove planning powers from elected local authorities and to promote urban and industrial redevelopment; further centralisation of the education system through a national curriculum coupled with measures to re-introduce selection and parent power; the introduction of a regressive poll tax instead of the current property tax (rates) to intensify electoral pressure against 'high spending' local councils; and further measures to promote privatisation and/or commercial accounting in local services. In addition there will be a further programme of privatisation and another round of legislation to weaken unions. In this sense the Thatcher governments are distinctive for the priority they have given to winning the political struggle over short-term economic crisis-management and/or dynamic economic efficiency.

Modell Duetschland and post-Fordism

The Kohl government has continued the *Modell Deutschland* strategy. But it has adapted it to conditions of growing austerity and also reoriented it towards the logic of post-Fordism. Thus it is still committed to promoting West Germany's dominant world market position in capital goods and high technology and it is still co-operating (somewhat less enthusiastically) with the unions as well as capital.

The Kohl government has continued the active industrial policy of the SPD-FDP coalition through its 'new research and technology policy oriented towards innovation' (Esser 1986). This is still oriented to the overall coherence of West Germany's industrial core and does not, as is true of Japan, aim to promote only selected high-tech products or sectors. Instead there is concern for everything from special steels to value-added cars, from new machine tools to telecommunications, from railways to aero-space. Often this is associated with 'societal guidance' or 'technocorporatist' programmes rather than the earlier tripartite corporatist arrangements linking unions, business and the state. These programmes seek to advance research on key technologies relevant to all industrial sectors (information technology, biotechnology, new materials, laser technology) and are based on a close, wide-ranging co-operation among the business, state and science community without significant union involvement (von Alemann *et al.* 1986; Esser 1986; Junne 1984; Willke 1986). Other elements in this technology policy are the growing West German interest in space travel and research, closer Franco-German co-operation to establish Europe as an independent aero-space power; and continued support for the energy industry. In turn this is reflected in more extensive federal co-ordination of technology policy (von Alemann *et al.* 1986). Another post-Fordist element is found in the state promotion of small business through venture capital, science parks, technology parks and so on. This policy is backed by more general measures (such as deregulation, tax breaks on profits and public sourcing policies) to favour German industry.

There are certainly neo-classical supply-side and monetarist currents within the coalition parties comparable to those in the Thatcher and Reagan regimes. But, as a separate political force, the monetarists are marginal (largely due to the comparative success the *Bundesbank* has long recorded in controlling inflation); and the supply-siders can be readily integrated into the modernisation strategy. Thus, whereas crude supply-siders and monetarists are relatively uninfluential, the more interventionist high technology modernisation currents have gained in influence (Saage 1985). This current has long-term institutional bases in the West German state system and receives strong and continued backing from the more competitive sectors of German industry. It is also advantaged by the powers enjoyed by *Land* governments to promote regional and industrial development so that sunrise industries can move to CDU/CSU areas in sunrise regions where a modern infrastructure is most readily available. Particularly important in this respect are Spaeth's Baden-Wurtenburg and Strauss's Bavaria. But SDP governments in sunset regions are also active in promoting rationalisation and re-industrialisation. In this sense the North-South divide has much less resonance in West Germany than in Britain (Esser and Hirsch 1987).

The christian-liberal strategy towards the unions is twofold. Firstly, it is supporting employers in their efforts to make production more flexible, to resist union attempts to slow or reverse job losses, and to press for legislation favouring more flexible working time (Leithauser 1986). This is reflected in legislative changes to restrict the rights of workers regarding hours and conditions, dismissal, and so forth; and to undermine the rights of established unions in representing workers at plant level and undertaking secondary action (Adamy and Steffen 1985). This is part of an attempt to redefine the 'terms of trade' among capital, organised labour, and the state and to induce the unions to develop a 'new realism' towards flexibility. Its effect will be to push the unions towards a selective corporatism in which core workers gain and others (typically non-unionised) are marginalised.

Secondly, the government is co-operating, as before, with the unions in high-tech sectors through codetermination and concertation (Esser 1986). No attempt is being made to exclude the unions (as in Britain) and the aim is to tie them into the transition process. The effect of this dual strategy in the political field has been to reduce the significance of national-level corporatism (Chancellor Kohl himself only met union leaders formally in late 1984) and to promote regional and local corporatism (especially in the form of crisis-cartels in declining industries) (Brandt 1985, p. 9).

The Kohl regime has also been reconstructing the welfare state. Initially it continued the austerity programme of the social-liberal coalition, especially in restricting support for the unemployed and transferring more of the burden of pension provision to individual contributors. This has been motivated by a desire to improve the economic climate for business as well as to save money when conjunctural and demographic factors have put budgets under strain. One effect of these changes has been a stronger differentiation than hitherto of social policies between employees and the economically inactive poor — to the latter's disadvantage. There is a gradual movement towards minimising guaranteed state provision and encouraging people to make their own earnings-related provision and/or to purchase services in the market or else to seek help in the community. Thus, as official state welfare services and norms have been cut back, the state has encouraged an informal welfare state and the privatisation of social risk. Various measures have been taken to devolve state responsibilities to community care, self help and neighbourhood help (*Subsidiaritaet*). The overall result of these policies is to strengthen the 'two nations' tendencies of the post-Fordist welfare state with such 'subsidariary' help constituting a self-financed bonus for the privileged and stigmatising, disciplinary charity for the disprivileged (Hirsch and Roth 1986, pp. 144–7; Baecker 1986, pp. 201–3).

Finally, discontinuities in the West German state are less marked than in Britain. This reflects two features of the state. On the one hand, the movement towards a strong, security state was already developed in West Germany (Hirsch 1980).[12] The Kohl government has simply presided over its further development, building on recent developments in information technology. On the other hand, the economy's greater strength and the adaptability of its institutional structures means that pressures for a radical break are less evident (Hirsch and Roth 1986, p. 142). The opportunities offered for local experimentation by the federal system are as significant here as they are in areas such as industrial policy.

Overall, then, the continuities are more marked than the discontinuities and a radical break involving 'Kohlism' (or its equivalent) is not needed. Instead what is required and what is occurring is a correction and modification of the strategies pursued in the 1970s in the light of the technical and economic developments of the 1980s. The new coalition is better able to achieve this re-orientation because it faces fewer legitimation problems *vis-à-vis* the unions than an SDP-dominated government but it nonetheless represents a basic continuity with past political and economic strategies which have proved relatively successful.

Some comparisons

To illustrate these general contrasts we can compare some broad areas of reorganisation involved in the transition to post-Fordism in both Britain and Germany. These areas show how existing modes of growth and regulation influence the politics and strategies of the transition. We deal in turn with attempts to flexibilise financial institutions; privatisation; industrial policy and industrial relations.

Deregulating financial institutions

In Britain the Thatcher government is strongly committed to the deregulation and liberalisation of the financial sector. This has been accompanied by radical changes in financial institutions and financial products. Above all the first Thatcher government abolished exchange controls and the second established the framework for 'Big Bang', that is, the liberalisation and deregulation of financial services. Together these changes have transformed the City into the world's leading international financial centre — which is all the more remarkable in the light of its weak domestic industrial base compared with its New York and Tokyo rivals. In West Germany changes in the banking system, the stock exchanges and financial regulations have occurred but they are less marked and have been undertaken reluctantly rather than from political zeal.

This contrast reflects several aspects of the modes of growth and regulation. Firstly, the universal banking system in West Germany is very flexible and can already provide financial products serving functions similar to the innovative products in Britain; secondly, the inflation and instability which prompted innovation in Britain (and the US) did not produce such a large demand for financial innovations (for a survey of the most important recent financial innovations, see van Horne 1986); thirdly, until recently, the Bundesbank has blocked Deutschmark-denominated financial instruments in order to limit West Germany's exposure to international interest rate and exchange rate shocks and to discourage the use of the Deutschmark as an international reserve and investment medium; fourthly, the Bundesbank had always operated in market terms rather than through administrative measures so that deregulation was less necessary; and, finally, West German rules were already relatively liberal for domestic and foreign activities so that there was no need to find loopholes (on these issues, see especially Dudler 1986).

Yet international competition and the fear of losing business to foreign institutions and/or foreign financial centres has led to a partial liberalisation. Some financial innovations from abroad can now be employed in West Germany (see Clarich 1987). But the impression remains that, whereas British financial institutions are moving in the direction of internationally competitive specialists in financial services, the West German banks are still more oriented to the West German industrial core (including its operations abroad) (Grou 1985). This is one area where the mode of growth has shown inertia and modes of regulation have been adapted.

Privatisation and liberalisation

This also provides an interesting contrast. Whereas nationalised industries in Britain are state-owned and have often been run on non-commercial lines, West Germany's public enterprises are more often controlled at *Land* or communal level, enjoy more commercial autonomy, and are often used to promote technological change and modernisation. Moreover, whereas nationalisation has usually divided political parties in Britain, the postwar SDP has never campaigned for a state sector. These factors are reflected in the nature of privatisation programmes in the two countries. For, whereas privatisation in Britain was initially motivated by ideological commitment and the need to raise revenue to finance tax cuts and sustain public spending, West Germany's programme is subordinated to the needs of industrial coherence, national security, maintaining stability in financial markets and preserving continuity in management (Uhel 1986; Abromeit 1986; Young 1987). Thus the christian-liberal rhetoric of privatisation has been tempered by pragmatism; proposals are also subject to negotiation rather than being imposed from above (Uhel 1986, pp. 77–8).

We can illustrate this contrast by considering the liberalisation and privatisation of the telecommunications industry in Britain. For the Thatcher government has adopted a market-driven strategy in liberalising telecommunications, putting market-led *demand* before indigenous *supply* capacity. Domestically this has mainly benefited the City and those involved in supplying value added network services. But it is consistent with the Thatcherite strategy of promoting *cosmopolitan* re-industrialisation in so far as supply has been met by incoming firms interested in doing business with Europe as a whole (Morgan and Webber 1986, pp. 59, 62). In contrast, the West German strategy has been much more solicitous of German 'electro-capital' (Luethje 1986, pp. 67–71). Nor is there a social basis for liberalisation in the German telecommunications sector because the union parties are more solicitous than the Conservatives for lower income groups, the rural population, small and medium manufacturing firms and so forth (Webber 1986b, pp. 408–10); and must also take greater account of its implications on jobs, incomes and the regions (Morgan and Webber 1986, p. 76).

It should also be noted that privatisation in Britain has major political aims. It represents an attempt to roll back the post-war settlement and socialism and to create a 'popular capitalist' base of support for a neo-liberal accumulation strategy. And it has served to disguise the government's failure to control the PSBR (since privatisation counts as negative public expenditure). So far privatisation in West Germany has only concerned the federal level.

Industrial policy for the private sector

As regards British industrial policy, we must distinguish between rhetoric and reality under Thatcherism. The first Thatcher government disengaged loudly from the unsuccessful policies on older nationalised industries, (pre-)Fordist lame ducks and regional aid. This period of doctrinal palaeo-liberalism ended in the latter half of 1980 under the combined impact of rising unemployment and criticism from business. Since then the government has been active in promoting rationalisation and re-industrialisation in declining industries and in supporting innovation in sunrise industries. It has developed a wide range of initiatives through several government departments and quasi-government agencies and is now particularly active in partnership with private industry in promoting small business, rationalisation, new wave technologies and so forth (Wilks 1985). Indeed, in the five key future technologies (micro-electronics, telecommunications, robotics, optics and opto-electronics and biotechnology), Britain has programmes which are similar to those in Japan, the US, France and Germany (Junne 1984, pp. 143–4). Whether or not the sums available are adequate, spent wisely and adequately co-ordinated is debateable but the existence of these programmes does reveal the state's importance in the transition to post-Fordism even if in neo-liberal guise.

In West Germany there is less reluctance to proclaim this strategy because it continues the earlier *Modell Deutschland*. The main elements of this strategy have already been outlined in the preceding section and only two further comments are needed. The neo-statist strategy is particularly clear in crisis sectors. Here one finds state-sponsored, union-supported rationalisation, concentration and upgrading together with moves to export low-tech products to production sites abroad using low-wage, unskilled labour. The high-tech sectors are also receiving more financial support under the Kohl government with the federal state playing a more directive role (Esser 1986, Vaeth 1984). In contrast to Britain the state plays a more active role and this is reflected in the greater coherence of the industrial strategy as well as the greater coherence of the industrial core.

Industrial relations

Strategies towards industrial relations also differ. The weak institutionalisation of trade union rights in Britain has greatly helped the Thatcher government in withdrawing them along with privileged access to the institutions of government. The onslaught began before the inexorable rise of mass unemployment and exploited the political unpopularity of the unions and their organisational weakness borne of easy expansion during the post-war boom. It involves direct state intervention into unions' internal organisation as well as more general economic, labour, financial and social policies (Kastendiek 1987, pp. 2–3). And, above all, it involves action against public sector unions in industry and public services.

In the private sector the reform of industrial relations is much more market-generated than state-imposed. On key issues business has rejected the government's strategy (for example, on the closed shop or regionally differentiated wage agreements). And it is actively developing forms of micro-corporatism based on the 'new realism' and internal labour markets. This is reflected in continuing wage drift in the private sector as well as wildcat co-operation, employee bailouts, formal agreements or collective bargaining over new technology and so forth. Conflicts are largely confined to the public sector, to new modern firms outside greenfield sites and to firms faced with the choice between bankruptcy or confronting the unions (Terry 1986).

Conversely, juridification, co-determination, and involvement in parafiscal bodies (such as health insurance, unemployment pay and pension organisations) have blocked a frontal political attack on the unions in West Germany and encouraged cooperation between unions and employers. Thus, although right-wing fringe groups have raised doubts about *Tarifautonomie* and demand more pluralism at plant level, neither employers' associations nor the CDU leadership want to touch co-determination (Streeck 1985; Markovits 1986, p. 426; on the main legal measures against unions and ways in which unions are excluded from the workplace, see Wendeling-Schroeder 1986). Indeed, after remaining aloof for two years, the Kohl government restored tripartite consultation at national level (Markovits 1986, p. 424); and IG Metall, the largest union, reached an agreement with state and employers over vocational training in 1984. Within this framework, however, changes are occurring. For the Kohl government is trying to work within the legal and corporatist systems to overcome unions' opposition to flexibility. It is changing the law on working time (length of working day, Sunday working, night work for women, fixed duration contracts and so on) and helping to divide the workforce into a stable core and precarious margin (Leithauser 1986, pp. 183, 197).

Moreover, within the two-tier system of worker representation, it is possible to discern a shift towards micro-corporatism at plant level based on works councils at the expense of meso-corporatism involving the unions (Markovits 1986, p. 419). Indeed, the works councils appear to be the nucleus of an emergent company unionism (Streeck 1984, p. 27). In turn this continues the pattern of effective consensual interest accommodation at enterprise level which has long been a crucial precondition of West German success in world markets (Streeck 1984, p. 42). The continued willingness to bargain can also be seen in the conclusion, in April 1987, of a three-year agreement between IG Metall and the employers over flexible working time in exchange for the stepwise introduction of a 37.5 hour week and wage increases.

Interim conclusions

The Thatcher and Kohl governments are conservative regimes which cannot avoid being involved in the transition to a post-Fordist economic, political and social order. Nonetheless, the Thatcher governments have adopted policies different in key respects from those pursued in West Germany. Where the post-Fordist industrial logic is particularly strong (in the high technology areas), some similarities between the two regimes have emerged under the impact of international competition. These similarities can also be seen in the emergent post-Fordist industrial and service sectors where management and unions play the leading role within a framework established by government. In both societies, for example, we find a movement towards micro-corporatism at plant level. The similarities are weakest in areas where the scope for political action is greatest and the logic of post-Fordism less clear. The contrasting approaches to privatisation are especially noticeable and so too are those in the field of industrial relations and union legislation. If politics makes a difference, however, we must enquire why it has taken different forms in Britian and West Germany.

WHY IS THERE NO KOHLISM IN WEST GERMANY?

In their different ways both Britain and Germany have embarked on a transition towards a post-Fordist economy. We will now examine how political factors have helped shape this general process. For, alongside differences in their forms of Fordism and its crisis, political structures and forces have also significantly moulded the transition. These can be approached by asking why there is no Kohlism in West Germany as long as this question is not reduced simply to matters of personality and political style.

In Britain the beginnings of the transition to post-Fordism have coincided with the rise and consolidation of Thatcherism. The latter certainly has populist ideological aspects and a plebiscitary political moment and is closely identified with the distinctive personality and political style of Mrs Thatcher. But it also involves a new economic and political strategy for the central state which transcends particular personalities and indeed parties. It now dominates the Conservative Party; the SPD in Britain soon acquired the soubriquet of 'Thatcherism with a human face'; and the Labour Party is gradually accepting the need for flexible accumulation, even if it still rejects the 'two nations' aspects of popular capitalism. Different parties would pursue somewhat different strategies but the break with the Keynesian welfare state mode of regulation is clear.

In Germany the transition to post-Fordism involves not so much a break with the past as a correction in the earlier course. It involves no populist movement or ideological current which one could term Kohlism and it is not associated with a radically new economic and political strategy. In part this reflects two simple facts. Kohl himself is no charismatic, conviction politician; and he entered office at the hands of the FDP through parliamentary machinations rather than through a critical, realigning election campaign. These facts are related in turn to basic structural features of the West German electoral and party system. This is structurally predisposed towards coalition government and creates conditions in which small parties (such as the FDP or, perhaps, the Greens) can make or unmake governments. Indeed three major governmental changes in the BRD since 1949 have been secured in parliamentary manoeuvres rather than directly through realigning elections at federal elections: Erhard's fall in 1966, Kiesinger's in 1969 and Schmidt's in 1982 (Irving and Paterson 1983, p. 422). Likewise the recent *Machtwechsel* had more to do with shifts from radical liberalism to economic liberalism in the FDP than with the gradual rightward drift of the CDU/CSU (Bulmer 1983, p. 19; Kastendiek and Kastendiek 1985); and it was helped by Kohl's centrist commitments which made the shift from SPD to CDU less dramatic and ruptural. It sometimes seems, indeed, that Kohl's job is to hold the 'middle ground' and secure moderation in domestic and foreign policy so that market, corporatist and molecular social forces can refashion German society.

But explaining the absence of a radical break in terms of Kohl's personality and the circumstances of his accession to the Chancellorship could be misleading. Other leading figures (such as Strauss) do have an authoritarian populist style and there are also significant neo-conservative and neo-liberal currents in the West German political system. Thus at least two preconditions for something akin to Thatcherism and Reaganism exist but nothing like them has gained power in West Germany. Indeed, whilst Kohlism has never emerged, Straussism actually failed on the national political stage in 1980.[13]

And, despite loud calls for a neo-liberal and neo-conservative break, the union parties still follow a centrist line. Thus a more satisfying explanation for the absence of Kohlism (understood as a successful political movement arguing for a radical break in West German modes of regulation and growth) should be sought in more general structural and conjunctural features of German society.

In Britain there is a long-term structural crisis in the polity which can be exploited by a dominant leader. It involves a peculiar dual crisis of the state, that is, a crisis in the functioning of the parliamentary and party system and a failure to consolidate alternative corporatist strategies of economic and political crisis-management. In turn this has had two effects. It means there is a political vacuum into which authoritarian politics can enter and appeal directly to the masses without significant intermediation. It also means that there has been limited resistance to the Thatcher regime from party political or corporatist forces. This has given Thatcherism one of the most vital of political assets in securing the relative autonomy of the state: time. In turn this has helped the three Thatcher governments to make mistakes, correct them, try new policies, choose the moment when to confront opposition and gradually to broaden the fronts in a war of position aimed at a fundamental and long-term transformation of British society in all spheres. Only through the structural crisis has Thatcherism been able to ride out frequent bouts of electoral unpopularity, internal dissent within the Conservative Party, opposition from vested interests and a disastrous first two years in office. At the same time this crisis has created the opening for a new style of conviction politics.

In contrast the parliamentary and party systems in West Germany, despite much talk to the contrary in the 1970s, seem much more stable and effective. The *Machtwechsel* itself was the culmination of a long run trend in favour of CDU/CSU support since the 1972 election (with 1982 an aberration due to the Schmidt-Strauss confrontation). Likewise the Greens have already been incorporated into government at *Land* level and seem prepared to share in federal power. The operation of the voting and party systems is also less conducive to a purely populist or plebiscitary politics since it encourages coalition government and the FDP's stabilising role. There are also close bargaining relations between the federal and provincial governing systems: an intricate web of continuous bargaining, carried on by various political and administrative hierarchies, working within clear rules and structures and often involving close links with all main parties (Dyson 1984; Katzenstein 1987). Finally, West Germany also has long-established, stable corporatist features which would provide the basis for resistance to a purely neo-liberal strategy within the CDU-state – should this even become the dominant tendency.

Thus the complex web of legal, administrative, party political and corporatist relations makes a drift to authoritarian populism and/or a radical political rupture far less likely. At the same time, of course, the modes of regulation and growth associated with the *Modell Deutschland* have also proven more effective in sustaining high and stable living standards for the majority as well as maintaining West Germany's place in the international economy. Given the strong neo-statist elements in this mutually reinforcing set of structures and strategies, therefore, a break along neo-liberal lines seems implausible.

CONCLUDING REMARKS

The arguments in this chapter have moved between abstract theory and historical description. Thus we should conclude with two sets of remarks. The first set concerns the heuristic value of the regulation approach as deployed here; and the second concerns the prospects for Thatcherism in Britain and the revamped *Modell Deutschland* in West Germany.

Reflections on the Regulation Approach

Attentive readers will have discerned a problem in the regulation approach employed in this chapter: ambiguity concerning the scope of Fordism. Neither Britain nor Germany reveal a clear-cut case of Fordism if this is defined simply in terms of mass production and mass consumption. Britain failed to secure the productivity growth which Fordist methods could have brought to mass production and was hard-hit by de-industrialisation as a result. West German growth owes as much to the capital goods sector as to mass production of consumer goods and has also relied as much on its highly qualified *Facharbeiter* as on semi-skilled, Fordist mass workers. In its minimal sense, therefore, 'Fordism' serves mainly as an 'ideal type' against which to assess the specificity of the British and German regimes of accumulation. The broader concept of Fordism is, however, both directly relevant and powerful. For the Fordist wage relation based on institutionalised collective bargaining around a wage tied to rising productivity and inflation characterised both Britain and West Germany. Likewise private credit and monopolistic competition played key roles in capital accumulation; and state credit and tax expenditures were central elements in economic managment. If we adopt the broader concept of Fordism as a regime of accumulation, therefore, we can treat both Britain and West Germany as having Fordist regimes.

The related concepts of 'mode of regulation' and 'mode of growth' have proved even more relevant for our analysis. They are clearly more concrete concepts and can generate significant insights into the differential dynamic of the British and West German regimes. The institutions of collective bargaining, the relations between banks and industry, and the state play key roles in a mode of regulation; and their contrasting natures in the two cases investigated emerges very clearly. Likewise the modes of growth in Britain and Germany are also significantly different — reflecting their different industrial profiles and modes of insertion into the international economy.[14] By examining the contrasting modes of regulation and growth in these two economies we can better grasp the specificity of their post-war development and of the forms assumed by the crisis of Fordism. It is also interesting to speculate how far these modes of growth seem to have a structural and institutional inertia transcending the specific Fordist logic.

For West Germany is trying to build up its relatively coherent industrial core, its high technology export industries, and its skilled workforce to exploit the opportunities offered by flexible specialisation in batch production as well as traditional Fordist mass production industries. Even so fears are often voiced that West Germany is losing out in the technological race with Japan and the US. Likewise Thatcher's Britain is pursuing an accumulation strategy based once more on a leading role in international financial services — albeit this time as the centre for transnational banks rather than purely indigenous British banking and commercial capital. But industry is being further balkanised among multi-nationals from different economies so that its long-term re-industrialisation will depend on how Britain fits into the global accumulation strategies of MNCs rather than on a coherent industrial strategy pursued by the British state. This does not exclude regeneration through the synergy of high-tech centres created through interaction among various MNCs, home-grown subcontractors, services and so forth, in a neo-liberal fiscal and regulatory environment. But such synergic effects are no more guaranteed than the continuing international competitiveness of a national industrial core favoured in the neo-statist strategy.

But even the more concrete concepts of the regulation school must be supplemented by much greater attention to the *sui generis* dynamic of the political system. The state apparatus and political system has been seriously neglected by the French regulation school[15] and the American radical political economy tradition.[16] In contrast the leading West German contributors (Esser, Hirsch, Roth) to the regulation approach have consistently emphasised the state's role and the political dimension in developing a more general analysis of different forms of societalisation (*Vergesellschaftung*).[17]

Hopefully the present analysis has shown how important political factors can be in explaining the forms assumed by modes of regulation and growth, the crises which they undergo, and the nature of the strategies which emerge to resolve them. The specificity of the British and German post-war settlements, the contrasts between the Keynesian welfare state and the CDU-Staat in the 1950s, and the different experiences with corporatist concentration in the 1960s and 1970s surely provide evidence enough for this view. But the contrast between the break between the Social Contract and Thatcherism and the continuity between the social-liberal *Modell Deutschland* and the present christian-liberal strategy provide even more convincing evidence for the need to 'bring the state back in'. In this sense the regulation approach needs modifying to take account of the state to a much greater extent.

The prospects for Britain and Germany

The prospects of Thatcherism and the revamped *Modell Deutschland* depend on three sets of factors. Firstly, there is the changing balance of forces mobilised for and against them; secondly, there are the institutional obstacles, structural constraints, and policy dilemmas which might block them; and, thirdly, in an increasingly international-alised global economy, the complementarities among different national strategies and crucial elements in ascent or decline in the international hierarchy. These factors are inter-related. In the short run, no strategy, however rational in narrow economic terms, can succeed without a favourable balance of forces; in the medium-term, a strategy which was once irrational could eventually succeed because it can be sustained long enough for changing circumstances to render it more plausible and/or to enable its protagonists to improve it through trial-and-error; and, in the long-term, no strategy which is inconsistent with the long-run trends emerging from the clash of all strategies in the world economy can provide the basis for movement up the international hierarchy.[18]

The development of Thatcherism illustrates all these points. Its initial survival was related to the demoralisation and disorganisation of the opposition (there *was* no alternative) and to various short-run political concessions. In the medium term it has gained economically and politically. Thus it has benefited from the weakening of bases of resistance in manufacturing and the trade union movement as the economy has been restructured and from the emergence of a more coherent supply-side strategy which better reflects the competitive pressure to move beyond Fordism. And it has benefited from the recomposition of political forces through its hegemonic project of popular capitalism and its reorganisation of the state system. Yet to be decided is the long-term compatibility of this strategy with the strategies of the three dominant economic powers (Japan, the US and Germany) as well as the host of other players.

A comparison of the two conservative regimes led by Thatcher and Kohl is revealing in at least two different ways. This involves more than the question of the overwhelming presence of Thatcherism versus the apparent absence of 'Kohlism'. This can easily be explained in personal, conjunctural and institutional terms. At stake is not merely the form taken by the transition to post-Fordism but also the reasons behind the relative continuity or discontinuity of specific accumulation strategies and hegemonic projects.

Thatcherism was significant initially because it represented a specific response to the crisis of flawed Fordism in Britain and its accompanying 'Keynesian-welfare-state' political shell. Mrs Thatcher knew instinctively that there could be no return to the old Keynesian welfare state ways: but in rejecting these crisis-management and crisis-avoidance responses, she invoked a return to even earlier values and institutions. The dual crisis of the British state gave Thatcherism (which is not purely a vehicle for Thatcher's aggrandisement but also a project for radical transformation of British society) enough breathing space to engage in trial-and-error policy-making and to find a relatively coherent strategy for the transition to post-Fordism in Britain. Thus, having come to power promising a return to a pre-Fordist, liberal capitalism, the third Thatcher government is now paving the way for movement towards post-Fordism.

In contrast the union and liberal parties were more aware of the need for *forward* movement and rejected a simple return to the social market economy of the 1950s – let alone to a mythical *laissez-faire* approach absent from the German state tradition. They were committed to 'high technology modernisation' alongside sound money and sound finance. In this regard they are seeking to exploit the peculiar features of West Germany's export-oriented Fordism. Flexible specialisation is particularly useful in the batch production of capital goods which was previously resistant to Fordist methods; and West German employers still retain a relatively skilled workforce which can operate flexible manufacturing systems. What Boyer (1986b) has termed 'flexi-Fordism' provides a good basis for movement to a flexible post-Fordism.

The broad aims of Kohl and Thatcher are the same: what differs is the conditions in which they are being pursued and the route that has been chosen. In both countries there is a movement towards post-Fordism: in Britain this involves new forms of populist and plebiscitary politics closely associated with (but not reducible to) a dominant political personality; in West Germany there is much greater concern with business as usual. But the British road to post-Fordism also involves specialising in trans-national financial services for the world economy and reinforcing the commercial and *rentier* character of British society. In contrast the West German road involves continued specialisation in high technology manufacturing as the industrial workshop of the European Community. The dangers involved in these strategies may be overcome if the modes of growth which these contrasting strategies involve can be rendered complementary and reinforcing.

NOTES

1. In writing this chapter I have benefited from discussion with Kevin Bonnett, Simon Bromley, Alex Demirovics, Harald Dueren, Josef Esser, Klaus Friedel, Klaus Gretschmann, Joachim Hirsch, Hans Kastendiek, Emil Kirchner, Tom Ling and Doug Webber. I have also drawn freely on my earlier work on these themes, especially 1980, 1985 and 1986a–c. The final responsibility for the arguments presented here naturally remains with me.
2. This sketch is drawn above all from: Blackburn *et al.* 1985; Boyer 1986a; de Vroey 1984; Galbraith 1967; Hirsch and Roth 1986; Hurtienne 1986; Kundig 1984; Lipietz 1985; Piore and Sabel 1985.

3.   It is worth repeating that Fordism is treated here in terms of the overall organisation of the production–wages–consumption nexus and its associated modes of growth and regulation rather than in the narrower terms of the Fordist labour process in mass production industries.

4.   The post-war settlement was basically concluded during the war itself and its institutional embodiment was largely completed by the post-war Labour government by 1948: see Addison 1984; Barnett 1985; Middlemas 1986.

5.   It is debateable how far this is due to management failures, to union veto power over management initiatives and to government macro-economic policy (Coates and Hillard 1986; Nichols 1986).

6.   Middlemas correctly identifies a persisting pattern of corporatist bias in the governing institutions of Britain: in the inter-war years this was more concerned with political crisis management, during the war it was conditioned by the dominance of labour in the market hierarchy, and during the 1950s it had been attenuated by the dominance of liberal strategies (Middlemas 1979).

7.   Domestic forces were not passive during this period but sought to advance their own interests and strategies under the imprimatur of the occupying powers.

8.   Conversely it has prompted collaboration among *Laender* and the federal government as well as concertation with organised interests (Dyson 1981; Webber 1986, p. 7).

9.   German firms are more highly organised than their workers – among whom around two-fifths are unionised: the BDA has an 80 per cent enrollment among all firms, co-ordinates lockouts and imposes a taboo catalogue of non-negotiable issues. In addition, 95 per cent of industrial firms belong to the BDI, and all firms are legally obliged to belong to local chambers of commerce.

10.   For this reason I disagree with the unqualified use of the terms Fordism (Hirsch and Roth 1986) or neo-Fordism (Deubner 1984) as well as the qualification, 'flexi-Fordism' (Boyer 1986b), to describe the West German model. Collective bargaining assumed the typical Fordist form but it was coupled to an atypical mode of growth due to Germany's industrial profile.

11..   This control is exercised through their own shares and/or proxies entrusted by customers or borrowed from other banks.

12.   The British state has been perfecting a security state apparatus in Northern Ireland for decades but its extension to the mainland is far more restrained and also limited mainly to the inner cities.

13.   It is also worth noting that Strauss's Bavaria has an interventionist state which is deeply committed to promoting flexible accumulation.

14.   The importance of modes of growth is neglected in Hall's otherwise interesting comparison of Britain and France in terms of what we would call their modes of regulation (Hall 1986).

15.   The main exception here is the work of André and Delorme (1983) with its emphasis on the state as the site of an institutionalised compromise; but even their magisterial work neglects the relative autonomy of political processes and the specificity of political struggles. Lipietz has

invoked some Gramscian concepts in his analyses but they remain essentially underdeveloped: for example, Lipietz 1986.
16. For a critique of its state theory see Verhagen and Elshout 1986.
17. To the extent, indeed, that they run the risk of politicism.
18. This last argument should not be interpreted in a narrowly economic fashion: strategies are never purely economic but always have significant political, social and ideological dimensions.

REFERENCES

W. Abelshauser, 'West German Economic Recovery, 1945–1951: a Reassessment', *Three Banks Review* 135 (1982) pp. 34–53.
H. Abromeit, 'Veraenderung ohne Reform. Die britische Privatisierungspolitik (1979–1985)', *Politische Viertel jahresschrift* 27 (3) (1986) pp. 271–89.
A. Accornero, 'Social Change and Trade Union Movement in the 1970s' in O. Jacobi *et al.*, (eds), *Technological Change, Rationalisation, and Industrial Relations* (London: Croom Helm, 1986) pp. 219–37.
W. Adamy and J. Steffen, *Die Wende Stoppen* (Hamburg: VSA, 1985).
P. Addison, *The Road to 1945* (London: Quartet, 1984).
D. Albers *et al.*, *Lotte sociale en Europea 1968–74: Francia, Gran Bretagna, Repubblica federale tedesca* (Roma: Editori Riuniti, 1976).
U. von Alemann *et al.*, 'Technologiepolitik – Ansichten und Aussichten in den achtziger Jahren' *Gewerkschaftliche Monatshefte* 5 (1986) pp. 305–15.
C. Andre and R. Delorme, *L'Etat de l'économie* (Paris: Seuil, 1983).
G. Baecker, 'Sozialpolitik durch soziale Dienstleistungen – Zukunftsperspektiven des Sozialstaates', *WSI Mitteilungen* 3 (1986) pp. 201–16.
C. Barnett, *The Audit of War* (London: Macmillan, 1985).
V. R. Berghahn, *Modern Germany: Society, Economy, and Politics in the Twentieth Century* (London: Cambridge University Press, 1982).
P. Blackburn, R. Coombes, K. Green, *Technology, Economic Growth and the Labour Process* (London: Macmillan, 1985).
S. Bowles and R. Edwardes, *Understanding Capitalism* (New York: Harper and Row, 1985).
R. Boyer, *La Théorie de la Régulation: une analyse critique* (Paris: La Découverte, 1986a).
R. Boyer, (ed.), *La Flexibilité du travail en Europe* (Paris: la Découverte, 1986b).
R. Boyer and B. Coriat, 'Is the new Mode of Development Emerging?' in R. Boyer *et al.*, *Aspects de la Crise*, vol. 1 (Paris: CEPREMAP, 1987) pp. 509–86.
G. Brandt, 'Beyond Neo-Corporatism?' in idem (ed.), 'Labour Exclusion or New Patterns of Worker Cooperation?' (Frankfurt: Institut fuer Sozialforschung, 1985).
S. Bulmer, 'The Changing Government in West Germany', *Politics* 3 (2) (1983) pp. 14–20.
M. Clarich, 'The German Banking System: Legal Foundations and Recent Trends', *EUI Working Paper 87/269* (Firenze: EUI, 1987).

D. Coates and J. Hillard, (eds), *The Economic Decline of Modern Britain* (Brighton: Harvester, 1986).

C. Crouch and A. Pizzorno, (eds), *The Resurgence of Class Conflict in Western Europe* 2 vols (London: Macmillan, 1978).

C. Crouch, 'Conservative Industrial Relations Policy: Towards Labour Exclusion?' in O. Jacobi *et al.*, (eds), *Economic Crisis, Trade Unions and the State* (London: Croom Helm, 1986), pp. 131–55.

S. W. Davies and R. E. Caves, *Britain's Productivity Gap: a study based on British and American Industries 1968–1977* (London: Cambridge University Press, 1986).

M. Dauderstaedt, *Social Consensus and International Competition* (Bonn: Friedrich Ebert Stiftung, 1983).

C. Deubner, 'Internationalisierung als Problem alternativer Wirtschaftspolitik', *Leviathan* 7 (1) (1979) pp. 97–116.

C. Deubner, 'Change and Internationlisation in Industry: toward a Sectoral Interpretation of West German Politics', *International Organisation* 38 (3) (1984) pp. 501–34.

M. de Vroey, 'A Regulation Approach Interpretation of the Contemporary Crisis', *Capital and Class* 23 (1984).

M. Drupp *et al.*, '"Ohne Hast, aber beharrlich!" – Zum Stand der Entstaatlichungspolitik im Bereich der oeffentlichen Wirtshcaft und des Wohnungswesen', *WSI Mitteilungen* 5 (1985) pp. 293–303.

H-J. Dudler, 'Geldmengepolitik und Finanzinnovationen', *Kredit und Kapital* 4 (1986) pp. 472–92.

K. Dyson, 'The Politics of Economic Management in West Germany', *West European Politics* 4 (1) (1981) pp. 34–55.

K. Dyson, 'The Politics of Corporate Crises in West Germany', *West European Politics* 7 (i) (1984) pp. 24–46.

K. Dyson, 'The State, Banks and Industry: the West German Case' in A. Cox, (ed.), *The State, Finance and Industry* (Brighton: Wheatsheaf, 1986) pp. 118–41.

G. Esping-Andersen, 'Power and Distributional Regimes', *Politics and Society* (1986) pp. 223–56.

J. Esser, *Gewerkschaften in der Krise* (Frankfurt: Suhrkamp, 1982).

J. Esser, 'Auf dem Weg zu einer neuen Partnerschaft', *Gewerkschaftliche Monatshefte* 11 (1985) pp. 650–61.

J. Esser, 'State, Business and Trade Unions in West Germany after the "Political Wende"', *West European Politics* (April 1986).

J. Esser and W. Fach, 'Internationale Konkurrenz und selectiver Korporatismus', Paper for 10th meeting of working group on 'Parties-Parliaments-Elections' of German Political Science Association (Neuss: 24 February 1979).

J. Esser and J. Hirsch, 'Der CDU-Staat. Ein politisches Regulierungsmodell fuer den nachfordistischen Kapitalismus', *Prokla* 56 (1984) pp. 51–65.

J. Esser and J. Hirsch, 'Stadtsoziologie und Gesellschaftstheorie von der Fordismum-Krise zur "postfordistischen", Regional- und Stadtstruktur'. Unpublished manuscript (1987).

J. Esser and R. Staudhammer, *Zwischen Gesundschrumpfem und Modernisieren – Industriepolitik in Krisensektoren'* (Bonn: Friedrich Ebert Stiftung, 1986).

J. K. Galbraith, *The New Industrial State* (Harmondsworth: Penguin, 1967).

P. Grou, *The Financial Structure of Multinational Capitalism* (Leamington Spa: Berg, 1985).

W. Hager, 'Germany as an Extraordinary Trader' in W. L. Kohl and G. Baseri, *West Germany: a European and Global Power* (London: Gower, 1980) pp. 3–20p.

P. A. Hall, *Governing the Economy* (Cambridge: Polity, 1986).

W. Hankel, 'Germany: Economic Nationalism in the International Economy' in W. L. Kohl and G. Baseri, *West Germany: a European and Global Power* (London: Gower, 1980) pp. 21–44.

J. Hirsch, *Der Sicherheitsstaat* (Frankfurt: VSA, 1980).

J. Hirsch, 'Fordismus und Post-Fordismus: die gegenwaertige gesellschaftliche Krise und ihre Folgen', *Politische Vierteljahresschrift* 26 (June 1985a).

J. Hirsch and R. Roth, *Das neue Gesicht des Kapitalismus* (Frankfurt: VSA, 1986).

K. Heubner, '"Modell Deutschland": Karriere einer "oekonomischen Kampfformation"', in H-G. Thien and H. Wienold (eds), *Herrschaft, Krise, Ueberleben* (Muenster: Westfaelisches Dampfboot, 1986) pp. 374–93.

T. Hurtienne, 'Fordismus, Entwicklungstheorie und Dritte Welt', *Peripherie* 22/23 (1986).

R. Hyman, 'Trade Unions and the Law. Papering over the Cracks', *Capital and Class* 31 (1987) pp. 93–114.

R. E. M. Irving and W. E. Paterson, 'The Machtwechsel of 1982–83: a significant Landmark in the Political and Constitutional History of West Germany', *Parliamentary Affairs* xxxvi (4) (1983) pp. 417–33.

B. Jessop, 'The Transformation of the State in Post-war Britain' in R. Scase (ed.), *The State in Western Europe* (London: Croom Helm, 1980).

B. Jessop, 'Thatcherismo: fallimento economico o successo politico?' *Transizione* 4 (1985) pp. 37–60.

B. Jessop, 'Warum es keinen Kohlismus gibt', *Links* (January 1986a).

B. Jessop, 'The Mid-Life Crisis of Thatcherism', *New Socialist* (March 1986b).

B. Jessop, 'Der Wohlfahrtstaat im Uebergang vom Fordismus zum Post-fordismus', *Prokla* 65 (1986).

B. Jessop, (ed.), *Accumulation, Regulation and the State* (London: Century-Hutchinson, 1988).

B. Jessop et al., 'Popular Capitalism, Two Nations and Left Strategy', *New Left Review* 165 (1987).

G. Junne, 'Der Strukturpolitische Wettlauf zwischen den kapitalistischen Industrielaendern', *Politische Viertelsjahresheft* (1984) pp. 134–55.

H. Kastendiek, 'Regierungen, Parteien und Gewerkschaften in Grossbritannien, Italien und der Bundesrepublik. Einige Probleme vergleichender Politik- und Sozialforschung'. Unpublished paper (November 1986).

H. Kastendiek, 'Zwischen Ausgrenzung und Krisenpolitische Konditionierung. Zur Situation der britischen Gerwerkschaften' in W. Mueller-Jentsch, (ed.), *Gerwerkschaften im Umbruch. Chancen fuer eine Neuorientierung?* (Frankfurt: Campus, 1987).

H. and H. Kastendiek, 'Konservative Wende und industrielle Beziehungen in Grossbritanien und in der Bundesrepublik', *Politische Vierteljahresschrift* 26 (4) (1985) pp. 381–99.

M. Katzenstein, *Policy and Politics in W. Germany* (Philadelphia: Temple University Press, 1987).

M. Kreile, 'West Germany: the Dynamics of Expansion' in P. Katzenstein, (ed.), *Between Power and Plenty* (Madison: University of Wisconsin Press, 1978).

B. Kundig, 'Du taylorisme classique à la "flexibilisation" du systeme productif. L'impact macro-économique des differents types d'organisation du travail industriel', *Critiques de l'Economie Politique* 26/27 (1984).

G. Leithauser, 'Des flexibilitiés... et pourtant une crise: la République fédérale d'Allemagne' in R. Boyer, (ed.), *La Flexibilité du travail en Europe* (Paris: la Découverte, 1986) pp. 181–99.

A. Lipietz, 'Akkumulation, Krisen und Auswegen aus der Krise', *Prokla* 58 (Maerz: 1985).

A. Lipietz, 'Behind the Crisis: The Exhaustion of a Regime of Accumulation', *Journal of Radical Political Economy*: 18, 1–2 (1986) pp. 13–33.

B. Luethje, 'Regulierungskrise im Telekommunikationssektor in der BRD', *Prokla* 64 (1986) pp. 64–84.

A. Markovits, *The Politics of the West German Trade Unions* (Cambridge University Press, 1986).

A. Markovits and C. Allen, 'Trade Unions and the Economic Crisis: the West German Case' in P. Gourevitch *et al.*, *Unions and Economic Crisis* (London: Allen & Unwin, 1984) pp. 89–188.

J. Mazier *et al.*, *Quand Les Crises Durent* (Paris: Maspero, 1985).

K. Middlemas, *The Politics of Industrial Society* (London: André Deutsch, 1979).

K. Middlemas, *Power, Competition and the State*, vol. 1 (London: Macmillan, 1986).

J. Mistral, 'Regime internationale et trajectoire nationale' in R. Boyer (ed.), *Capitalismes: fin de siecle* (Paris: PUF, 1986) pp. 167–201.

K. Monse, 'Post-Fordismus: vor einem neuen Konsummodell?', *Mehrwert* 29 (1987) pp. 7–29.

K. Morgan and D. Webber, 'Divergent Paths: Political Strategies for Telecommunications in Britian, France and West Germany', *West European Politics* 9 (4) (1986) pp. 55–79.

P. Morville, *Les nouvelles politiques sociales du patronat* (Paris: La Découverte, 1985).

T. Nicholls, *The British Worker Question* (London: Routledge & Kegan Paul, 1986).

M. Piore and C. Sabel, *Das Ende der Massenproduktion?* (Frankfurt: VSA, 1985).

A. Przeworski, *Capitalism and Social Democracy* (Cambridge University Press, 1985).

M. Regini, 'The New Lexicon of Industrial Relations: Flexibility, Micro-corporatism, Dualism' in G. Brandt *et al.* (eds), *Labour Exclusion or New Patterns of Cooperation?* (Frankfurt: Institut fuer Sozialforschung, 1986) pp. 73–90.

A. Roobeek, 'The Crisis of Fordism and the Rise of the New Technological System', Research memorandum no. 8602, Department of Economics, University of Amsterdam (1986).

R. Saage, 'Gesellschaft, Staat und Technik im Neokonservatismus', *Gewerkschaftliche Monatshefte* 7/36 (1985) pp. 573–79.

C. St. John-Brooks, *Who Controls Training? The Rise of the Manpower Services Commission*, Fabian Society Tract 506 (London: 1985).

J-J. Santini, 'Les denationalisations au Royaume Uni' in idem (ed.), *Les privatisations à l'étranger* (Paris: La Documentation Française, 1986) pp. 25–62.

F. W. Scharpf, *Sozialdemokratische Krisenpolitik in Europa* (Frankfurt: Campus, 1987).

F. Schlupp, 'Modell Deutschland and the International Division of Labour' in M. Kreile (ed.), *West German Foreign Policy* (London: Sage, 1982) pp. 33–100.

H. Schmidt, 'Zwischenbilanzbericht', *Muenchener Parteitag* (April 1982) cited in *Sozialismus* 6 (1982).

W. Streeck, 'Neo-Corporatist Industrial Relations and the Economic Crisis in West Germany', *EUI Working Paper 97* (Firenze: EUI, 1984).

W. Streeck, 'Industrial Relations in West Germany 1974–1985: an overview', *Discussion Paper IIM/LMP 85–19* (Wissenschaftszentrum Berlin 1985).

J. Terry, 'Shop stewards are Getting Weak', *British Journal of Industrial Relations* 24, 2 (1986) pp. 161–79.

P. Uhel, 'La privatisation des entreprises publiques en RFA' in J-J. Santini (ed.), *Les privatisations a l'étranger* (Paris: La Documentation Française, 1986) pp. 63–80.

T. Ward, 'De la crise rampante à la rupture: le Royaume Uni' in R. Boyer (ed.), *La Flexibilité du travail en Europe* (Paris: la Découverte, 1986) pp. 65–88.

W. Vaeth, 'Konservative Modernisierungspolitik – ein Widerspruch in sich?', *Prokla* 56 (1984) pp. 83–103.

J. C. Van Horne, 'An Enquiry into Recent Financial Innovations', *Kredit und Kapital* 4 (1986) pp. 456–69.

M. Verhagen and L. Elshout, 'Der Staat in der Theorie der Radicals', *Mehrwert* 28 (1986) pp. 122–32.

D. Webber, 'The Politics of the New Industrial Revolution in the Federal Republic of Germany'. Unpublished paper (13 May 1985).

D. Webber, 'The Framework of Government-Industry Relations and Industrial Policy Making in the Federal Republic of Germany' (University of Sussex: Working Paper Series on Government-Industry Relations, no. 1, 1986).

D. Webber, 'Die ausbleibende Wende bei der Deutschen Bundespost', *Politische Vierteljahresschrift* 27 (4) (1986b) pp. 397–414.

D. Webber, 'Eine Wende in der deutschen Arbeitsmarktpolitik?' in H. Abromeit and B. Blanke (eds), *Arbeitsmarkt, Arbeitsbeziehungen und Politik in den 80er Jahren* (Opladen: Westdeutscher Verlag, 1987) pp. 74–85.

H. Weber, 'Technokorporatismus: die Steuerung des technologischen Wandels durch Staat, Wirtschaftsverbaende, und Gewerkschaften', in H-H. Hartwich (ed.), *Politik und die Macht der Technik*, (Opladen: Westdeutscher Verlag, 1986) pp. 278–97.

U. Wendeling-Schroeder, 'Die Zukunft der Gewerkschaften im Rechtssystem', *WSI Mitteilungen* 3 (1986) pp. 238–45.

S. Wilks, 'Conservative Industrial Policy 1979–83' in P. M. Jackson (ed.), *Implementing Government Policy Initiatives: the Thatcher Administration 1979–1983* (London: RIPA, 1985) pp. 123–44.

H. Wilke, 'Political Intervention – Organisational Preconditions for Generalised Political Exchange', *EUI Colloquium Papers* (Firenze: EUI, 1986).

S. Young, 'Privatisation and the Fiscal Crisis of the State', *Politics* 7 (1987) pp. 29–35.

12 Political Regulation: The Crisis of Fordism and the Transformation of the Party System in West Germany

Juergen Haeusler and Joachim Hirsch

The contours of transformed economic and social structures in advanced capitalist countries, stemming from the continuing crisis of the 1970s, are becoming more and more visible. In contrast, the understanding of future developments of political systems, especially of political parties, remains vague. The era of social democratic dominance has ended and neo-conservative political regimes have been established in several relevant capitalist countries. Additionally, in West Germany both large parties, the Christian-Democrats and the Social-Democrats, face growing competition from the smaller parties, the Liberals and the newly formed Greens. Is the era of 'Volkspar-teien' (catch-all-parties) that managed to integrate a multitude of diverse sections of the population coming to an end? Will the crisis of Fordist capitalism be accompanied by the establishment of a new, 'post-Fordist' party system?

Established theories of political parties provide no answers to these questions. Thus, we attempt to outline a theoretical approach that will interpret political parties within the context of a more comprehensive mode of regulation of historical social formation. This interpretation is based on a 'non-linear' theory of capitalistic development which is seen as a sequence of specific social formations, mediated by crises and each characterised by specific modes of accumulation and regulation. The theory of political parties is thus formulated as part of a comprehensive historical theory of social development.

The concrete empirical analysis of the development of political parties is confined to West Germany. This seems necessary, if only because existing national party systems exhibit a high degree of variation due to historical and political national peculiarities. It can be assumed, however, that those tendencies surfacing in the case of West Germany will prove to be of a more general character. The West German Fordist mode of regulation, termed *Modell Deutschland*, achieved a high degree of international success and political dominance. It is still unclear if there will be a revised 'post-Fordist' edition of the successful model, although there are signs that point in that direction. This will to a large degree depend upon the parties' capability to adapt their own structure and the institutional arrangement of the mode of regulation as a whole to the changing conditions of the post-Fordist phase.

THE CAPITALIST SOCIAL FORMATION: A THEORETICAL OUTLINE

Our attempt to formulate a 'non-linear' theory of capitalist development is based upon analytical approaches that were developed by the so-called 'regulationist' school (Aglietta 1976; Boyer 1979; Coriat 1982; Boyer and Mistral 1983b; Mazier *et al.* 1984; Lipietz 1984 and 1985; Jessop 1985; Hirsch and Roth 1986). We thus argue against such versions of historical-materialistic theory that see historical development as a set pattern, that is, the 'logic' inherent in the economic structure of the capitalist mode of production, thereby reducing the complex fabric of society to a simple model of bases and superstructure. In contrast, we assume that the history of capitalism on a world-wide scale has to be understood as a sequence of specific social formations that are, on the one hand, characterised by an invariable basic structure (private production, wage labour, appropriation of surplus value mediated by commodity exchange), but also, on the other hand, exhibit distinct differences in the forms of production and exploitation, social and class relationships and finally, the character of the state and political rule. The transitions between these capitalist social formations take on the form of 'secular' crises that are defined by long-term variations of the rate of profit. However, the development of the rate of profit as well as the eruption and form of these secular crises do not follow any objective logic but are determined by the economic, social and political conditions within any given formation.

Accumulation regime, mode of regulation and hegemonial structure

All capitalist social formations are characterised by a specific accumulation regime linked with a mode of regulation. An accumulation regime refers to a specific form of organising production and labour based on specific technologies; thus, it encompasses the way in which surplus-value is produced and realised and it describes specific forms of the reproduction of capital (investment cycles, form of competition, modalities of capital devalorisation, sectoral divisions, especially the relationship between the division of means of production and consumption, consumption models), the wage relation (including social wage funds), class structure, state intervention, the relationship between capitalist and non-capitalist sectors and integration into the world market. Regulation refers to the way in which the existing elements of this complex process of reproduction are connected or 'The way in which the system as a whole functions, the conjunction of economic mechanisms associated with a given set of social relationships, of institutional forms and structures' (Boyer 1979, p. 100). It encompasses a multifarious configuration of economic, social and political institutions and norms that lend a certain degree of stability to the reproduction of the system as a whole. It describes the 'sum of institutions, networks, explicit or implicit norms that secure the compatibility of modes of behaviour within a regime of accumulation' (Lipietz 1985, p. 121). Consequently, all accumulation regimes need regulation but can exist with very different concrete modes of regulation (for example, different modes of interest organisation, varying degrees and kinds of state intervention).

A hegemonial structure refers to the historically existing concrete combination of accumulation regime and mode of regulation that ensures the stable economic (value-realising form of capital reproduction) and political-ideological (legitimacy, compulsion and consensus) reproduction of the system as a whole under the dominance of the ruling class(es) (Boyer and Mistral 1983a). All capitalist formations are characterised by specific forms of exploitation and class relations, as well as institutional and normative reproduction. This is not to rule out long-term 'non-hegemonial' phases that stem from crises of formation and exhibit continuous conflicts over a new mode of accumulation and regulation.

The concepts of accumulation regime, mode of regulation and hegemonial structure enable us to leave behind the abstract contrasts of 'economy', 'politics' and 'ideology' or 'bases' and 'superstructure'. The economic reproduction of capitalist societies takes place within the institutional and normative network of regulation and is simultaneously tied to the conditions set by the laws of capital accumulation. However, the law of value does not govern in its 'pure' form, external to politics, but is always enforced *within* and *via* historically specific regulative arrangements. Consequently, the way in which the law of value prevails cannot be determined in abstract and logical terms but only historically and specifically for an existing formation.

The secular crisis of capitalist formation, that is, a hegemonial accumulation and regulation regime, has to be distinguished from cyclical crises (economic fluctuations and sectoral adaptive difficulties) *within* a mode of accumulation and regulation (Lipietz 1985, p. 112; Mazier 1982, p. 41; Mazier *et al.* 1984). Secular crises occur because the stability of the rate of profit can be secured over longer periods, but never permanently, within a relatively firm, institutionalised and – within limits – flexible hegemonial structure. In general terms, crises of formations are rooted in collisions of the dynamics of the economic process and the economic and social consequences of an accumulation regime with a rigid institutional and normative mode of regulation. The socially and technologically cataclysmic effects of capital accumulation will sooner or later break up that mode of regulation, within which it has evolved. This causes a structural disturbance in the reproduction of the system, expressed by a 'secular' fall of the rate of profit. The historical form in which the law of value governs, institutionalised in a specific regime of accumulation and regulation, thus turns into a barrier to capital accumulation.

The Theory of Regulation

Next, the concept of regulation shall be examined in more detail. In general terms, 'society' is constituted as a social relation, in which individual and collective activities interact. For material reproduction and the reproduction of unity, society needs mechanisms to connect and stabilise behavioural norms and expectations of individuals and groups. The norms that guide behaviour can be distinguished according to achieved stages of historical development, the degree of development of productive forces, social differentiation, division of labour, class relations and forms of exploitation, among others. They include traditional norms and hierarchies as well as social and political institutions (family, associations, churches, media, the political and administrative system, law, market). In this context, regulation refers to the interaction of a complex configuration of norms and institutions that guide behaviour in a concrete social formation.

The structural antagonism of capitalist society, based on exploitation in the exchange of commodities, prohibits the harmonious working of the 'invisible hand' of market forces as well as the establishment of consensual 'general will'. Capitalist society breaks up into opposing classes, class factions and groups, rendering its reproduction structurally crisis-prone and insecure. Thus the state is created as a distinct entity, formally separated from the immediate production process of capital and from the classes and equipped with the 'monopoly of legitimate use of physical force' (Max Weber; for the 'derivation' of the state see Holloway and Picciotto 1978). The state represents a central precondition for successful reproduction of society and for social coherence among classes. The state cannot, however, abolish commodity and capital relations and the resulting contradictions and conflicts; it is rather, based upon them. The 'relative autonomy' of the state is the characteristic feature of capitalist-bourgeois rule and gives rise to the seeming antagonisms of state and market, politics and economy.

The state represents the institutionalised condensation of legitimising and repressive class relations (Poulantzas 1978) established by its relationship to the complete network of regulative instances. In this way it forms the centre of the institutionalised regulative network (Lipietz 1985, p. 112; Boyer and Mistral 1983a, p. 495). The state does not constitute a subject but an institutionalised class relation, a complex of apparatuses with divergent class connections and therefore provides the ground for inter- and inner-class conflicts. The antagonisms that have to be handled regulatively also exist within and among state apparatuses or the institutions of the 'political system' respectively.

This suggested definition of regulation is intended to avoid a functionalist misinterpretation. To the contrary, the regulationist theory can be seen as the materialist alternative to a conceptualisation of the reproduction process of society in terms of a functionalist systems theory. As a result of a 'process without subject', regulation cannot be understood as a well-planned order but rather developments within specific formations as an expression of the socio-economic structure of society.

The acting individuals and groups are forced to accept the need for regulation in two ways: by the compulsion to maintain their material reproduction within given socio-economic structures and by the dynamics of the world market.

The general form of the regulative system is derived from the basic structure of capitalist relation of production, exchange of commodities and wage labour. This structure brings about the emergence of money, civil law, competition among capitalists and workers, wage relation, and the constitution of the bourgeois subject as an individual participant on the market. On this basis, capitalist private property, the family, the free association of individuals to safeguard common interests and the specific form of the state can be established. Mediating between state and individuals and institutions in society, political parties play a central role in advanced capitalist societies. The institutional system of regulation is founded on these general determinants and is thus characterised by a basic structure invariant throughout the development of capitalism.

Within and between the elements of the regulative system, contradictions exist — and they have to exist to allow disparities and antagonisms in society to develop within limits that permit the reproduction of society. Market and state intervention, formal law and traditional norms, bureaucracy and family represent different forms of regulation that correlate (for example state regulation of money, guaranteed private property) as well as contrast (such as compulsory production limits). The regulatory process is based on the institution-alisation of social antagonisms and (class-)conflicts, and therefore can never be functionally secured but always entails conflicts and confrontations. Regulation is thus fundamentally a crisis-prone process and 'disturbances' represent a functional principle. However, crises 'within' regulation and (secular) crises of historical regimes of regulation should be distinguished.

POLITICAL PARTIES AS REGULATIVE INSTITUTIONS

The following attempt to develop a theory of political parties is based upon the most important elements of the theory of capitalist formation as outlined above. Parties are understood to be parts of a complex regulative network, the concrete form and functioning of which are determined by the mode of regulation that developed historically within the context of an accumulation regime. Excluded from our analysis are revolutionary parties that radically oppose the existing parliamentary system.

In our perspective, the analysis of parties cannot exclusively focus on any single party but has to acknowledge that parties are components of a complex regulative network and above all, can only be understood as competing and co-operating elements of a party system. Also the analysis of parties has to proceed from the state as the centre of the capitalist regulative network. Parties hold a very specific and strategic position in that network as they nominate candidates, organise elections and compete for electoral votes.

The party system represents that component of the regulative network of institutions within which antagonistic and pluralistic interests and attitudes are produced, articulated, adjusted, formed and connected in such a way that relatively coherent state action, safeguarding the reproduction of the system as a whole, is rendered possible and legitimate. Content and legitimacy ('coercion' and 'consensus') of state action are not exclusively determined by parties (but also, for example, by state apparatuses themselves). In the long run, however, in advanced capitalist nations and within formally democratic systems, they cannot be established without parties. It should be noted that parties never merely transform or transmit given interests or norms but that the party system simultaneously serves as a medium to produce and articulate them. Both structure and functioning of the party system heavily influence social and political interests and practices.

The parties' regulative capacities are due to a large degree to their internal structure: they hardly ever constitute hierarchically and rigidly organised, closed, homogeneous and single-purpose oriented apparatuses but rather decentralised, heterogeneous organisational networks, relatively open to their environment (Wiesendahl 1983; Jäger 1983; Esser and Hirsch 1984). Parties represent complexes of a multitude of 'vertically' (internal factions and groups) and 'horizontally' (regional and local subdivisions) divergent separate organisations. Their heterogeneous internal structures enable parties to entertain 'pluralistic' relations within an intricate and contradictory institutional 'environment' of corporations, interest groups, churches, media and the general public. Manifold personal or institutional connections, often across party lines, with other regulative institutions (such as unions) and vague differences between formal members, activists and supporters document the fluidity of boundaries between the 'explicit', formal party and the 'environment' (Jäger 1983). Parties remain open to the state apparatus whose personnel they actually or potentially recruit, as well as towards a diverse societal environment ('party in a wider sense').

The party's internal and external plurality and heterogeneity represents a decisive precondition for its regulative function of articulating and processing antagonistic interests and norms. Simultaneously, however, this structure produces a permanent contradiction that has to be dealt with internally between the incorporated plurality of interests on the one side and programmatic and political unity and the administrative capacity to act on the other. This contradiction is institutionalised in the antagonisms between the 'party outside of the state apparatus' and the 'party within the state apparatus' (with the parliamentary faction as mediator), between heads of state bureaucracies recruited by the party and party organisation. A structural and at the same time necessary divergence among government/parliamentary factions, central party organisations and decentralised local party organisations with their respective relations to the 'environment' results from the described structure. (We exclude here the somewhat, but not completely, different situation in non-parliamentary systems such as the US.) Besides traditional, ideological and milieu-bound orientations, the heterogeneous network of organisations and relations is politically unified within parties by the double and also contradictory pressure to maximise votes and formulate a relatively coherent government policy that acknowledges the imperatives of capitalist reproduction. This in turn puts parties in a position to apply political leadership and thus unify the similarly heterogeneous complex of state apparatuses exhibiting contradictory relations towards classes, class factions and interests (Poulantzas 1978, p. 214ff.). The regulative function of parties include two homogenising activities: in a competitive environment, a distinguishable political profile has to lend coherence to divergent interests and motives and this profile has to be translated into a relatively coherent political programme (the capacity to rule). Both aspects are interrelated but also represent an insolvable contradiction (since state action remains bound to conditions of capital reproduction on the world market) that has to result in permanent conflicts within parties. Because the bureaucratic state apparatus itself constitutes a heterogeneous complex of institutions with distinguishable functional principles and relating interests, its relative political homogeneity is dependent upon political leadership established by parties. The party form and its regulative potential are, to a high degree, responsible for the 'relative autonomy' of the state which is by no means a functional given but always needs to be re-established within permanent conflicts and proves necessary for the reproduction of the system. The 'relative autonomy' of the state remains especially critical in those countries where parliamentary parties do not exist, such as the US.

The party form produces a series of systematic ruptures and connections during the process of regulative articulation and the processing of interests and actions: Parties polarise and sort individuals on an abstract level relatively distant from real life situations and discriminate between office-holders, activists, members and supporters (Jäger 1983). This distinction gains importance as party activities are more and more professionalised and party membership proves necessary for a successful career. Although formal party membership remains relatively low, parties are comprised by almost all members of society: 'Parties are an almost total phenomenon because only a few individuals are indifferent towards them in such a way that they could not be ascribed to one of them' (Steininger 1984, p. 115). This does not exclude, however, that individuals ascribe to several parties at the same time. The 'implicit' party thus reaches much further than the formal, 'explicit' party organisation (Jäger 1983). Parties are forced by elections and the goal to maximise votes to develop a general programme extending beyond manifold, concrete interests. This leads to political polarisation on the party level that has to counter structural conflicts in society: pure 'interest' or class parties, as a rule, never gain the status of a majority party, especially when societies exhibit several cleavages along different conflict lines (as in the case of a Catholic, rural, female worker). In a system with several parties, the obligatory process of forming coalitions achieves the described separation of party programme and concrete social interests. Counter polarisation is reinforced by the fact that every party is a potential ruling party and thus potentially the 'state'. Thereby, parties are forced to exclude from public debate or neutralise in an institutional arrangement, systematically, such antagonisms that endanger reproduction of the system as a whole.

The party form implies a (relative) monopoly for access to public offices and for shaping political decision-making processes. Thus, every articulation of social interests has to be aimed — positively or negatively — at parties. The parties 'policy monopoly' also enables them to tightly control chances for political participation, especially in terms of impeding or obstructing the successful foundation of new parties by using legal regulations of the political process such as majority voting, restrictive clauses, prohibition of parties, public funding of parties and access to public media. This potential to control the political process permits parties to restrict societal interests and groups to marginal political and institutional status (by their power to define what is accepted as being 'political' and thus, to influence the decision-making process). This ability to marginalise is paralleled by a similar capacity to integrate: being open and approachable to all citizens. In a consolidated and split corporative society, parties are able to reintegrate those individuals ahd interests into the political regulative network that are excluded from the corporative bloc. They 'catch' rebellious groups by forcing them to voice their protest in 'parliamentary terms' (Jäger 1983).

The relationship between parties and the network of social interest groups (business and farmers associations, trade unions, churches and so on) is similarly contradictory, simultaneously developing cleavages and unity. Connections with these regulative institutions stabilise the 'implicit party organisation' and provide parties with essential personnel, funding and propaganda. Parties differ according to their specific connections with the network of organised interests exemplified by the relationship between Social-Democratic parties and unions on the one hand and conservative parties and business or farmers associations, as well as churches, on the other. However, parties cannot too closely establish ties with the existing corporative structure of associations: they are forced by the imperative to gain majorities and to govern to keep in touch with *all* interest groups, just as these groups in turn have to maintain ties with all parties (at least with those that have the potential to become ruling parties). Thus, the party form structures the network of interest groups, shapes their internal power structures and policy formation processes, while concurrently, parties themselves are influenced by their environment of interest groups.

One of the parties' regulative functions thus consists of polarising and unifying the institutionalised corporative interest structure according to the logic of policy formation and decision-making processes within the state. And because they have to remain accessible to a multitude of uninstitutionalised or only weakly institutionalised social interests, parties are, when necessary, able to mobilise against existing corporative blocs. Such operations not only serve to weaken or reorganise established networks of interests but also attempt to reintegrate interests and groups into the political regulative network that are marginal to corporative blocs — a function that only the party form can perform. Should parties neglect this aspect and tie themselves too closely to consolidated corporative structures, a version of 'non-hegemonial' politics is established (Buci-Glucksmann 1982) and, at least in the long run, threatens the parties' ability to gain majorities and to take over government responsibility and possibly even the existing mode of regulation as a whole. Thus, the risk is run that 'non-institutionalised' political forms and movements appear that cannot be integrated into the existing mode of regulation.

The process of contradictory articulation, the splitting and unification of interests and norms, depends on the plurality of parties in a party system, especially on the recurrent change of government and opposition: party competition is essential for this process. The party 'system', a plurality within a unity, simultaneously organises disposal of aggression, diversion from problems, adjournment of decisions and paralysation of social revolts (Jäger 1983). Individual electoral decisions always have to be made among the lesser evil and insofar the voting act represents a renunciation of vital interests.

Consequently, the party system seems to guarantee the 'relative autonomy' of the state, separating 'state' and 'society'. Additionally, however, it serves to 'expand the state' into society. As a regulative instance mediating between the 'articulation of interests' and 'system imperatives', the party system forms interests and establishes norms in such a way as to shield the bureaucratic state that works in accordance with the 'inherent necessities' of capitalist reproduction and thus 'unpoliticised', from 'dysfunctional' forms and contents of interest articulation (Buci-Glucksmann 1982, p. 56, our translation). It sorts social interests in accordance to the logic of the state, focuses political orientations and individual behaviour towards the state and plays a major role in coordinating the politics of interest groups and state ('social contracts' and 'concerted actions' mediated by parties). Essentially, the party system imparts the imperatives of capitalist reproduction on the world market to the smallest segments of society and lastly, individuals — not in the sense of a simple enforcement from 'above', but in such a way that the mode of interest articulation remains in accordance with the otherwise flexible forms of enforcing those imperatives (Poulantzas 1978).

Regulation, understood as the formation and articulation of interests and norms, always takes on a discursive character. Interests never exist prior to the political process and only need to be filtered, steered and channelled within a process of political treatment. Rather the form of the political and institutional regulative network, as well as imbedded discourses, combine material conditions, experiences, *Weltbilder* (world-view), traditional norms and 'values' in such a way that they can appear as politically relevant 'interests' (Esser and Hirsch 1984, p. 53). 'Objective' social conditions and experiences based on them are transformed into 'interests' within a very complex and contradictory mediating network: 'It is ... impossible that economic agents have "interests" that can be represented by political and ideological instances because how should interests exist prior to those discourses in which they are determined and articulated?' (Mouffe 1982, p. 29; Conolly 1983). And:

In so far every individual entertains a multitude of different social relations, a plurality of determinations exists within the individual to which different discourses correspond. And each of these discourses produces 'interests' and positions by the subject. Thus, every individual is necessarily multifarious, heterogeneous and represents the intersection of several discourses [Mouffe 1982, p. 31, our translation].

The individual is, for example, dependent on wage labour, a member of a church or union, a family member or a car driver. This plurality of experiences and discourses overlapping within the individual represents the basis of the production, the splitting and recombining of interests which occurs in the process of regulation or, in other words, under similar living conditions, individuals can develop different and even contradictory interests depending on the kind of discursive field within which they exist.

Because social conditions and the experiences based on them are structurally contradictory, manifold and contradictory discourses are possible and necessary. Since parties are 'implicitly' present in all social arenas and to almost all individuals, they have the capacity to readily participate in the process of developing and articulating interests. Their heterogeneous internal structure as well as multifarious relations with their 'environment' enable them to transport contradictory discourses. This represents one precondition for the parties' ability to develop discourses, play off one discourse against another and recombine discourses that are all based on manifold material conditions, experiences and actions. In the long run, however, discursive contradictions can only persist on the grounds of a general 'basic consensus' that parties do not produce but at the most, stabilise or expand. Insofar, their regulative function is dependent on the existence of a stable 'hegemonial structure' that in turn is based on the compatibility of social experiences and political forms of interest regulation (as was the case in the 'Keynesian' consensus of growth and progress during the Fordist period).

Electoral competition forces parties to develop distinguishable discursive strategies and to support them with different forms of relations with their 'environment'. Thus, they may differ not only in their official programmes and electorate but also in the mode of regulation that they represent (Esser and Hirsch 1984, p. 53). Changing regulative conditions necessitate adaptions in the organisation and political mode of the ('broader') parties. These adaptations are to a large degree initiated and accelerated by electoral competition: in adapting to new conditions and by developing a new mode of regulation (connections with the electorate, with business, the system of interest groups, social milieux and the public), opposition parties can prove their 'ability to govern'. At the same time, successful parties force their losing competitors to adapt not only their programmes but also their discursive strategies and organisational arrangements.

Thus, the electoral mechanism induces continuous adaptation and differentiation in the mode of regulation as far as it is structured by the party form. Therefore, a change in the mode of regulation, originating in a crisis of the hegemonial structure does not necessarily lead to an open political crisis but can take the shape of a change in the ruling party or party coalition.

This also explains why the importance of parties seems to diminish in political 'fair-weather' periods, that is, in periods of relatively undisturbed accumulation and well-established regulation within a stable hegemonial structure. Then, parties are seemingly reduced to 'unideological' and 'statist' appendages of government and administrative apparatuses; opposition parties have limited possibilities and corporative arrangements between state apparatuses and established interest groups gain dominance. The parties' hour comes during crises of the mode of regulation when traditional forms of interest articulation are ripe for change and new discursive strategies have to be developed. Changes in the mode of regulation are always also 'moral', that is, discursive changes during which parties become decisive factors in getting a new mode of regulation accepted and stabilising it.

THE CRISIS OF FORDISM AND CHANGING CONDITIONS OF REGULATION

Fordist capitalism – the post-World War II hegemonial structure established on a world scale under the dominance of the US and notwithstanding national differences, is in a crisis (for a detailed discussion of the origin and dynamic of this crisis, see Coriat 1979; Boyer and Mistral 1983a; Mazier *et al.* 1984; Hirsch and Roth 1986). The present stage is characterised by fierce conflicts over fundamental societal reorganisation, that is, establishing a 'post-Fordist' accumulation regime and mode of regulation. Parties play a major role in this confrontation during which their internal structure is transformed and their position in the regulatory network is changed. These developments are still ongoing and it is therefore not yet possible to depict a definite 'post-Fordist' party type. Some essential tendencies can be described, however.

During the Fordist period of capitalism, Taylorised work processes became dominant in relevant economic sectors, wage labour expanded considerably (by diminishing forms of subsistence production in agriculture and household) while simultaneously, differences in living and working conditions of wage labour were levelled (*'Arbeit-nehmergesellschaft'* – 'middle-class society'). Industrial mass production of consumer goods led to extensive capitalisation of reproductive sectors and reproduction of labour became an integral part of capital reproduction on the basis of a generalised consumption model. Large productivity gains and the coupling of mass income with those productivity gains made large increases in gross products and the general standard of living possible. Accelerated capitalisation of production and reproduction caused the traditional socio-cultural milieux to dissolve.

This mode of accumulation was connected with a 'monopolistic' mode of regulation that differed substantially from the previously existing liberal-competitive form of regulation (Boyer and Mistral 1983a, p. 49; Boyer and Mistral 1983b; Lipietz 1985, p. 121). It was based on processes of massive economic concentration and the development of new industries (especially automobiles and electronics), the establishment of bureaucratised and centralised unions representing nearly all employees and charged with negotiating centralised industrial agreements, the expansion of the welfare state which substantially changed the conditions of the reproduction of labour and effectively supported the stability of the mass consumption model. Within the party system, 'reformist' and bureaucratised mass integrationist parties were established that were based on redistributionist measures by the state and which loosened their ideological and class orientations ('catch-all-parties'; Kaste and Raschke 1977). A centralised corporatism, based on contractual co-operation among business associations, unions, parties and state administration and Keynesian state intervention developed. Full employment and economic growth, expansion of the welfare state and global macro-economic regulation, applying fiscal and monetary instruments, corporative bargaining structures and macro-economic prognoses became characteristic of the Fordist hegemonial structure.

The crisis of Fordism in the 1970s led to the collapse of the 'Keynesian' mode of regulation. Some of the defining properties of the developing new mode of accumulation include:

(1) the transformation of post-Tayloristic forms of production and the labour process based on new information and communication technologies. This will not lead to an 'end of mass production' but to a technological reconstitution that creates mass unemployment, initiates massive social marginalisation and fragmentation of working conditions and wage relations;

(2) accelerated industrialisation of services based on new information and communication technologies ('hyper-industrialisation') that create unemployment as well as forced mobility and drastically change the social structure of the labour force (that is the relation between 'white' and 'blue-collar' workers) in the service sector. At the same time, changes in information and communicative behaviour will have strong individualising consequences for the form of societalisation;

(3) a new push of capitalisation based on the industrialisation of services as well as of agriculture that will initiate an increase in forced mobility and an accelerated collapse of traditional milieux;

(4) uncoupling of increases in productivity and mass income and thus, the transformation of accumulation with slower growth rates combined with increased differences in levels of income and consumption;

(5) 'individualisation' and 'pluralisation of life-styles' based on fragmented wage and labour relations, societalisation mediated by information technologies, differentiation of consumption levels, increased competition for jobs, weakened disciplinary effects on standardised wage labour and psycho-social liberation. In connection with these developments, a new mode of regulation begins to emerge that attaches new importance to existing elements of monopolistic regulation but still combines elements of statist market regulation. Some features are:

(6) new divisions in and integration of industrial sectors on the basis of advanced production technologies and in connection with massive international concentration processes and reorganised relations between finance and industrial capital. More market

oriented and innovative, small industrial companies gain new importance in high-tech sectors as well as marginal economic spheres while differences between self-employment and wage labour increasingly disappear;

(7) quantitative reduction and institutional fragmentation of the welfare system and additional cleavages within wage labour, induced by the welfare state;

(8) unions weakened by mass unemployment, increased relevance of the 'third sector', heterogenised work conditions and added social cleavages within wage labour;

(9) new corporative forms, consisting of close state-industry collaboration in technological development, selective integration of privileged segments of the labour force in corporative arrangements at the company level and above, and abandoning full-employment and reform policies aimed at the reproduction of the work force as a whole ('selective-decentral corporatism').

PRESENT TRANSFORMATIONS IN THE PARTIES' ORGANISATIONAL STRUCTURE AND POLICY MODE

In West Germany, the crisis of Fordism is accompanied by a crisis of the dominant party type: the *Volkspartei* (catch-all-party). The *Volkspartei*, that is, 'the modern bureaucratic party with mass membership and socially diverse, heterogeneous electorate most adequately represents *the* party form of a developed "Fordist" capitalist society facing severe competition on the world market' (Esser and Hirsch, 1984). *Volksparteien* were established as bureaucratic, centralised and statist mass integration agencies, primarily oriented towards fulfilling control functions: securing government stipulations for reproduction of the socio-economic system. Their foundation within traditional social and political milieux has steadily weakened. Professionalisation and bureaucratisation of the party apparatus resulted in centrally organised, more selective and tactical interest representation and was accompanied by an almost exclusive orientation of party strategies on the maximisation of electoral votes.

Both *Volksparteien*, CDU and SPD, consensually transcribing to a limited 'distributive pluralism', supported a model of regulation (corporatist interest mediation, political Keynesianism, security state) that harmonised exceptionally well with the requirements of the West German model of accumulation (export orientation, highly specialised and well integrated modern industrial structure). The Social-Democratic party was especially successful in providing a system of material concessions and compromises (welfare state, wage-oriented co-operation between capital and labour) to manage likely conflicts between 'system imperatives' (adapting to developments on the world market) and individual interests (resisting forced mobility or disintegration of traditional milieux, intensification of labour in Taylorised labour processes).

Facing increased pressure on the world market and specific conflicts within the Fordist model, this mode of mass integration turned increasingly crisis-prone and finally collapsed (Hirsch and Roth 1986, p. 71). On the party level the crisis therefore appears to be primarily the crisis of the Social-Democratic party – a crisis which, however, turns out to be paradigmatic for the present situation of both *Volksparteien*.

The Crisis of *Volksparteien*

Both *Volksparteien* experience some common difficulties, in spite of obvious differences with respect to their electoral success and the condition of their respective party organisations. Thus, the federal elections of 1987 caused similarly critical reactions in both parties. After decades of steadily growing electoral support, the percentages of votes attained in 1987 were comparable to the results in the 1950s. Evidently, heterogenising and fragmentary tendencies in society had begun to work in favour of smaller parties. Additionally, conclusions drawn by both parties show striking similarities: programmatic and organisational renewal is the order of the day.

The bureaucratic organisations, with all their election campaign apparatuses to identify and influence their voters, see themselves being challenged by the increasing incalculability of the electorate (Radunski 1986). Thus, party specific abstentions become increasingly important in determining election results in spite of still relatively high turn-outs. In addition, abstentions possibly signal impending voter 'reorientations'. The number of those people who have not decided if they will vote or for which party they will vote shortly before election day is growing. Party strategists in an 'emotional democracy' (Radunski) devise their election campaign with those voters in mind who intend to abstain or frequently change their party preferences.

At the same time parties find it increasingly hard to define their electorate; confused by a tangle of regular voters, voters only loosely tied to a party, and floating voters, they are 'searching for their typical voter' (Zundel 1987). Help is expected from social science studies. These, however, only state a far-reaching differentiation of electoral behaviour on the basis of increasing socio-economic segmentation. Several distinctive 'milieux' or 'life-styles' are defined that also differ with respect to party preferences. They are relevant to parties since potential voters of both parties are found in all milieux and in order to gain a majority of votes, both parties have to fully activate their respective potentials in all milieux.

The *Volksparteien* thus face an electorate that votes with an increasing degree of flexibility, that is structured more heterogeneously and that, finally, becomes increasingly indifferent towards party activities. Differences between parties are noticed to a lesser degree and less political importance is given to possible changes in government. These developments tend to threaten the legitimising essence of periodical elections: voters have to assume to be able to decide between sufficiently different alternatives.

Voters are demotivated as much by their doubts with regard to political parties' competence as by a feeling of powerlessness in the face of party omnipotence. According to party managers, parties are rightfully 'blamed for extending their influence ever further into societal areas' (Geissler 1982, p. 277; similar: Glotz and Wagner 1982).

Whether impotent or omnipotent, parties are increasingly met with voter indifference. Ever closer identification of parties with the state and the strategic concentration on bureaucratic, centralised and tactical efforts to maximise votes are beginning to work against the 'inventors' of the party strategy. The accelerated process of splitting (party) apparatus and (party) people ('simple' members and voters) produces unpleasant effects for party managers.

Strategically thinking party managers are especially startled when indifference from the 'silent masses' — which an Americanised party system could at least live with – is accompanied by rejection of the 'politically mobile' (Glotz and Wagner 1982, p. 290; Geissler 1982, p. 267). For both *Volksparteien*, citizen's initiatives, new social movements and finally, the emergence of the Greens signal a disturbing 'tendency towards alternative organisational forms' of political activity (Glotz and Wagner 1982, p. 284). Obviously, the growth of political activities and organisations outside and besides *Volksparteien* show that it would be short-sighted to expect a future 'voters market' consisting of individualised, disoriented and apolitical 'consumers' that could be reached by one or the other *Volkspartei* simply with clever political PR-efforts — as assumed in prevailing Americanised party strategies. Parallel to tendencies of dissolving traditional milieux — including total 'individualisation' — counter-tendencies exist towards newly established networks that also promote political orientations. However, traditional political institutions can either hardly or not at all politically organise these networks (for example 'anarchist scenes' in metropolitan areas).

Parties (in a narrow sense) do not merely entertain 'external relations' with voters — although this is the dominant orientation of debates within *Volksparteien* primarily trying to maximise votes. Manifold connections with their respective *Vorfeldorganisationen* (interest groups surrounding parties) are of prime importance for parties in their efforts to deal with the 'pre-political arena' (*vorpolitischer Raum*). However, these traditional ties are loosening up too. Tendencies towards a more heterogeneous and divided society also restructure memberships of interest groups and associations; whole economic sectors or regions are threatened by increased competition and, consequently, interest group leaders are faced with new and radicalised requests 'from below'; traditionally identical interests and group solidarities are destroyed as a result of restructured industrial sectors and transformed labour processes. Within interest groups and associations, these developments produce new and different interest constellations and conflict lines as well as intensify internal quarrels causing *Volkspartei* and party specific pre-political arenas to drift apart.

A more heterogeneous electorate and disintegrating traditional institutional networks linked to specific parties are mirrored in parties in two ways: firstly, a plurality of 'life-styles' emerges within parties and secondly, and more importantly, divergent strategies are developing as to how the party should react in the face of a splitting and disappearing traditional electorate. Simultaneously, the parties' lack of social and political concepts further strengthens disintegrationist tendencies. So far, debates over post-Keynesian global concepts produce at the most programmatic diversity and not coherence established by precise programmatic statements. A build-up of factions and conflicts and fierce strategic confrontations characterise the situation of today's *Volksparteien*.

A structural dilemma, inherent in the development of *Volksparteien*, surfaces in the present situation of major economic, social and political changes. Plural and heterogeneous internal structures, programmatic statements and connections with the 'environment' are preconditions for the parties' integrationist capacities. At the same time, however, they permanently undermine the parties' internal integrationist capabilities, they enable *and* limit strategies to maximise votes, they render difficult production and existence of unifying programmatic and political orientations and thereby finally endanger the state bureaucracies' ability, supposedly secured by political parties, to adequately react to world market pressures.

The described potential dilemma and latent danger is presently developing into a manifest crisis. Internal and external party critics successfully challenge *Volksparteien* with aspersions such as 'ungovernability', 'leadership crisis', 'a party within the party', 'split party image' and so on. Strategic debates following these verbal attacks severely divide both *Volksparteien* (Fach and Simonis 1987, p. 170; Jäger 1986). Attempts to rebuild *Volksparteien* into 'traditional' parties with limited membership and electoral ambitions as well as traditional programmatic orientations are confronted with strategies to further strengthen the concept of the 'catch-all-party' which tears down traditional party barriers and reaches for practically all voters with the help of a centrally organised and 'depoliticised' discourse using most advanced technologies to adequately address specific target groups.

An analysis of the fragmentation of party organisation must take these confrontations into account. Widening differences between government and parliamentary faction or party apparatus establish the image of parties torn by inner conflicts. Increasing spatial differentiations in the transformation to Post-Fordism support ambitions within regional party organisations to reach for larger autonomy. State governments, constituted by the same parties, experiment with completely different economic, social and political strategies to overcome the present crisis. Regional differentiation, pluralist programmatic diversity and a lack of identity establishing concepts help render the parties' search for their voters very difficult.

Structurally inherent dynamics in the development of the *Volkspartei* party type lead to noteworthy consequences in West Germany. The heterogeneous electorate is further differentiated, traditional social and political networks disappear, new networks are established, the voter and the 'voter market' are less and less calculable for parties so exclusively focused on maximising votes; bureaucratisation, professionalisation and an increasingly autonomous party apparatus, the dominance of 'control functions' (statification) and finally the tactical and selective use of societal interests are disintegrating the social, political and ideological context within which *Volksparteien* exist; consequently, 'party weariness' in and outside of parties becomes a more widespread phenomenon, cleavages in the electorate become more numerous, party organisation and membership are further separated, political engagement is substituted by careerism, indifference, fatalism or even aggressive rejection. *Volksparteien* are presently undergoing changes characteristic of party types in general: they are becoming 'outdated in line with those conditions that produced them' (Raschke 1983, our translation).

Modernisation strategies

The party system gains prominence in times of political and economic crises and societal change (Fach and Simonis 1984). In a specific way, it manages phenomena of political and ideological crises. In it, confrontations take place as to how heterogeneous and diffuse conflict lines and interest differences should be restructured so that a new and stable connection between accumulation regime and mode of regulation can be established.

The Christian-Democrats and Social-Democrats strategic-conceptual blueprints and political and organisational modernising efforts take place within the prevailing crisis constellation as well as from within the emerging contours of a new, 'post-Fordist' mode of accumulation and regulation: increased competitive pressures on the world market inducing new labour processes and industrial structures; trenchant changes in social structure and political and ideological norms (rearrangements, differentiation and fragmentation; 'individualisation', the 'silent revolution' and 'pluralisation of life-styles'); reorganisation of the welfare and security state and new, 'selective' corporatism. On the other hand, the 'new face' (Hirsch and Roth 1986) of the future West German accumulation and regulation model will, to a large degree, depend on the transformation process of the *Volksparteien*.

Presently, the Social-Democratic party finds itself forced to 'modernise'. As *the* party representing the *Modell Deutschland*, the SPD is especially hard hit by the crisis. After the collapse of Keynesian hegemony, the Social-Democrats are left with a programmatic and strategic vacuum; decomposition and reformation of political and social milieux have split up the potential Social-Democratic electorate; new social movements and the Greens in particular have caused Social-Democratic votes to decline.

The Social-Democratic party has reached with hyperactivity and with various attemps at organisational reform. Modernising strategies include Americanisation of the party (reducing the party to an 'election machine' or political PR agency, personalising and depoliticising politics) as well as 'reinstalling' the party as a 'workers party'. The debate has focused on organisational renewal — in spite of manifold programmatic efforts. The loss of traditional ties between voters and party as well as the party's lack of ability to attract new segments of the electorate has caused the party to think about reorganisational strategies. Both crisis phenomena call for rebuilding the pluralistic complex of relations with classes, groups, milieux and institutions. The establishment of the party's omnipresence in the 'pre-political arena' (clubs, associations, the recreational sector as a whole) is the goal.

In the pre-political arena, independent Social-Democrats are of special interest to the party as 'multiplicators' or 'opinion leaders'. Intellectuals are of strategic importance in the party's daily 'fight to conquer minds'. New organisational forms have been set up and party media expanded to establish the integration of independent Social-Democrats. Communication with the party environment has to be achieved by organised discussion forums, open to manifold opinions and up-to-date themes. Increasingly, documented programmes and party platforms have been charged with the limited task of 'serving' the discourses within the party and between the party and the 'outside' and thus, adhere to principles of flexibility, openness and plurality. Programmatic debates become ends in themselves staged according to the discursive requirements of a 'modern *Volkspartei*': the party has to prove readiness to communicate, commonality and diversity between parties has to be signalled, openness, plurality *and* unity has to be documented.

Parallel dialogues with manifold heterogeneous target groups presuppose a high degree of discursive autonomy of responsible party subdivisions (Glotz 1981, p. 4). However, close ties between party headquarters and these subdivisions are to safeguard against a degree of autonomy that could be dangerous to the party. Additionally, activities of institutionalised subdivisions (*Arbeitsgemeinschaften*) traditionally attending to target groups are increasingly taken over by conferences with experts and commissions organised by the party centre. Party headquarters now initiate and organise manifold subject and target group specific discourses – also and above all with the intention to thereby control the activities of the party as a whole.

In order to successfully address target groups, organisational forms need to be applied that are 'adequate' for respective target groups. 'Depoliticised' music and neighbourhood festivals, afternoon coffee parties and party schools exemplify a 'personalised organisational policy' (Glotz 1986). An expansion of services offered by the party reflects the party's understanding of 'politics as a service activity' (Wentz 1987).

Traditional 'target groups' are in a transitory stage of differentiation, transformation and reconstitution. Therefore, parties experience growing pains in dealing with them and thus, party strategies are increasingly oriented towards the individual voter (Wentz 1987). Party activities follow the needs of 'a modern election campaign in the era of mass communication' (Radunski 1986). Party politics are turned into media events. Themes that are in vogue — as reflected by the media — have been promptly taken up by flexible parties. The parties' comments and statements have addressed specific sectors of the public and necessarily differ or are even contradictory at times. 'Model argumentations' have been proposed by the parties' centre to achieve, at least in a formal manner, the desired unified party image. Politics as 'media events' (Glotz) have applied 'suggestive pictures, great abbreviations, archetypes', stage controversies, have led image campaigns developed by PR agencies and established commissions to worry about political semantics (Glotz 1986). The 'politician as a personality' has moved into the centre of political competition (Wentz 1987). The Americanisation of political campaigning has turned degrees of professionalisation, commercialisation and technicalisation into indicators of success in party competition (SPD 1983 and CDU 1987).

The party apparatus, and especially party headquarters, has been strengthened by the described transformation process — and not weakened or even abolished as frequently implied in the thesis of Americanisation of West German parties. The party headquarters acts as a 'communication centre', and as such initiates and organises the 'great societal communication process' (in this sense: the political process) as well as establishing and stabilising the parties' 'campaign and discourse capabilities' (Glotz 1986). Differentiation and pluralisation of the parties' connections with its 'environment' are internally accompanied by a centralisation process. While parties are 'opening up' towards their 'environment', party apparatuses are further bureaucratised and party headquarters become more dominant: the latter organise the strengthening, professionalisation, standardisation and technicalisation of party organisations.

The process of modernisation has been accompanied by an 'erosion of affective party loyalties'. As in other large organisations, the members of the party apparatus need to be constantly motivated anew. 'Corporate identity' has to be achieved by 'depoliticising' and 'emotionalising' party activities, by offering services or reviving traditions.

CONCLUSION: A NEW PARTY SYSTEM?

The 'post-Fordist' party type accentuates and emphasises organisational and political elements already present in traditional *Volkspar-teien* and thereby adapts to new societal regulative conditions. However, the process of restructuring the party system is in progress and some of the described phenomena may turn out to be merely peculiarities of a transitory stage. The specific features of the traditional system of *Volksparteien* are responsible for the fact that the crisis of Fordism in West Germany did not develop into a crisis of the political institutional system as a whole. The party system, driven by the mechanisms of party competition, provides for continuous transformation without open political ruptures.

The new party form is essentially characterised by continued centralisation that, based on rapid introduction of new communication technologies, increases the weight of party centres. A differentiated expansion of regional subdivisions or interest-specific functional divisions increasingly turns these 'lower' segments of the party organisation into target group-oriented multiplicators or transmission instances. Organisational centralisation, however, is accompanied by clear signs of regional fragmentation. Since, firstly, parties have not yet produced a consensual and effective regulative concept for post-Fordist capitalism and secondly, regional disparities increase as a result of accelerated economic change, state party organisations try to achieve a more autonomous status in spite of efforts by party centres to contain such efforts. Regional pluralisation of parties is caused by increased competition among states to formulate and enforce respective crisis policies following the collapse of the Keynesian-Fordist mode of regulation.

The process of bureaucratic centralisation reduces the importance of traditional interest groups institutionalised within parties. They are rendered marginal for internal decision-making processes by the possibility, created by communication technologies, for strengthened central apparatuses to instantly get in contact with local organisational units. As party ties with traditional socio-cultural milieux weaken and social networks, scenes and life-styles fluctuate, it becomes more important for parties to use all available technical means to keep communication with this differentiating arena outside parties alive. By now, parties function as depoliticised social service institutions, not only instrumentalising but also organising senior citizen meetings or street festivals. Thus, the creation of positive corporate identity is intended, which is accompanied by personalisation of politics. Contradictory discourses with different specific target groups can only be successfully established on the basis of general confidence detached from concrete politics.

Institutionalised connections with interest groups and associations reach a critical stage if only because of their social and political heterogenisation and weakness. Thereby, parties are increasingly forced to organise 'their' respective 'political environment'. However, they permanently run the risk of neglecting vital interests or active political-social milieux. The stability of the party system remains primarily threatened by uninstitutionalised and uncontrollable political networks.

It seems unlikely that gains in recent elections by small parties suggest the establishment of a heterogeneous multi-party system and the disappearance of the dominant mass integrationist parties. These developments rather reflect temporary difficulties of the *Volksparteien* to adapt to a changing environment. Decentralisation of the party system seems unlikely in the face of monopolising effects stemming from the increasing importance of technical apparatuses and therefore necessary financial resources. And even more importantly, the fact that society, in spite of social differentiation and fragmentation, remains a class society, supports the establishment of contradictory political blocks with respective dominant parties – even more so when the relevance of traditional 'cleavages' decreases. Assuming that societal heterogeneisation and pluralisation will further increase, it appears equally unlikely that the factual two-party system of the Fordist era will return. Rather, the party system will take the form of an uneven oligopoly, in which small, milieu- or interest-specific corrective or protest parties play an important role. They will function as a twofold flexibility reserve: as additional competitors, they will firstly, increase the pressure on the party system to continuously transform itself and adapt to new social, economic and political constellations and they will secondly, provide for reintegration into the representative mechanism of scenes, groups and movements outside the established political patterns.

In spite of organisational and political continuities, a rather different mode of regulation is evolving within the transformation to 'post-Fordism'. Parties will not continue to act as political mediators within a highly organised corporative arrangement institutionalising the class conflict in a centralised fashion. One pillar of that arrangement collapsed when large mass associations (such as unions and farmers' associations) showed increasing signs of weakness and internal polarisation. The Fordist-corporative form of regulation undergoes modifications with far-reaching social implications. This is based on enormous industrial concentration and further autonomisation of the security state following increasing pressure for economic transformation exercised by the world market. The mode of regulation remains monopolistic since a return to liberal market regulation is rendered impossible by a high degree of economic monopolisation and the continuing need for centralised administrative control of market processes and consequently, the existence of a state-monopoly complex.

The 'liberalism' of the new mode of regulation is restricted to the subsidiary mobilisation of innovative potential in small enterprises and the privatisation of individual destinies and risks. A 'depolitisation' follows in which personal destinies are turned into matters of individual capabilities and forcefulness — an ideological development based on the reality of growing societal polarisation and eroding social security systems. Political decisions and state activities thereby become seemingly less relevant for individual perspectives. This might help explain decreasing party ties and increasing abstentions which in turn force parties to assume their discursive strategies with an orientation towards target groups: structurally privatised interests are mobilised in an *ad hoc* fashion, in tactical terms and in a quasi-populist manner and without establishing stable coalitions and interest complexes.

NOTES

1.   The authors gratefully acknowledge the help of John Ely, Margit Mayer and Susan Wylegala-Haeusler in preparing this translation.

REFERENCES

M. Aglietta, *Régulation et crises du capitalisme. L'experience des État-Unis* (Paris: Calman-Lévy, 1976).

R. Boyer, 'Wage Formation in Historical Perspective: The French Experience', *Cambridge Journal of Economics* (September 1979).

R. Boyer and J. Mistral, 'Le Temps Présent: La Crise, *Annales* Jg. 38 nr. 3(I) u 4(II) (1983a), pp. 483–506, 773–89 (a).

R. Boyer and J. Mistral, *Accumulation, Inflation Crises* (Paris: PUF, 1983b).

C. Buci-Glucksmann and G. Therborn, *Der sozialdemokratische Staat. Die 'Keynesianisierung' der Gesellschaft* (Hamburg: VSA, 1982).

CDU, 'Wahlkampfbericht der Bundesgeschäftsstelle zum Bundestagswahlkampf' (1986/87). Unpublished manuscript.

W. E. Connolly, *The Terms of Political Discourse* (Oxford: Martin Robertson, 1983).

B. Coriat, *L'Atelier et le Chronomètre* (Paris: Christian Bourgois Editeur, 1979).

B. Coriat, 'Relations industrielles, rapport salarial et régulation: l'inflexion neolibérale' *Consommation 3* (1982).

J. Esser and J. Hirsch, 'Der CDU-Staat: Ein politisches Regulierungsmodell für den "nachfordistischen" Kapitalismus', Prokla 56 (1984) pp. 51–66.

W. Fach and G. Simonis, 'Die politische Funktion der politischen Partei. Konsequenzen aus dem westdeutschen Atomkonflikt' in J. W. Falter, C. Fenner, M. Greven (eds), *Politische Willensbildung und Interessenvermittlung* (Opladen: Westdeutscher Verlag, 1984) pp. 131–39.

W. Fach and G. Simonis, *Die Stärke des Staates im Atomkonflikt. Die Bundesrepublik im Vergleich mit Frankreich* (Frankfurt, New York: Campus, 1987).

H. Geissler, 'Das Verhältnis zwischen Bürgern und Parteien aus der Sicht der SCU' in J. Raschke (ed.), *Bürger und Parteien. Ansichten und Analysen einer schwierigen Beziehung* ('Schriftenreihe der Bundeszentrale für politische Bildung' Band 189) (Bonn, 1982) pp. 264–82.

P. Glotz, Zusammenfassung der Diskussion' (Organisationspolitische Tagung der SPD am 2–3 Oktober 1981 in Bonn-Bad Godesberg) (1981). Unpublished manuscript.

P. Glotz, 'Kampagne in Deutschland', *Politisches Tagebuch 1981–1983* (Hamburg: Hoffmann und Campe, 1986).

P. Glotz and R. Wagner, 'Das Verhältnis zwischen Bürgern und Parteien aus der Sicht der SPD' in J. Raschke (ed.), *Bürger und Parteien. Ansichten und Analysen einer schwierigen Beziehung* ('Schriftenreihe der Bundeszentrale, für politische Bildung' Band 189) (Bonn, 1982) pp. 283–93.

J. Hirsch and R. Roth, 'Modell Deustchland und neue soziale Bewegungen', Prokla 40 (1980) pp. 14–39.

J. Hirsch and R. Roth, *Das neue Gesicht des Kapitalismus* (Hamburg: VSA, 1986).

J. Holloway and S. Picciotto (eds), *State und Capital. A Marxist Debate* (London: Edward Arnold, 1978).

M. Jäger, 'Über Macht und Parteien, in Marxismus und Theorie der Parteien', *Argument-Sonderband* AS 91 (Berlin: Argument, 1983) pp. 38–121.

T. Jäger, 'Verlassen die Konservativen die CDU/CSU?' CIVIS 4 (1986) pp. 15–23.

B. Jessop and N. Poulantzas, *Marxist Theory and Political Strategy* (London: Macmillan, 1985).

H. Kaste and J. Raschke, 'Zur Politik der Volkspartei' in W. D. Narr (ed.), *Auf dem Weg zum Einparteienstaat* (Opladen: Westdeutscher Verlag, 1977) pp. 26–74.

A. Lipietz, *L'Audace ou l'Enlisement. Sûr les Politiques Economiques de la Gauche* (Paris: Editions La Découverte, 1984).

A. Lipietz, 'Akkumulation, Krisen und Auswege aus der Krise. Einige methodologische Anmerkungen zum Begriff der "Regulation"', Prokla 58 (1985) pp. 109–37.

J. Mazier, 'Growth and Crisis – a Marxist Interpretation' in A. Boltho (ed.), *The European Economy. Growth and Crises* (Oxford: 1982) pp. 38–71.

J. Mazier, M. Basle und J-F. Vidal, *Quand les crises durent...* (Paris: Economica, 1984).

C. Mouffe, 'Arbeiterklasse, Hegemonie und Sozialismus' in *Neue soziale Bewegungen und Marxismus*, Argument-Sonderband AS 78 (Berlin 1982) pp. 23–39.

N. Poulantzas, *Staatstheorie. Politischer Überbau, Ideologie, Sozialistische Demokratie* (Berlin: VSA, 1978).

P. Radunski, 'Wahlkampf in den achtziger Jahren. Repolitisierung der Wahlkampfführung und neue Techniken in den Wahlkämpfen der westlichen Demokratien', *Aus Politik und Zeitgeschichte* B 11/86, (15 March 1986) pp. 34–45.

J. Raschke, 'Jenseits der Volkspartei', *Das Argument* 137 (1983) pp. 54–65.

SPD, Analyse und Konsequenzen der Bundestagswahl 1983 (Vorstand der SPD). Unpublished manuscript.

R. Steininger, *Soziologische Theorie der politischen Parteien* (Frankfurt, New York: Campus, 1984).

M. Wentz, Sozialer Wandel, 'Dienstleistungsgesellschaft und sozialdemokratische Politik', *Die Neue Gesellschaft/Frankfurter Hefte* 4 (April 1987) pp. 347–52.

E. Wiesendahl, 'Wie politisch sind politische Parteien? Zu einigen vernachlässigten Aspekten der Organisations-wirklichkeit politischer Parteien' (1983). Unpublished manuscript.

R. Zundel, 'Auf der Suche nach dem typischen Wähler', *Die Zeit* (15 January 1987) p. 5.

Part IV
Capitalist Restructuring and Spatial Change

Part IV

13 The Change of Regional Inequality in the Federal Republic of Germany

Hartmut Häusermann and Thomas
Krämer-Badoni

The regional development of population and employment in the Federal Republic of Germany subsequent to World War II has been characterised by a stronger growth of the southern regions whereas the western regions (Saarland, North Rhine-Westphalia) and the northern German centres have lost in importance. The resulting structure presents a new outline of regional imbalance which can be explained by the history of industrialisation in Germany, by the restructuring of economic relations after World War II and by political decisions (Friedrichs, Häusermann, Siebel 1986). Due to changes in international trading and corresponding investment strategies by capital the long-term transformation has considerably accelerated since the onset of the economic crisis in the 1970s. While up to the mid-1970s the discrepancy of development, between rural agrarian areas and industrial agglomerations was considered the main problem of regional development it is now the dissimilar development of those agglomerations that holds the main attention in regional politics. The economic instability of the centres of previous industrial growth on the one hand and the persistent growth of the economic centres in southern Germany on the other hand present a new historical situation. The core cities of the traditional industrial areas are particularly affected by this course of development and in some cases are confronting severe losses of employment and population.

CAPITALIST DEVELOPMENT AND THE PATTERN OF SPATIAL STRUCTURE

There are always imbalances to be found in the course of the economic and spatial development of a society but their specific social shape was first systematically established by the development of capitalist

331

industrial societies. The mechanisms of capitalist production – competition, concentration, maximisation of profits – lead to a systematic exploitation of natural space, thereby socially overlaying natural space. The natural conditions of space become integrated into the new social structure of space, differing in each case according to the stage of development of capitalist production.

This is not to say that the spatial structure of industrial capitalism is determined exclusively by mechanisms of competition, concentration and maximisation of profits. The development of productive facilities, the utilisation of energy resources, the technical and technological development of production and transport, the deposits of natural resources, the structure of the labour market, and, not least, political intervention link a society's spatial development to a combination of production preconditions involving natural and political ones and those inherent in the logic of capital development. Spatial structure is composed of the sum of these conditions. Therefore, the history of industrialisation — if it can be deciphered — is the history of successive phases of industrialisation, each one revealing the ideal type of a specific spatial structure accompanied by agglomeration and deglomeration processes, by regional losses and gains in importance. The ideal types of spatial structures are rarely to be found in pure form in the actual histories of societies. The coexistence of different stages of capital development generates an actual spatial structure necessarily appearing contradictory and inconsistent. Thus, ideal types of spatial structure can only be enlarged upon in theoretical analysis.

The history of industrialisation, however, is at the same time the history of a progressive mastering of natural and spatial barriers of production. The independence from the locations of natural resource deposits, from natural energy resources and from labour reserves already has largely become reality. The independence from natural resources by way of their synthetic substitution, the minimisation of energy demand and material requirements in the line of production, the tendency to replace live labour in the immediate line of production by automated and computer-based systems of production, the substitution of immediate proximity by networks of information and communications systems, and finally the independence of agricultural business from climatic conditions as a matter of manipulations by genetic technology, will be realised within the immediate or near future. The resulting spatial structure will be independent from the factors that previously determined the spatial distribution of production and to such extent that the former theories of regional inequality

— at least the ones that were based upon an interconnection of spatial structure and the mechanisms of capitalist production — will lose their explanatory powers. This is not to say that they were initially false but the reality of capitalism they tried to explain up to now will have completely changed.

The presently observable re-formation of capitalism will prepare the ground for a new capitalist formation having only little in common with the spatial structure of traditional industrial capitalism. According to our estimation there are two main trends which may be subsumed under the notion of an 'abstractification of space': firstly, a trend towards increasing independence of capital allocation from socially generated spatial structures; and secondly, a trend towards independence of capital from national territories.

The deciphering of spatial structures in their connection to certain phases of industrialisation is a very complex enterprise as both the process of establishing new technologies and products and the decline of former systems of production represent prolonged processes which are temporally and spatially overlapping. Besides, there are only a few industrial locations to be found that are monostructurised to such an extent that the decline of the industries in question has immediate and clearly evident effects. Therefore, historical inspection outlines necessarily complex spatial structures as they are to be observed in reality at a given time.

In the following our analysis will operate on two levels. On a first level we will outline the historical development of regional structure up to the new pattern of regional inequality that has taken on the shape of a south-north-decline in Germany. We will examine where and under what conditions the regionally dissimilar development within the urban agglomerations — representing the dynamic centres of capitalist production — may result in new social problems. On a second level we will present a rough sketch of the new trends in capitalist development and show that the new structural elements of this development render the former Marxist models of explanation obsolete.

HISTORICAL DEVELOPMENT OF REGIONAL STRUCTURE

Due to Germany's division into numerous small absolutist states economic development prior to industrialisation was largely decentralised. Within the basic agrarian structure numerous isles of crafts and functions of the third sector had emerged. A relatively tight network of cities, linked to each other by extensive trade relations, overspread the German Reich. Iron production and manufacturing of semi-finished products were located in the sub-alpine mountain range because water and wood were the most important sources of energy (Otten 1986).

After having continuously developed for several centuries this pattern changed with the beginning of the 19th century because of the employment of mineral energy (coal) in processing ore for iron production. The Saarland and the Ruhr district, where the largest deposits of coal were discovered, developed into centres of heavy industry. New cities came into being because the advancing iron and steel production attracted the population of the agrarian areas. Since the turn of the century the population on the whole had grown to such an extent that it could no longer be maintained by the agrarian regions. The rural districts eventually were pauperised, a situation that was gradually mitigated by migration to the industrial areas (Marschalck 1984).

In the course of this first wave of industrialisation the southern German regions remained 'backward' because they lacked natural resources, the main condition of the new industrial growth. The surplus population of these regions was reduced mainly by emigration to the US. The specific pattern of hereditary succession in agricultural production (division of the farmstead among all heirs) stabilised the decentral distribution of the population. But as the steadily shrinking farms did not yield the necessary means of subsistence, a specific combination of agricultural and specialised manufacturing production evolved. Only by the end of the 19th century, when the shortage in energy could be eliminated by the construction of electric power stations and overhead cables, did a rapid industrialisation of the southern regions begin. From the very onset, however, the main emphasis was placed on electrical and mechanical engineering. The regional disadvantage of being remote from the coal mining districts (*Revierferne*, Salin 1928) had to be compensated for by specialisation and emphasis on quality (Kunz 1986).

Apart from the establishment of heavy industry in the coal mining districts and the emergence of new cities in connection with the rise of the chemical industry around the turn of the century, the existing regional structure all over Germany was being industrialised (Reulecke 1985). Beyond that, industrialisation did not generate fundamentally new regional structures. Compared to the other regions, however, the coal, iron and steel industries showed exorbitant growth rates up to World War I.

The development following World War II was characterised above all by a restoration of the previous structures. The large requirements of the capital goods industry initiated a new boom of the coal, iron and steel industries. Up to 1959, when full employment was attained, *all* regions were marked by high growth rates in employment and gross national product. However, indications of regional change were to be observed even in this phase of growth: mineral oil and synthetic materials already substituted for a part of the 'old' natural resources of coal and iron. But within a growing economy this was not yet perceived to be a structural problem. Even the severe job losses that occurred in coal mining in the 1960s could still be absorbed by growing industry elsewhere without great difficulties.

The beginning of the world-wide crisis in the mid-1970s altered the situation. The trends of economic development in the southern regions and the 'old' industrial areas to the west and north of Germany have taken different courses. Further growth of employment, population and the real net output as well as low unemployment rates on the one hand, job losses, low growth rates, public poverty and high rates of unemployment on the other hand characterise a development that has since dominated the discussion of regional policy under the catchword of a 'south-north-decline'.

Explanations for the dissimilar development trends

The development of the regional economic structure is characterised by processes of deindustrialisation, tertiarisation and neo-industrialisation. The resulting effects act upon the regions in different ways and add up to contrary perspectives. As Germany's industry is highly export-reliant, the regional shifts of employment and the different growth rates are closely linked to changes in international trading.

The selective industrialisation of Third World countries, directed by international capital (Fröbel *et al.* 1986), has caused a reduction of shares in international trading for certain sectors of German industry. Those industrial sectors that rely heavily on the availability of natural resources and cheap labour lost their ability to compete on the world market (Läpple 1985). This had previously happened to the textile and lumber industries and has now extended to the core sectors of heavy industry. Deindustrialisation spreads wherever the development of a region has been dominated by the manufacturing of a single product because the formal economic sector creates no other jobs. Deindustrialisation accordingly is a phenomenon of monostructural regions that are deprived of their industrial basis because of international developments.

The newly industrialised countries and Japan in particular have entered into competition with German industry in the area of industrial mass-production. The establishment of free exchange rates according to the Bretton Woods agreement caused production costs in the Federal Republic to increase relatively to such an extent that the labour-intensive sectors were no longer competitive in international trading. The capital investment of German business, mainly consisting of expansion investment on a traditional technological basis until the late 1960s, now concentrated upon the rationalisation of production. In addition, capital investment abroad increased (Welzk 1986). Thus, the traditional industries had to register job losses in the manufacturing sector. The reduction of employment due to rationalisation mainly affects large-scale industry where, firstly, production is Taylorised and thus suitable for further rationalisation and automatisation and, secondly, where the necessary capital equipment is available.

Neglecting low cost mass-production, the export strategy of German industry instead switched to technologically advanced products, particularly those of the capital goods sector. This involved a restructuring of employment: the number of technicians and engineers employed in the areas of research, development and construction largely increases relative to the number of those working within the direct line of production. Job losses due to rationalisation and job creation in the course of development and production of modern technologies as well as tertiarisation of productive enterprises, result in a balance of employment which differs regionally. The southern regions, too, have to put up with job losses due to rationalisation, but these are altogether overcompensated for by job creation in tertiary functions of the production sector and by the development of the third sector. To simplify matters: capital goods for rationalisation purposes, particularly micro-electronic units of control, are developed and produced in the south while they are employed mainly in the 'old' industrial regions.

The accumulation of high-tech industries in the southern part of Germany can be accounted for by several factors. Firstly, one particularly important factor is the transfer of the electronic industry from the former centre of electrotechnical industry in Berlin to the Munich region after World War II. Siemens, at present a multi-national trust and the largest employer in Europe, then transferred its head office to Munich and in this region established its most up-to-date departments of research and development which expanded significantly during the last 20 years. Other firms in the area of electronic data processing likewise sought the American occupied part of southern Germany. Large trusts of the motor vehicles and electrical industries (for example Daimler-Benz, Porsche, BMW, Bosch) developed into enterprises with a steady world-wide market or were integrated into multi-national trusts.

Secondly, at present the Munich region is the centre of high technological development and production, in the hardware as well as in the software sector. Today the development of modern electronics in all advanced industrial countries is closely interlocked with the armaments industry. The ambitious goals of the former Minister of Defence, Strauss, at present the Bavarian Prime Minister, to reconstruct an aeronautic industry and a modern armaments production led to a progressive concentration of the most advanced technological production in Bavaria. By now the centralisation of armament, aeronautic and electronic industries in and around Munich has produced such an effect of agglomeration that it has grown permanently self-amplifying. The most important forces in this respect are a specialised labour market and, as a result of the interconnections typical of this region, a favourable market even for new and smaller firms.

Interlocking capital arrangements among the aeronautic, electronic and motor vehicles industries meanwhile have originated stable multi-national trusts with a most up-to-date range of products. They are largely co-operating with numerous public research institutions in their regions. Taking into account that Germany is a rather small country, it seems highly improbable that another productive potential of this kind, tightly interlocked with the industrial co-operation within the European Community, will be developed in another region. In addition, the historical development of industrialisation in the southern federal states has established a decentral structure enabling them to adapt the most advanced techniques far more rapidly, and this holds for product development as well as for manufacturing. The advantages of rationalisation which were previously based on a Tayloristic organisation of production are, meanwhile, available in smaller units and for smaller firms because of micro-electronic control systems. This has stabilised employment also for smaller firms in these regions whereas rationalisation is accompanied by severe job losses in traditional large-scale industries.

The relatively late industrialisation of southern Germany, for a long time referred to as 'industrial backwardness', has by now turned into an advantage as there are only insignificant proportions of industries stemming from the first phase of industrialisation. The specific historical situation and purposeful political interventions have by now created the fact that the former 'second' has become the leading growth region. In addition to these historical factors the old industrial areas reveal 'repellent' structural properties responsible for the fact that the 'new growth' took place in other regions.

For a long time the labour market of those areas that were shaped by the first wave of industrialisation was exclusively dominated by large trusts. Professional careers and high earnings could best be realised on the internal labour market of the large firms. Whoever aspired to professional success and social reputation tried to obtain a position in one of those firms. Krupp, Thyssen, Mannesmann – those were the names that incarnated 'German efficiency' during the nationalist flush of the first half of the century and which formed part of the stable core of industrial growth during the reconstruction period subsequent to World War II. The entire vocational training system was directed towards the dominating industries because vocational training in the Federal Republic is predominantly performed by firms on their own accord. The trusts were able to offer high wages and secure employment. Even today they still dominate the real estate market though it is no longer required by the shrinking industries.

Political coalitions among capitalist entrepreneurs, trade union leaders and municipal politicians allowed little possibility for the development of other industrial branches. The image of the biological effect of the upas tree vividly illustrates this (Hall 1985). Now that the large firms recurrently shed labour on a large scale the local political culture is ruled by efforts to master the ensuing problems. Given these conditions it was initially improbable that new industrial branches and employment sectors would develop in these very regions. Taking the aforementioned historical and political situations into account the discrepancy of economic development between old and new growth centres becomes explicable.

Regional policy

Up to about 1975 the federal government's policy of regional economics aimed at mitigating or eliminating the economic inequality between the urban agglomerations and the rural areas. In order to attain this goal, 'structurally weak' regions were differentiated by way of indicators of growth. Those regions that were characterised by only a slight degree of industrialisation were defined to be structurally weak. After Germany had reached full employment in 1959 the industrialisation of rural districts was considered a strategy to open up labour reserves. Tax exemptions and investment assistance were set up as incentives for capital investment in peripheral regions.

During the 1960s these measures appeared to be successful when numerous firms opened branches in rural areas. But since the onset of the crisis in the mid-1970s these 'extended workbenches' frequently closed down because simple assembly jobs were either entirely automated or could be performed at an even lower cost of labour in countries of the Third World. When the sales crisis and the effects of rationalisation shed labour and increased the unemployment rate mainly in the industrial centres, regional economic aid was extended to the areas of early industrialisation. But the results have as yet been insignificant because public subsidies hardly have any effect on the selection of production locations. However, the transfer and extension of regional economic aid from rural districts to the centres of early industrialisation indicate that the dissimilar perspectives of industrial agglomerations representing a new spatial inequality have turned into a political problem. Many empirical studies have demonstrated that the effect of state subsidies on regional development is insignificant because the incentives are irrelevant to the firms' decisions in favour of a location. The traditional factors of location like communication lines, land prices, channels of trade, and so forth which may be influenced by public investment have lost in importance considering the shrinking volumes of transport, the ubiquitous extension of the transportation system and the slight relevance of these expenses in cost accounting. Government incentive strategies are hardly able to influence the decisions of multi-national trusts, which hold for Germany for the reason alone that by now all locations without exception offer the same advantages. Thus, not even slight differences in expenses present a decisive factor. Recent years provided abundant instance of how large trusts, procuring fat profits, were additionally supported by public subsidies though these did not influence the decision in favour of a location in any way. By now, public subsidies are taken for granted in the competition among regions and cities.

The polarisation of development

The core cities of industrial regions are particularly affected by the new trends of regional development. The locations of both employment and population are shifting to the periphery of agglomerations in times of economic growth as well as during stagnation (Bade 1987). While in times of growth the suburbanisation of employment and population was due to the growth pressure upon the core cities, the fluctuation of population and employment in times of economic stagnation represents a result of structural change affecting the different regional units in different ways.

The large cities of Germany began to lose population continuously by migration and low natural increase from the 1960s. The German population's shift to the periphery showed a socially selective pattern: mainly groups of young and high-income population migrated to the surrounding communities because there the real estate prices allowed them to settle down and start acquiring property. Up to the mid-1970s the resulting decline in population could be compensated for by a large-scale immigration of foreign workers. Since this flow subsided in the course of the employment crisis and, as the immigrant workers have partly returned to their native countries, the population of the large cities is decreasing absolutely.

Employment likewise moved continually further into the outskirts of the agglomerations. This is due partly to the lack of space for expanding firms and partly represents a result of business closures in the large cities (Massey, Meegan 1982). Those sectors of industry that are mainly affected by the present restructuring are usually located in the large cities. Their reduction of employment leaves tracts of derelict estates which can only be reutilised for other purposes by long and expensive procedures. As there is only little demand by prospective users in the large cities of western and northern Germany, increasing numbers of previously industrial tracts remain without further use. As the third sector business, being occupied with supplying to households and rendering service, follows the migration to the environs of the large cities the latter show higher unemployment rates than their surroundings.

The large cities have high losses in employment in the second sector, particularly in manufacturing. That is to say that mainly those working in the line of production lose their jobs. The areas of trading and transportation likewise show negative development with regard to employment in large cities. Service activities are still increasing but not as much as they do in the surroundings. The only employment sector showing high growth rates in the cities is represented by high quality service professions such as research and development activities, electronic data processing and marketing, organisational assistance and legal aid. These fields of activity grow most rapidly in those cities where the head offices of the prospering branches of business, mainly the multi-national trusts, are located.

The structural change in the economy is accompanied by processes of economic concentration. A progressively shrinking number of large firms employ an increasing share of the entire labour force. The head offices of large firms concentrate in fewer and fewer cities of Germany, which produces a new hierarchy among them: the previously decentralised structure of economic power is being altered to the advantage of a few locations that are integrated into the international turnover of capital and goods. Frankfurt, a stock market of international importance, and Munich with its accumulation of high-tech business are the preferred locations of multi-national trusts. Stuttgart (motor vehicles and electrical industries), Düsseldorf (steel industry) and Hamburg (oil and newspaper trusts) also rank among this category. The remaining large cities in part looking back upon centuries of international importance are reduced to the status of provincial capitals.

In some cases these cities have to bear severe consequences through the loss of population and employment. Infrastructural expenditure cannot be reduced to the same extent to which population and employment decrease. Taxation, however, drops rapidly. The rising unemployment in these cities consumes a growing share of municipal public expenditure in the form of social benefits as the latter represent an obligation of the cities by federal law. With regard to their expenditure many cities by now are completely dependent on federal or state government support. Those cities that have not established supra-regionally important functions in the fields of cultural, educational and other services are hardly able to devise successful strategies to secure their own existence under these conditions.

Fortunately, cities receive financial investment assistance mainly for infrastructural measures which are supposed to stimulate the local economy. Assistance includes funds for road construction, for the development of prospective business tracts, the establishment of technology centres and so on. Though this kind of investment creates temporary employment for the local building and construction industry it neither has noticeable effects upon employment nor does it fulfill the function of a pump primer for new industrial growth.

The present changes in the regional economy take place against the background of a structural change in industrial production with the result that economic growth is no longer necessarily coupled to a growth of employment. In Germany this process concurs with a period of a drastic decline of the native population. Quite possibly a quantitatively balanced labour market will evolve beyond the year 2010. But this future labour market will be characterised by frictions in qualifications, on the one hand, and by severe regional fluctuations, on the other hand. This implies that those regions that at present are trying to master the problems resulting from the first wave of industrialisation in the long run will be facing a prospect of depopulation and decay. Germany will perhaps turn into an immigration country but even now the flexibility of internationally- operating capital renders it unneccessary to transfer labour from those countries with a 'superfluous' population to the industrial centres. On the contrary, the lower costs of reproduction in the industrially less advanced countries are taken advantage of by capital in its globally interlocked production processes.

Social and political consequences

The disparate economic development of the regions corresponds to different political majorities. While the old industrial regions (Saarland, North Rhine-Westphalia, Bremen, Hamburg) are ruled by Social-Democratic state governments, the Christian Democratic Union possesses the political majority in all of the growth regions. This fact is being exploited ideologically in such a way that a state policy of strict orientation towards growth allegedly becomes the guarantee of economic success. This serves as a means to discredit the social state direction of the SPD-governed states as well as to oppose their policy of subsidising the declining industries. This political situation indicates that the economic and regional reorganisation that has been observed in Germany for roughly a decade is linked to the reorganisation of the regulation mode.

The Fordian model of a long growth phase during the post-war period, characterised by a growing real income for the majority of the nation, by the extension of social state security systems and by the political integration of the working class, has taken a critical turn because those industrial sectors that represented the core area of this model themselves confronted a crisis. The social structure resulting from the trends of production organisation and qualification in modern industries is characterised rather by a polarisation into highly qualified and well-paid labour on the one hand, and a growing number of insecure low-wage employment, demanding only low qualifications, on the other hand. From the overall viewpoint, the described polarisation is reflected in a pattern of growing and shrinking regions but it also occurs *within* the agglomerations in the shape of a social division into those employees integrated in the formal system of employment and a large number of marginally and insecurely employed or unemployed workers. The restructuring of the economy in Germany, closely connected to processes occurring in international trading, will therefore make way for a new social formation differing substantially from the previous *Modell Deustchland*.

STRUCTURAL ELEMENTS OF A POST-FORDIAN SOCIETY

So far we have described empirical phenomena which may be described by the formula 'economic growth involving a decrease in employment'. At the same time these phenomena imply more than merely a process of rationalisation of the kind that capitalist development exhibited necessarily and recurrently. Rather, the process in question appears to be a fundamental change of the organisational structure of capitalism which does indeed have spatial effects but is not dependent on the exploitation of location factors in the course of its dynamic development. The spatial structure of post-Fordian capitalism is not an entirely new structure but represents the dissolution of an old one: the presently evolving structure of socio-economic spaces in Germany is a result of the decline of those industries that are linked to the Fordian phase of high industrialisation. While these required the necessary locations, this is not the case with the high-tech industries, the representatives of the new economic growth. As we showed in our historical sketch their locations are mainly a result of historical coincidence and political decisions. Only when the presently still vague structures have consolidated may new locational restrictions appear. Various reasons suggest, however, that the further development of communications techniques will counteract the development of these locational necessities.

J. Hirsch and R. Roth (1986) attempted to delineate the new trends of capitalist development by means of a prognostic sketch. Though the 'new face of capitalism' does not appear consolidated yet, its basic features are already perceivable. In the following we will list some of the most important features:

(1) From industrial assembly-line mass production to a flexible computer-based production; a trend to automated production;

the establishment of new industries (in the sector of information and communications technologies); the decline of traditional labour-intensive industries (steel, ship yards, coal mining and so forth). On the whole this means a new model of production involving considerable consequences with regard to firstly, the organisation, the quantity, the qualifications and the spatial distribution of labour; and secondly, the destruction and creation of capitals as well as their branch-conditioned and spatial distribution.

(2) The emergence of a new 'model of consumption' implying a polarisation into cheapened mass consumption on the one hand and individual consumption of high quality goods, partly substituting personal services, on the other hand. At least in the latter area this will lead to the formation of a demanders' market in place of the present suppliers' market, made possible by the flexibilisation of production.

(3) A sweeping transformation of the social structure not only implying that a large proportion of the present wage workers will lose employment and consequently be exposed to marginalisation but also that the middle class – having increased on the whole – will be divided and polarised into a professionally unstable part, sinking in the social scale, and a professionally stable one, rising in the social scale; the latter becoming the representatives of the new model of consumption (Dangschat, Krüger 1986).

(4) The formation of contradictory subject structures due to a 'thrust of individualisation' (Beck 1983) producing at the same time isolation and extreme other-directedness but also a re-orientation towards individual creativity released in the process of a dissolution of old ties.

(5) A re-evaluation of culture and education. Given the altered conditions of access to an altogether considerably reduced labour market, culture and education represent neither status symbols nor do they guarantee employment. Instead, they represent luxury spending and an interest in meaning.

(6) The long-term decline of traditional constituencies which will affect mainly (though not exclusively) social-democrat parties and trade unions. This will lead to a redistribution, above all, however, to an increasing flexibility of social power blocs because there has yet to materialise systematic planning schemes that can solve the various social problems consistently and in a way unambiguously pertinent to political positions.

(7) A progressive institutional and political autonomy on behalf of state authorities (government and administration, police and armed forces) while simultaneously the national political system becomes increasingly dependent on international and highly differentiated trusts which are able to react swiftly by simple spatial transfer in the case of unfavourable development. The lack of political means of control will be substituted by an expansion of the repressive instruments and by binding international trusts with the help of armament orders.

Thus, the predominant changes may be defined in terms of three complementary processes consisting of the simultaneous re-formations of economic foundations, social structure and political rule within capitalist society.

The essence of the transformation of economic foundations has repeatedly been described as the development of 'new concepts of production' (Kern, Schumann 1984; Läpple 1986). The development of new concepts of production (and new management strategies) will have to be completed by the increasing internationalisation and concentration of capital. R. J. Johnston (1986) maintains the hypothesis that in the course of the internationalisation and concentration processes, the state's influence upon capital has continually diminished. Today the process has reversed and the national state's development depends on the decisions made by international capital. This certainly does not imply that a state policy towards capital can be dispensed with, but it has to fulfill two additional functions: on the one hand, the state has to make compensation for the employment losses by way of social policy; on the other hand, the growing proportion of a marginalised population has to be kept under control, which implies an expansion of the repressive apparatus.

Of course, there are also assumptions about the relation of post-Fordian capitalism to a new spatial structure. Empirical evidence indicates that the new structures of production will mainly develop where Fordian mass production has not reached an advanced stage, that is where at least the remains of a production structure of small-scale trade and crafts are available (Bagnasco 1977; Läpple 1986; Piore, Sabel 1985). Considering the international structures of trust, however, this spatial relation remains highly abstract. The reference frame of capital is no longer an actual national territory with its advantages and disadvantages, but is the 'world' space instead. Seen this way, the spatial structure of a post-Fordian society represents a result of *political* decisions made by capital rather than a systematic and necessary exploitation of spatial factors. Consequently, the possibilities to manipulate spaces, regions and entire nations have significantly grown. Capital is no longer dependent on space whereas space is indeed dependent on capital. The initial relation between capital and space has thus principally reversed. This is another result of the logic of capital development, yet the actual spatial structures can no longer be explained by the logic of capital, they have to be explained by its policy instead.

REFERENCES

F-J. Bade, *Regionale Beschäftigungsentwicklung und produktionsorientierte Dienstleistungen* (Berlin: Duncker and Humblodt, 1987).

A. Bagnasco, *Tre Italie* (Bologna: Il Mulino, 1977).

U. Beck, 'Jenseits von Klasse und Staat?' in R. Kreckel (ed.), *Soziale Ungleichheiten, Soziale Welt, Sonderheft* 2 (Göttingen: Schwartz, 1983).

J. Dangschat and T. Krüger, 'Hamburg im Süd-Nord-Gefälle' in Friedrichs, Häussermann and Siebel (1986).

J. Friedrichs, H. Häussermann and W. Siebel (eds), *Süd-Nord-Gefälle in der Bundesrepublik? Sozialwissenschaftliche Analysen* (Opladen: Westdeutscher Verlag, 1986).

F. Fröbel, J. Heinrichs and O. Kreye, *Umbruch in der Weltwirtschaft* (Reinbek bei Hamburg: Rowohlt, 1986).

P. Hall, 'The geography of the Fifth Kondratieff' in P. Hall and A. Markusen (eds), *Silicon Landscapes* (Boston: Allen & Unwin, 1985).

J. Hirsch and R. Roth, *Das neue Gesicht des Kapitalismus* (Hamburg: VSA, 1986).

R. Johnston, 'The State, the Region and the Division of Labour', in A. J. Scott and M. Storper (eds), *Production, Work, Territory* (Boston: Allen & Unwin, 1986).

H. Kern and M. Schumann, *Das Ende der Arbeitsteilung?* (München: Beck, 1984).

D. Kunz, 'Anfänge und Ursachen der Nord-Süd-Drift' in *Informationen zur Raumentwicklung* Heft 11/12 (Bonn: BfLR, 1986).

D. Läpple, 'Internationalisation of Capital and the Regional Problem' in J. Walton (ed.), *Capital and Labour in the Urbanised World* (London/Beverly Hills: Sage, 1985).

D. Läpple, 'Trendbruch in der Raumentwicklung. Auf dem Weg zu einem neuen industriellen Entwicklungstyp?' in *Informationen zur Raumentwicklung* Heft 11/12 (Bonn: BfLR, 1986).

P. Marschalck, 'Bevölkerungsgeschichte Deutschlands' in *Jahrhundert 19/20* (Frankfurt/M.: Surrkamp, 1984).

D. Massey and R. A. Meegan, *The Anatomy of Job Loss* (London: Methuen, 1982).

D. Otten, *Die Welt der Industrie. Entstehung und Entwicklung der modernen Industriegesellschaften*, 2 Bde. (Reinbek bei Hamburg: Rowohlt, 1986).

M. J. Piore and C. Sabel, *Das Ende der Massenproduktion* (Berlin: Wagenbach, 1985).

J. Reulecke, *Geschichte der Urbanisierung in Deutschland* (Frankfurt/M.: Suhrkamp, 1985).

E. Salin, 'Standortverschiebungen der deutschen Wirtschaft' in B. Harms (ed.), *Strukturwanddlungen der deutschen Volkswirtschaft* (Berlin: de Gruyter, 1928).

S. Welzk, *Boom ohne Arbeitsplätze* (Köln: Kiepenheuer & Witsch, 1986).

14 From National to Local: The Janus Face of Crisis

Nicos Komninos

A lot of work has been done recently concerning the impact of crisis and capitalist restructuring-rationalisation processes on urban and regional space, local policies, planning institutions, physical form of space and so forth. Their main interest focuses on a one-directional causality between contemporary socio-economic changes and spatial effects, continuing the argument of the 'production of space' during the period of crisis. We may begin by retracing these arguments in order to arrive at a different question: that of the new forms of capitalist relations and patterns of accumulation emerging within new spatialities, characterised by the so-called high-tech *savoir-faire*, productive flexibility, individuality and individual commitment.

RESTRUCTURING

The present major crisis of the post-war regime of capital accumulation soon introduced multiple and combined restructuring processes of production and labour organisation, of social strata, of consumption models and regulation practices, as research for ways out of the crisis intensified along with efforts for recovery and amelioration of the crisis' destructive effects. In these processes, some authors (Castells 1980 and 1985; Carnoy and Rumberger 1983) recognise the seeds of a new model of economic accumulation, social organisation and political legitimation (still being capitalist but also quite different from the Keynesian model of the 1945–73 period); others recognise the basis for the rise of the 'restructuring school' (Storper 1985), combining the changing organisation of production and investment with the macro-economic crises of capitalism; or the turn towards new but contradictory social projects, carried out by opposing social forces and groups (Soja 1983; Massey 1985; Lipietz 1985).

Starting with the level of production, we may note that restructuring concerns the development of science-based industry, the rationalisation and modernisation of traditional industry, as well as the

348

adaptation of services to information technology and organisation. In all cases, the restructuring of labour processes aims either at the reversal of the Taylorist and Fordist methods of work organisation in favour of more flexible, labour saving and higher-productivity ways of production, or at the functioning of production units under the conditions of the over-accumulation crisis.[1] Through the generalised recomposition of work processes, in terms of functions and numbers of places, a capitalist rationalisation is introduced confronting the problems of timing in the spatial shift of activities, of overspecialisation, of large stocks according to a 'just in case system',[2] of large numbers of controllers, as well as of the wider proliferation of tertiary activities and work places.

The role and significance of 'new or high technology' in the changing organisation of labour processes are major. They permit a general transition from mechanically structured production technologies to electronically guided flexible productive systems; automation as immediate industrial application of 'new technology' increases homogeneity as well as further specialisation and the hierarchical structure of task execution. All manufacturing work is subject to a process of simplification, while the conception and design of production becomes extremely sophisticated and complex (Anquetil 1983; Toft Jensen *et al.* 1983; Coriat 1985). And this change has important social implications.

As far as skills are concerned, in most cases of information technology and automation applications, the non-manual group of middle-level administrators is reduced; the numbers of engineers and technicians have quickly expanded, while their internal composition has shifted from production-based engineering toward research and development activities. Clerical work has also increased as a proportion of the workforce, while all manual categories have declined (Cross 1983; Massey 1985; Thwaites 1983). On the skilling-deskilling process a dual social structure is established, giving rise to a polarisation between the highly educated engineering, scientific and managerial strata on the one hand, and the unskilled or semiskilled workers on the other. Mass consumption, environmental conditions, housing conditions, educational opportunities also follow the above pattern of duality, separating economically and spatially the levels of work specialisation. So, a new social structure is being established in the sphere of middle and working classes altering their composition and characteristics, and replacing the social base of the post-war mass production mass consumption model. Decomposition of the middle class, overall decrease of the white-collar and rejection of blue-collar workers from the production process are present tendencies of a production system incorporating smaller masses of labour force.

Productive restructuring and new forms of labour organisation go along with the restructuring of policies, institutions and procedures of social regulation. Keynesianism belongs to the past, together with its entire institutional superstructure. Today, as the form of the state gradually changes, new elements intervene in the structuring of its two basic functions of regulation, and establishment of a hegemonic system.

Policies of the post-Fordist regulation correspond to an apparently different relationship between politics and economy, to a relationship of separation which is said to ascribe to the restoration of market forces and the reduction of state interventions in the economy. However, although new policies permit a greater flexibility in the private economy, they do not lead to a reduction of global state intervention. Simply, they lead to the decomposition of the welfare state, to diminution of real wages and to reorientation of public expenditures towards selective capital accumulation (Boyer and Mistral 1983; Cohen and Combemale 1980). It is easy to understand that a growing popular consumption has no reason to exist when section II is under stagnation or decline conditions. If the total amount of value-added in section II is more or less stable, then any increase in popular consumption is translated into profit squeeze. So, the main character of the post-Fordist regulation seems to be the redistribution of value-added in the profits of particular multi-national and war industries in the direction of a new equilibrium between the growing parts of section I (high-tech and electronic industry) and specific parts of section II (military equipment).

New redistribution policies, reductions of indirect wages, decollectivisation of collective consumption, austerity policies and the simultaneous rise of a 'warfare state' constitute the bases of an authoritarian political scene. The evident and unconditional state support to capital raises social contradictions and changes the previous social-democratic contract. The social cohesion and regulation achieved in the immediate past through welfare policies and institutions is no more valid. So, this aspect of regulation, related to the formation of a hegemonic system and to the establishment of social cohesion becomes uncertain. The question is whether and how post-Fordist regulation may lead to a new class hegemony replacing the defeated bloc of social-democracy and achieving, though differently, social cohesion. To this question we will come again.

SPATIALITY

Economic and political restructuring had a direct impact on the geography of social activities and the spatiality of social relations. Empirical evidence from OECD countries shows a decline in the rates of urbanisation (Long and De Are 1983; Van den Berg *et al.* 1982; Fothergill and Gudgin 1979), a faster growth of rural areas in comparison to urban ones in terms of numbers of industrial work-places and value-added or regional income (Keeble *et al.* 1983), a crisis of the urban centres of traditional industry related to the new geographical mobility of industrial firms (Bade 1983; Ortona and Santagata 1980; Damesick *et al.* 1982; Aydalot 1980; Dennis 1978; Chombart de Lauwe 1982), a change in rates of growth of the major European metropolitan areas (Van den Berg *et al.* 1982; Frost and Spence 1984), and an intra-metropolitan change of industrial and office location (Dicken and Lloyd 1978 and 1979; Ducreux, 1983; Elias and Keogh 1982; Daniels 1977; Damesick 1979, 1982). On the other hand, new regions and urban centres emerge as production centres with respect to the diffusion of the productive system (Antonelli 1979; Planque 1983), the spatial clustering of high-tech activities, and the centrifugal behaviour of R & D (Malecki 1980; Oakey *et al.* 1980; Chombart de Lauwe 1984). A new spatial dualism is also taking place within urban and metropolitan centres corresponding to the economic and social dualism developed through crisis and restructuring conditions. It concerns housing conditions, social services and collective consumption illustrating the fiscal crisis of the local regulation system (Elliot and McCrone 1984; Marcuse 1983; Flockton 1984; Harloe and Paris 1984; von Einem 1982).

Expressing this shift in a caricature form, as proposed by Massey (1985, p. 306) for the UK, one would point out the change of the social and economic geography from a predominantly sectoral and urban pattern to one increasingly less dominated by the great urban concentrations, and in which the differentiator between regions is the occupational rather than the industrial structure. One could also point out, following P. Hall (1985, p. 45), the emerging geography of high technology that incorporates a spatial structure characterised by the progressive deconcentration of a dominant metropolitan city into a polycentric city region wherein some important controlling functions remain in the urban core, while R & D, some headquarters and specialised producer services decentralise. In my opinion, it is not obvious that for the moment it is possible to formulate a model integrating the above summarised spatial mobility of population, of production, of services and of state intervention; even in a caricature form. On the contrary, it is possible to avoid inappropriate generalisations by considering the supporting processes of emerging spatialities, like de-industrialisation, re-industrialisation, high-tech clustering and decentralisation (Komninos 1986a and 1986b).

De-industrialisation accelerated during the present crisis period in terms of industrial production, and even more in terms of employment. This shift is the direct outcome of a twofold process: a short-term strategy which manages overproduction in many industrial branches and mainly in the automobile, chemical, textile, steel and coal, electric machines, heavy engineerings and ship production (*L'Expansion*, 1975 and 1985 special issues). Secondly, it is an effect of over-accumulation. Over-accumulation occurs when introduction of new surplus-value into production does not yield the previous rate of profit. This decline in profitability leads productive investments to a decline, and capital to a reproduction crisis. It is worth noting that over-accumulation has been confronted via inflation and austerity policies attempting a temporal re-establishment of profits in their previous levels. In both cases, production rationalisations and cuts, labour reductions and plant closures, in other words a functioning of firms at lower levels, was inevitable.

De-industrialisation affected mainly the major centres of the post-war accumulation like metropolitan areas, assembly and mass-production urban centres. It is expressed via plant closures, locational shifts of industrial firms (relocations or branch movements) towards low cost localities, like the outer metropolitan rings or the medium-size cities, massive metropolitan unemployment, fiscal crises of local regulatory institutions and crises of local autonomy and democracy. As far as the spatial aspects of these phenomena are concerned, environmental and fiscal crisis couple the socio-economic dualism based on income and employment variations. Places of production rapidly deteriorate as firms do not modernise, reduce their capacity or move away. The images of devastated places extend to housing and infrastructure conditions, as reductions of the local tax base, of central state expenditures and of individual consumption do not permit a normal replacement of the general conditions of production.

However, all industries do not function under over-accumulation conditions. In branches of electronics, scientific instruments, plastics, some subsectors of chemicals, where new technologies transform the production process (automation, multifunctional workshop, alternative production), the resulting gains in productivity sustain profitability, industrial growth and expansion. So, a new round of technological innovation and work intensification produces an expanding spatiality based on reindustrialisation processes. This is the case of the science-based industry or high-tech industry.[3]

Although high-tech industry does not obey a uniform locational pattern — and why should one expect certain shared technological characteristics such as rapid product development or high automation to have uniform locational effects across otherwise different industries in different countries? — specific spatialities emerge due to innovation and its industrial applications: science parks, high-tech production centres, techno-cities, rapid development corridors, neo-urbanised areas and so forth. The evidence about these localities is extremely fragmented (Oakey *et al.* 1980; Malecki 1980; Kellerman 1984; Planque 1983; Glasmeier 1985; Kerorguen and Merland 1985). However, it seems that these forms of development follow *two different spatial patterns* with respect to different socio-economic realities. On the one hand, we may observe small scale units under the form of science and industrial parks, which solidify the co-operation among industrial activities, university-based research institutions and state finance; a form corresponding mostly to the European experience with about 40 high-tech centres, parks and zones in France, UK, Italy, West Germany, Spain and the Netherlands. On the other hand, we may observe more important development schemes, based on innovative firms where R & D is incorporated and specified within industries; this leads to more spontaneous forms of urbanisation as has happened in the Turin metropolitan area, in southern England or east France. In both cases firstly, the new processes of growth were located in quite different places from the old areas of decline; secondly, government supported policies played a significant role either through military oriented projects which constitute the major market for high-tech products, or by establishing organised centres for the promotion of high technology industry; and lastly, clustering and decentralisation characterised high-tech activities, thus justifying the literature about the diffusion of the productive system and the concentration of high-tech employment.

All these aspects of socio-economic restructuring and changing spatialities are well-known and a growing literature focuses on these immediate consequences of the crisis. What is less analysed is the form of a 'modern capitalism' emerging and growing with respect to spatial changes.

Emerging and declining spatialities are considered as combined parts of a new model of capitalist development based on polarised growth, selective accumulation, productive diffusion, hierarchy and functional interconnectedness (Castells 1985); or, as spatial aspects of a new regime of accumulation based on a flexible organisation of labour (industrial paradigm) and new modes of regulation (Leborgne and Lipietz 1987); or, as a spatial fix arising in response to the failure of the state-managed and directed capitalism to assure continued expansion. As has happened during the past prolonged crisis and restructuring periods, the present restructuring processes (like a 'long-wave') are contingent on opening up new room for capitalist accumulation and seeking new forms of labour discipline (Soja 1983).

But, to what degree have new development models and regimes of accumulation been achieved? Which overall socio-economic balance do they involve? Which hegemonic systems and major social changes are related to them? Affirmation of the 'new equilibrium' is rather risky when massive unemployment, low growth rates and profit squeeze are persisting. On the other hand, it is clear that the restructuring approaches describe rather the 'creative destruction' than the new developmental dynamic. And the 'long-wave' argument about the periodicity of the capitalist development still is in need of its ex-post verification. Development today applies no more to the same meaning and connotations that it held in the post-war period.

On the contrary, according to my point of view, de-industrialisation and re-industrialisation processes constitute just the go-between to a new articulation among accumulation, regulation, class hegemony and spatiality. Their global pattern, determining also a new 'articulated period', far from being established is simply showing a few segments of the 'post-modern capitalism' puzzle.

FROM THE NATIONAL TO THE LOCAL

Industrial activities based on systematic scientific research and innovation were the ones which during the generalised decline of the 1970s presented positive results in the promotion of products, productivity and the creation of new places of work.[4] So, the logic of their quantitative growth and their particular geography constitute a preliminary version of a different developmental dynamic. As we have already mentioned, two spatial patterns specify, for the moment, the above selective growth: the pattern of the 'technopole' and the pattern of 'metropolitan restructuring-reorganisation'.

The main characteristic of technopoles is the synergy among innovative industry, research institutions and state support. The scene of their collaboration is placed in the fields of electronics, aeronautics, chemistry, biotechnology, information technology, telecommunications, artificial intelligence and automation (Kerorguen and Merland 1985). The nuclear geography of technopoles and science industrial parks is based on the characteristics and spatial behaviour of R & D, and the production of innovation. According R. Oakey (1984), the poor performance in product innovation by the small and medium-size firms is due to their low 'local resource environment'. As product innovation demands a positive environment and a dense network of high-tech producers, of firms developing R & D or using external research services, of overspecialised labour and finance possibilities, the clustering of firms becomes inevitable. Nevertheless, this pattern of co-operation is supported by:

(1) a new concept of investment by the so-called community of venture capital; in many cases, traditional finance is replaced by university sources and others related to scientific expertise, who can better evaluate the risks of high-tech investment;

(2) a new entrepreneurial behaviour which accepts the possibility of failure and the progress through experimentation; it flourishes in relation to less formal and less hierarchically structured organisations of work, and to ideologies of individualism, individual effort and commitment[5];

(3) the state which may finance directly R & D activities, thus providing the needed general conditions of production and creating the also needed markets for new products.

So, this new form of 'incubator' establishes a developmental strategy capable of experimenting on a new social co-operation, of mobilising investments of a particular type, of promoting particular products and of creating conditions of profitability. However, these new centres of growth do not emerge on their own; on the contrary, they demand the creative intervention of regional or local institutions.

The scheme of technopoles cannot be applied to all regions; in cases of traditional industrial concentrations, where crisis is more severe and apparent, other selective strategies are taking place and different experimentations are introduced.

One may note the massive introduction of information technology and automation into traditional industries. This modernisation does not concern the big firms only; small enterprises in co-operation with research institutions can change their technical base and production techniques. One may also note the efforts for development of new products, production processes and know-how with respect to local and regional resources, aiming at the rational use of scientific personnel and labour skills as well as at the exploitation of local natural resources. These kinds of modernisation are coupled by modernisation in management and organisation. The point is to support flexible patterns of work organisation, forms of collective non-linear production and ways of reducing non-productive labour power.

In industrial relations it becomes very important to possess a policy of harmonisation. In return for a better place of work, the firm achieves flexibility in organisation, transfer of personnel and its specialisation in more than one place of work, creation of multifunctional workshops and so forth. The previous posts of controller and of syndicate representative are replaced by a new one, that of 'facilitator' whose mission is to activate the autonomous production teams. Flexibility becomes the major feature of a new productive system together with the ideology of individual commitment and combined actions between the syndicate and management. We must also note that many firms proceed to unprecedented reselection of personnel and retraining to new production tasks, a procedure which sometimes lasts for two years.

Spatially, the modernisation of production and management are related to regional development programmes (in contrast to national ones or the absolute absence of planning). But, this time the initiatives belong to the private sector and to local institutions of industry and research. Mixed organisations of interested parties, of industry, of research, of communities and consumers support the local and regional developmental actions. The financial sources are also very diversified, based on joint ventures between local or regional institutions and private enterprises.

All these spatio-economic strategies of high-tech application and re-industrialisation mentioned very briefly above bring along at least a new concept for development. In the first place, growth and change are no more compatible with the long-term national strategies of the post-war era. It is quite easy to write down the slide of interest towards productive processes. The level of production, the question of productivity, the networks of co-operation which support industrial performance and which are different from place to place, gain in significance. The same applies to the local environment with its specificities which cannot be evaluated at a macroscopic level; the development of industrial research and co-operation with research institutions, the specialisation of the labour force and the characteristics of the community of venture capital. The spirit of selectivity, specificity and particularity supersedes the previous aspects of homogeneity and global growth.

So, the conditions of crisis and the issues proposed by the use of new technology (information technology, automation, multi-functional workshops and so forth) transform the established rationality of development and its strategies, transferring the problems from the general to the particular and from the national to the local: the local being the field of experimentation and concretisation of new forms of co-operation. However, this interest in the local, in the context of long-term accumulation, is equivalent to a spatial shift of centres and creation of new ones.

But, the significance of the local is not supported only by the changes in the processes of capital accumulation and its new locus. Inside the structures of regulation, locality plays a more fundamental role, as new policies and normative ideologies replace that kind of regularity, which was achieved up to now through Keynesian, welfare practices and institutions. In my opinion, the shift towards the local, as an important level of regulation is a result, mainly, of the contemporary 'ineffectiveness' of national regulation.[6]

During the post-war years of rapid development, accumulation and growth were stimulated and regulated via hierarchically structured national, regional and local plans. Through this institutional intervention general conditions of production were produced, labour force reproduction was socialised, the growth of important but non-profit industrial sectors was secured, and a redistribution of income was realised. In reality, what was regulated was the wage relation (duration and intensity of work, value of labour force, salary consumption, division and skill structure of the labour market and so forth), as well as the distribution of money-capital in the various sectors of the social division of labour, and the problems of currency and money reproduction (Lipietz 1984). In the hierarchy of interventions and plans, regulating the realisation and distribution contradictions of capital accumulation was the particular role of the nation state.[7] All measures, policies and incentives of national intervention were specified locally by regional or urban planning actions. The national state was the major level of decision-making, co-ordination and evaluation of plans and actions, although a significant number of them had regional or local character.

Gradually and through conditions of capital internationalisation, national regulation becomes more and more restricted. In the first place, the transnational strategy of firms, together with the growing control of national markets by internationalised capital left the field of wage relation as the only field of nation-state intervention. On the other hand, national regulation supported the rise of bureaucracies, and a 'political proliferation' was developed which led to high cost regulatory intervention, to the growth of non-commodity sectors and to different power relations between politics and the economy. The limits of the welfare national state were reached.

Within this new framework of contradictions, local institutions seem to assume some of the previously national roles. Multiple decentralisation, in most advanced industrial countries reinforces local decision-making and management (Ghotta-Gobin 1984; Flockton 1984; Beekmans 1984). In many cases co-operation among localities is less important than autonomy and locally based decision-making. And it is very interesting to observe the simultaneous promotion of local decision autonomy by liberal, social democratic or left-wing political parties. However, there is something more than simple decentralisation in this matter. It is the problem of securing social cohesion which is being damaged by the adventures of modernisation, by the intense class struggle and by the changing logic of regulation.

CONCLUSION

Based on the above, we can underline two points. The first is that re-industrialisation comes along with a new scheme of co-operation among capital, state and labour (research) which sustains accumulation and development; in this case, the spatiality of the developmental co-operation is no more national but local. New localities and growth poles assume leading roles, mainly through the constitution of models and concrete examples of growth. The national context is no more relevant as a strategic framework for development. And, if we wish to look for new accumulation regimes, we must examine how production and consumption are redistributed into the new growth poles, into the local rather than the national level. Nation and state, once again in recent history, are introduced in a process of separation. This does not mean that the role of the state is diminishing, but that the nation as a socio-geographical context for organising co-operation among the agents of capital accumulation is no more adequate for the continuation of accumulation.

The second point to stress is, on the other hand, that the achievement of social cohesion, or the regulation of realisation and distribution contradictions of capital accumulation, is attributed to local communities. However, one could question the permanency of this political shift towards the local. If we are moving towards a system of market regulation, of fragmented and unequally growing economic places, then the local could be the field of social cohesion, based on ideological and cultural particularity. In this case, we would have to deal with a form of 'local state' where the establishment of the hegemonic system prevails over the political intervention in the contradictions of capital accumulation. On the other hand, the importance of local communities could be just temporal; as long as restructuring is taking place, hegemonies and social contracts are negotiated and austerity policies intensify class struggles.

But what is the real meaning of the rise of the local in the field of regulation (through the role of local communities) or in the experimentations of accumulation (through new growth poles)? Instead of an answer we will simply propose a hypothesis; that the shift towards the local presupposes an understanding of the 'Janus face of crisis', the interrelations of a combined system of four elements (accumulation, regulation, class hegemony, space) before and after crisis.

Before crisis: capital accumulation was centred on mass consumption goods and growth concerned all industries; realisation and distribution contradictions of accumulation were regulated via state intervention, an important part of the labour force reproduction was based on state expenditure, and the state also provided the general conditions of production; accumulation processes and regulation practices were supported by a coalition between bureaucracy and state-based capital, which assumed the interests of all fractions of capital; space, where these developments could manifest themselves was defined at the national level because in this territory inter-capital struggle was politically restricted and the state-based hegemony bloc could dominate.

However, crisis constituted a point of global reversal of the above. After crisis: accumulation becomes selective, it is centred on high-tech products while the growth performance of capital depends on industrial research and innovation; political regulation is partly replaced by market regulation, signifying a return to a sort of

19th-century economic Darwinism where stability comes through conflict and supremacy; the state-based hegemony bloc is defeated and replaced by a big capital coalition, which controls private industrial research and innovation production; space, where the new processes are articulated, is no more defined politically, it may be local, regional or whatever, since it is now delimited economically.

Within this framework, spatial change and the rise of localities follow the experimentations of capital accumulation, its selectivity, its successes or failures. Fragmented space, local or regional, becomes the spatiality of a hegemonic bloc emerging through economic conflicts, and of growth experimentations during post-Fordist forms of capitalism. However, this change must not be interpreted as a shift towards 'disorganised capitalism' without regulatory mechanisms providing coherence to accumulation, but, as a shift towards 'localism' and 'regionalisation' of capital, coupling the process of internationalisation and supported by a neo-liberal hegemonic bloc.

NOTES

1. The shift towards post-Fordist methods of work organisation may be specified as follows: as far as production objectives are concerned, it is mainly the flow of information that is regulated; at the level of the means of production, the recomposition of execution, the fragmentation of conception and the incorporation of know-how into the system of machines replace the previous working norms and production fragmentation; in the field of applications, new types of organisation are used in the tasks of production, conception and management, in large- or small-scale production, and in industries of continuous and non-continuous processes (see Pastre 1985).

2. A very interesting analysis of this topic is that by A. Sayer (1985).

3. We must note that the existing literature shows great confusion as to just what constitutes high-technology industry. Such confusion has allowed the term 'high tech' to be used for most types of firms, industries and processes. Even official reports use the term very vaguely, often referring generally to electronics or electronics-related activities. On the other hand, existing work on defining high-tech has tended to relate it to the production and application of innovations. More precisely, Oakey *et al.* (1980) claim that high-tech branches in the UK – where post-war innovations are mainly concentrated – are those of Chemicals, Mechanical, Instrument and Electrical Engineering. Based on a more recent work by Rothwell (1982) relating to the role of technology in industrial transformation in the UK, it follows that five industrial branches make

up for 72 per cent of total innovations, innovation being defined as the first industrial application of a new technique. These branches are Chemicals (271–9), Mechanical Eng. (331–3), Instrument Eng. (351–4), Electrical Eng. (361–9) and Vehicles (380–5). Norton and Rees (1979) in their study of manufacturing in the US, classify industrial branches in high and low technology groups according to the increase in value-added and their degree of technological intensity. With this set of criteria, branches of high technology are defined as those of Electronics (SIC 36), Transport Equip. (37), Scientific Instruments (38), Chemicals (28) and Plastics (30). Finally, the approach of Hall and Markusen (1982, 1983) is different. They consider as high-tech branches those which exhibit a 2 per cent per annum growth rate in employment, coupled with a ratio of production workers to total employment of 20 per cent below the national average. This definition rests on two assumptions: that high technology industries create higher than the average employment opportunities, and that their occupational composition is of higher than average professional and technical nature. The application of these hypotheses by Langridge (1983) in the UK, defines as high-tech branches those of Electronic Computers (366), Radio, Radar and Electronic Capital Goods (367). Further analysis of the performance of manufacturing in terms of production output, capital labour ratios, capital output ratios and occupational composition ratios includes Chemicals in the above group. So, although there is no adequate definition of the high technology industry, it is possible to relate it to the branches of Chemicals, Electronics, Vehicles, Electrical, Mechanical and Instrument Engineering. Although computer and micro-electronic industries are generally considered as high-tech, the inclusion of other technology intensive industries such as chemicals and machinery is controversial.

4. During 1970–82 annual production in the electronic sector was increased by 11.8 per cent in the UK, by 19 per cent in France and by 19 per cent in West Germany (Dunford and Perrons 1986).

5. 'image: staying on into the night, struggling over that knotty problem on the frontiers of science' (Massey 1985).

6. On the concept of regulation and the internal link to capital accumulation, as well as on the historical transformation and correspondence between regimes of accumulation and modes of regulation, see Lipietz (1982 and 1984) and Aglietta (1979).

7. In the process of capital accumulation, two different levels of contradictions may be defined: those related to the conflict between commodity producers and to the realisation of surplus value (contradictions of the commodity relation), and those related to the distribution of value-added between wages and profits (contradictions of the wage relation). The former places commodity producers against each other within the same or different branches, and the latter places workers against capitalists, workers against workers, also sustaining conflicts due to intensification and control over the technical division of work.

REFERENCES

M. Aglietta, *A Theory of Capitalist Regulation* (London: New Left Review Editions, 1979).

D. Anquetil, 'Automatisations et Organisation du Travail dans l'Automobile', *Critique de l'Economie Politique* (January–March 1983).

C. Antonelli, 'Innovation as a Factor Shaping Industrial Structures: the Case of Small Firms', *Social Science Information* XVIII (1979).

P. Aydalot, *L'Enterprise dans l'Espace Urbain* (Paris: Economica, 1980).

F. J. Bade, 'Locational Behaviour and the Mobility of Firms in West Germany', *Urban Studies* XX (1983).

H. Beekmans, 'Amsterdam à l'Ecoute de ses Quartries', *Urbanisme* no. 204 (1984).

R. Boyer and J. Mistral, 'La Crise: Pensateur et Potentialité des Années Quatre-Vingt', *Annales – Economies, Sociétés, Civilisations*, no. 4 (1983).

M. Carnoy and R. Rumberger, *A New Social Contract* (New York: Harper & Row, 1983).

M. Castells, *Economic Crisis and American Society* (New Jersey: Princeton University Press, 1980).

M. Castells, 'High Technology, Economic Restructuring and the Urban-Regional Process in the United States' in M. Castells (ed.), *High Technology, Space and Society* (London: Sage, 1985).

P. H. Chombart de Lauwe, 'Peripherie des Villes et Crise de Civilisation' *City and Region* no. 3 (1982).

P. H. Chombart de Lauwe (ed.), *Culture-Action des Groupes Domines* (Paris: RCI, 1984).

A. Cohen, P. Combemale, *Croissance et Crises: Elements d'Analyse* (Paris: Hatier, 1980).

B. Coriat, *L'Atelier et le chronomètre* (Paris: Bourgeois, 1979).

M. Cross, 'Technical Change, the Supply of New Skills and Product Diffusion' in A. Gillespie (ed.), *Technological Change and Regional Development* (London: Pion, 1983).

P. Damesick, 'Office location and Planning in the Manchester Conurbation' *Town Planning Review*, no. 50 (1979).

P. Damesick *et al.*, 'Economic Regeneration of the Inner City: Manufacturing Industry and Office Development in Inner London', *Progress in Planning* vol. 18, part 3 (1982).

P. W. Daniels, 'Office Location in the British Conurbations: Trends and Strategies', *Urban Studies*, vol. 14 (1977).

R. Dennis, 'The Decline of Manufacturing Employment in Greater London: 1966–1974' *Urban Studies* vol. 17 (1978).

P. Dicken and P. Lloyd, 'Inner Metropolitan Industrial Change, Enterprise Structure and Policy Issues: Case Studies of Manchester and Merseyside', *Regional Studies* vol. 12 (1978).

M. Ducreux, 'Les Mutations de la Banlieu Dûes au Retrait des Grands Etablissements Industriels', *Actes du Colloque Banlieu* (Paris: CESP, 1983).

M. Dunford and D. Perrons, 'Waht's Growing Where in Britain', *Thesis*, no. 19 (1987).

E. von Einem, 'National Urban Policy: the Case of West Germany', *Journal of*

APA vol. 48, no. 1 (1982).

P. Elias and G. Keogh, 'Industrial Decline and Unemployment in Inner City Areas of Great Britain – a Review of the Evidence', *Urban Studies*, vol. 19 (1982).

B. Elliot and D. McCrone, 'Austerity and the Politics of Resistance' in I. Szelenyi (ed.), *Cities in Recession* (London: Sage, 1984).

C. Flockton, 'France: Ambitious Gaulist Designs and Constrained Socialist Plans', *Built Environment* vol. 10, no. 2 (1984).

S. Fothergill and G. Gudgin, 'The Regional Employment Change: a Sub-regional Explanation', *Progress in Planning*, vol. 12 (1979).

M. Frost and N. Spence, 'The Changing Structure and Distribution of the British Workforce', *Progress in Planning*, vol. 21 (1984).

C. Ghotta-Gobin, 'Le Nouveau Fédéralisme Americain', *L'Urbanisme*, no. 204 (1984).

A. Glasmeir, 'Innovative Manufacturing Industries: Spatial Evidence in US' in M. Castells (ed.), *High Technology, Space and Society* (London: Sage, 1985).

P. Hall, 'Technology, Space and Society in Contemporary Britain' in M. Castells (ed.), *High Technology, Space and Society* (London: Sage, 1985).

P. Hall and A. Markusen, *'Innovation and Regional Growth: Proposal to National Science Foundation'* (California: Institute of Urban and Regional Development, 1982).

M. Harloe and C. Paris, 'The Decollectivisation of Consumption: Housing and Local Government Finance in England and Wales 1979–1981' in I. Szelenyi (ed.), *Cities in Recession* (London: Sage, 1984).

H. Toft Jensen *et al.*, 'Capitalist Technology and the Change of the Labour Process' in A. Gillespie (ed.), *Technological Change and Regional Development* (London: Pion, 1983).

D. Keeble *et al.*, 'The Urban-Rural Manufacturing Shift in the European Community', *Urban Studies*, vol. 20, no. 4 (1983).

A. Kellerman, 'Telecommunications and the Geography of Metropolitan Areas', *Progress in Human Geography*, vol. 8, no. 2 (1984).

Y. Kerorguen and P. Merland, *Technopolis: L'Explosion des Cités Scientifiques – USA, Japan, Europe* (Paris: Autrement, 1985).

N. Komninos, *Theory of Urbanity: I. Crisis, Metropolitan Restructuring and New Urban Planning* (Athens: Sychrona Themata, 1986a).

N. Komninos, *Theory of Urbanity: II. Urban Planning and Social Regulation* (Athens: Sychrona Themata, 1986b).

R. Langridge, *Defining High-Technology Industries* (University of Reading: Working Paper, 1983).

D. Leborgne and A. Lipietz, *New technologies, New Modes of Regulation: Some Spatial Implications* (Paris: CEPREMAP, 1987).

A. Lipietz, *De la Nouvelle Division Internationale du Travail à la Crise du Fordisme Périphérique* (Paris: CEPREMAP, 1982).

A. Lipietz, *Accumulation, Crises et Sorties de Crise: Quelques Réflexions Méthodologiques autour de la Notion de 'Régulation'* (Paris: CEPREMAP, 1984).

A. Lipietz, 'Le National et le Regional: Quelle Autonomie face à la Crise', *Lesvos Seminar Proceedings* (Thessaloniki: 1985). Unpublished paper.

L. Long and D. De Are, 'The Slowing of Urbanisation in the US', *Scientific American*, vol. 249, no. 1 (1983).

E. J. Malecki, 'Corporate Organization of R & D and the Location of Technological Activities', *Regional Studies*, vol. 14 (1980).

P. Marcuse, 'Distribution Spatiales et Crise Fiscale Urbaine aux Etats-Unies', *Actes du Colloque Banlieu* (Paris: CESP, 1983).

D. Massey, 'Which New Technology?' in M. Castells (ed.), *High Technology, Space and Society* (London: Sage, 1985).

R. D. Norton and J. Rees, 'The Product Cycle and the Spatial Decentralisation of American Manufacturing', *Regional Studies* vol. 13 (1979).

R. P. Oakey *et al.*, 'The Regional Distribution of Innovative Manufacturing Establishments in Britain', *Regional Studies*, vol. 14 (1980).

R. P. Oakey, *High Technology Small Firms: Innovation and Regional Development in Britain and the United States* (London: Francis Pinter, 1984).

G. Ortona and W. Santagata, 'Industrial Mobility in the Turin Metropolitan Area', *Urban Studies*, vol. 20 (1980).

O. Pastré, L'Informatisation de l'Emploi (Paris: La Découverte, 1984).

B. Planque, *Innovation et Dévelopment Regional* (Paris: Economica, 1983).

A. Sayer, 'Spatial Implications of New Flexible Manufacturing Technologies and Working Practices and of Producer-User Relations to Information Technology', *Lesvas Seminar Proceedings* (Thessaloniki: 1985). Unpublished paper.

E. Soja, 'The Contemporary Restructuring of Regional Development: Politics, Periodicity and the Production of Space', *Naxos Seminar Proceedings* (Thessaloniki: Department of Urban and Regional Planning, 1983).

M. Storper, 'Technology and Spatial Production: Disequilibrium, Inter-industry Relationships and Industrial Development' in M. Castells (ed.), *High Technology, Space and Society* (London: Sage, 1985).

A. T. Thwaites, 'The Employment Implications of Technological Change in a Regional Context' in A. Gillespie (ed.), *Technological Change and Regional Development* (London: Pion, 1983).

L. Van den Berg *et al.*, *Urban Europe: Study of Growth and Decline* (New York: Pergamon Press, 1982).

15 Crisis Theory and Socio-Spatial Restructuring: the US Case

M. Gottdiener

The concept of industrial and socio-spatial restructuring is on the agenda of the 'new' urban analysis with a vengeance. This academic flowering is ironic from the perspective of the US because processes underlying change have been at work in that country for more than 30 years. While not using the currently fashionable terms of neo-Marxists and post-structuralists, mainstream analysts of social change in the US have been charting the patterns of restructuring for some time. In fact, studies of this kind are the bread and butter of regional analysts, urban economists and ecologists. Well established in the literature are proximate explanations for fundamental change that have only been repeated by the new discourse on restructuring including: the de-industrialisation of manufacturing; the rise of service related industries; the regional dispersal of industry, retailing and finance from the central city; technological change and its impact on both business and space; and regional shifts in prosperity and depression, such as the north-south or the sunbelt-frostbelt distinctions.

To be sure, restructuring discourse has isolated some new and different aspects of change that are quite important. The real claim to the uniqueness of this approach, however, rests with the assertion that mainstream work possesses theoretical perspectives on change that are false. Contending, in contrast, several contemporary analysts of restructuring have claimed that they are providing *new* theories that can replace the old. It is precisely this contention which marks off restructuring theory from extant perspectives on socio-spatial change.

In this chapter I shall assess this claim and also evaluate the alleged link between the crisis tendencies of capitalism and socio-spatial change. However, in doing so I do not wish to indulge in an extended discussion and critique of the efforts of restructuring theorists *per se*.

365

Instead, given the content of the papers in this volume and considering treatments of restructuring appearing elsewhere, I am more concerned with raising a specific issue. Namely, that, because much of the recent work on restructuring and socio-spatial change has been conceptualised by Europeans, the theoretical importance and comparative differences represented by the US case might be overshadowed by current work which is more applicable for the moment to the case of the European OICs. Capitalist development in the US is not only different from Europe, in many respects it represents advanced stages of tendencies found elsewhere. Hence, it is a grievous error to work theoretically solely in the direction of east to west. For quite some time, and due to the theoretical backwardness of much American social science, this tendency to import ideas without proper domestic insight has been a mixed blessing – stimulating but also confusing work in the US. I wish to contend that socio-spatial and industrial change in the US are best understood both through an appreciation of their long history and the complex links among several factors involved in the maturation of US capitalism. Consequently, this understanding calls forth a theoretical perspective that is at variance in a number of respects with important European work.

AMERICAN EXCEPTIONALISM: WAR, SPACE AND THE STATE

Changes that apparently have signalled aspects of maturation in US capitalist development over the years include the following. First, since the turn of the century, but especially increasing to a scale unprecedented elsewhere since World War II, American cities (built without enclosing walls) have overgrown the classical bounded urban form characteristic of industrial capitalism. Sprawl and hinterland expansion occurred in a growth environment with limited planning controls and a public philosophy that systematically ignored green belt or clustering ideas in favour of an ideology equating development of any kind with progress. At present most American cities are really specialised agglomerations embedded in a multi-centred urban region of immense scale involving marketing networks, sprawling housing patterns, industrial decentralisation and an extensive infrastructure of auto commuting routes. Within the confines of the US most people live in suburban areas outside central cities and the most typical type of housing is home ownership. By contrast in most European OICs it is the less affluent that have found residences outside the city.

The phenomenal form of industrial capitalism was the factory and its associated spatial form was the bounded, industrial city. The phenomenal form of late capitalism, in contrast, is the modern, vertically and horizontally differentiated corporation and the associated spatial form is the sprawling, multi-realmed, multi-centred urban region. This spatial phenomenon of late capitalism is illustrated in the US explicitly by the deconcentrated growth of urban areas which has caused both central city and suburban restructuring (Gottdiener 1985).

Second, and beginning with the 1950s, most of the urban areas in the US became racially segregated. An immense exchange of populations occurred as a consequence of suburbanisation, the maturation of industry, the effect of organised unions with power, and government policies regulating agriculture. These factors affected the locational status of black people in an unprecedented way during the 1950s and 1960s. Many cities not only experienced a surge of black in-migration but also a rapid influx of hispanics from Puerto Rico and Mexico. During this same period white flight to the suburbs virtually emptied cities of the child-rearing middle class. As a result urban areas in the US by the 1960s became marked by racial distinctions and problems with an inequitable flow of resources that prejudiciously disadvantaged minority areas. There has been nothing in Europe that can quite compare with the ghetto riots that occurred in the middle 1960s in the US and which brought the world's attention to this form of segregation.

Third, while defence budgets were reduced in the US immediately after World War II they began to rise again in the 1950s with the advent of the cold war and have never since decreased. Defence related spending amounted to almost $500 billion alone in 1986. This massive commitment for so long a time has assumed the features of what Mandel (1975) calls the permanent war economy. State defence spending is a major reason for the spatial transfer of value across regions because areas with the most per capita taxes are not necessarily those that receive their fair share of contracts. Over the years military related spending has shown a preference for suburban and southern locations, thereby helping to provide a base for regional sprawl and the more notorious frostbelt to sunbelt shift, although it is but one of several factors involved in the spatial transfer of value.

Initiatives in research and development, associated military expenditures and defence-related industrial expansion all supported by federal and state governments have combined to create a new industrial base that does not conform to capital logic and which is the outcome of what has been called 'Pentagon capitalism' (Melman 1970, 1983). This mode of economic activity, associated in the recent restructuring literature with the shift to high technology industries, cannot be analysed by current models of economic behaviour. When companies are allowed to enjoy profits without production (Melman 1983), theories of location, capitalist competition, pricing, investment, profit rates, and so on, are all thrown out to make room for a new logic underwritten by the state subsidisation of the permanent war economy. To suggest, as is the present case, that neo-classical, neo-Ricardian or neo-Marxian analysis remains applicable to the study of economic activity under these conditions, is to miss the fundamental importance of defence-related spending on the spatial transfer of value.

Fourth, as a frontier country, US development involves a relationship with land speculation and real estate that is quite unique among the OICs. In fact, investment in real estate has always been a principle way of making money in the US. At the bottom line, the approximately 60 per cent of the population who are homeowners have a vested interest in housing speculation as a major source of income. This aspect has been made especially effective due to the easy availability and tax write offs of home equity loans.

The flow of capital into land was aided by the many subsidies for new construction and for infrastructure development associated with the restructuring of capital following the Great Depression. Especially important was the link created between the real estate sector and banks which had the capacity to channel investment into housing on an unprecedented scale. Housing programmes were not, however, solely products of restructuring. They were also political prizes provided by government to the vast majority of working and middle class people as subsidies for single home ownership. In addition, much of the legislation supporting land development was initiated and passed under pressure from several successful political lobbying groups, such as the asphalt lobby, banks, construction trade unions and housing and real estate interests.

The sum total of state initiatives and preferential tax laws coupled with private sector innovations in banking, credit and construction combined over the years to produce a second circuit of capital in real estate (Lefebvre 1974; Gottdiener 1985) capable of channelling enormous investment funds into and out of different land development forms. In the US this second circuit of capital is so active that real estate investment, speculation and development comprise a major economic sector that rivals the industrialised first circuit of capital as a site of both valorisation and realisation. In fact, due to its low organic composition of capital, real estate has the capacity to siphon off capital during times of crisis in the primary circuit, thereby complicating crisis adjustment in ways that cannot be analysed by the logic of capital alone as it is commonly understood, that is, as it operates in the primary circuit. This issue, however, cannot be developed here (Gottdiener 1985).

Investment in the second circuit of capital has a direct impact on space. Real estate development is relentless and can take any number of different forms. While regulationist interventions exist in the US that govern land development, such as zoning codes, these restrictions are circumvented in a variety of ways, including political bribery, so that they remain weak or ineffective. Turnovers in use and sprawling growth seem to occur with only limited constraints. No place or person is immune from its effects. Due to the vast exchanges of population between cities and suburbs and the deconcentration of millions of people from the frostbelt to the sunbelt, housing development and infrastructure construction have taken place on a scale unprecedented among the OICs since World War II. As both the central city and the suburbs shift land uses to accommodate this relentless change, new forms of real estate investment constantly appear, thereby making the second circuit of capital immune to the kinds of crises associated with the primary circuit, although real estate does possess a crisis logic of its own that is linked to industrial production.

Finally, and among features of the US case that are distinct and which have led to early socio-spatial restructuring are all the government programmes aimed at domestic housing and infrastructure needs which have involved the expenditure of billions of dollars in local places since the 1950s. Due to the active, powerful interests involved in the second circuit of capital, state intervention in supplying the general conditions of production with regard specifically to settlement space have been more pronounced in the US than in other OICs. I have in mind here, for example, the well known record of urban renewal which transformed almost single-handedly the central city areas of the US and which created a 'boondoggle' of real estate investment bonanzas for combined business interests and construction trade unions, sometimes known as growth networks. In addition, and as already mentioned, housing programmes have also subsidised home ownership leading to and sustaining massive suburbanisation. Not the least of these subsidies is the generous VA loan programme for war veterans which enables them to qualify for home purchasing with only a small down payment. Together state intervention and regulation, therefore, since 1950 have underwritten the patterns of socio-spatial restructuring which exist in both central cities and suburban areas to this very day. The massive extent of this state intervention falsifies on the surface other approaches, such as neo-classical location theory, neo-Ricardian location theory, urban ecology and political public choice theory, that are commonly encountered in the literature on metropolitan restructuring and change which ignore completely the state's role in the subsidisation of both housing and industrial location and of investment and capital realisation in the permanent war economy.

In sum, the causal factors operating in the US that have produced socio-spatial restructuring and which are comparatively unique up to this time but which may now be appearing elsewhere include: racism, the role of the interventionist state in urban renewal programmes and the subsidisation of single-home ownership as the dominant mode of housing, the operation of the second circuit of capital, and the transfer of value through the permanent war economy. These factors have been at work in the US for at least the last 40 years. There are additional structural forces, however, that are also fundamentally responsible for the restructuring of society and of space that are more familiar features shared by other countries as well.

First, it is important to note the accelerated way that technology has influenced socio-spatial relations. Communications and transportation innovations have altered the space-time dimensions of social action. Recent advances in micro-computing, in particular, have resulted in the burgeoning component of information processing work as a constituent sector of society. This has altered labour needs and enabled the growing specialisation of downtown districts in the activities of finance capital and corporate decision-making. Finally, recent advances in robotics and in custom production machinery have altered the factory regimen and point towards new relations between workers and capital. Flexibilisation, small batch runs, just-in-time subcontracting, automation of mass production, and the like, all represent formidable restructuring of basic industry with consequent effects on socio-spatial relations.

Over the past two decades, in fact, new relations have emerged between state-directed spending, private sector strategic and defence-related production, public and private research and development, and the new technologies. These new relations do not either follow capital logic alone, or share its crisis base. They are responsible for the spectacular growth of the new technopoles during a time when traditional centres have undergone decline in a crisis of de-industrialisation.

A second factor active elsewhere as well as in the US involves structural changes in the corporate-bureaucratic form and the shift to the internationalisation of capital through the phenomenal form of the multi-national corporation. In the past business was vertically integrated, often having administrative and industrial functions existing in close proximity. Presently, it is more common for corporations to be vertically disintegrated with different functions located in different places. This shift coupled with the internationalisa-tion of capital into a quasi-global system takes its ultimate form in the multi-plant, multi-product, multi-national corporation. Existing bey-ond the control of any one nation state, multi-nationals have reshaped industrial relations to conform more closely to the needs of global investment flows made easier by microelectronic modes of administra-tion and decision processing. One important outcome of such changes involves the feasible adoption of labour sourcing strategies, namely, the splintering of functions by multi-business corporations and the location of facilities in places offering the best combination of trained and inexpensive labour. However, theorists of the labour theory of location and those that subscribe to the 'new international division of labour' have neglected the important role that exchange rate differences and their shifting nature play in labour sourcing decisions. As 'modification theorists' above have suggested (see Busch and Milios above) considerable volatility still remains in relations of capital and labour across the nations of the globe.

The practice of labour sourcing has followed in the wake of other factors responsible for the spatial transfer of value, such as state initiated defence spending, and helps explain the de-industrialisation of traditional, unionised central city factories. Labour sourcing is also an active means for the integration of production by multi-nationals making possible a shift towards a global system of capital.

In sum, the following six factors are the main ones responsible for the present patterns of socio-spatial restructuring in the US and they constitute the primary dimensions along which the transition to a new societal conjuncture can be analysed for the US case: racism, changes in the corporate-bureaucratic form, labour sourcing, knowledge and information processing as a force of production, the relatively independent effects of the second circuit of real estate, and, finally, the multiple forms of the interventionist state and its various effects on the transfer of value. It is wrong to suggest that these factors follow a well defined logic, such as the logic of capital, some alleged global system, or world division of labour, or even that they contain mechanisms that orchestrate separate spheres of change according to some kind of periodisation of Fordist relations. There are enough degrees of freedom among these several causal forces to create patterns that cannot be explained by the affinities of structural concordances alone. A contingent articulation of these six factors is a more likely way of understanding the interplay responsible for current social change. Consequently, my approach to the explanation of restructuring departs from those that stress the pre-eminence of capital logic arguments or which explain change simply as altered relations between capital and labour that are generated by technological innovations in a global system. I find it remarkable that so much variation exists among industrialised yet restructuring societies. A more precise concept than the regime of accumulation, namely, the mode of development, has been added to the regulationist lexicon specifically to deal with the non-determinate, contingent nature of the post-Fordist transition.

After considering the long history of socio-spatial changes in the US and the contingent nature of the present conjuncture it is possible to argue that the current crop of restructuring theories have made exaggerated claims regarding their relative explanatory power. No single causal factor, such as high technology or flexible accumulation, can capture the depth of change or provide the basis for some determinate theory of post-Fordism. In short, theories developed in Europe to account for social change may have only limited applicability across the Atlantic. Ironically, because the original theory of Fordism was based on the US case (Aglietta 1979), it can even be argued that those Europeans using regulationist theory to explain change in their own societies may be overlooking the limited applicability of Fordist phases outside the US (see Jessop, ch. 11).

Yet we cannot end here. Certainly socio-spatial changes are occurring in the US and crisis tendencies are implicated in them. Consequently, it is still necessary to explore the link between these two dimensions and this will serve as a means of specifying further the nature of the present conjuncture and also, perhaps, refining further the understanding of the post-Fordist transition.

CRISIS RELATED RESTRUCTURING IN THE US

For the case of the US, the devalorisation and redevelopment of central city areas, the spatial transfer of resources to suburban and sunbelt locations, the flight of the middle class from the central city, new flexible modes of production and the appearance of high-tech and defence-related growth poles are all historical products of capitalist development that are only contingently or, in some cases, independently related to crisis tendencies of domestic capital. This observation is analogous to the discovery that the fiscal crisis of central cities is not related directly to economic crisis tendencies (Gottdiener 1986). In both cases the explanatory value of crisis theory for socio-spatial restructuring remains limited.

Yet, it should also be noted that economic restructuring in response to crisis has an equally long history in the US and that crisis related changes have accelerated since the 1970s. Restructuring in response to these concerns has had a significant impact on space. It is the contention of this paper, however, that socio-spatial changes associated with crisis restructuring are also related to other factors that prevail in the general composition of capitalist development and which are components of the production of space that are typically characteristic of the US case, such as land development according to second circuit dynamics. Consequently, crisis related change and factors belonging to the production of space are interrelated. Furthermore, it is precisely by appreciating this linkage that contemporary restructuring patterns can be most fully understood. In what follows I shall discuss those socio-spatial changes associated with crisis restructuring from the perspective of the theoretical approach outlined above. That is, I shall show how restructuring has both a longer history than is often asserted and that it is contingently linked to the general factors in the production of space, namely, racism, labour sourcing, corporate changes, state intervention, knowledge and technology and the action of the second circuit of capital.

Among the host of changes associated with contemporary crisis related economic restructuring, Feagin and Smith (1987, p. 13–14) call attention to five distinct ones that have been central in affecting spatial changes. These include: plant closures, plant start-ups, corporate

centre development, expansion of service and other jobs related to
office employment, and, corporate expansion to areas outside the
central city. Feagin and Smith unfortunately explain these changes
according to a world system perspective and its new international
division of labour. Enough has been said by the preceding papers in
this volume to question their approach. Let us re-examine these five
trends in the light of the remarks above in order to illustrate a more
contingent interrelated perspective.

Plant closures: de-industrialisation

Among the OICs in general unproductive industries have been hit
hard by international competition. Mergers and buy outs associated
with a greater centralisation of capital on a global scale have also had
an impact on local firms and plants. As a consequence productive as
well as unproductive industries have been subjected in recent years to
the spectre of plant closings. For the most part this phenomenon
represents a clear case of economic restructuring, especially as
manifested by the plague of de-industrialisation (Bluestone and
Harrison 1982) or in response to rising local labour costs after the oil
shocks of the 1970s. Plant closures, however, have also been the
consequence of developmental patterns consistent with new investment in physical plant, especially the process of capital deepening
and the shift to more automated forms of mass production. Consequently, job loss can be the product of new investment patterns
following the logic of domestic capital as well as disinvestment
according to world system capital flows (see below for further
discussion).

The process of de-industrialisation, contrary to restructuring
theories, has been operating in the US for some time — at least since
the 1950s. The now familiar shift out of manufacturing and blue
collar jobs and into service took place on an immense scale during the
two decades prior to the 1980s in the US (Sternlieb and Hughes
1975). The cumulative decline in manufacturing for the 15 years
between 1960 and 1975 far outweighs the more spectacular and rapid
decline of industry since 1975 which has been more directly related to
'world system' crisis restructuring. To be sure the general shift out of
manufacturing involves some crisis related change and clearly there
are no grounds for the post-industrial explanation of this phenomenon because services have not replaced manufacturing but are
ancillary to it.

In the post-war period, however, the intensive regime of accumulation worked well because of the relation between labouring and the hypertrophic expansion of 'Department II', that is, commodity production, which was not a direct product of crisis restructuring. The social generalisation of the 'new consumption norm' (Aglietta 1979) helped to produce a consumer society and this process involved important political and cultural changes as well as economic ones. This more organised form of capitalism had its origins in the crisis adjustments of the 1930s but cannot be reduced to them. The cultural and political accommodations sustaining a consumer society became relatively independent from crisis tendencies as such. This was most evident in the growth of suburbia and the emergence of a middle class, family oriented life style organised around high consumption. Fuelling this change and coupled with it was the phenomenal post-war expansion in services. The needs of consumerism worked backwards to affect industrial production and stimulated further the changes taking place there, especially capital deepening and increased automation. As a labour intensive mode of work, services enjoyed an expansion in its employment base taking up the slack from the declining need for mass armies of labourers in industrial production. Plant closures and plant reorganisation played an important role in maintaining an organised form of capitalist expansion within the boundary constraints of the intensive regime of accumulation. This was not a process of de-industrialisation but of structural change associated with the maturation of the Fordist regime of accumulation and the general tendency of capital deepening (that is investment rather than disinvestment). As mentioned, this developmental process bears only a limited resemblance to the rapid de-industrialisation and spectacular changes associated with the current crisis of this same intensive regime, or what some have called the contemporary shift from an organised to a disorganised phase of capitalism.

New plant start-ups: re-industrialisation

The literature on crisis restructuring quite rightly includes analysis of plant start-ups or re-industrialisation. This effort is almost exclusively focused either on the central city and the relation between re-industrialisation and labour intensive business or on spectacular examples of technopoles and new R & D growth centres. Operating all along as a kind of baseline process of industrial development, however, has been the steady shift of manufacturing plants from the central city to suburban locations since the 1950s. This is not a process of re-industrialisation but is, rather, part of the growth pattern associated with the general process of deconcentration in the US and the changing relation between central city and suburban hinterland (Gottdiener 1985).

Some restructuring analysts attribute the suburbanisation of plant locations to a direct outcome of capital deepening with suburban locations more suited to the larger land needs of new plants (Scott 1986). Yet, this is merely one factor among an entire constellation of causes associated with deconcentration, while capital deepening itself cannot explain suburbanisation of new plants. In particular, the shift to larger, capital intensive plants was facilitated greatly in the US by its tax laws and its generous appreciation allowances (Marcuse 1981). Against neo-Ricardian reductionism, it must be pointed out that the dominance of suburban locations in the post-war boom of new plant construction occurred despite the general availability of an immense quantity of industrial floor space of good quality already existing and languishing within traditional central city areas. Capital deepening could have occurred within the city at these sites but due in part to tax laws it was more profitable to build new plants rather than refurbish existing ones.

A second factor in the deconcentration of industry involves the racial shifts afflicting American cities. By the 1960s most of the blue collar, industrial labour force among whites had moved to suburban locations. Plant building in suburbia was a means of locating facilities closer to labour pools. The greater presence of industrial workers in suburbia explains why such areas experienced an increase in manufacturing activity at the same time that the country as a whole and central cities in particular experienced fundamental decline. To this day suburban locations are attractive because they contain the bulk of the country's population. Labour sourcing location strategies result from these demographic changes and the institutional shifts in labour militancy that followed.

A third neglected factor in deconcentration of industrial activity is the role of real estate speculation. Especially important in this regard is the operation of the attractive locational changes promoted by developers and called 'industrial parks' (Feagin 1983). These parks often offered tax write offs, subsidised rent, low interest development bonds or 'cheap money' and free land and infrastructure development as speculators worked in tandem with local suburban government officials to promote locations outside central cities in an attempt to capitalise on new growth. This combined public-private sector effort was especially effective in capturing new plant construction that was associated with the massive amount of defence spending unleashed by the cold war. As indicated above, defence related industries do not operate by capital logic, hence the shift to capital deepening in this case and the construction of new suburban plants were trends subsidised by the federal government rather than outcomes produced by capitalist competition as traditional observers suggest (Scott 1986).

Corporate centre development: recentralisation

The renovation of central city areas as sites for new corporate headquarters with its associated explosion of service and other support jobs associated with office work is a third feature often underscored by restructuring analysts and which is referred to as recentralisation. Explanations for recentralisation emphasise the role of the world system and the centralisation of global capital within multinational corporations that have carved up the earth. In addition, emphasis is also placed on Third World immigrants and minority in-migration as the new exploitable labour force of recentralised industry. In both cases an attempt is made to come to terms with the change in US cities from bastions of manufacturing with associated and robust working class cultures to the present case of combined multi-national corporate centres and industrial sweatshops relying on the working poor. Currently, urban dwellers inhabit a central city landscape consisting of a skyscraper existence during the day with the night-time given over to abandoned streets and random violent crime.

In the US central city redevelopment began in the 1940s and with the massive investment of federal dollars in the urban renewal programme. This complex of public-private initiatives organised by growth networks included labour as well as capital (Friedland 1983; Mollenkopf 1983). The federal bulldozer (Anderson 1964) was responsible for the eradication of many culturally distinct and traditional central city areas and the forced devalorisation of sound urban real estate in addition to slum clearance. Combined with the subsidisation of single family home ownership, urban renewal programmes fuelled the middle class abandonment of the city. And, combined with the glut of real estate speculation that the programmes encouraged, renewal sustained a bonanza for speculators of all kinds who tore up the traditional fabric of urban life (Boyer 1973). Big winners in this process, in addition to speculators, were both the construction trade unions that enjoyed steady, highly paid work and the banks who not only helped finance new construction but also realised gain through the construction of their own business headquarters buildings in speculative efforts (Leinsdorf *et al.*, 1973). It is not by accident that the new skyline of most American cities features prominently the headquarter buildings of banks and insurance or investment companies. This outcome is not a consequence of recentralisation or contemporary crisis restructuring, but rather represents a very opportunistic effort launched under cover of the questionable, multi-billion dollar intervention of the state that was known as urban renewal.

Quite clearly, the headquarters function of the central city for global multi-nationals has grown since the 1950s and elements of downtown construction are intimately connected with the current phase of crisis restructuring. But this complementary growth is not rooted in the same factors which earlier on irrevocably changed the face of the traditional American city. Rather the two processes have melded together in a persisting trend of greater functional specialisation for all downtown areas, brought about by several decades of deconcentration.

Corporate and industrial expansion outside the central city: decentralisation

This process, which is often referred to in the restructuring literature as decentralisation, has also been covered above in connection with new plant start-ups where the role of local tax and other related subsidies was noted. Evidence suggests that the deconcentration of corporate locations is in large part a consequence of the maturing functional specialisation of American capitalism. A study by Armstrong (1972) notes that suburban office locations have been taken up not by the large multi-national firms characteristic of the central city, but mostly by small- and medium-sized businesses almost wholly, if not exclusively, involved in domestic operations. For the most part these firms are located in areas outside the city in order to be closer to the centre of gravity of their own local market as well as in response to land development subsidies. In addition, it has also been noted (Gottdiener 1985) that suburban office construction, which outstrips in the aggregate the figure for central cities, is related to the explosion of administrative and public service districts in urban hinterlands. Since the 1950s public sector employment has mushroomed at the local and county levels as a consequence of massive suburbanisation. The vigorous real estate market for office buildings in suburbia is a reflection in part of this trend.

To be sure a spectacular example of decentralisation is the emergence of the silicon landscapes that heralded the movement to post-Fordism. However, too much has been made of the role of high technology in the creation of such spaces. When the influence of defence spending is taken into account, a better picture emerges and one which views the phenomenon of technopoles as characteristic of general trends since the 1950s rather than the immediate product of crisis restructuring, as is often suggested. For example, important hinterland regions, such as Suffolk County outside New York, became high technology growth poles, albeit with a diverse rather than a relatively homogeneous economic base, in the 1950s and due to massive defence spending during the Korean War (Gottdiener 1977). In sum, decentralisation possesses, like the other components of restructuring, a firm base in trends related to the general maturation of American capitalism since World War II and the link between the crisis of Fordism and socio-spatial restructuring in the US is less solid than restructuring theorists like to suggest (see below).

POST-FORDIST RESTRUCTURING AND SPACE

The crisis of Fordism is real. Recent socio-spatial restructuring in the OICs can in part even be attributed to it. Having argued for a limited view of the relation between crisis and socio-spatial change, it is profitable at this point to examine the nature of the Fordist transition and its effects on socio-spatial organisation.

Among regulationist scholars, Roobeek (1986) is quite right to caution against the substantive periodisation of Fordism. With this in mind it is still possible to acknowledge at least two separate phases of this capitalist stage and to contemplate social movement to a third, and most probably 'post-Fordist' phase. The basis of Fordism, which occurred in many of the OICs between the world wars, was the correspondence established between mass production in industry, on the one hand and mass purchasing of commodities by labour, on the other. This so-called 'intensive regime of accumulation', because it relied for growth on domestic rather than foreign circuits of capital, also required political and cultural accommodations that constituted a 'mode of regulation'. Regulation assured an organised adjustment over time among capitalist growth factors, productivity changes of labour and the level of consumption.

After World War II Fordist regimes enjoyed spectacular success. Growth was rapid as were the increases in labour's standard of living. With prosperity certain problems arose that threatened the peace of Fordist accommodations. Among all the disequilibrating factors (see Roobeek 1986; Hirsch 1985; de Vroey 1984; for a more extensive discussion) perhaps the most significant was the internationalisation of capital along with the concommitant rise of multi-nationals to the top of the capitalist pantheon. On the one hand, rapid increases in wages during the 1960s and 1970s fuelled a domestic demand for consumer goods that outstripped the ability of domestic industry to supply it. In a sense the consumer society or culture which is a product of Fordism began to work too well. Imports of consumer goods from other industrialised countries became a significant way the gap was plugged, thereby aiding the multi-national globalisation of capital. The voracious demand for consumer goods allowed some countries to specialise in export production while controlling their own internal demand, thereby following a growth path that did not follow the Fordism of other OICs; that is, not every industrialised country can be said to serve as a clear example of Fordist organisation (see Jessop, above). This difference led to spectacular growth, in particular, in the cases of West Germany and Japan. Secondly, the internationalisation of finance capital led to the penetration of industrial capitalism into less developed countries including eastern Europe and what has now come to be called the NICs. This mobilisation of capital flows across the globe mushroomed to billion dollar levels following the oil shocks of the 1970s with the leap in the price of crude and the consequent 'superprofits' that oil rents engendered.

The internationalisation of capital violated the conditions of the Fordist intensive regime and modulated that phase to produce 'neo-Fordism' (Lipietz 1982; van der Pijl 1984). This phase, however, quickly produced problems and showed itself to be an essentially unstable one. In particular, the greater global reach of multi-nationals coupled with the persisting voraciousness of domestic consumer demand led to a rapid increase in competition among all industrial corporations for significant pieces of the consumer markets. During the 1980s the heated race for the consumer dollar produced the monumental crisis of industrial capital in most of the OICs among all sectors that simply could not compete with foreign trade. The structural effects of this crisis have been described in many of the papers in this volume. Furthermore, investment by finance capital in the NICs, despite initial successes, led to the current debt crisis which has no means of solution save the writing off of immense debt levels (see chapter 9 in this volume). This characteristic feature of neo-Fordism further exacerbated the crisis of domestic economies in the OICs by failing to provide capital there with easy access to liquidity. In sum, and at present, we find a crisis of neo-Fordism afflicting the OICs and as a result there are restructuring efforts under way (as described in several papers above) that will move such countries to a new, and perhaps post-Fordist phase.

Haeusler and Hirsch in this volume (chapter 12) have suggested some characteristic features of this new phase following the present crisis of restructuring (Hirsch 1985; Roobeek 1986). These include: a new technological basis for labour leading to a new division of labour characterised by sharp distinctions between skilled and non-skilled workers and leading to a 'massive social marginalisation and fragmentation of working conditions and wage relations' (Haeusler and Hirsch, above); what Hirsch calls 'hyper-industrialisation' or the industrialisation of services, thereby extending the above division of labour to all sectors of capital; a concommitant penetration of capitalist relations into all sectors of society including agriculture and traditional economies; the uncoupling of the Fordist correspondence between worker incomes and productivity increases, thereby changing the basic relation between workers and capitalists as well as altering the regulatory needs of the new phase to a scaled down, partly privatised level of government intervention; and, finally, a 'pluralisation of life styles' due to labour force changes under the new conditions and reflecting gross disparities between the affluent and the working poor, greater insecurities of employment and extreme differentiation in consumption levels.

Roobeek (1986) has added to these forecasted aspects of post-Fordism several additional features. A principal change, for example, involves movement of both capitalist production and labour force supply to greater institutionalised forms of flexibility. 'Flexibilisation' assumes the decline in power of unions and the presence of workers who are trained in and are willing to perform a variety of tasks. Production itself will shift to smaller batches, 'flex-time' work shifts, 'just-in-time' flexibility among suppliers, and a deregulation by the government of many industries. In post-Fordism businesses will have to move fast to accommodate to changes and new market demands and so will have to eliminate present constraints which tie up labour and capital in commitments that cannot easily be changed. Micro-computing will be essential to this task.

A second feature suggested by Roobeek concerns a predicted expansion of the informal economic sector. This changes the nature of households from their previous specialisation in consumption to a combined consumer-producer unit. Production at home will be capital and technology intensive following the new conditions of post-Fordist work. As Roobeek observes:

> A new type of mass employee has therefore made his debut, whose work is not concentrated in one place and for which no homogeneous working conditions apply but which is clearly individualised, flexible and fragmented [1986, p. 25].

In sum, if the hallmark of capitalist society is uneven development, then post-Fordism promises more of the same with inequities differentiating to a finer degree capitalist businesses as well as the structure of the working class.

Post-Fordism and space

To what extent will the coming changes associated with post-Fordism be manifested in new spatial forms? In addressing this question for the case of the US it is necessary first to return to certain observations that are the premise of this paper. Briefly put, the European theory of post-Fordism can be applied to the US case only with extreme caution and awareness of its limitations.

I do not believe, for example, that the complex of high technology and knowledge industries will provide the basis for a new stage of capitalism, or that there already exists a new regime of accumulation based on flexibility. This is not to say that such arrangements will not constitute an important segment of economic activity. Clearly such trends have already made a significant impact in the other OICs as well as the US. New forms of technology and knowledge have already articulated with all aspects of social organisation changing the shape of institutions such as education, medical care and government as well as business and factory production. However, I wish to suggest that post-Fordist theorists overemphasise the impact of high technology on industry, in general, and socio-spatial organisation, in particular. Furthermore, most observers who have rushed to proclaim a qualitatively new regime of accumulation, such as 'flexible accumulation', have ignored the lack of specificity adhering to that concept itself and the variety of problems associated with periodising Fordism. As indicated in the previous section, while the US has experienced a growth pattern that is uniquely different form the previous bounded city form, this deconcentrated pattern possesses roots already well developed in the earliest stages of capitalist industrialisation. It is wrong to periodise socio-spatial changes by linking them directly with the stages of capitalist development (see Gottdiener 1985) because there is no direct one-to-one correspondence between the two. Furthermore, while capitalism in the US is maturing to a new phase, I do not subscribe to the view that it will be based on flexible, 'process oriented' high technology alone.

I contend, instead, that the core technological innovations based on micro-computing, flexibility, research and development and so on, which constitute the post-Fordist response to capital's current crisis, will affect aspects of deconcentration in limited yet distinct ways. Provided we understand, according to the argument in the previous sections, that both central city restructuring and mature suburban development have their roots primarily, although not exclusively, in other causes, it is possible to venture some observations about how the nature of deconcentration will be altered as further post-Fordist restructuring in response to crisis unfolds.

The central city

By the 1970s *prior* to many 'post-Fordist' changes, American cities already exhibited an urban milieu representing the extreme form of racial and class inequities characteristic of the mature, deconcentrated metropolitan region. With the middle class moved to the suburbs, a stark contrast existed between the wealthy and the poor. Functional specialisation of 'downtown' sectors further polarised a once diverse city landscape into distinct enclaves for work, for residence and for consumption.

Post-Fordist restructuring will accentuate what already exists within central cities. Gentrification, for example, which created new forms of residential living within the city, will not reverse the fundamental urban polarisation of class and race; nevertheless, it will constitute a greater proportion of real estate activity than at present. New housing will be expensive. The continued expansion of the specialised city economy will ensure that gentrified areas will expand. This latter trend does not mean a return of families to the city. As in the recent past, gentrified urban areas are more typified by single occupant households and this segment makes up the fastest growing new household component among the city population.

Keeping pace with active speculation in and eventual, although not immediate, occupancy of office buildings will be expanded commercial and service sectors. We can expect a greater return of small businesses to the inner city after several decades of urban renewal that removed such entrepreneurs from the centre. Speciality shops and consumer outlets of all kinds will reappear. In the 1970s the mall form invaded the central city and such fully enclosed marketing areas are a significant way the new gentrified urban professionals will be serviced with commodities. In addition, the small business life of the city should be enriched by subcontractors and just-in-time suppliers who will expand their presence. Hyper-industrialised services should also be another growth sector for the central city including private sector suppliers of former public goods provided by city government.

The increased presence of small businesses will mean a growing proportion of low wage but employed minority and immigrant workers. Added to this will be jobs in the new 'sweatshops' and in cheap labour, often illegal, manufacturing which has recently re-invaded downtown urban districts. The presence, of the working poor will increase (Gordon *et al.*, 1982) as these trends remain with us.

A trend which might become a well-defined characteristic of post-Fordism will be the increasing presence of pedlars selling wares or services on city streets. It is expected that there will be a growing percentage of pedlars selling products produced by the home economy as well as those selling stolen or illegally imported commodities.

In sum, it can be expected that central cities will continue to experience an expansion of the type of specialised real estate, manufacturing, commercial and service sectors characteristic of the crisis period of Fordism rather than transforming into some unique post-Fordist milieu. A greater percentage of immigrants, minorities and the working poor, on the one hand, coupled with the relatively highly paid professionals residing in gentrified ghettos, on the other, will mean an increasing polarisation of the city along racial, ethnic and class lines. Linked to this trend are the effects from a retreating public sector and the abandonment in the US of the social engineering mandate which characterised city regimes in the 1960s. With less government intervention in pursuit of social justice, city life will increasingly become punctuated by crime and other pathological social forms deriving from uneven and inequitable development. Consequently, there will have to be an increase in the surveillance and policing role of the local state. Expenditures by local government on these functions may well come to comprise the greatest proportion of municipal budgets during the coming era of post-Fordism. Whatever type of economic recovery which may be in store for central cities, an improved economy will be overshadowed eventually by this growing crisis of uneven development.

Perhaps the most important transformation which occurred as a consequence of recent post-1970 events involves changes in the way cities are being run politically. In the past cities functioned to concentrate wealth, industry and labour. There was a concordance between their political boundaries and the economic power that produced wealth. Over three decades of progressive deconcentration, however, and with the general effects of de-industrialisation, global flows of capital investment and the rise to power of multi-nationals, cities no longer enjoy the concordance of political jurisdication and economic resources. The city has, as a result, experienced a kind of retreat of the economic sphere from the domain of its own influence and it now must compete with other places for the opportunity of harbouring value-generating activities. In recent years, furthermore, there has also been a concomitant retreat of the political sphere from the city's public reach as well. A decade of fiscal crisis and retrenchment combined with tax revolts and the intense competition between places for new economic resources has forced a fundamental change in the political relations of the local state. More and more traditional urban public policy based on the twin initiatives of providing for the general conditions of production, on the one hand, and the redistribution of value in favour of increasing the social wage for the entire working class, on the other, has come into ill repute. Instead, city regimes have shifted to the promotion of a 'good business climate' and the subsidisation of growth. This change has been accomplished, especially by measures such as tax abatements, the funnelling of cheap money to business through development bonds, outright grants, the institution of non-elective 'superagencies' responsible for development, and all manner of public/private partnerships — measures that are all generally beyond both the participation and control of the polity. In effect, then, as the urban political sphere has been placed in the service of capital, both the economic and the political domains have retreated beyond the reach of public life. Democracy itself has declined (Gottdiener 1987).

Recent changes of this nature trivialise the activity of local politics and make it extremely difficult to visualise how the local state can serve at some future time as a mechanism of social engineering to alleviate the growing crisis of inequality that lies at the heart of contemporary urban growth patterns. At the same time, the debilitating crime rate already present in places that have been pursuing growth has redefined the local state as principally a policing agent of social control. The shifts from more to less regulation of business and from liberal, welfare policies to regulation based on social control constitute the seeds of a new mode of regulation that includes the transformed local state.

The suburban hinterland

There is little question that the vast bulk of metropolitan regional development will take place in the areas outside the central city in the future. This phenomenon is but an extension of already existing trends. Post-Fordist changes do not suggest any alteration of present growth patterns in favour of the hinterland nor any abatement of deconcentration in manufacturing to areas outside the city. More importantly, it will probably be the case that trends discussed above with regard to the central city will also characterise suburban development as well. For example, hinterland areas will no doubt experience an increasing polarisation between the wealthy and the poor. Low wage manufacturing and service industries will be just as active here as in the central city. To make room for a greater, de-skilled labour force there will be an expansion of multiple family or apartment housing in suburban areas. As in the past, the more affluent communities will be better able to defend themselves against the construction of less expensive rental housing. Consequently, greater polarisation of class and race will occur with sharp distinctions among communities in wealth and well-being.

Among the changes that are associated with post-Fordism two seem most likely to affect suburban areas in unique ways, namely, the greater social role of high technology and the growing importance of the home economy. Defence-related high technology industries have had a greater impact on the suburban hinterland than in the central city. Much of defence-related spending since World War II has been funnelled to suburban and/or sunbelt locations. Areas such as Suffolk County in New York or Orange County in California owe most of their industrial growth to the well-being of such industry. These counties and other high-tech growth areas, such as Silicon Valley (Santa Clara County in California) may find their growth potential further enhanced by the projected increasing role of high-tech related industry in manufacturing that is envisioned by post-Fordist theorists (Roobeek 1986). Such a future may not materialise, however, for a number of reasons, in which case the suburban industrial base will have to diversify in order to expand.

Among the reasons to doubt the further expansionary ability of high-tech industry are: the role of foreign competition in stifling consumer-oriented domestic high-tech industry — an outcome already apparent in Silicon Valley; the growing centralisation of defence contractors who obtain the lion's share of new government spending – a factor contributing to the decline of important defence-related industry in Orange County; and, finally, the reassertion of product rather than process related industries after a decade of economic restructuring. The latter requires further comment. Some analysts preaching the high technology gospel have suggested that technology is responsible for a new 'stage' of capitalism that will feature process-rather than product-oriented economic activity (Castells 1985). Technological change of this type involves the production and circulation of information and knowledge (Lyotard 1984). Economic activity based on this change consists of flows to and from functionally specialised units that are fragmented but hierarchically structured (Castells 1985, p. 14). As envisioned by Castells, in particular, the new mode is coherently organised by the 'world system' and locational decisions are functions of the 'new international division of labour'.

As indicated in this volume there are ample reasons to be suspicious of this argument. More importantly, studies of urban industrial activities reveal that traditional product-oriented manufacturing remains the backbone of the economy. This is especially the case for suburban areas which have been the beneficiaries of manufacturing decentralisation (Gottdiener and Kephart, forthcoming). Furthermore, and due to the restructuring of the capital/labour relation, basic manufacturing is returning to the US. Although physical plants are more capital intensive and automated, de-skilling and union busting of the labour force, combined with the retreat of the welfare state have brought about a renewed attractiveness for domestic industrial locations thereby falsifying the alleged trend of global sourcing under the world system. In short, while high technology and process-oriented knowledge industries comprise part of the future wave of change for capitalism, in the US these trends are overrated and such activities remain secondary to basic product-oriented manufacturing following the present period of restructuring.

One post-Fordist trend that will affect suburban areas is the new role of the home economy. As families differentiate their domestic activities into producer as well as consumer units with an increase in home-related work, fundamental socio-spatial changes can be expected in suburbia. These include: a greater need for specialised services within easy reach of suburban housing developments; an increase in traffic flows proceeding in all directions which may reach prohibitive levels in some places, thereby stifling future growth; and alteration of traditional family sex roles as both women and men switch to some work-at-home arrangements. The advent of the home economy will make obsolete the concept of the suburban bedroom commuter shed and will add further fuel to the already powerful forces of deconcentration resulting in the persistent expansion of metropolitan regions.

In brief, post-Fordist changes will not mean new spatial forms in the US, because such restructuring was already underway in the 1950s. The profound shifts in the mode of production associated with contemporary developments will have their greatest impact on the fabric of social life. Polarisation of the population, increased use of surveillance, the massive fragmentation of the population by racial and subclass distinctions, and the relentless activities of the second circuit of real estate will comprise the socio-spatial counterpart to post-Fordist restructuring at the place of work. For the case of the US socio-spatial restructuring producing a space of deconcentrated development involves the contingent articulation of six factors: racism, technology and knowledge as forces of production, labour sourcing, state intervention, corporate reorganisation and differentiation, and the effects of the second circuit of capital.

Surprisingly, for all the talk of crisis and the use of metaphors, such as 'disorganised capitalism', to represent the contingent nature of social change, present transitions have taken place in the OICs with relative social stability and working class acquiesence. To be sure, severe traumas have been experienced by labour; however, these have manifested themselves less as collective responses than in private misfortunes, and conservative regimes have gone largely unchallenged. Furthermore, it can be observed that while crisis tendencies exist they remain immanent in the system. We have yet to witness the full effect of what present crisis tendencies potentially represent. For example, the extreme polarities of wealth and power in central cities are manifested principally as a war on crime. Powder keg potentiality of the kind actually manifested in the ghetto riots of the 1960s remains with us today lying beneath the surface of urban life. The same can be said for the volatilities and instabilities of investment flows. Money managed capitalism has, so far, held crisis tendencies, such as those manifested in the stock market crash of October 1987, in check. The real crisis tendencies of a weakened dollar and of enormous fiscal and trade deficits have yet to be felt.

Industrial restructuring has moved incrementally perhaps towards some new regime of accumulation and changes in the social and political fabric have also accompanied this transformation, but theorists proclaiming the advent of some new stage have tended to assume that this transition will proceed smoothly. In effect, such analyses have neglected the antagonistic basis of all capitalist relations. Surely, smooth and incremental social change is still highly dependent on the continued economic influence of the permanent war economy, the absence of trade wars, and on the success of surveillance and social control forces within cities. Were this combined economic and political underpinning removed, the violence done to the working class in the form of displacements, insecurity due to flexibility, deskilling, split labour markets, the growing expense of commuting, housing, and medical care, the retreat of the state from welfare provisions, and the toll of crime, might surface in a reaction that could sweep away the nice linkages between regimes of accumulation and modes of regulation celebrated by academic champions of the transition to post-Fordism. As we neglect the continued presence of real crisis tendencies and the smouldering power of working class interests in a crisis theory without real crisis, we ignore perhaps a more formidable potential for social change that might have to be reckoned with at some future time.

REFERENCES

M. Aglietta, *A Theory of Capitalist Regulation: The US Experience* (London: New Left Books, 1979).

M. Anderson, *The Federal Bulldozer* (Cambridge: MIT Press, 1964).

R. Armstrong, *The Office Industry* (Cambridge: MIT Press, 1972).

B. Bluestone and B. Harrison, *The Deindustrialisation of America* (New York: Basic Books, 1982).

B. Boyer, *Cities Destroyed for Cash* (Chicago: Follet, 1973).

M. Castells, 'High Technology, Economic Restructuring and the Urban-Regional Process in the United States' in M. Castells (ed.), *High Technology, Space and Society* (Beverly Hills, California: SAGE, 1985).

M. de Vroey, 'A Regulative Approach Interpretation of Contemporary Crisis', *Capital and Class* 23 (1984).

J. Feagin, *The Urban Real Estate Game* (Englewood Cliffs, New Jersey: 1983).

J. Feagin and M. Smith, 'Cities and The New International Division of Labour' in M. Smith and J. Feagin (eds), *The Capitalist City* (Oxford: Basil Blackwell, 1987).

R. Friedland, *Power and Crisis in The City* (New York: Schochen Books, 1983).

D. Gordon *et al.*, *Divided Workers* (New York: Cambridge University Press, 1982).

M. Gottdiener, *Planned Sprawl* (Beverly Hill, California: SAGE, 1977).

M. Gottdiener, *The Social Production of Urban Space* (University of Texas Press, 1985).

M. Gottdiener, (ed.), *Cities in Stress* (Beverly Hills, California: SAGE, 1986).

M. Gottdiener and G. Kephart, 'The Fully Urbanised County' in S. Olin *et al.* (eds) *The Fragmented City* (Los Angeles: University of California Press, forthcoming).

J. Hirsch, 'Fordismus und Postfordismus', *Politische Vierteljahressschrift* 26, 2 (1985).

H. Lefebvre, *La production de l'espace* (Paris: Anthropos, 1974).

D. Leinsdorf *et al.*, *Citibank* (New York: Grossman, 1973).

A. Lipietz, 'Towards a Global Fordism', *New Left Review* 132 (1982).

J.-f. Lyotard, *The Postmodern Condition: A Report on Knowledge* (Minneapolis, MN: University of Minnesota Press, 1984).

E. Mandel, *Late Capitalism* (New York: Velos, 1975).

P. Marcuse, 'The Targeted Crisis', *International Journal of Urban and Regional Research* 5 (1981).

S. Melman, *Pentagon Capitalism* (New York: Columbia University Press, 1970).

S. Melman, *Profits Without Production* (New York: Knopf, 1983).

J. Mollenkopf, *The Contested City* (New Jersey: Princeton University Press, 1983).

A. Roobeek, 'The Crisis in Fordism and the Rise of the New Technological System', Research Memorandum no. 8602, Department of Economics, University of Amsterdam (1986).

A. Scott, 'High Technology Industry and Territorial Development', *Urban Geography* 7, 1 (1986).

A. Scott and M. Storper, *Production, Work and Territory* (Boston: Allen & Unwin, 1986).

G. Sternlieb and R. Hughes (eds), *Post-Industrial America* (New Jersey: Rutgers University Press, 1975).

K. van der Pijl, *The Making of an Atlantic Ruling Class* (London: Verson, 1984).

16 Financial Crises and the Evolution of Capitalism: The Crash of '87 — What Does it Mean?[1]

Hyman P. Minsky

INTRODUCTION

The world-wide crash of financial markets on 19 and 20 October 1987 furnishes prima facie evidence that modern capitalist economies, which are characterised by complex, sophisticated and ever evolving financial structures, are by their very nature endogenously unstable. The crash and its aftermath also show that the structures of intervention and control that emerged over the decades since the Great Depression of the 1930s are able to contain the endogenous processes that in earlier times brought on great and serious depressions. As a result of the successful containment of instability, the evolution of capitalism in the main capitalist economies has been dominated by the result of government and market adjustments to isolated or contained crises, that take place within an on the whole adequately performing system, rather than by market participants and government reactions to overriding crises and failed performance. One need but note that Thatcherism survived a full term of deindustrialisation and unconscionable unemployment, mainly because welfare state transfers sustained the Andy Capp's of Britain at a tolerable standard, to recognise that the evolutionary dynamics of capitalism has changed.

In earlier times the stock market crash of October 1987 combined with the Third World debt crisis, the imbalances in international trade, and the virtual bankruptcy of savings and loan institutions and their deposit insurance organisation that characterise 1988 would have been more than enough to bring about a serious recession.[2] In 1988, even as serious financial disruptions take place, unemployment rates decline and corporate gross profits are unscathed. Capitalisms that successfully sustain incomes and contain crises are different from capitalisms that are subject to serious depressions, especially in how they change through time.

Financial crises still occur. However, modern capitalisms, characterised by governments that make up a big portion of Gross National Product and central banking that is active and interventionist, have the ability to contain the effects of crises upon income, employment, profits and prices. This means that the evolution of capitalism is not now dominated by private and public responses to traumatic breakdowns but is the result of the adaptive behaviour of markets and individuals in the context of interventions, by governments and central banks that, in a broad sense, are successful (although adverse 'side effects' of the interventions do occur). Traumas, such as that of 19 and 20 October 1987, show the fragility of modern financial capitalism; the subsequent behaviour of the world economy illustrates the resiliance of today's capitalism.

Over the years since World War II economics has been dominated by doctrines that were formulated to yield the conclusion that decentralised markets result in either a static or a growth equilibrium.[3] Comments in the press on the events of October 1987 showed that eminent practitioners of today's standard economic theory are as barren of insights into why financial crises occur as their predecessors in distinction were in 1929. Purveyors of the conventional wisdom stand as the weavers and tailors stood after the little boy cried out 'The Emperor is naked'.

Monetarism and supply-side economics are big intellectual and political losers, for in these views, largely based upon an extreme and unwarranted interpretation of the substance of the aforementioned general equilibrium theory, a virtual breakdown of the financial system, such as occurred on 19 and 20 October, is not supposed to happen. In general, the neoclassical synthesis (the technical label for today's dominant economic theory) which in its modern guise reduced all economic behaviour to the result of maximising behaviour by individuals, has been hurt. This is so even though some economists are getting what they call Keynesian results out of the preference system, production function and maximising behaviour structure of neoclassical theory.[4] However, even the best of these neoclassical theorists do not expressly consider investment, its financing, the financing of capital asset holdings, and banking relations: that is, they do not consider the economy as a structure that sets up cash flows through time.

The behaviour of the economy since the late 1960s points to the need to reconstruct economic theory to emphasise the intertemporal relations that mainly centre on investment and finance. The economic theory that goes by the label Post-Keynesian, which holds that an understanding of the behaviour of a capitalist economy requires that financial considerations be fully integrated into the explanation of the path of the system through calander time, and which also holds that financial instability is a normal evolutionary outcome of periods of financial and economic tranquility, seems to be validated by the behaviour of the economy.[5] Henceforth institutionalist and Keynesian concerns, as well as analytical structures that lead to a recognition of the flaws in capitalism due to various time-dependent relations that are specific to capitalist finance, should carry more weight and the neoclassical theories, that have served as apologetics for capitalism, should carry less weight.

CASH FLOWS

What happened on 19 and 20 October cannot be explained as normal, albeit not everyday, events by the neoclassical synthesis. It is a theorem of post-Keynesian theory that it is normal for conditions conducive to financial instability to develop in a capitalist economy. This is so because bankers, business men and portfolio managers react to profit opportunities by adjusting their asset and liability structures so that, over a period of time, payments on liabilities become more closely articulated to receipts from assets. In this construct the income, employment and production system generates cash flows and a portion of these cash flows are precommitted to the validation of various liabilities.

In a world characterised by uncertainty, in the sense of Keynes and Knight,[6] successful functioning of a capitalist economy leads to changes in perceptions of the likelihood of alternative outcomes and therefore in the bets that are made. The bets that firms make to finance their holdings of capital assets and their purchase of investment outputs are revealed by the structure of their liabilities. Bankers and managers of money place bets as they acquire the liabilities of businesses, households and governments and as they structure their own liabilities. Specifically successful functioning of a capitalist economy means that there is an increased acceptance of liability structures that pledge ever greater proportions of the expected cash flow from operations or assets to servicing liabilities.

Financial robustness exists when firms and households have little indebtedness and as a result bank portfolios are heavily into government debt: this situation ruled for about 20 years after World War II. History has shown financial robustness to be transitory. Analytically financial robustness leads to low short-term financing rates and therefore it offers large payoffs to those who are willing to stretch the accepted bounds of liability structures by financing long positions with short liabilities. Financial robustness leads to liability experimentation and institutional innovation, whose effects cumulate over time, so that initially robust financial structures become fragile. Financial fragility leads to conditions in which from time to time a substantial need to try to make position by selling out position arises. Financial fragility is a necessary condition for markets to perform in the manner that was witnessed in mid-October.

LENDER OF LAST RESORT

The necessity for intervention to thwart a destabilising thrust and the power of such intervention were once again made evident in October. The US Federal Reserve increased the reserve base of banks by some 2 per cent in the immediate aftermath of the crisis.[7] This was the fifth time the Federal Reserve acted as a lender of last resort in the 1980s. (The five are the Hunt silver affair in 1980, Drysedale and the Chase Bank in 1982, Mexico in 1982, Continental Illinois in 1984, and the stock market collapse in 1987: this Goldman Sachs chronicle does not include the Penn-Square episode of 1982, which occurred simultaneously with the Mexican crisis.) Each time the Federal Reserve reacted by substantially increasing the reserve base.

The critical and most interesting day for economic analysis was Tuesday 20 October. As the *Wall Street Journal* described it, by noon of Tuesday the stock market was ready to close, for sell orders so outweighed buy orders that if orders to sell had been fulfilled the market would have experienced a free fall.[8] In particular the specialist system on the floor of the exchange and the block trading (position-taking activity) of the great street houses had ground to a halt. Bank financing was being withdrawn and the specialists and houses were unwilling to commit what was left of their equity to position taking in what they feared was a free fall market.

As this was taking place President Corrigan of the New York Federal Reserve Bank was in direct contact with both the banks and the houses. It would be consistent with the responsibilities of the lender of last resort (although a deviation from conventional Federal Reserve behaviour) for the New York Federal Reserve Bank to have lent directly to the specialists and the block traders and to have guaranteed the banks and the affected Wall Street houses against further losses from taking positions. As the *Wall Street Journal* reported, after Corrigan intervened the market turned around. The day ended with a gain.

It is worth observing that by the actions of 20 October the domain of responsibility of the Federal Reserve was extended to include the prevention of a free fall in the prices of common stocks and other financial instruments. The prevention of a full fledged debt deflation seems to require that the domain of responsibility of the Federal Reserve be continuously expanded.

It is worth noting that in the aftermath of the crash, Fidelity Investments, which offers over 100 funds and which manages about $80 billions, announced that it intends to increase its bank lines of credit so that a flood of orders to redeem its funds will not lead to a need to sell securities. The distress of October is inducing a financial innovation which makes the managers of money beholden to banks and changes mutual funds, which are now prepared to finance some of their holdings with bank debt.

FORMS OF CAPITALISM

We might characterise the crisis of 19 and 20 October as the first financial crisis of THE NEW CAPITALISM OF 'MANAGED MONEY'. Although any neat stages and ages view of economic evolution should be taken with the proverbial grain of salt, capitalism is such a changeable system that it is useful to think of varieties of capitalism as differentiated by the forms of organisation and financing. We could well think of there being as many varieties of capitalism as Heinz had of pickles.

In particular we can distinguish forms such as commercial, industrial, financial, managerial-welfare state and managerial capitalism, recognising that any real world capitalism will be a combination of these types. Because of space limitations we will consider only two forms: the managerial-welfare state capitalism of the post-war era and the newer managed money capitalism.

After World War II a combination of managerial and welfare state capitalism was dominant in the United States, Western Europe and the other advanced capitalist economies. Managerial capitalism can be defined as a form of corporate capitalism in which industry, transportation and trade are largely dominated by firms that are characterised by heirarchical management styles, where the management is drawn from self-perpetuating professional bureaucracies that are committed to technical progress and industrial 'statesmanship': these managements exercise constraint in their perquisites and income and are not largely beholden to financial market organisations. The stockholders are widely dispersed and largely individuals — the widows and orphans that the Bell System used as a protective shield — who are largely satisfied with modest but steadily growing returns. As long as returns are steady, management is largely independent of stockholder influence and shows only minor concern about the course of the price of its stock.

In this post-war model, corporate capitalism recognised the legitimacy of the New Deal reforms (transfer payments, trade unions), even as the New Dealers backed off from the interventions, as envisaged in the prospective third New Deal of the Temporary National Economic Commission, that would have forced competitive market conditions upon business. In the United States the post-war consensus was largely the work of the Committee for Economic Development, a group of liberal businessmen. The model guiding economic policy was of firms which operate in the absence of strong banker constraints and which possess market power but which use their market power with discretion. Furthermore, firms shared the benefits of market power with their workers: labour was not to be sweated.

This paternalistic industrial arrangement took place in the context of a welfare state, which consisted mainly of a system of transfer payments, and Keynesian fiscal policies. This combination assured the economy against any large shortfall of aggregate demand and of business profits. The very success of this managerial-welfare state capitalism assured that it would run into difficulties, for the stabilisation of profits against large downside deviations meant that the debt-carrying capacity of firms increased. Bankers and firms were sure to experiment with increasing debt, and the 'market' rewarded those who understood that the interventionist economy put a floor to the downside risks on aggregate profit flows.

MONEY MANAGER CAPITALISM

In the past decades, as a response to the success of managerial-welfare state capitalism, a new form of capitalism has emerged which reflects the increase in the 'clout' of managed money. Pension funds, mutual funds, insurance companies, and bank-administered trusts are now much more important than they were earlier in the capitalist epoch. This money is managed by professional money managers who aim to obtain the largest short-run total return from their portfolio, that is, to maximise the combination of short-term cash flows, in the form of dividends and interest, and asset appreciation. Because of the weight of short-term asset price movements in determining the total return, managed money is active money: managers pursue short-term asset appreciations by actively trading their portfolio.

Keynes distinguished between the returns from enterprise and the returns from speculation; enterprise returns are dividends, interest and retained earnings that are usefully invested, whereas speculative returns are asset appreciations that are not due to retained earnings. Managed money conforms to Keynes's definition of speculation, for the appreciation or depreciation of asset prices can dominate in the determination of total return. We can recall Keynes's remark to the effect that if enterprise is a mere bubble on a sea of speculation the capital development of an economy is likely to be poorly done. Money manager capitalism emphasises the value (price and positive changes in price) of financial assets and in particular ordinary shares. Money managers press the management of firms to act so as to sustain the market value of shares. This usually implies increasing indebtedness without any obvious increase in profit flows unless it is possible to exploit market power or sweat labour. Money manager capitalism implies that the Committee on Economic Development consensus breaks down: in particular, firms are no longer managed on the basis of a longer view that entails investments in innovation, research and staff development.

The growth of managed money bought into being institutions and usages (ways of doing business) in financial and other markets that facilitated (and made money from) the operations of the money managers. Multi-billion and even multi-million dollar funds deal in large blocks of shares. If these blocks of shares were sold or bought on the open market they would move the market, appreciably changing their price. To prevent this large blocks are not bought or sold in the normal market manner; large blocks are first bought and then sold by the block trading desks of the major houses. These block traders buy for their own account (take a position) and then either dribble their holdings out in the market or find some other body of managed money that wants to acquire these shares or bonds. (Block traders will also shop for stock for clients). Block trading facilitates the merger and hostile takeovers that have become a conspicuous part of the economics of managed money capitalism.

The growth of the funds (pension, mutual, bank-administered personal trusts, and insurance) were a result of the absence of a major depression during the years since World War II. (Pension funds are part of the welfare state apparatus.) During the debt deflation phase of a great depression, asset values are written down even further than income and employment declines; the surviving mutual and other funds would be those that appreciated the wisdom of portfolio prudence. Those whose portfolios were heavily weighted with liabilities of strong financial institutions would do better than those whose portfolios were heavily weighted with financial market assets. Great depressions induced portfolio conservatism, what Keynes called a shift to liquidity preference and what was called a shift to quality in the aftermath of 19 and 20 October.

The viability of money manager capitalism depends upon not having a serious depression: the continued absence of a serious depression fosters experimentation with portfolio managing techniques that increases the likelihood of system threatening crises, that is, increases the likelihood of depressions. There is a basic contradiction in money manager capitalism, which makes continued success ever more dependent upon an apt structure of supportive government interventions. Money manager capitalism rests upon the power of government to prevent a sharp decline in aggregate business profits.

Over 19 and 20 October, even as money managers were trying to sell securities, the block traders were both reluctant and increasingly unable to take positions. Furthermore, because the losses of 19 October had compromised the equity of some position takers (these organisations mark their holdings to market at the end of every business day) on 20 October banks began to withdraw credit from block traders as well as from floor specialists.

INTERVENTION BY THE FEDERAL RESERVE

At this juncture the New York Federal Reserve Bank intervened. Its guarantees freed the flow of credit and got the block traders and specialists to once again take positions. The 1987 crisis was resolved in a manner analagous to the way the much studied British crises of the 19th century were resolved. The Central Bank intervened to assure that a market worked, not to protect an individual bank or some exposed speculators.

Economists and market participants should now appreciate that one reason why the fragile financial structure did not collapse between 1980 and 1987 is that the Federal Reserve, fulfilling its responsibilities as a lender of last resort, intervened at least five times to sustain institutions as diverse as the Hunts, the Chase Bank, lenders to Mexico, the depositors of huge sums in Continental Illinois, and the normal functioning of the stock exchanges. The Federal Reserve has demonstrated it can contain the dynamics that lead to chaotic financial markets and which would have strong immediate impacts upon income and employment: the Federal Reserve can sustain orderly conditions in financial and output markets.

The same history of the 1980s shows that the Federal Reserve cannot effectively determine the target level or trend of money or High Powered Money. The periodic threat of market instability forces the Federal Reserve to feed its liabilities, which become bank reserves, into the financial structure: the money supply is endogenously determined.

Lender of last resort responsibilities throw light on Paul Volcker's tenure as Chairman of the Federal Reserve. He was more successful as a lender of last resort than as a controller of the money supply or of the economy. Because of the recurrent threat of financial crises the quantity of reserve money was endogenously determined by the need to maintain orderly conditions. The transitory success that was achieved in containing inflation in the 1980s was due more to wage constraint, resulting from the Administration's trade union bashing, tolerance of unemployment, and accepting of imports, than to money supply constraint.

THE IMPACT OF GOVERNMENT

'Will the events of October herald the onset of another Great Depression?' is a question that is often asked. The first thing to remember is that the Great Collapse took 40 months. It started with the stock market crash of October 1929 and ended as Roosevelt was being inaugurated in March 1933. Much took place after 1929 that compounded the initial downward destabilisation.

One great difference between the 1930s and the 1980s has to be emphasised: today the Federal Government is some 25 per cent of GNP. In 1929 government was about 3 per cent of GNP. There is a greatly simplified formula for profits, usually identified with Kalecki,[9] that reads

profits = investment + the government deficit.

If investment is 16 per cent of GNP there is no way the deficit of a 3 per cent government can offset the effect upon profits of a sharp fall in investment. If government is 25 per cent of GNP then a fall in investment can be offset, or even more than offset, by the automatic increase in the deficit that a decline in income brings about and by some rather slight adjustments in tax and spending programmes. Profits collapsed in 1929–33; they can not do so with today's structure of aggregate demand. A big government capitalism cannot repeat the collapse of 1929–33.

In the 1929–33 contraction the stock market indices eventually fell to some 15 per cent of their prior peak. One reason for this was the drastic decline in the net and gross profits of business over 1929–33. The decline in gross profits greatly diminished the ability of business to validate debts, which adversely affected banks and other financial institutions.

Today, through its deficits, big government sustains profits when investment declines. The true beneficiaries of government deficits are profit, dividend and interest receivers, whose incomes are sustained during recessions by government deficits. Money manager capitalism is viable only to the extent that potential government deficits assure that profits will not collapse as they did in the 1930s.

INTERNATIONAL EFFECTS

The Kalecki profit equation opens up to

profits = investment + the government deficit −
the foreign trade deficit.

The great turn around in the United States trade picture during the Reagan years, largely a result of the short sighted monetarist anti-inflationary policies of the early 1980s, resulted in a drain of profits from the United States, mainly to Japan and West Germany. The result was a great growth in the holdings of United States-based assets by the rest of the world: primarily Western Europe and Japan but also the newly industrialised export-based economies of the Pacific basin. The United States' trade deficit and the continued growth of the United States' international indebtedness are not viable longer run situations. International economic adjustments will have to shift a larger part of the responsibility for maintaining global business profits to the countries that have recently accumulated international assets. This means that Japan and Western Europe, as well as the export platforms of Asia, will have to become in the aggregate net importers of goods and services. It is obvious that there will have to be great internal adjustments: economies that have been dependent upon exports will have to become dependent upon domestic consumption demand.

Japan, West Germany and the other rich countries whose prosperity has been export driven will have to maintain their prosperity by domestic expansionary fiscal and monetary policies if global prosperity is to be sustained. Whether or not global prosperity is maintained depends to a large extent upon whether Japan and West Germany can maintain their prosperity without the help of a massive United States trade deficit. If they cannot open their markets to increased imports even as they maintain prosperity by domestic policies that abet their evolution into high consumption, low savings economies, then a new round of beggar-my-neighbour policies is possible.

Money managers seek profits by international portfolio diversification and are sensitive to exchange rate fluctuations; positions are taken on the basis of exchange rate expectations. Money manager capitalism is hospitable to financial innovations such as the globalisation and securitisation of finance and to the growth of financing through markets relative to financing through institutions.[10]

CONCLUSION

The events of October and since constitute prima facie evidence that the price of non-interventionist, unregulated and small government capitalism is so high that it is a non-starter as a possible economic structure. But this does not mean that the 1980 or 1987 structure of big government interventionist capitalism is in any way best. It is now evident that a structure of regulation and intervention once in place may lose its power as time goes by and business and households learn how to avoid, evade and accommodate to the structure. Avoidance, evasion and accommodation are words that summarise the process of economic evolution in capitalist economies that do not experience the trauma of severe and long lasting depressions. Policies and programmes that are not modified as avoidance, evasion and accommodation take place are likely to become counter-productive: to lead to results that were not initially envisaged.

Managerial-welfare state capitalism gave the main capitalist countries an unprecedented period of success. The economic growth and the wide distribution of the benefits of economic growth that characterised the first two or so decades after World War II were clearly without precedent. However, this success planted the seeds of a transformation in the mode of functioning of the economy, in that the mass savings and asset appreciation that characterise successful managerial capitalism gave rise to institutions that managed large blocks of money. The objectives of money managers are different from those of the management of the non-financial businesses that were the dominant institutional form under managerial capitalism. The result is a fragile financial structure that, as was shown on 19 and 20 October, may require intervention on a massive scale to prevent the collapse of asset values. It is clear that apt government intervention is even more important if a semblance of successful functioning for money market capitalism is to be sustained than it was for managerial capitalism. Furthermore, it is more difficult to determine what constitutes apt intervention for this new and more complex form of capitalism. We can expect future crises to be met with some form of *ad hoc* intervention which will in part reflect an unwillingness by policy-makers to appreciate that once again capitalism has changed.

NOTES

1. A prior version of this paper was presented at a session on 'The Crash of '87 — What Does It Mean? that was arranged by URPE at the Applied Social Science Association's Meeting in Chicago Ill. on Tuesday, 29 December 1987.
2. Irving Fisher, 'The Debt-Deflation Theory of Great Depressions', *Econometrica* 1 (October 1933) pp. 337–57.
3. Kenneth J. Arrow and Frank H. Hahn, *General Competitive Analysis* (San Fransisco and Edinburgh: 1971).
4. N. Gregory Mankiw, *Recent Developments in Macroeconomics: A Very*

Quick Refresher Course. Working Paper No. 2474 (National Bureau of Economic Research, Cambridge, Mass.: 1987).

5. Among the key works in the post-Keynesian tradition are: Victoria Chick, *Macroeconomics after Keynes* (Cambridge, Mass. and London: 1983); Paul Davidson, *Money and the Real World* (New York: 1972); Jan A. Kregal, *The Reconstruction of Political Economy* (London: 1973); Hyman P. Minsky, *John Maynard Keynes* (New York: 1975) and *Stabilizing an Unstable Economy* (New Haven: 1986).

6. John Maynard Keynes, *The General Theory of Employment, Interest and Money* (New York: 1936); *A Treatise on Probability* (London: 1921); Frank H. Knight, *Risk, Uncertainty and Profit* (New York: 1921).

7. Robert M. Giordane, *Financial Market Perspectives* (Goldman Sachs, New York: 1987).

8. *Wall Street Journal*, 19 November 1987.

9. Michael Kalecki, *Selected Essays on the Dynamics of the Capitalist Economy (1933–1970)* (Cambridge: 1971).

10. Hyman P. Minsky, *Global Consequences of Financial Deregulation* (Washington DC: 1986).

Index

SUBJECT INDEX

404

AUTHOR INDEX